Praise for the First Edition

"Jordan Young's coverage of Spike Jones' career is worth a clang on the cowbell and a toot on the auto horn...By the time you're finished, you'll know more about the music business than perhaps you wanted to—and you'll also have a nifty perspective on American social history in the 1940s."

— *San Francisco Examiner*

"A fantastic book. An encyclopedic look at Spike's marvelous career...a book that's been needed for a long, long time. Any Spike Jones fan will love it."

— Gary Owens

"Young reveals the private world of Spike Jones and expands on the public career. Highly recommended.

— Tony Middleton, *Jazz Journal*

"Spike Jones, warts and all...Jordan Young has done a brilliant job."
— George Putnam, KIEV, Los Angeles

"This is a real fun book...but it's also a serious work of scholarship."
— W. Royal Stokes, *Washington Review*

"A wonderful book. It brought tears to my eyes as I lived again my years with Spike and his City Slickers."
— Dr. Horatio Q. Birdbath

Spike Jones
Off the *Record*

The Man Who *Murdered* Music

by Jordan R. Young

Foreword by Dr. Demento
Discography by Ted Hering and Skip Craig

BearManor Media
2005

In memory of Allen J. Desmaretz,
the wildest, funniest man I ever met

Spike Jones Off The Record: The Man Who Murdered Music
(The 20th Anniversary Edition)

First published as *Spike Jones and his City Slickers*
by Disharmony Books/Moonstone Press in 1984.

Printed in the United States of America

BearManor Media
P. O. Box 750
Boalsburg, PA 16827

bearmanormedia.com

Cover design by John Teehan
Typesetting and layout by John Teehan

ISBN—1-59393-012-7

Table of Contents

Foreword

Welcome to the 20th anniversary edition of the first book ever published about Spike Jones. Here's a man whose name was synonymous with laughter in America for more than a decade. The mere mention of that name still brings smiles to faces far too young to remember the days when "Cocktails for Two" and "Two Front Teeth" topped the record sales charts and people from all walks of life tuned in weekly to Spike's network radio show, and flocked to his spectacular live performances.

Spike never had time to tell his own story. He was far too busy performing, rehearsing and overseeing every detail of his incredibly complex and fast-moving stage shows, and planning future ventures—some of them remarkably far removed from the brand of entertainment that made him rich and famous. Even if his body hadn't yielded at a lamentably early age to the immoderate demands he made upon it, it's doubtful he would have ever retired to write his memoirs in peace. Rest and rumination simply weren't his style.

With the kind of energy and persistence Spike would have appreciated, Jordan Young has made sense out of Spike's chaotic career. Through diligent research and thorough interviews with ex-City Slickers and other longtime friends and associates, Mr. Young has not only put the facts of Spike's public life in perspective, but also discovered much for us about his turbulent private life.

Here was a man of exceptional self-contradictions: a man who operated for most of his career on the theory that show business was mainly *business,* yet increasingly yearned for respect as a serious musician; a man whose sense of humor offstage as well as on endeared him to many, but who could become a ruthless martinet at the slightest sign of incompetence or disloyalty; a man whose persistence in maintaining a strenuous performance schedule (and a five-pack-a-day habit) eventually reached suicidal proportions. It's all here in these pages, as are the stories of George Rock, Doodles Weaver, Del Porter, Red Ingle, Billy Barty and other partners in laughter, many of them as colorful as Spike himself.

I've been a Spike Jones fan ever since my dad brought home a 78 of "Cocktails for Two" when I was four. His records are still the cornerstones of my syndicated radio show, and I hear their influence even in the latest new "demented discs." Now, thanks to this book, we can learn at last just how Spike Jones made his magic, and what sort of magic man he was. Music lovers can well paraphrase one of Spike's favorite catch lines— "Thank You, Jordan Young!"

Dr. Demento

Preface

Now and then I give out with a good belch, which is generally met with a look of disapproval. "I'm auditioning for Spike Jones," I hasten to explain. To be honest, I don't think I would've passed such an audition; the truth is, I can't belch on cue.

Jones, the pistol-packing bandleader whose cowbell-washboard-and-gunshot renditions of popular songs brightened the darkest hours of World War II—and have been rediscovered by new generations—was an enigma in his day. Beneath the belches, the sirens and the larger-than-life public persona was a complicated, little understood man.

He was an immensely private individual who took great pains to hide the truth. His love of classical music was kept carefully under wraps, as were his razor-sharp tongue and ribald sense of humor. "If the real me were ever known," he once confided to Tom Prideaux of *Life* magazine, "my entire image would be shot."

I was introduced to Spike's peculiar genius in the early 1960s, by a pair of friends who drove up to my house with "Der Fuehrer's Face" blaring from a tape in their car. I promptly embarked on a musical scavenger hunt, scrounging for old 78s in neighborhood thrift stores and garage sales, like most other collectors in the days before eBay made child's play of such noble endeavors.

The seed for this book was sown one evening in 1976, at a spirited Hollywood banquet where I found myself seated next to Doodles Weaver. Despite my every intention of pumping him for anecdotes about Jones, he made me laugh so hard, I didn't have a chance. The following year I interviewed Mickey Katz for *The Los Angeles Times*. His amusing and unexpected remarks about his former employer further aroused my curiosity.

Five years later, I followed up a phone tip about a box of sheet music in a used furniture store, discovering instead six file boxes of long lost memorabilia—including the remnants of the band's music library and Jones' business correspondence, which revealed the inner workings of the band he had so skillfully concealed. Fired up by my serendipitous find, I began to track down and interview the survivors of Spike's organization and draw out their recollections of the man who assaulted popular and classical music with unparalleled artistry.

I didn't consider *Spike Jones and his City Slickers* a work-in-progress when it was first published in 1984. But not too many years later, when I realized a third of the people I had interviewed for the book had passed away, it occurred to me I hadn't told the whole story, and that a part of history was fast disappearing. I dusted off my tape recorder and began interviewing again, for an extensively revised and expanded edition that came out in 1994.

When Ben Ohmart of BearManor Media implored me early this year not to let the book go out of print, I was inspired to revisit the text, and the mountains of research material I have collected over the years. With new discoveries surfacing regularly—especially in the heretofore unexamined diaries of Doodles Weaver, courtesy of his son Win—how could I not be inspired?

This 20th anniversary edition of the book, like the previous one, digs deeper into the past and hopefully gives a much more complete picture of the bandleader and his largely unsung accomplices, the niche they inhabited in the entertainment world and the circumstances under which they worked.

Although many people have called this the definitive book—and I am deeply gratified by the public and critical acclaim received over the years—I do not feel it is possible to exhaust a subject as complex and fascinating as Spike Jones. The subject will surely exhaust the author first.

A conventional biography of Jones is not possible. This is a man who defied convention and conformity, and a story that in some respects defies logic. Because Jones was firing his gun in every direction at once—stage revues, records, radio and television shows, movies—each chapter follows the trajectory of a bullet, as it were. It's the only way to make sense of the nonsense. The Chronology places things in perspective, while Notes & Sources (following the appendices) adds further dimension to the story.

Spike Jones Off the Record is largely an oral history, of necessity, a story told by the men and women who lived it, on the road and in the studio. The additional research for the second and third editions shed new light on many facets of Jones' life and career and yielded much previously unpublished information. New discoveries, however, have led to further contradictions.

Every attempt has been made to corroborate the statements and anecdotes in this book, a task complicated by the passage of time and the scarcity of documentation. It is not possible to record the history of an era that has vanished, or reconstruct a man's life—certainly not a man as prolific, or as complicated as Spike Jones—with absolute accuracy.

Jones himself never let the truth get in the way of a good story; he would sacrifice almost anything for the sake of a joke. This is an effort to separate fact from fiction and delineate reality from fantasy. It is not my intent to exalt or depreciate Jones; neither hagiography nor sensationalism is appropriate.

In regard to the spelling of names: record labels, program notes, contracts and even official RCA Victor data sheets and musician's union contractor's reports are rife with inaccuracies and inconsistencies. The song denoted on record labels as "Hotcha Cornia," for example, was published as "Hotcha Cornya" (and spelled a variety of ways in print). Doodles Weaver used "Fietlebaum" and "Feetlebaum" interchangeably, but eventually settled on the latter. The author has attempted to be somewhat more consistent.

I am indebted to many for their assistance on this project. My special thanks to Ted Hering, for making available his interview with the late Del Porter and other rare memorabilia, including several previously unpublished photos for this edition; Skip Craig, for being so generous with his time and trusting with his remarkable archive of Jonesiana; and both for the painstaking effort that went into the discography, as well as their infinite patience.

I am grateful to Dr. Demento for taking time out from his demanding schedule to write the foreword, and for his erudite commentary on the manuscript. I am obliged as well to two old friends, Randy Skretvedt and Jim Curtis, for their continued advice, assistance and encouragement. Scott Corbett and Warren Dexter shared materials from their collections; Mark Cantor, Jack Mirtle and Don McGlynn were generous with their research.

Thanks are due also to: Jeff Abraham, John Adams, Ray Avery, Dick

Bann, Eric Blackford, Steve Blankenship, Bob Bowen, Nancy Cahen, Bill Cappello, Carol Capito, Russ Cheevers, Casey Maxwell Clair, Rich D'Albert, Eddy Davis, Virginia DePew, Allen Desmaretz, Roger Donley, Marc Eagan, Mark Evanier, Janet Fischer, John Fitzer, Susan Fox, Frances Gluskin, Howard Halasz, James S. Harris, Mimi Harris, Mike Hawks, Ray Heath, Ronnie James, Hal Kanter, Mark Kausler, Eleanor Keaton, Mike Kieffer, Margaret Trotter Kinghorn, Methabelle Kline, Steve LaVere, Ruth Leithner, Carl Mack, Leonard Maltin, Vi Marks, Skip Marrow, Shepard Mencken, Robert Michel, Alan Nitikman, Estelle Nitikman, Jay Nitikman, Kathy O'Connell, Michael Oldfield, Abe Nole, Dan Pasternack, Hub Phelan, Andrew C. Pinchot, Abe Ravitz, Paul Reid, Dave Robinson, Bill Rothwell, Gerald Ruark, Herm Shultz, Walt Solek, George Stewart, Carol Vernier, Nan Webster, Manny Weltman, John Wood, Pam Young, Pearl Young and Stanford Zucker.

ABC; Howard Prouty, Academy of Motion Picture Arts and Sciences, Center for Motion Picture Study; Norma Painter, American Federation of Musicians (AFM), Local 47; Arena Stars, Inc.; Bernadette Moore, BMG Music; *Billboard*; British Broadcasting Corporation; Lucy Banaga, Calipatria High School; Frank Pinkerton, Chaffey College; Cinema Shop; CBS; Columbia Pictures; David R. Smith, Disney Archives; Larry Edmunds Bookshop; Bob Morgan, Good Music Company; Mark Rogister, Hollywood Fotolab; Bob Colman, Hollywood Poster Exchange; Hoosier Hot Shots Museum; Miles Kreuger, Institute of the American Musical; Sally Guthrie, Jonathan Club; KLAF, Salt Lake City; Las Vegas News Bureau; Lippert Pictures; Bob Livingston Photo; Los Angeles County, Hall of Records, Registrar-Recorder; Irv Letofsky and Thomas Lutgen, *The Los Angeles Times;* NBC; New York Public Library at Lincoln Center; Peer-Southern Music; Society to Preserve and Encourage Radio Drama, Variety and Comedy (SPERDVAC); Spike Jones International Fan Club; Stanford University, Alumni Records Office; Tribune Media Services, Inc.; Turner Broadcasting System; Universal Pictures; Ned Comstock, Archives of Performing Arts, University of Southern California; Peter Kiefer, Fred Waring's America, Pennsylvania State University.

Last but not least, I am obligated to Spike Jones' associates, friends, family members and contemporaries for helping me to excavate the man behind the legend. I am particularly indebted to Earl Bennett, Joe Siracusa and Eddie Brandt, without whom this book would have been impossible altogether; and Linda Jones, for graciously cooperating with the project. I also thank Gina Jones, Leslie Ann Jones and Spike Jones Jr.

My gratitude to those interviewed: Don Anderson, Billy Barty, Buddy Basch, Gil Bernal, Dr. Horatio Q. Birdbath, Don Blocker, George Boujie, Carl Brandt, Dorothy Buehler, Skip Craig, Herman Crone, John Cyr, Bill Dana, Dwight Defty, Arthur Ens, Ray Erlenborn, Rex Finney, Ruth Foster, Stan Freberg, Paul Frees, Blanche Fritts, Eileen Gallagher, Dick Gardner, Gloria Gardner, Mousie Garner, Harriet Geller, Harry Geller, Bob Gioga, Lud Gluskin, Marty Gold, Duke Goldstone, Jack Golly, Phil Gray, George Hackett, Candy Hall, William Harris, Paul Harrison, Tony Hawes, Jim Hawthorne, Walter S. Heebner, C. Robert Holloway, Bruce Hudson, Don Ingle, Charlie Isaacs, Peter James, Ray Johnson, Bernie Jones, Ish Kabbible, Mickey Katz, Ward Kimball, Bill King, Wally Kline, Charlie Koenig, Eddie Kusby, Frances Langford, Beatrice Lee, Beau Lee, Jr., Frankie Little, Carolyn Livingston, Wally Marks, Willie Martinez, Eddie Maxwell, Zep Meissner, Eddie Metcalfe, Nell Michel, Betty Phares Murphy, Leighton Noble, Jad Paul, Tommy Pederson, David Raksin, Herschell Ratliff, Thurl Ravenscroft, Robert Robinson, George Rock, Luther Roundtree, Gordon Schroeder, Harry Sosnik, Cliffie Stone, Glenn Marlin Sundby, Frank Thomas, Charlotte Tinsley, Al Trace, Paul Trietsch, Jr., Danny Van Allen, George Van Eps, Bob Vincent, Gabe Ward, Doodles Weaver, Win Weaver, Dick Webster, Eve Whitney, June Wilkinson, Joe Wolverton and Bud Yorkin.

Jordan R. Young
October 2003

About the Author

Jordan R. Young is an entertainment historian and travel writer whose work has appeared in *The Los Angeles Times, The New York Times, The Washington Post, The People's Almanac* and other publications. His books include *Reel Characters: Great Movie Character Actors, The Laugh Crafters: Comedy Writing in Radio and TV's Golden Age, Acting Solo,* and *The Beckett Actor.* His plays include *Hollywood Is a State of Mind,* a trilogy broadcast on public radio, and *Picasso's Mustache.* He produced "Spike Jones: The Man Who Murdered Music" for Good Music Records and has acted as a consultant on various Jones projects for the Grammy Awards Hall of Fame, BBC Radio, BMG and Rhino Records.

Chronology

1911

Lindley Armstrong Jones is born to a railroad depot agent and a schoolteacher in Long Beach, Calif. (Dec. 14).

1912-1922

Jones grows up in Calexico, Calif. By the age of seven he decides to become a musician, and takes trombone and piano lessons.

1922-1926

Spike gets his first set of drums for his eleventh birthday, and soon organizes his first band. He also excels scholastically.

1926-1929

Jones studies music at Long Beach Polytechnic High School. He plays for dances and local radio stations with his own dixieland-style combo, Spike Jones and his Five Tacks, and other groups.

1929-1930

After a disastrous gig at the Ship's Cafe, Jones enrolls in Chaffey College in Ontario, Calif., but soon drops out to his later regret. He joins Ray West's band at a popular country club.

1931-1934

Spike plays drums with various dance bands around Southern California, including Sam Coslow, Kearney Walton, Fuzz Menge and George Hamilton.

1934-1935

Jones joins Rube Wolf's orchestra at the Paramount Theatre in Los Angeles. While employed there he meets his first wife, chorus girl Patricia Ann Middleton (they get married Sept. 7, 1935). He also forms his first novelty band, reusing the name Spike Jones and his Five Tacks.

1935-1936

Jones plays drums with Everett Hoagland, Freddie Slack, Earl Burtnett, Al Lyons and other dance bands.

1936-1939

Jones begins working as a freelance studio musician for recordings, radio and motion pictures. Victor Young, Harry Sosnik, Perry Botkin and others employ him frequently at Decca, Victor and elsewhere. On radio, he drums in the house bands on *Al Jolson, Burns and Allen, Eddie Cantor, Fibber McGee and Molly* and other shows, most notably in John Scott Trotter's orchestra on *Kraft Music Hall.* Spike's first daughter, Linda Lee, is born (1939).

1939-1941

While continuing his studio jobs, Spike becomes business manager for The Feather Merchants, a comedy band led by singer Del Porter. Meanwhile Spike and Del make their first novelty recordings at Cinematone Records, where Jones is music director. Their embryonic group also appears briefly in the film *Give Us Wings,* and plays for dances at the Jonathan Club in Los Angeles, with violinist Carl "Donald" Grayson fronting the band. King Jackson (trombone), Stan Wrightsman (piano) and Perry Botkin (banjo) help develop the City Slicker sound.

1941

The City Slickers make their radio debut on *Point Sublime*, in July. After circulating audition records around town, they sign a contract with RCA Victor and begin recording for the company's Bluebird label in August. Don Anderson joins the band on trumpet.

1942

The Slickers appear in a group of Soundies, the precursor of music videos. In July, Spike and the band record "Der Fuehrer's Face," a song

The boys in the back room: Del Porter, Don Anderson, Carl Grayson, Luther Roundtree (banjo), Hank Stern, King Jackson (trombone), Mel Blanc, Spike (behind counter) and dancer Valmere Barman in the Soundie, *Clink! Clink! Another Drink*, 1942. *(Scott Corbett)*

from a forthcoming Donald Duck cartoon. The record is soon issued and becomes a surprise hit; within a month, the band is signed for a regular slot on Bob Burns' radio show, and the all-star Warner Bros. film, *Thank Your Lucky Stars*. A record ban imposed by the American Federation of Musicians will keep them out of RCA studios for two years. Bassist-arranger Country Washburne is added to the troupe.

1943

The Slickers film *Meet the People* at MGM and embark on a cross-country tour. They are heard weekly on *Bob Burns* and *Furlough Fun*. Comedian-saxophonist Red Ingle joins the band. Jones does his part for the war effort by recording V-Discs and visiting army hospitals; he is crowned King of Corn by *Down Beat*.

The object of Spike's derision tries to pull the plug on his success. (*Scott Corbett*)

1944

    After filming *Bring on the Girls,* Jones and company entertain American and allied forces in England and France on a USO tour. They return to find their V-Disc of "Cocktails for Two" an unexpected hit; with the record ban lifted, they return to RCA to record Country Washburn's arrangement of the tune. Dick Morgan joins the group on banjo; George Rock is hired on trumpet, and soon becomes the dominant sound in the band.

1945

The Slickers adopt a new look with garish checkered and plaid suits. The band records "Chloe," "You Always Hurt the One You Love" and "The Nutcracker Suite" in between vaudeville appearances at movie theatres. They provide comic relief in two films (*Breakfast in Hollywood* and *Ladies' Man*) and make weekly appearances on radio's *Chase and Sanborn Hour* during the summer. Del Porter quits the group. Singer Helen Grayco (nèe Greco) plays her first engagement with the band.

1946

Jones puts together a large dance band he calls his Other Orchestra, but disappoints an unsuspecting public. He reorganizes the City Slickers for a new two-hour variety show, *The Musical Depreciation Revue*, and begins touring the country on a punishing itinerary. The band films *Variety Girl*. Red Ingle quits the group; Carl Grayson and several others are fired. Comedian Doodles Weaver, clarinetist Mickey Katz, drummer Joe Siracusa and dwarf Frankie Little are among the new members. "Laura" and "Hawaiian War Chant" are recorded. Jones divorces his first wife.

1947

Spike and the Slickers begin a two-year run on CBS Radio in *The Spotlight Revue* (later retitled *The Spike Jones Show*), broadcast from various cities on their itinerary. The band records "My Old Flame," "The William Tell Overture" and "Two Front Teeth" before the start of another year-long record ban in December. Mickey Katz quits; banjoist Freddy Morgan and comedian Earl Bennett (aka Sir Frederick Gas) are hired.

1948

Public appearances and radio broadcasts keep the band busy during the record ban. The London Palladium makes them an offer but the British musician's union kills the deal. The City Slickers have the honor of performing for President Truman in Washington, D.C. Jones marries Helen Grayco (Jul. 8).

1949

The Slickers return to RCA studios to record "Riders in the Sky" (to the displeasure of Vaughn Monroe), "Morpheus," "Rhapsody from Hunger(y)" and "Spike Jones Plays the Charleston." Spike and the band

Spike takes a spin in one of his midget racers, on the back lot at Paramount.
(*Gordon Schroeder*)

are parodied by Chester Gould in his "Dick Tracy" strip. The Coca Cola-sponsored CBS radio series is canceled. Spike Jones Jr. is born.

1950

The Slickers film two television pilots under the direction of Eddie Cline; the films circulate without a buyer for two years. The band records two controversial discs—"Chinese Mule Train" and "Tennessee Waltz"—along with "Pal-Yat-Chee" (not released until 1953). Bernie Jones joins the band on saxophone.

1951

The band makes its network television debut on NBC's *The Colgate Comedy Hour.* Doodles Weaver is fired, leaving after a tour of Hawaii; he is replaced by Peter James. "Alto, Baritone and Bass" is recorded but unissued. Daughter Leslie Ann is born.

1952

Departing from the expected, the Slickers record a polka album ("Bottoms Up") and a series of country and western records. The band hosts two episodes of NBC-TV's *All-Star Revue.* Joe Siracusa leaves the band.

1953

Jones records a parody of "Dragnet" and a series of uninspired children's records for RCA, in between tours with his *Musical Insanities* revue. A European tour is slated but fails to materialize. Dick Morgan dies of a heart attack; Billy Barty joins the group.

1954

Jones and the Slickers star in a film for Universal, *Fireman, Save My Child*, but Spike is dissatisfied with the finished product. The band gets its first TV series on NBC, directed by Bud Yorkin. Earl Bennett quits the band.

1955

Jones parts company with RCA Victor. While the Slickers' popularity begins to wane at home, huge crowds welcome the band on a tour of Australia. Spike plans an ambitious daytime TV variety series, but fails to sell the idea. Gil Bernal joins the band on sax.

1956-1957

Jones records "Spike Spoofs the Pops" and a number of LPs for Verve, notably "Dinner Music for People Who Aren't Very Hungry." The Slickers abandon their loud plaid suits for pastel tuxedos and become The Band That Plays for Fun, for a CBS TV series that marks a departure in style.

1958-1959

Spike serves as bi-weekly host for the summer of 1958 on NBC's *Club Oasis*. Another daughter, Gina Maria, is born that year. The bandleader records "Spike Jones in Stereo" for Warner Bros. Records and "Omnibust" for Liberty. Freddy Morgan quits the band.

1960-1961

Spike, in failing health, is diagnosed with emphysema. Nevertheless, he records "60 Years of Music America Hates Best" and "Rides, Rapes and Rescues" for Liberty. Spike and Helen host two summer series for CBS TV and continue to make personal appearances in Las Vegas. Jones pitches several TV projects around town, with no takers. George Rock and Billy Barty leave the band.

A rare moment of recreation. (*Ted Hering*)

1962-1964

Jones records four Liberty albums with his so-called New Band—actually led by arranger Carl Brandt—ranging from "Washington Square" to "Hank Williams Hits." Spike and Helen tour with a revue called *The Show of the Year*. He begins work on two additional albums, "Persuasive Concussion" and "Ghoul Days," but does not live to complete them.

1965

Jones fulfills a February engagement in Las Vegas, despite his illness. In March, he collapses at Harrah's Club in Lake Tahoe, and is flown to a hospital in Los Angeles. The maestro dies at his Beverly Hills home (May 1).

Der Furor
How It All Began

Ven Der Fuehrer says,
"Ve iss der Master Race,"
Ve Heil! *phbbt!*
Heil! *phbbt!*
Right in Der Fuehrer's Face.
Not to luff Der Fuehrer
iss a great disgrace,
So ve Heil! *phbbt!*
Heil! *phbbt!*
Right in Der Fuehrer's Face.

On a mid-September day in 1942, as Adolf Hitler's war machine wrought havoc in Stalingrad, America enjoyed a much-needed laugh at his expense. For that was the day an obscure bandleader's raspberry-flavored rendition of "Der Fuehrer's Face" made an audacious assault on the nation's airwaves, courtesy of a Manhattan radio station.

The silly lyrics, the nutty vocal and the imitation oom-pah band sound, not to mention the raspberry—also known as *the bird,* or the Bronx Cheer in those days—instantly caught the fancy of a nation fraught with anxiety, and catapulted a relatively unknown musician to stardom almost literally overnight.

"This, brother, is the first big war-tune—and it fulfills every requirement that was put down here," declared Mike Levin of *Down Beat.* "It has an easy melody, with a refrain that a bunch of guys can scream at the top of their lungs. The lyrics are not only funny, but they also poke brutally at some of the Nazis' worst weaknesses. A good 50% of what makes this look like *the* record of the year is the terrific job that the Spike Jones gang

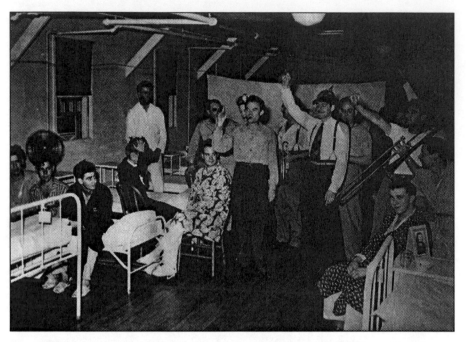

Hitler gets the "the bird" in a live performance, circa 1944. (*Warren Dexter*)

do on it. I've been raving about their stuff for months and am certainly glad to see that they're going to pick up some chips now for their fine work."

Lindley Armstrong Jones was making a comfortable living drumming in recording studios and on radio shows, notably in John Scott Trotter's orchestra on *Kraft Music Hall.* But there was a hunger, less a physical want than an artistic need, a yearning unfulfilled by the repertoire of popular songs he was required to play.

In his spare time he rehearsed with a group of studio musicians, sounding out his frustrations with a collection of cowbells, washboards, automobile horns, firearms, doorbells, flit guns and other assorted junk. But despite a regular Saturday night gig at a private club, an occasional radio guest appearance and a contract with RCA Victor, Spike Jones and his City Slickers were going nowhere fast.

"Der Fuehrer's Face" was not something Spike—or anyone else—visualized as a ticket to fame and fortune; it was simply chosen to round out a last-minute recording session. Just how the song found its way into Spike's hands, and what happened once it did, is not easy to discern. Due to Jones' resounding success a legend has grown around his rendition of the number, the details of which have been distorted not only by time but by design.

The tune came from the pen of an unlikely source. British-born composer Oliver Wallace, a one-time silent movie organist who wrote the score for *Dumbo,* was well known for his sour disposition. But with the war accelerating, and Hitler's path of destruction ever widening, it wasn't hard to ridicule the Nazis. Even a dour old Englishman could sink his teeth into that assignment, especially since it was for a Walt Disney cartoon.

Wallace brought the tune to Jones' standby pianist, his friend and neighbor Carl Hoefle, according to Del Porter, who wrote the arrangement. Jones himself recalled however that *his* friend, song plugger Nat Winecoff, "found the tune and gave it to me."

A third possible route from songwriter to bandleader has been suggested. "I think it was probably someone in music publicity," ventured veteran Disney animator Frank Thomas. "They were so delighted at this meeting where somebody walked in and said, 'Hey, we got Spike Jones to record it.' Walt said, 'Hey, that's good.'

"No one thought of that when they were writing the piece, but after that's all done, publicity's part of it is to come in and figure out ways to promote sales. They were trying to get different bands to record the thing. Someone said, 'Hey, you ought to get Spike Jones. He's the guy to do that.'" That someone in Disney's music promotion department could have been Nat Winecoff, who worked in both Disney's and Jones' employ at various times.

A song plugger reportedly gave an advance copy of the song to another novelty band, the Hoosier Hot Shots. The group—which was featured on NBC's *National Barn Dance* and enjoyed far greater renown than the City Slickers at the time—was forced to turn the number down, asserted clarinetist Gabe Ward. "We weren't allowed to make it, because we were under contract to the Wade Advertising Agency. They thought the raspberry thing was obscene on 'Der Fuehrer's Face.' We had too good a contract with Alka Seltzer to argue with them," said Ward.

When Spike decided to record the number, the studio's legal advisers objected—according to a *Saturday Evening Post* article bylined by Frederick C. Othman, and filled with half-truths and fabrications: "Spike called Wallace, who agreed that the recording would be an excellent idea. The Disney lawyers didn't. Contractual relationships made it necessary, they said, for the tune to be published as sheet music before it could be recorded."

Such difficulties seem unlikely, although *Donald Duck in Axis Land*

Carl Grayson lampoons the enemy in concert, circa 1943, while Country
Washburne and John Stanley provide support. (*Skip Craig*)

was still in production at the time. "I don't think there was any problem
at all about getting the rights to it," Del Porter recalled. "We had no
trouble at all."

Frank Thomas contended that negotiations with recording artists
were generally conducted during production "so they could have [a record]
out about the same time the picture came out. Something as important
as this…I would think they'd try to get it out early. The legal department
would say, 'No, you can't.' But Walt would say, 'Oh, yes, you can.'"

In any case, there was no time to lose in putting the tune on wax.
Jones cut the record on July 28, 1942, just days before the musicians'
union banned their members from recording studios for a long duration.
The City Slickers, with violinist Carl Grayson doing the vocal and Spike
himself on drums and sound effects, gave it their all. First, they did the

tune with a trombone blaring out the insult to Hitler and his stooges; then, after Jones reportedly told the band, "It stinks," they did it again with a toy rubber razzer—which he promptly dubbed *the birdaphone*—emitting a spirited Bronx Cheer.

"We recorded it both ways, hoping that maybe Victor would take the one with the raspberry, but they kicked like the devil," Porter stated in an interview. "They didn't want to do that at all."

"It didn't seem like such a good song to me, but I got to thinking that if it were to get anywhere, it would have to be released with the bird included," Jones told the *Post*. "So I drew $1,000 out of the bank and Pat [his first wife] and I went to New York to talk the Victor Company's private board of public morals into letting us use the bird." Jones arrived to find company executives already in agreement with him, according to the *Post* article. Another version of the incident by Chicago columnist Irv Kupcinet claimed executives relented only after a long session on said morals.

Despite Jones' and Porter's assertions—and the widely circulated falsehood that the raspberry had never been heard on record or radio before—RCA Victor's reluctance would seem improbable. Rudy Vallee ("The Old Sow Song"), English comedian Jack Hodges ("Everything is Fresh Today") and the western group, the Sweet Violet Boys ("Jim's Windy Mule"), had already etched such rude noises on wax. Furthermore, Teddy Powell's "Serenade to a Maid"—which preceded "Der Fuehrer" on Victor's Bluebird label by several months—featured a much juicier and more potentially offensive raspberry, but was greeted by mild reaction.

However, Walter S. Heebner, the Artists & Repertoire (A&R) representative in charge of Jones in the late '40s, gave some credence to stories about the company's reluctance. "The A&R man, the sales manager and so forth, they were afraid of what the reaction would be from the top floor," ventured Heebner. "General [David] Sarnoff was quite a straight-laced gentleman. He was a rabid union man, and he was socially conscious…and 'Der Fuehrer' had more political overtones than 'Serenade to a Maid.' The brass had the word; that would be my thinking. I'd say Spike is telling the truth."

RCA's publicity department wasted no time in their promotional efforts once the record was scheduled for release. They devoted the front page of their *Phono-Graphic* newsletter to a cartoon illustrating the lyrics, and attributed a blurb to Nazi minister of propaganda Joseph Goebbels

calling it "a laugh-provoking sensation!"

Given the promotional push, reports of the company having so little confidence in the song that they pressed only 500 records seem unlikely. Within weeks however, *Down Beat* noted, "Victor has been caught flat-footed and is racing desperately to catch up."

Setting a career precedent, Jones himself jump-started the record's success, making the rounds of disc jockeys with test pressings in hand during his visit to New York. Alan Courtney played it three times on the same show on station WOV. But Martin Block went one step further at WNEW.

Block, the preeminent deejay of his time, created a furor over "Der Fuehrer" by playing it repeatedly on his *Make Believe Ballroom* as part of a campaign to sell war bonds. Every time the pledges increased $2,500, he would spin the anti-Hitler song again, recalled one of his faithful listeners. "We just couldn't get enough of it," said Abe Ravitz. "Boy, did that ever relieve the tension!"

The disc jockey—a master pitchman who once persuaded his listeners to run out and buy refrigerators during a blizzard—offered a free record to anyone in his listening audience who bought a $50 war bond, giving away 289 records the first day. He sold over $60,000 worth of war bonds in the first week.

Such a stunt was all in a day's work for Block. "He was the guy that brought disc jockeydom to America," asserted Jones' longtime publicist, Buddy Basch. "The Lindbergh kidnapping trial was coming over the wire from Flemington, New Jersey, and for minutes and hours on end nothing would happen, and they wanted to leave the wire open and not put anything else on. Block came in and said, 'What if I play some records and talk between 'em? They can cut away from me any time they want.' The general manager of WNEW said, 'That's not the worst idea I ever heard'—and that's how disc jockeydom started."

Things started popping for Jones like champagne corks on New Year's Eve. Within four weeks of "Der Fuehrer's" September 18th release and its launch into orbit, he accepted an offer to appear in the all-star Warner Bros. extravaganza *Thank Your Lucky Stars;* signed a deal to headline his own show on NBC; agreed to provide the music for Bob "Bazooka" Burns' coast-to-coast radio program, following a guest appearance; and jammed with Count Basie, Tommy Dorsey and Lionel Hampton on Armed Forces Radio's *Command Performance.* With sales nearing the half-million mark, he signed a new contract with Victor.

Walt Disney also capitalized on Spike's success. By the time the record came out, his yet-to-be-released cartoon—which was built around the song, and depicted its web-footed star working in a Nazi munitions factory—had been retitled *Donald Duck in Nutziland.* In October Disney did what any savvy producer would have done; he renamed it *Der Fuehrer's Face.* Promoted heavily on the strength of the hit record, the January

1943 release won an Academy Award for Best Cartoon Short.

"It did the job of boosting morale…" noted animator Jack Kinney, who directed the cartoon. "Prints [of the film] were sent all over the world, even to Russia, which used its propaganda message to encourage their troops. I don't think it was very popular with the Nazis. In fact, we heard that Hitler burned every copy he could find. We loved that."

While Jones' recording of the tune was not the only one, it proved far more durable than its competitors, enjoying ten weeks on *Billboard*'s Hit Parade. Singing cowboy Johnny Bond recorded his own version on Columbia's Okeh label, which enjoyed some success; Arthur Fields' gravelly-voiced rendition, on the short-lived Hit label, and Charles Brook's version on Victory, fared less well. Spike was the only one who dared to give the Bronx Cheer to Hitler. Bond and Fields used a squeaky duck call; the Donald Duck cartoon substituted a blast on the tuba and a munitions factory whistle.

There is some question about the actual number of copies Jones' version sold, but it is certain the number was diminished by the unavailability of materials. "I imagine all sales were hurt, because shellac was damn important to the war effort," said Walt Heebner. "They were conducting drives for shaving brush handles, tooth brush handles, all that stuff—and that's why we used only a mix of vinyl at RCA; it wasn't a pure vinyl."

The leader of the so-called Craziest Band in the Land continued to do his raucous hit song long after the war was over, as he toured the country with his mad ensemble. In live stage performances they improved on the recording. Spike Jones and his City Slickers did what any red-blooded American in Uncle Sam's Armed Forces would have done; arms outstretched in mock salute, they gave Der Fuehrer der finger.

Drummer Boy
Youth & Education, 1911–1929

Eleven days to Christmas, prompted the advertisement. *Don't forget father. Get him that gift now.*

Ada Armstrong Jones didn't forget. Nor did she need the prodding of the Long Beach, California, *Daily Telegram.* That very morning, December 14, 1911, in Long Beach's Bethlehem Inn, she delivered a Christmas present her husband would always cherish—a blue-eyed, sandy-haired baby boy.

While it is clear his childhood was far from ordinary, the circumstances of his birth—like so many other aspects of Spike Jones' life—have become somewhat muddled over the years, thanks in part to Jones himself. The bandleader gave varying accounts of his past for public consumption, without regard to inaccuracies and inconsistencies.

Privately, he was not one to reminisce about his youth. "These are things he never told us about, or talked about," reflected Spike's eldest daughter, Linda Jones. "When we would sit at the dining room table, there were no stories about his childhood, or his parents, or what he had done, or life as a little boy—ever. We missed out on all of that."

In an as-told-to article in *True Story* magazine, Jones cited Calexico, California, as the first hometown he could remember, pointing out he lived with his parents in Long Beach until he was ten weeks old. The birth announcement in the *Long Beach Press,* however, identified the parents of the newborn as "Mr. and Mrs. L.M. Jones, of Calexico."

The town where his parents lived, 230 miles to the south—all three square miles of it—did not always meet their needs. Lindley Murray Jones was a depot agent for the Southern Pacific Railroad, a company man who went where the job took him. Although he lived and worked in California's hot, barren Colorado Desert, there was no reason his schoolteacher-wife had to give birth to their child in that desolate wilderness.

The future music wrecker, circa 1916.
(*Spike Jones International Fan Club*)

The Joneses were first-time parents, but they were not a dreamy-eyed young couple. They were staid, set-in-their-ways Midwesterners—"the salt of the earth," according to a family friend. They were long past the normal child-rearing age. Lindley Armstrong Jones was their first-born, and because they were in their early forties, they knew he would be their last.

Imperial Valley wasn't the worst place to raise a child. Calexico, a sleepy little town on the U.S.-Mexican border of some 797 people (as of 1910), provided plenty of room to grow. And the Joneses, who hailed from Iowa, could appreciate the climate; as a result of the surrounding desert, the sun shone nearly every day of the year.

Little Lindley lived with his parents above the railroad depot. At seven he started grammar school in or near the neighboring town of El Centro, where his mother was not only the teacher, but the bus driver. As if that were not enough, she also served as principal, according to her son.

"At school I was troublesome boy No. 1," Jones volunteered years later, in an interview with an Australian newspaper. "On my first day I was sent to the principal's office to meet Mama in a new capacity—and what a licking I got!"

Mrs. Jones was a no-nonsense woman who did not play favorites. "Another day Mama came into the classroom and a great big bully was throwing his weight around. Mama let fly and socked him across the room. That night the bully gave me a licking—and from then on every time one of the kids got a going over I got one too, from them after school."

When he wasn't defending himself against his classmates, Lindley was seldom to be found in their company. His middle-aged parents gave him an unusually mature outlook on life, one that allowed little patience for the childish games of his peers.

"The only play I got was through music," he recounted. "Dad's parents were Quakers, and his father was the first man to introduce music to

Quaker services. Both he and Mother were fond of hymns and old songs, and I acquired a liking for music from them."

Becoming a bandleader, however, was not a respectable ambition for a seven-year-old boy—not as far as the Joneses were concerned. They wanted their only child to be a doctor or a lawyer, anything but a musician. They were not alone in their way of thinking. "Anybody in showbiz or music or anything, that was about as low as you could get," affirmed trumpeter George Rock, the backbone of the City Slickers. "I would assume his parents were proud of him later on—they would have had to be. But they didn't associate with the band; we were a pretty low form of life."

On Saturday, her one day off, Lindley's mother drove him 24 miles each way over rugged dirt roads, to the home of a trombone teacher. The boy also took piano lessons, and showed evidence of some ability. But his parents hoped he was simply going through a phase.

The family followed the tracks from one town to another in the sprawling Imperial Valley, moving from Calexico to Niland, near the Salton Sea. The stairway leading up to their new second-floor home was too narrow for a piano—as Jones later recalled—forcing the boy to abandon the instrument. It was a fortuitous move.

Lindley, who continued his education at Fremont School in nearby Calipatria, soon found a sympathetic friend at the railroad lunch counter. "Having no piano, I became interested in the sounds produced by the colored chef of the station restaurant, who rattled knives and forks and other tools of the eating trade into catchy rhythms," Jones recalled.

A station porter—or the cook, according to the most frequently-told version of the incident—fanned the flames of the sixth-grader's youthful curiosity by whittling the boy a pair of drumsticks from the rungs of an old wooden chair. Jones also attributed his "affinity for noise" to his environment – "listening to the trains, the whistles, the bells, the telegraph keys, all the sounds of a railroad depot."

Chair rungs and breadboard were all right for a start, but before long he decided he had to have the real thing. On Christmas morning, 1922, just after he celebrated his eleventh birthday, Lindley got his first set of drums. About the same time a telegrapher, "seeing me hanging around the tracks so much," gave him the nickname by which he would one day be recognized around the world. But while he was Spike to his peers—and later, his public—he was always to remain Lindley to his parents.

Jones, who took lessons from a local orchestra leader, did no sooner acquire his first real percussion instrument than he organized his first group, the Jazzbo Four. "I suppose if I had been an ordinary kid I would have been content to join a fife and bugle corps," he later explained. "But though I wore knee pants, and Mother still told me to be careful how I crossed the tracks, I had adult ideas."

While the members of his dance band were between 15 and 18, Spike was only 11 or 12. His father objected to the idea of his son playing professionally at such a tender age but eventually softened; he reluctantly gave his consent after band members campaigned one by one on Spike's behalf. Jones was apparently part of a group called the Calipat Melody Four—"the loudest four-piece orchestra in the Imperial Valley"—during the same period, although this could have been an alternate moniker for the Jazzbo Four.

Spike attended the ninth grade and the beginning of the tenth at Calipatria High School. He excelled scholastically during his brief tenure there, during which he was chosen from thousands of California students to be a member of the All State High School Symphony Orchestra. The opportunity changed his life.

When the young drummer attended an All State contest in Sacramento, he realized school, as it existed in the barren desert region he called home, left a lot to be desired—at least in regard to the music department. He had only to meet the band director of Long Beach Polytechnic High School and some of the musicians, and his mind was made up.

"Spike wanted to be in Long Beach because of the music program," affirmed William T.J. Harris, who became one of his closest friends at Poly High. "We had two orchestras, two bands; they were pretty well known. When John Philip Sousa would come to town, he would always direct our band. Spike met George Moore at this state contest, and that's when he decided he wanted to come to Long Beach."

Poly High was built the year Spike was born. By December 1926, when he returned to his birthplace, Poly had garnered a reputation as the number one high school in the United States. Its students had the highest grade average in the country.

"Poly was a terrific school," enthused Herschell E. Ratliff, who played tuba and string bass alongside Spike. "It was set up just like a college;

that's why it was number one. There was a four-block square of schools and you could enter any department, take any course."

Long Beach itself had blossomed in Jones' absence. Its population had increased nearly ten-fold, and the city, beribboned by 125 miles of paved roads and three transcontinental railroad lines, was growing ever rapidly to meet their needs. Buses were beginning to replace trolley cars, and the harbor was taking shape, growing out of the mud flat Long Beach had once been.

"We had a town center, we had a municipal auditorium; any big event was held there. There was a wonderful

The first set of drums, circa 1922.

hotel, the Virginia, and they had an orchestra," said Bill Harris. "It was a good Methodist town. People went to church, they had socials; they had lots of small dances and everybody would attend. It was a good, wholesome town." It was also a town with money, thanks to the oil wells now dotting the landscape – providing much-needed income for the school district.

Though Jones noted, "Dad was transferred to a station near Long Beach," his classmates recalled that "Spike was on his own" during his years at Poly High. "When he first came to Long Beach, his mother got him a room on Third Street with an older couple," stated Harris. "That didn't last very long; I never figured out whether it was Spike or the old couple. Then he went over on 16th street, and roomed with a clarinet player he had met in the All State Orchestra by the name of John Healy. Spike lived with him when they started Poly."

"During the summer, we were jobbing and everything," said Harris, then a budding trombone player himself. "Spike decided he'd like to go out on his own, so he talked his mother into letting him rent this apartment. It was a nice apartment, right over near the school; it was owned by the old fire chief. And Spike had this place in the back. It sort of became a hangout."

While he was a remarkably independent 15-year-old, Jones' freedom from home was tethered by one proviso—that he maintain good grades at Poly. Spike entered the three-year high school as a sophomore, enrolling in band and orchestra. The 125-piece orchestra, one of two which met daily in the music room above the boy's gym, was unique in that it offered practical experience in ensemble playing. Before long, Spike was drumming in the 85-piece Advanced Orchestra, which gave radio concerts and provided the music for the senior play.

There were three teachers in the music department, one of whom taught nothing but harmony. George C. Moore, who taught band and orchestra, had played flute with the Boston Symphony; his successor, Dwight S. Defty, had been a cellist with the Los Angeles Symphony for many years. "Neither had college degrees, but they had years of experience. As a result," said Hersh Ratliff, "our orchestra won every contest in the State of California."

Although the musical education Spike received in Long Beach was far superior to what was available at Calipatria High, it was still lacking in one regard. His instructors didn't teach him how to "play it hot," so he augmented his formal studies by listening to—and playing along with—the radio.

The walls of Spike's one-bedroom apartment, unfortunately, were not soundproof. "He used to drive the neighbors nuts. He'd turn on the radio, set up his drums and practice like mad," recalled Ratliff. "There were a lot of complaints."

Intent on becoming a jazz band drummer, Jones turned a deaf ear to the noise other people made about the noise he was making. "Spike was determined. He was so concentrated on learning to be a good drummer, so imbedded with this idea of what he was going to do when he got out of school," ventured Ratliff. "His whole energy went to that, and his studies."

Jones soon found himself playing drums for Al Rowland's Varsity Six dance band. Day or night, he was focused on his goal. On Sundays, he could be found in church—playing in the First Methodist Junior Orchestra.

"We played every Sunday and rehearsed once a week. Spike heard about it and he wanted to play in it, so we got him in," related Bill Harris.

"John Rankin, the local Cadillac dealer, was our Sunday School teacher. He would get us jobs playing at automobile shows; anybody that had a dollar, we would play. The same group became Rankin's Cadillac Eight on weekdays, and the church orchestra on Sunday."

Despite the experienced counsel available to him at school, Spike never asked for advice in pursuing his career. "He had his own ideas," observed teacher Dwight Defty. "He was an independent cuss; he did what he wanted to do when he wanted to do it. One day I said something and he sassed me. That was one thing I wouldn't take from anybody, and I kicked him out of the band. I got a box of oranges from his family with regards."

Among Jones' "own ideas," naturally, was another band under the leadership of a certain drummer. A number of boys from the Poly High orchestra had formed a group called the California Tantalizers. They played over radio station KFOX before school started, and earned their lunches by providing meal-time entertainment for patrons of the campus cafeteria. Spike knew a good thing when he saw one, and when the Tantalizers disbanded circa 1927, he stepped in with his own group.

Spike Jones and His Five Tacks was a typical jazz combo patterned after Red Nichols and His Five Pennies, as were the Tantalizers, who often copied his records. The Tacks—a name allegedly suggested to Jones by Nichols himself—sometimes numbered six, despite their moniker.

In addition to KFOX, the Tacks reportedly played for station KGER on behalf of an adjacent shoe store, Dobyn's Footwear, billing themselves as The Patent Leather Kids. But Harris remembered the Kids as a different group, "just in between Spike and the pros," led by someone other than Jones. "Maybe Spike played with them," suggested Harris. "But I knew the guy who had the band; If Spike had the band, it had his name on it."

There was no question who led the Five Tacks, but not everyone was as enamored of the group as its irrepressible leader. Defty, who was witness to a few of the group's rehearsals, was not an ardent fan. "It was a good band, all good players, but it didn't address me too much," he reflected. "I like better music than what they were playing."

Ada Jones could not have expected her son to play the hymns his parents taught him—as she had hoped, when he first started taking music lessons—but she was predictably horrified when she got a chance to listen to his band. "We played our music hard and hot, and when Mama heard us she was deeply shocked," recounted Spike. "But it was too late. I was on my way."

During the Tacks' two-year existence the members included Bill Woodard and Noble Montaro on trumpet; Bill Harris and Linwood Howe on trombone; Carl Vidano and Stanley Sheriff on piano; Rex Finney and Gilbert Scott on banjo; Paul Harrison and Guy Laraway on clarinet and tenor sax; and Hersh Ratliff on bass sax.

The teenage jazzmen had more in common than their classes at Poly High. They were bonded by "this strong desire to be musicians when we grew up, and we all sensed that in each other. There was nothing going to get in our way. Nobody was going to stop us," maintained Ratliff, a member of both the Tantalizers and the Tacks.

"The Five Tacks never made history," conceded Harris. "It was just a get-up orchestra of a bunch of ambitious kids who didn't know any better, and thought they were better than they were. We kept workin' at it; when we could get jobs and carry a dance all the way through, then we began to feel like we were doin' something. But the Five Tacks started out as just a group of guys playing any place we could. We played in Mt. Baldy for some girls; we got a dollar a night and lodging.

"I can remember many a dollar-a-night job," said Harris. "I used to kid Spike. He'd say, 'We're going up here to do this... we're not going to get anything for it, but they'll feed us and so on.' I'd say, 'You know, Spike, you'd play for nuthin' if they put your name up in lights.'"

"We all played in different groups," noted saxophonist Paul Harrison, who roomed with Spike for about a year. "If somebody had a job Saturday night and we weren't working, we played a job with them."

The earnings were minimal, but the bandleader hustled plenty of work. When he found out the Demolays held dances, he joined the organization; he then had the members of his band join the Junior Elks and various other clubs and organizations that sponsored dances. "They had to have us, or nothing. And we were just about better than nothing," quipped Bill Harris.

Despite their less than spectacular achievements, the bandsmen persevered. "We got laughed at and ridiculed and everything else when we said we were going to be musicians, but we hung in there," affirmed Ratliff. "No one expected Spike to end up like he did; no one expected our trumpet player to end up with Paul Whiteman. We didn't know what direction we were going to go in, except we wanted to be musicians. You've got to have that determination."

Spike's devotion to the practice and performance of music in and

out of school required sacrifice as well as discipline. "He
forfeited a lot of other things,"
averred Ratliff. "He didn't
have a lot of friends; he wasn't
an easy guy to get close to in
high school."

Jones was so short and
skinny, the opposite sex paid
little attention to him. "I don't
remember him going out with
girls hardly at all," said Ratliff.
"He was too small. Most of
the girls his age were much
bigger than he was and way
much more mature." Harris
observed: "Spike never chased
the women much. I generally
had to chase them for him; he
was always too busy to fool
around with them."

Senior portrait, Long Beach Polytechnic High
School, 1929. (*Herschell Ratliff*)

The aspiring musician went to the movies with friends on occasion, but
he was choosy. "Spike generally was too busy looking for a band to listen to,
to go to a movie. If the movie had Fred Waring or Paul Whiteman in it, he
might go," noted Harris. The boys also went to vaudeville shows in downtown Los Angeles. "We saw every big show, Eddie Peabody and Paul Whiteman
and all the stage shows. Mr. [John] Rankin would drive us up there in his big
Cadillac, and pay for everything," said Harris. "Spike and I sat through four
shows up at the Orpheum, watching Whiteman; Spike sure went for
Whiteman a lot."

He was not one for other types of recreation. "I don't ever remember
Spike going swimming; he wouldn't have taken time off. Spike just didn't
have any interest in that type of thing. He used to get out of physical
education if he could, at school," said Harris. "There was a special class
he was in—The Sick, Crippled and Useless, we used to call them."

Many of the Tacks shared his disdain for this aspect of school. "We
were too busy with music. We had no time for football and all that stuff,"
contended Paul Harrison. "We went into ROTC purposely so we didn't

have to go. In ROTC you got to play in the band—that took care of physical education."

Jones, who suffered from asthma as a child, at first ran with a clean crowd that didn't drink or smoke, which was of no small benefit to his health. He apparently took to cigarettes for the same reason little girls play dress-up. "Spike started out smoking because he thought that's what the big boys did," ventured Harris. "He started smoking, and it became a habit."

Clearly this only child who had never been very childlike now wanted to be perceived as a young adult. "I became so self-conscious about my youth that I used to fuss a lot to make myself look more mature," he reflected. "I began to dress too old for my years, assumed a sophisticated expression, talked smart."

The aspiring musician soon found he could talk his way into almost anything, and adopted a demeanor to match. The many occasions on which he went to see Red Nichols at the Cotton Club—across the street from Hal Roach Studios in Culver City—were no exception.

"We got pretty well acquainted with the band. There was a booth right close to the band; once in a while we were able to get in there, then the guys would come talk to us," said Paul Harrison, who recalled paying to get into the club "the first time or two—then I think some of Red's band told us how to get in the back way."

Mused Bill Harris: "We had no money. We sneaked in through the kitchen. We learned that that was the way to go in. The musicians were pretty nice to us; they kinda felt sorry for us, I think. Spike used to even get those guys to stay after work and teach him licks on the drums. He learned a lot from Nichols' drummer [Chick Condon]."

One night their departure was rather sudden, however. Remembered Carl Vidano, the Tacks' pianist: "The maitre d' comes over and says, 'Mr. Nichols, you'll have to pardon me a second. Hey, you fellas, what are you doing in here?' 'We're just talking to Mr. Nichols.' 'Did you come through the front door?' 'No, sir.' 'Well, you better leave the way you came. And I mean right now.' So with that we immediately headed for the back door…

"Evidently they had been tipped off in the kitchen, 'If those guys come though here again, you better be sure they go out.' As we exited, we were followed by this chef with a long knife, and we certainly did exit the place," said Vidano. "I don't think we went back for a while," conceded Harrison. "We were not angels in those days."

The boys' getaway car that night was Spike's Hupmobile, which his parents had bought him to carry his equipment—and facilitate the "Have Drum, Will Travel" lifestyle he was rapidly developing. "Spike and I did some jobbing together when we were kids in high school," recalled bass player Russell "Candy" Hall, who attended Santa Monica High.

"We worked many jobs together. Sometimes we'd try to save a car; we'd meet someplace and drive together. I remember on one job we ran out of gas, going to San Bernadino. Drums and bass were late on the job," mused Hall, who rejoined Spike as a City Slicker years later.

During high school Jones augmented his education at every opportunity. The Long Beach Municipal Band offered one of many extracurricular classes in music appreciation and technique. "Ninety percent of that band was with Sousa. He had a guy by the name of O.F. Rominger, who was one of the best timpanists in the country. Who was down there at intermission? Spike. He went down, and Rominger gave him timpani lessons for about 50 cents apiece," said Bill Harris. "Spike wasn't bashful. He always had an angle; he was always working at it.

"He used to write to Isham Jones and Fred Waring. He'd go tackle 'em. Spike carried on a lot of correspondence with them. I remember he asked Waring in a letter, what advice he would give to a fellow like him, who wanted to have a band. Spike had that letter [reply] framed for a long time."

But Jones was a doer, not a daydreamer. Among his accomplishments at this time was his appointment as drum major of the 60-member Poly High School Band, a sure triumph of baton over brawn. "In selecting Jones for this position Mr. [Dwight] Defty departed from precedent and chose the shortest, rather than the tallest, man for the position," noted a local newspaper. "Jones barely passes the five-foot mark, but makes up for his lack of height with a magnetic personality and considerable drum major flair, according to Mr. Defty."

Harris recalled with amusement how his "scrawny" friend pulled off this feat. "Spike, here's how alert he was, he knew this was coming up," marveled Harris, "so he hunted up a guy who had the championship drill team for the American Legion. Spike went over and took lessons from him. The first day when the band came out and they were going to have tryouts for the drum major, he brought his baton and boy, ol' Spike, he strutted hell out of the end of that contest. He put on a pretty good show."

Apparently, he was only doing what came naturally. "Spike was quite a character. He was a regular clown," asserted Defty. "He was a darn good drummer, though. He wasn't very big, but we gave him a great big baton, about seven feet long. We had lots of fun with him. One day we played a trick on him during a parade in downtown Long Beach. Spike was out in front of the band. At a certain signal, the band turned left and went down a side street, and Spike kept going right on down the street with the baton, all by himself."

Jones remembered the incident a little differently, but not always the same way. In one version of the story he told, as he marched along Pine Street with the procession behind him—and his mother in attendance—he continually gazed at himself in shop windows. "I was so wrapped up in my own reflected glory," he noted, "that the band turned down a side street—as it was supposed to do—and I kept going straight ahead, wondering why the music was getting fainter."

The band, which had recently swapped their khaki ROTC uniforms for green and gold sweaters with white trousers and beanies, provided Spike his first real turn in the spotlight. The group's yearly invitation to play in the California's annual Tournament of Roses Parade gave him the opportunity to strut his stuff before a sizable crowd.

Jones earned an A in every subject except chemistry at Poly High, according to one account, although he cited a B plus average elsewhere. He graduated in June 1929, with 467 other hopeful young people ready to make their mark on the world.

Their glorious alma mater was leveled to the ground just four years later, by the devastating Long Beach earthquake of 1933. By then many of Poly's alumni had gained a firm footing on the road ahead, including one somewhat frail but very energetic and determined boy who yearned to be a bandleader.

Man About Town
Dance Bands & Studio Work, 1929–1941

Upon graduation from Long Beach Poly High, Spike Jones joined the Los Angeles chapter of the American Federation of Musicians, Local 47—apparently lying about his age to do so—and began working odd jobs. "He'd play a single here, maybe two nights in Balboa, a single over in Santa Monica. He was substituting all around...just making enough to pay for gasoline," recalled Bill Harris of the Five Tacks, who was accustomed to having the itinerant musician spend the night at his house, and make himself at home.

Spike's first regular job on graduating school was an engagement at the Ship's Cafe in Venice, a popular nightspot next to the pier in the form of a Spanish galleon—a replica of the flagship sailed by Portuguese explorer Juan Cabrillo. Where Cabrillo discovered California, Jones would begin his exploration of the New World.

The gig was a testament to Spike's abilities as a salesman if not a musician. "He didn't even have a band. He went down there with some pictures and sold those guys on the fact he had a band that would come in there and put it over. He got the job, and he literally went out and recruited that band," revealed Harris. "It was kind of a game of bluff. The Ship's Cafe didn't have any money and neither did Spike." Jones got a sour taste of the real world when the colorful establishment went broke that fall—during the Crash of '29—owing him a substantial amount of money.

With the country in the throes of financial collapse, Spike enrolled at Chaffey College in Ontario, California. Concurrent with his participation in the school's busy Concert Orchestra, under the guidance of Fred Wilding, Jr., he played in Ray West's band at the Lake Norconian Club, a popular hotel and country club in nearby Norco.

During his tenure at Chaffey, Jones entered a public speaking contest.

He won the first and second elimination rounds, only to be disqualified because he was a professional musician. "You can take such a let-down philosophically or you can say, 'To heck with it!' I took the latter way and entered no more contests," he recalled. "Soon after, I quit college. Partly this was due to my disappointment and partly to the urge to give my whole time to band playing."

In 1930 or thereabouts, Jones joined the California Revelers. The eight-piece dance band was led by Paul Harrison, who had played sax and clarinet with the Five Tacks, and included several of Spike's former bandsmen. The group was heard weekday mornings and Sunday evenings on KGER, advertising a real estate development called Cambria Pines By the Sea.

Spike also took the opportunity to advertise himself. "He would do anything to get his name on the air," asserted banjoist Rex Finney, who graduated from the Tacks to the Revelers. "Spike was serious, but he always wanted to cut up, have fun. The idea of fun was to get publicity.

"One time during the commercial—we were in a glass room, and you were supposed to be real, real quiet—he dropped his cymbal and made a lot of noise. 'Oh, that was Spike Jones who dropped his cymbal.' A couple of KGER officials were running up and down on the outside of this glass room, pointing their fingers at us; they were pretty upset. Spike would do things, but he always had a reason for it—get his name out in front."

"He had a good, fast brain," observed Harrison. "When Spike wanted something, he went after it; he knew how to do it. I would say he was a little unusual, a little faster than a lot of us."

He also put his name before the public at this time—or so he recalled—by organizing another band of his own, once more called Spike Jones and his Five Tacks. "I was 18 and my men were between 23 and 30," he recalled of the second incarnation of the group. "The band went pretty well for over a year, then the urge to return to college got me." Although he returned to Chaffey, "the spirit of academic learning was out of me," he conceded. At the end of the term he quit again and never went back—a "mistake" he later regretted.

In the early summer of 1931, he organized a short-lived dance band called the Baldy Four with at least two Chaffey classmates, trombonist Herbert Michel and trumpeter Ted Wing. Jones was apparently the leader, but not the drummer. The group performed at Mt. Baldy, a nearby resort, on behalf of Camp Curry—which also employed the band to entertain up at Yosemite National Park.

The group could have called themselves The Band That Plays For Fun, a name Jones used years later. "They probably got room and board, just enough to keep 'em up there. They were living on a string," mused Michel's sister, Dorothy Buehler. "One man at Mt. Baldy didn't pay them one week, and they took all the silver and linens when they left. They came home with a lot of silverware and napkins and things."

Herb Michel, who went on to teach music himself, remained in contact with Jones for the next three decades. "We went to see Spike somewhere in Los Angeles one time, when he came out with 'The Nutcracker Suite,' " remembered his widow, Nell Michel. "Spike autographed the album and gave it to our son, who was three. And he said, 'Listen, kid, you don't know this, but I'm tearing down everything your dad's trying to build up.' "

During the same summer he marked time with the Baldy Four, the future music wrecker auditioned for a job with composer-turned-bandleader Sam Coslow at the swank Hollywood Roosevelt Hotel, across the street from Grauman's Chinese Theatre. Coslow, who had hastily assembled a dance band when the Depression struck the movie industry, was suddenly in need of a percussionist.

Aspiring drummer joined fledgling bandleader in the Roof Garden of the Roosevelt at local scale, about $85 a week. It wasn't big money, but playing for sellout crowds on the open air terrace—where show people were tipping the maitre d' $25 and $50 for a table—was better than standing in a breadline, or working for silverware. It must've been heady stuff for a lad just two years out of high school; most of his jobs at the time were nowhere near as glamorous.

Three years later Coslow wrote himself a standard-of-living insurance policy called "Cocktails for Two," little dreaming he was also writing an annuity for the young drummer he had hired that summer.

Much of Spike's work in the early '30s was as a substitute. "Spike used to go over to the La Monica Ballroom in Santa Monica, where they played afternoons and evenings for dancing," recalled Bill Harris. "When the drummer would poop out or get tired, he'd say, 'C'mon, Spike, sit in.' Anyplace he went, if he could get acquainted with either the leader or the drummer, Spike would sit in. When Jimmie Grier took over the band at the Coconut Grove from Gus Arnheim, Spike sat in."

Jones bounced around from one job to another at this juncture of his career, at which time he shared living quarters in Hollywood with Carl

Vidano of the Five Tacks. During this period he played a two-year stint with Kearney Walton at the elegant Biltmore Hotel in Los Angeles, along with many more temporary engagements. But the job he really wanted was one he couldn't get.

Almost every weekend Spike made his way down to the beach with his pals, to listen to Everett Hoagland's group at the Rendezvous Ballroom in Balboa. "Hoagland had the only real jazz band in Southern California, and it was all of us young musicians' ambition to play for him, because he was considered *it*," observed Stan Kenton, who joined the band on piano about that time. "We all used to haunt the ballroom where he played. If you got a chance to play with Hoagland, you felt you had really arrived."

The young drummer would eventually get that chance, but not in Balboa and not at the Rendezvous, which burned to the ground some years later. As a result of hanging around the bandstand, however, he did get acquainted with Hoagland's drummer—a veteran entertainer named Beauregard Lee, whom he would one day hire himself. Spike also had a weekly rendezvous at that time with his aging parents, who had by now retired from the railroad life and moved to Monrovia, California, near Pasadena.

Throughout the early and mid-'30s Jones played a variety of short-lived gigs. Among those who frequently worked alongside him were Stan Kenton, who fruitlessly haunted the studios then; Freddie Slack, soon to become famous for his boogie woogie style of piano playing; Harry Geller, who later played trumpet for Benny Goodman; and his old pal Hersh Ratliff, former Five Tack and future City Slicker.

Jones, Kenton and Geller had a steady date, circa 1933, with a little orchestra accompanying singer Russ Columbo at the Cafe Montmartre on Seventh Street. In 1934 Jones and Slack joined trumpeter Fuzz Menge and his band at a night spot called the Club Ballyhoo on Sunset Boulevard.

While working at the Ballyhoo they took an apartment on the Sunset Strip together with two other band members—Willie Martinez, a jazz clarinet player they had met at a burlesque show, and saxophonist Bob Gioga. "These musicians would get an apartment together; maybe three of them would pay the bill," noted Bill Harris. "They'd just make enough to pay their overhead."

The Ballyhoo was an *in* spot for movie stars. Its 3 a.m. closing time was doubtless among the attractions. Another was the floor show, an entertainment which featured a teenaged Ann Miller in a specialty number. According to Martinez, Spike fell "madly in love" with one of the six young ladies in the show.

The lovestruck musician drummed the summer at Casino Gardens—a dime-a-dance joint two blocks from the Aragon Ballroom—in the resort city of Ocean Park, adjacent to Venice. The band was led in haphazard fashion by violinist George Hamilton, father of the latter-day actor. "Hamilton was a nowhere musician, yet he had some good men," said pianist Leighton Noble. "It was just a stepping stone along the line."

"Ocean Park was a scene to be remembered," asserted Harry Geller, who played second violin. "The place was so bad, during intermission Spike and I raced cockroaches across the back of the bandstand. At times people paid so little attention to the band, Spike would occasionally play the xylophone with one of his private parts—he'd use it as one of the hammers. That's how wild things were in those days. People paid no attention at all."

"Spike was a terribly funny man, great fun to be with," concurred Harriet Geller, who recalled racing cockroaches in her wedding dress. The Gellers had hardly consummated their marriage when Jones moved into their living room. "He came to live with us practically on our wedding night," she said. "We were living in an apartment in Santa Monica for $26 a month—all three of us."

While money and living quarters were equally tight in those days, Jones' fortune was soon to improve. Economic recovery was clearly on its way when the vaudeville theaters, their doors shut by the Depression and a Hollywood invention called "talking pictures," began to reopen.

Fanchon and Marco—a sister-and-brother team who had produced lavish stage shows for theatre chains in the '20s—made a deal with the musicians' union to put in an orchestra at the majestic Paramount Theatre in downtown Los Angeles, at a drastically reduced scale. Since the promoters were known only by their first names, few people were aware their last name was Wolf—and that bandleader-comedian Rube Wolf, who headlined many Fanchon-Marco revues, was their brother.

In any case, the arrangement had happy consequences for Jones. Shortly after Harry Geller joined Wolf at the Paramount—and became contractor—he got Spike a job in the showman's 16-piece orchestra at $40 a week. But given the limits of Jones' experience and the demands of the engagement, it was not an easy job to hang onto.

"Wolf was kind of tough. You really had to be on your toes," reflected Geller. "Spike had never played in a stage band before, and at one point Rube came to me and said, 'We can't keep this guy—he doesn't know how to read.' There's a whole technique of reading stage music as opposed to playing for records, catching cues.

"Fanchon and Marco used to put on such extravaganzas, you wouldn't believe. They would do an entire classical ballet. Spike had no real training as a drummer, formal training; he wasn't used to that kind of thing. But it didn't take him long."

It didn't take Jones and Geller long—together with Freddie Slack and Willie Martinez—to form a clique within the Paramount orchestra. "They felt superior to the rest of the group that was not jazz-oriented, and it was unmistakable," claimed pianist George Hackett. "They kept themselves aloof from the rest of the band. The other fellows were excellent musicians, but they weren't jazzhounds; they didn't talk the jive talk, and everything else."

"We had our own separate dressing room," said Martinez. "Between shows we often used to have sessions down in the basement, the four of us. Tremendous sessions, just jazz," he exclaimed. "People think of Spike only as a crazy guy, with the act he had. But he was a great drummer, believe me."

Martinez recalled one other characteristic that had surfaced by the mid-'30s. "He was tight with his money. There was a Coke machine in the alley at the Paramount. Cokes were a nickel—Spike never had change for a lousy Coke. All he ever had were quarters or half dollars; he was always mooching nickels."

A lack of pocket change didn't deter Jones from making acquaintance with the chorus girls at the Paramount. He began dating several of the Fanchonettes and soon forgot about the dancer he had fallen for at the Club Ballyhoo. One redhead in the line particularly struck his fancy, and within a year she agreed to marry him.

Just where and when Spike first met Patricia Ann Middleton of Pittsfield, Massachusetts, is uncertain. Adding to the confusion is the fact that Jones always seems have been in two—if not three or four—places at once. About the same time he drummed for Rube Wolf, Spike was substituting with Earl Burtnett's band, playing for daytime tea dances at the nearby Biltmore Hotel. He was also working with Al Lyons' society orchestra, which played casuals at the Biltmore as well as various auditoriums and dance halls around town.

Harry Geller, who was best man at Spike's wedding, maintained Jones met his first wife at the Paramount, circa 1934. "Spike and I had a double date, the first time he met Patty. I knew Patty before Spike did; I had worked

Jack Benny, Tommy Dorsey, Bing Crosby, John Scott Trotter and Spike, at an all-star version of Dorsey's Amateur Swing Contest, July 1938. (*Margaret Kinghorn Trotter*)

at the Paramount before I got him in the orchestra, and Patty was then dancing in the line."

Willie Martinez, however, asserted he was responsible for bringing the couple together. "I introduced Spike to Patty," he claimed. "I was in Al Lyons' orchestra; Patty was singing with the band. I got Spike into the band. Then he says, 'Introduce me to the singer.'"

According to *The Saturday Evening Post*, Spike met his wife in 1935 at the Biltmore Bowl—the lavish banquet room in the grand hotel—where he was playing, and she was singing with Lyons' orchestra. Linda Jones was reasonably certain her parents met at the Biltmore. "I think that's what my mother told me," she affirmed. "When she and my dad met, he was the drummer in Wolf's band."

In any case, the couple quickly found a common bond. "My mother was an only child," said Linda. "She went on the road with *The Desert Song*, as a child of 15 or 16. She traveled without her parents. She was very much like my dad being an only child, and out there on her own very young."

Spike and his first wife, Patricia Middleton. (*Warren Dexter*)

Patricia Middleton became Mrs. Spike Jones on September 7, 1935. They said their vows before an audience of musicians and chorus girls. Their friends brought groceries to the wedding, in lieu of more traditional gifts. Spike was not the only member of Rube Wolf's band to marry a Fanchonette. Several of his fellow bandsmen did the same, including Martinez and Wolf himself.

Spike and Pat moved into a one bedroom apartment off Seventh Street, near the Paramount Theatre. "The thing that impressed me most was that they were living on hamburgers, cigarettes and Coke. Patty was not the greatest cook," observed Geller. Fortunately, the 20-year-old bride did not have to cook every night; Sunday dinner at Spike's parents' house was almost ritual.

Following his stint at the Paramount, Spike joined Everett Hoagland— whose band was now more society than swing—at the Cafe de Paree near Westlake Park (now MacArthur Park) for a brief but memorable engagement. "People used to come just to listen to the rhythm section," recalled Hersh Ratliff, who played bass. Among the sidemen were Vido Musso and Bob Gioga (both of whom ended up with Stan Kenton) on sax; Freddie Slack on piano; and Bob Simmers, another of Wolf's sidemen and a close friend of Spike's, on guitar.

When the gig ended Slack organized a band, and asked both Jones and Ratliff to join him. "We tried to get a job at the Trocadero out on the Sunset Strip but the band was too big," reflected Ratliff. "It was a beautiful hotel-style band, but it was too big to hire—the Depression was on.

"Then Max Factor, Jr. wanted to start a band; he had a girlfriend who wanted to be a singer. We were going to make some transcriptions which would be sent to England, so Max asked me to organize a band. It was a big dance band—five sax, four brass, et cetera—and both Spike and Freddie Slack were in that.

"The first number we rehearsed—the first time we played it—the guys just stood and yelled. I just happened to get the right mix of guys together," reflected Ratliff. "But the union wouldn't let us send the transcriptions overseas, so the thing just kind of blew up. We tried to sell the band somewhere else, but it was just too big during the Depression. Spike said, 'If we could have kept it going, we could have gone right to the top.'"

Jones made a leap in that direction without the Factor ensemble when he finally won work in the recording studios. His long-sought entry into the Hollywood wax factories came about when composer-conductor Victor Young—or his contractor, Perry Botkin—began asking Spike to substitute for Vic Berton, a top-flight drummer who often had more bookings than he could handle. Jones' first known studio call was for an August 1936 session at Decca Records, backing singer Gene Austin of "My Blue Heaven" fame.

Once Victor Young cracked the studio sound barrier, Jones found himself being called to the waxworks on a regular basis. Decca musical director Harry Sosnik requested his presence behind Judy Garland, Dick Powell, Connee Boswell and others; under Young's baton, he found himself drumming for the likes of Bing Crosby, Tony Martin and Irene Dunne. He backed Crosby on over 110 selections for the label, including the original recording of "White Christmas."

Jones also cut sides with the Andrews Sisters, Hoagy Carmichael and others at Decca. "Spike was about the top drummer on the West Coast," said Harry Sosnik. "We all hired him. I used Spike whenever I could get him. So did everyone else. Victor Young and myself, a couple of the other guys, we all used the same men."

Beginning in 1937 Jones did several sessions at Decca with The Foursome, a popular vocal-and-ocarina quartet who were summer regulars on

Kraft Music Hall. Perry Botkin—who had recorded with The Foursome in New York—put together the quartet's instrumental support group: Jack Mayhew on sax and flute, Slim Jim Taft on bass, Spike on drums and sandblocks, and himself on guitar. Delmar Porter played tin whistle with the group in addition to his singing duties in the quartet.

Botkin, who played guitar on many of Young's sessions, frequently hired Spike to play with his own ensembles. A bandleader in name only, Botkin was an amazingly prolific musician who, nevertheless, lacked the respect of his peers. While he looked out for himself first—according to those who worked with him—he kept Spike busy whenever possible.

The peripatetic young drummer was also in demand at Victor, the American Record Corporation (where he was heard on the Brunswick and Vocalion labels) and CBS (on the Columbia and Okeh labels). Here Jones backed such diverse artists as Alice Faye, Jerry Colonna and Dorothy Lamour; at Victor he was often employed in Lou Bring's orchestra. So disparate were the gigs he used to get "the musical bends" going from one session to another—or so he later claimed.

The Columbia record of "I Ain't Hep to That Step But I'll Dig It" (1940)—on which Spike's drums do a snappy duet with Fred Astaire's feet— is perhaps the best example of Jones' talents during this period. "Me and the Ghost Upstairs" (from the same session), on which his cowbells are heard, is another. While he rarely had the opportunity to display his percussive prowess to such an extent, Ella Logan's Brunswick disc of "Cielito Lindo" offers further evidence of Spike's abilities in pre-City Slicker days.

Although there were no recordings made, Jones was also heard loud and clear when an international organization of clubs dedicated to the listening and appreciation of jazz—*hot clubs*—began springing up in metropolitan areas circa 1937. "These sessions were a big thing," said Harry Geller. "I remember one occasion with just Spike and myself. Hundreds of kids gathered around us. We played duets; I'd play a riff on the trumpet and Spike would imitate it on the snare drum. Then he'd play something and I'd imitate it, back and forth. This was the L.A. hot club's first concert."

Jones joined another hot club when he made his network radio debut about the same time on *The Al Jolson Show*, in the company of Victor Young—again as a sub for Vic Berton, whom he soon replaced. Before long he became staff drummer at CBS under the direction of Ludwig Gluskin, and found himself serving in the same capacity at NBC under Gordon Jenkins.

Other bandleaders who employed Spike's considerable talents on their radio programs were Henry King (*The Burns and Allen Show*), Oscar Bradley (*Screen Guild Theater*), Freddie Rich (*Tommy Riggs and Betty Lou*), Jacques Renard and Edgar "Cookie" Fairchild (*The Eddie Cantor Show*), William "Billy" Mills (*Fibber McGee and Molly*) and Dave Rubinoff.

There was no outlet for the young drummer's sense of humor on radio at the time, but his comic sensibilities were evident in social circles. "He hadn't actually crystallized as a comedian at that time—it was just the way his mind worked," reflected guitarist George Van

Spike's parents, Lindley and Ada Jones, with granddaughter Linda, circa 1940. (*Ted Hering*)

Eps, who was then part of Jones' social clique. "He could take fun poked at himself; a lot of kidders can't take kidding, but not Spike. If somebody made a crack about him, he'd always see something funny in it. Maybe from the opposite direction of the person who made the crack.

"Spike approached comedy through the back door. He had some funny contraptions on his drums, little things that didn't come out of the drum accessory catalog. Things he had put together himself. I can't single anything out, but they made an impression on me," said Van Eps.

It was often that little something extra that won Jones the job. "One of the key reasons he was asked to be on so many of these sessions was that he used to have additional traps, additional drums. Most drummers just had a xylophone and a basic set of drums," Spike Jones Jr. explained to an interviewer. "He would come in with cowbells and sound effects... and he was pretty much sought after because of this. His trap set was very embellished."

But while Spike was drumming regularly for a nationwide audience, it was hardly what he could call fame and fortune. Try as he might, Jones was one among many talented young musicians toiling anonymously on Radio Row. Even his longest and most prestigious stint—on NBC's *Kraft Music Hall* with Bing Crosby, under the baton of John Scott Trotter— failed to threaten that anonymity.

Jones took every job he could get at this point. When *Kraft* colleague Johnny Cascales put together a band for a 1939 summer engagement at Topsy's, a club in Southgate near downtown Los Angeles, Spike came aboard, along with several other Trotter sidemen. With pianist Charlie LaVere and singer-songwriter Bonnie Lake, both of whom joined him at Topsy's, Jones also put together a vocal quartet that year, which lasted long enough to cut at least one audition record.

The hours Spike languished between jobs were interminable. "The union had a rule no musician could play on the radio more than two hours a week unless the producers specifically insisted on him," he once observed. "Frankly, I like money. I always did like it and I could see I wasn't getting anyplace. There were too many other drummers in town for anybody to look me up."

"There was a quota," pointed out one-time *Kraft* contractor Wally Marks, explaining the restriction. "You could only play four shows—two hours maximum. But if you had four shows, that would have been about all you could handle. Our show was three hours work, including rehearsal. And there was always overtime."

Jones should have had no complaints about the money he was making either—at least not on the Crosby program. "Spike got 'doubles' for playing such extras as timpani, bells or vibraphone; on top of the basic scale of $37, he got 25% extra for the first one—if he played timpani for instance—and 10% more for a second or third extra," noted Marks, who made out the invoices.

"Actually, he got doubles whether he played extras or not; that was part of the deal. He got 45% more than the basic scale. But this wasn't unusual. The woodwinds and percussionists wouldn't work without extras."

But it wasn't near enough to satisfy the audacious young drummer. Struggling to support his wife and a recent addition to the family named Linda Lee, Jones turned his imagination loose. With his future at stake, he embarked on a campaign to make a name for himself and turn the world on its ear.

And Then Along Came Jones
Influences & Precursors

The newspaperman who caught Spike Jones' act during an engagement at the 1948 California State Fair hit the cowbell on the head, in summing up the band's appeal. "Anybody who attacks the banality, excessive sentimentality and poor taste which is often present in popular music," he maintained, "is doing the world a service."

Jones and his City Slickers were not the first to mine the lucrative field of "corn" or make use of funny sound effects in the name of such service, nor were they the last. As the newsman observed, they were simply "carrying out an old tradition of musical satire." But there is little argument today that they employed peculiar instruments and screwball orchestrations with far greater skill—and more spectacular results—than any band before or since.

Haydn and Beethoven were exceedingly fond of musical jokes, two hundred years before Victor Borge took his first dive off a piano bench. A sequence involving a deflating chromatic scale of brass in Verdi's comic opera, *Falstaff,* has been called "Spike Jones before his time." But the explosive possibilities of combining music and humor were not fully explored until the dawn of the record business.

With the advent of recorded sound, their compatibility soon became apparent. French musical comedy star Maurice Farkoa performed his famed "Laughing Song" for the 18-month-old Berliner Gramophone Company in 1896. Funny sound effects were no longer a novelty when Ed Meeker made his Edison cylinder recording of "I'm a Yiddish Cowboy" in 1909, but he was perhaps the first to use effects to accompany each line of a song, instead of throwing them in haphazardly.

The visual humor missing on record was abundant in the ensemble clown bands that were a fixture in American circuses by the turn of the last century. William "Spader" Johnson, a former minstrel, reportedly originated the clown band in 1897. Dressed and made up to resemble John Philip

Sousa—a recurring motif in clown bands of that era—cornetist Johnson led a ragtag group of Ringling Bros. funsters in a variety of costumes.

Vaudeville headliner Ted Lewis was perhaps the first to legitimize the concept, as it were, anticipating a musical trend by two decades when he put together his four-piece Nut Band in 1916. The sidemen were costumed "like the clown dog in an animal act" when the top-hatted clarinetist made his debut at New York's Palace Theatre three years later; by 1922, the clown suits had been replaced by tuxedos, but the laughing trombones which characterized his less than solemn instrumentals—and snickered at Lewis' own schmaltzy vocals—were still present. He later added comedy sketches.

Lewis has been called "the grandfather of corn" by musicologist Dr. Demento, who observed, "He was the first to record in real out and out corny style, right off the cob." Although Lewis employed the likes of Benny Goodman, Muggsy Spanier and other jazz greats over the years, when the master showman retired—after a career that spanned over half a century—he acknowledged, "They think I'm too corny."

Among the earliest bands to realize the creative and financial potential of novelty songs and nutty sound effects were Harry Reser's Six Jumping Jacks, a group of New York studio musicians, and Waring's Pennsylvanians, which pioneered in virtually every facet of the entertainment business under the durable baton of Fred Waring.

Reser, whose long career was nearly as accomplished as Waring's, recorded in a variety of styles under some two dozen names. The personnel varied little from one group to the next during the '20s; the Six Jumping Jacks was simply the identity Reser chose for the raucous comedy numbers he did for the Brunswick label beginning in 1926, including "I'm Just Wild About Animal Crackers," "You Oughta Hear Olaf Laugh" and "She's the Sweetheart of Six Other Guys."

The Jumping Jacks were a distinct predecessor to the City Slickers. Like Ed Meeker before him, and Spike Jones years after, Reser employed sound effects in precise and appropriate places—not merely at random, as so many others did.

The records credited to the Jumping Jacks sound like background for Max Fleischer cartoons; they could have easily underscored the animated antics of Betty Boop. Whistles, bells, kazoos, crying babies, cuckoos, whinnying horses, duck calls and cackling hens punctuate the instrumentals. Reser's virtuoso banjo predominates, but often takes a backseat to the clarinet and saxophone, or a spirited duet between piano and tuba. The jaunty vocals, by drummer Tom Stacks, are every bit as playful as the lyrics.

Fred Waring's organization could hardly be considered a comedy outfit, but his abundant sense of humor was evident in their '20s repertoire. "When My Sugar Walks Down the Street" might have been in keeping with his image as a purveyor of dance melodies, but "We've Never Seen a Straight Banana," "I Scream, You Scream, We All Scream for Ice Cream" and others hint at the broad grin behind the straight face of the group.

The band, which began in 1916, waxed a large number of novelty tunes for Victor in its "collegiate" days (they were "too young and exuberant" for Edison). Most of the fun in Waring's novelties derive from the clever lyrics and inventive use of standard instruments, along with drummer James "Poley" McClintock's gravelly Popeye voice, itself widely imitated.

Freddy Buck's arrangements employed no washboards or cowbells, and precious little in the way of sound effects—but Jones was well aware of Waring. The straight instrumentals on some of Spike's records are reminiscent of the orchestra's bouncy, highly-polished sound; Waring's trademark pep-rally atmosphere is also present in his work.

Irving Aaronson and his Commanders, perhaps best known as a training ground for Artie Shaw and Gene Krupa, was one of many outfits that emulated Waring. But unlike others who parroted the group's choral style, Aaronson led a top-flight dance orchestra that had its own inimitable sound.

While few jazz and dance band leaders were able to resist the temptation to cut at least one funny record during their career, Aaronson—like Britain's Billy Cotton—waxed several. The raucous rhythm was embellished with elements not frequently heard on disc in the late '20s—barking dogs, chirping birds and cute, childlike vocals—all of which Spike Jones would later claim as part of his trademark.

Frank and Milt Britton were another early influence on Jones, particularly on *The Musical Depreciation Revue* he would one day stage. By all accounts the Brittons had far and away the zaniest act of its day—they were the only "jazz band" whose members routinely fell into the orchestra pit, squirted water at one another, fired pistols in the air or broke violins over each other's heads. At least, they were one of a kind until other bands started borrowing wholesale from them.

The Britton brothers, who were actually neither Brittons nor brothers, were born when Milton Levy teamed with Frank Wentzel as a two-man vaudeville act, playing trombone and cornet. The shenanigans that became the meat and potatoes of their repertoire began as an accident six years later, in

1923, during an engagement of their Brown Derby Band.

As Milt Britton later recalled, "Benny Meroff had been quite flippant early in the act during my trombone solo, tuning his cello on stage among other interruptions. To get even I fell backwards from the bandstand during Benny's cello solo which followed. The audience howled and we discovered a sure-fire laugh."

Before long, the first "accidental howl" inspired all manner of lunacy. The Brittons' specialty was a jazz melody that started off in a purely conventional manner; halfway through the number, the trombone slide would knock the cornet out of its owner's hand. As Walter "Mousie" Powell imitated an airplane on the trombone, a fellow sideman would contribute sound effects at inopportune moments; when the trombonist began to emulate a fire engine, he was drenched with seltzer bottles. Soon the sidemen were throwing custard pies and maniacally smashing their instruments. By the time the Crazy Crew of Fiddle Wreckers was through, the bandstand was a complete shambles.

Frank tired of the fun and games and went straight in 1936; Milt carried on until felled by a heart attack in 1948, at the age of 54, ringing down the curtain on the maddest act that ever graced the stage of New York's legendary Palace Theatre or the *Ziegfeld Follies*. Meroff and Powell formed their own comedy bands after leaving the troupe, but neither enjoyed the success of their mentors.

The Brittons, who apparently made no phonograph records, left little evidence of their chaotic enterprise behind. A 1945 film short of their "Poet and Peasant" routine, as performed by Milt's band—a Soundie now on video—provides a teasing, all-too-brief glimpse of the insanity they flung onto the stage.

Ezra Buzzington's Rube Band, a nine-piece novelty orchestra led by banjoist Mark Shaffer, toured vaudeville throughout the 1920s with a much tamer act than the Brittons. This virtually forgotten outfit, which employed a large array of strange instruments, was a headliner in the pre-Depression era when novelty songs were plentiful; it is more noteworthy, however, for the experience it provided three young men from Indiana.

Brothers Paul and Kenneth Trietsch—who played drums and guitar under the stage names "Hezekiah" and "Rudy Vaselino"—and clarinetist Otto Ward, alias "Gabe Hawkins," met in the Rube Band in 1923; Ken, the eldest, was barely 20. They worked with Shaffer's unit (also known as Buzzington's Rustic Revelers) for the remainder of the decade, playing fairs and theatres, including the prestigious Hippodrome.

The Hoosier Hot Shots, 1950. Paul "Hezzie" Trietsch, Ken Trietsch, Gil Taylor and
Gabe Ward perform their stage act on film.

"When the Crash of '29 came, we were refugees from vaudeville," explained Gabe Ward. "And we had freak instruments, so we decided we would
just do silly, crazy stuff because everybody was so sad. And we weren't going to
make them any more sad."

The Trietsch Brothers and Ward, as they billed themselves, were renamed the Hoosier Hot Shots by a radio announcer while working at WOWO
in Ft. Wayne, Indiana. With the addition of Rube Band alum Frank Kettering
on bass, the group became a foursome in 1934, shortly after finding a home
in Chicago on WLS' *National Barn Dance*—a gig lasting 18 years.

Although they played such standards as "Ida" and "Sweet Georgia
Brown," the group was known for material as novel as their instruments.
Tunes like "I Like Bananas (Because They Have No Bones)" and "From the
Indies to the Andes In His Undies" were distinguished by zany lyrics and an
offbeat sound that propelled their records into jukeboxes throughout the
country. They were also in demand for USO shows, B-western movies and
TV appearances.

While Ken led the band, Paul—better known as Hezzie, as in "Are you
ready, Hezzie?"—set the tone, abandoning his drums to invent a contraption
that revolutionized music in its humble way. His widely-imitated Wabash

Washboard—an ordinary galvanized iron washboard flanked by tuned auto and bicycle horns, cowbells, pie pans, garbage can lids, a Klaxon, a slide whistle and other noisemakers—would later be copied by Spike Jones and many others.

Hezzie Trietsch, who discovered the musical potential of the washboard while helping his mother with the family laundry, was not the first to employ one for comic effect. The washboard bands and jug bands that proliferated in the '20s often belied their roots in the blues, offering a good-humored mix of folk and rural jazz; The Five Harmaniacs specialized in spirited renditions of novelty numbers ("Sadie Green, Vamp of New Orleans") that demonstrated the fun potential of scrub-boards.

Trietsch transcended such comparatively crude usage of homemade instruments, and inspired a whole generation of "corn bands." But the Hoosier Hot Shots outlasted all their imitators and competitors, performing until shortly before Paul died of cancer in 1980.

The Schnickelfritzers and their virtual clone, the Korn Kobblers, were two of the more successful groups influenced by the Hot Shots. They went several steps further into the absurd with a stronger emphasis on crazy sound effects and off-kilter instrumentation of the sort that would later become identified with Spike Jones.

Freddie Fisher toured the Midwest with various groups before he began the Schnickelfritz Band in 1934. His key sidemen were Nels Laakso on cornet, trumpet and slide whistle, and Stanley Fritts, who played trombone, jug and a more elaborate version of Trietsch's washboard. Fisher himself played washboard, ocarina, slide whistle and flute, in addition to the clarinet.

The Schnickelfritzers might have made a living playing dixieland jazz and polkas, but the bandleader had a habit of fooling around in the midst of tune, to cover for a weak memory. The echoes of Ted Lewis in his work were no accident, as witness the evening he found his niche at the Sugar Loaf Tavern in Winona, Minnesota.

"One night some drunk kept saying 'Play 'Tiger Rag,' play 'Tiger Rag.' So Fisher said, 'Let's play it corny,' " recalled bass player Charlie Koenig. "So we played it corny, and we did a lot of action along with it, mugging and so on—and the people gave us almost a standing ovation."

Fisher and company—who were often described as a swing band in the press —won a contract with Decca while packing the house at the Sugar Loaf, where a two-week engagement lasted two years. When Rudy Vallee "discovered" them in St. Paul he asked Warner Bros. to bring the troupe to

The Schnickelfritzers, 1937. Clockwise from lower left: Charlie Koenig, Stan Fritts, Kenny Trisko, Nels Laakso, Paul Cooper and leader Freddie Fisher. (*Susan Fox*)

Hollywood for *Gold Diggers in Paris*. Fisher's prospects were bright but most of his sidemen found him impossible to get along with, and parted company with their boss in 1939.

The nucleus of the Fisher band became the Korn Kobblers, choosing Stan Fritts as their nominal leader. They planned to call themselves The Original Schnickelfritzers—or at least Fisher thought so, and he filed a lawsuit to prevent them from using the name. Little else changed. The Kobblers continued to use the washboard, tuned auto horns, cowbells, frying pans and funny hats they had employed with Fisher; they even performed the same stage routines, including one based on Chic Sales' popular book about outhouses.

On the recommendation of Guy Lombardo—whose "sweetest music this side of heaven" was an acknowledged influence on the group—the Kobblers were booked to appear at the 1939 New York World's Fair. The band recorded for various labels, made hundreds of radio transcriptions and eventually had their own TV show. Fisher, meanwhile, replaced the bandsmen and continued for many years, making records and films, and playing nightclubs in Hollywood and Las Vegas; both he and Fritts retired in the early '50s, as musical tastes began to change.

The Schnickelfritzers had their counterparts in Great Britain as well as America. "It all started in the music hall," said comedy writer and vaudeville aficionado Tony Hawes. "There were several comics in the '20s who would do a fiddling act, and do jokes between, like Henny Youngman. There were a crowd of them. First came the violin comics, then the musical saw comics, then the comics who started with the horns. There were a lot of acts in that time who did motor horns, taxi cab horns..."

Edward Stanelli, who began his career as a serious musician—but won renown as a comedian in radio and vaudeville—distinguished himself on a contraption dubbed the Hornchestra. Manipulating every type of horn imaginable, Stanelli (who went only by his surname) ferociously honked his way through the likes of "Tiger Rag."

Sid Millward and His Nitwits was another act that grew out of the English music hall tradition. "That was a real Spike Jones-type band," enthused Hawes. "It was like a crazy concert orchestra that would do 'The William Tell Overture,' 'The Entry of the Gladiators,' things that were not copyrighted. They didn't do popular songs at all, the way Jones did. They had two drummers; an ordinary guy sitting behind a drum kit, and a lunatic boy who'd be hitting the big kettle drums everywhere."

Perhaps the preeminent act of its kind in England, the Nitwits surfaced on radio in the '30s and were featured as the resident band on BBC's quiz show, *Ignorance is Bliss,* during its maiden 1946-47 season. Millward and company toured English music halls and entertained U.S. troops stationed in Europe, enjoying perhaps their biggest success at Paris' famed Lido Club.

Charles Prentice was yet another Englishman who anticipated Jones by some years with his Orchestra of Novelty Apprentices. Their recording of "The Poet and Peasant Overture" sounds like a cartoon soundtrack with laughing trombones a lá Ted Lewis, singing birds, squawking ducks, whinnying horses, whimpering dogs and nutty voices.

Scott Saunders was a percussionist with a wholly unique act during the same era. "He came on with this knife-grinding machine, with knives, axes, everything that might need sharpening," recalled Tony Hawes. "When he finished sharpening them, he brought out two drumsticks and played them all, and got a tune out of them."

Not all Jones' precursors were flesh and blood; some were animated. In Walt Disney's first sound cartoon, *Steamboat Willie* (1928), a goat eats an arrangement of "Turkey in the Straw." As a girl cranks the tune out of the goat like a hurdy-gurdy, Mickey Mouse—whose name became synonymous with silly, corny music – bangs a garbage can, strums a washboard, squeezes a chorus out of a duck as though it were a bagpipe, and turns a row of cow's teeth into a xylophone.

When Mickey tries to conduct "The William Tell Overture" in *The Band Concert* (1935), the program is disrupted first by an incorrigible Donald Duck, then by a pesky bee Mickey tries in vain to swat with his baton. Finally, a tornado wreaks havoc during the frenzied storm sequence of "William Tell." The bandsmen are swept into the maelstrom but never stop playing; one by one they end up falling into a tree, with the percussionist crashing through his drum.

The bee reappears in Max Fleischer's *A Car-Tune Portrait* (1936), starting a chain reaction that turns a symphony concert into a shambles a lá Frank and Milt Britton. A donkey tries to bop the bee with his trombone slide, whacking the horn player in front of him; a group of monkeys employ a flute as a pee shooter. The finale comes in a huge onstage brawl. In Fleischer's *The Spinach Overture,* Popeye plays the piano with feet and elbows; Olive Oyl strums the harp with her bare toes, and Wimpy fries a hamburger on the cymbal.

Mike Riley was the proprietor of an outfit as loony as any Fleischer Studios cartoon—and more overtly funny in live performance than on record. His anything-but-subtle style owed more than a little to Frank and Milt Britton. Riley had played trumpet and trombone with Jimmy Durante, Irving Aaronson and others before teaming in 1934 with trumpeter Eddie Farley.

Together, Riley and Farley turned New York's Onyx Club upside down. "They were two characters," recalled guitarist Arthur Ens. "Mike was a wild guy. Eddie was the straight man; they were like Abbott and Costello. When we didn't clown, we played very good. That was a band that could really swing." But no one knew when Riley was going to swing the chair out from under the piano player, pour beer in the guitarist's new shoes or throw a pie at someone—or switch the signs on the mens' and ladies' rooms.

"It was a real nut band," said bassist Candy Hall, who worked with both Riley and Jones. "Mike was so much more raucous than Spike. In Spike's band you had to learn to belch and it had to be on beat—not necessarily in tune, but on beat. Everything was timed like that. With Riley, it was spontaneous, a lot of it. The girl singer, while a guy's playing a solo, she'd put a match in his shoe and light it, give him a hot foot."

Riley and Farley split up not long after the phenomenal popularity of their novelty number, "The Music Goes 'Round and Around." Riley later formed a dixieland band and opened a Hollywood nightspot called Mike Riley's Madhouse; although he continued touring into the '60s, he never enjoyed the success he and Farley won in the mid '30s.

The duo had made such an impact even Paul Whiteman borrowed from Riley and Farley's bag of tricks when he found his popularity slipping. The King of Jazz—who was often charged with desecrating music in the '20s, when jazz had many detractors—would not be outdone by his competitors' clowning; his orchestra swung left and right, and juggled their instruments in time to the beat. "But when Paul earned laughs instead of applause, he realized that he was making a fool of himself and of the entire outfit," noted his biographer.

Kay Kyser and Al Trace led dance orchestras that ventured into novelty—and built on it—when they discovered how lucrative it could be. Kyser, who recorded hot dance music in the late '20s, began employing corny instrumental effects in the mid '30s under the influence of Guy Lombardo.

When big band critic George T. Simon first saw the group, "their sophomoric antics distressed and confused me," he reported. "Enamored of Lombardo's band at the time, Kyser affected a mickey-mouse approach, with sugary, simpering saxes and clippety-cloppety brass tickings which were far from impressive musically." But the bandleader scored a direct hit on the audience at Chicago's celebrated Blackhawk restaurant, from which he broadcast on WGN, and the band eventually matured.

Though he employed the occasional kazoo or funny noise, Kyser generally eschewed the sound effects that characterized Spike's work—yet he had a greater repertoire of novelty numbers than any dance band of his day. "When Veronica Plays the Harmonica" and "Horses Don't Bet on People" were tunes Jones could have recorded just as easily.

Featured comedian Ish Kabibble—whom Kyser often admonished to "pop that corn" as he launched into his solos—reflected, "Kay didn't go for novelty so much as he figured it had to be different, in order to get the public to listen. It was more a matter of being different. Style meant everything; style was the thing."

Al Trace's Shuffle Rhythm Orchestra followed Kyser into the Blackhawk with a featured act as wild as any. The Silly Symphonists were "a band within a band" that caught fire at the Chicago World's Fair in 1933. Drummer Red Maddock, bass player Dave DeVore, and Nate Wexler, who played almost everything, were the primary funmakers; in Riley-Farley style, their antics were not confined to the stage, and could erupt anywhere they happened to be.

The Korn Kobblers, late 1940s. Clockwise from upper right: Eddie Grosso, Sid Connie, Charlie Koenig, Hal Marquess and leader Stan Fritts. (*Stanford Zucker*)

The band, which was featured on record, radio, film and TV, enjoyed its biggest success in popularizing "Mairzy Doats." Observed Trace: "We did better than some of the big bands, because we'd put on a 30-minute Silly Symphony show that would knock 'em right on their ears, and then go back to good solid dance music. We played the biggest ballrooms in the country."

In later years the bandleader downplayed the novelty aspect of his long career, preferring to be known for other accomplishments—notably over 300 compositions recorded by the likes of Frank Sinatra, Ella Fitzgerald and Louis Armstrong. "I'm not strictly known as a fun band," he stressed. "I didn't confine myself entirely to comedy ideas."

The Kidoodlers could not have made such claim. The group, which toured in vaudeville in the '30s and appeared on NBC Radio, was a novelty band that began as a male vocal quartet. They augmented their voices with a collection of over 100 toy instruments and props—whistles, horns, cymbals, bells, guns, xylophones and other noisemakers—drawing comparison with the Schnickelfritz Band.

Spike Jones drew similar comparisons, although his instrumentals were far more sophisticated than the Kidoodlers. If he was unaware of all his antecedents—some of whom influenced those who in turn influenced him—he unabashedly borrowed from many of them. He reportedly went so far as to bring a secretary to one of the Korn Kobblers' live performances, and copy down their routines.

Publicly, Jones rarely acknowledged the mere existence – let alone influence—of other comedy bands. Privately, he was more generous. "That's the way he was," said Paul Trietsch, Jr. "Privately, he would've given my dad credit for his washboard, and all those things he did. Spike told me that himself, as a matter of fact, when I had lunch with him one time. He always admired my dad."

Trietsch and the Hoosier Hot Shots, with their crazy percussion instruments and untamed sense of fun, made a substantial contribution to the City Slickers. Freddie Fisher, an Iowa farm boy who reveled in shucking particularly overripe corn, sounded more like Spike than any other precursor, especially on Decca recordings like "Colonel Corn" and "Washboard Man." But Jones left both groups—as well as all the others who mined the field before and after—in his dust, artistically and financially.

"There's no question about it, the Slickers were a superior group," observed Charlie Koenig of the Schnickelfritzers and the Korn Kobblers. "I'm not envious of Spike; he knew what he was doing. He was probably a better businessman that either Stan Fritts or Freddie Fisher, and that's the important thing."

Jones promotional efforts were as driven as his records. "One of the reasons for his success was that the other comedy groups didn't take it as seriously as he did," asserted Spike Jones Jr. "He took it one step further…"

Schnickelfritzer-turned-City Slicker George Rock concurred: "I think the reason none of them could really connect, they had no exploitation really, nobody pushing them. They made a few records but they weren't played enough; nobody really got behind the things. Spike had the right idea in that department."

Birth of a Band
The Evolution of the City Slickers, 1939–1941

Spike Jones could have likely been a Broadway producer, a motion picture studio czar, a Wall Street tycoon or an industrial magnate with equal success. He once boasted if he had become an automobile manufacturer, he would have been "one of the big three." It was not an idle boast; he was a man of determination and vision, possessed of phenomenal energy.

But try as he might to make headway in his chosen profession, throughout the 1930s Jones was little more than a cog in the wheel that made the music industry go around. He did everything he could to hone his technique; he even took tap dance lessons to improve his sense of rhythm. But he had a hard time progressing through the ranks.

"Spike wasn't getting anywhere. There were too many drummers— Gene Krupa, Buddy Rich—he wasn't in their class. He was a good technician, a good all-around studio drummer. But they were a dime a dozen; there were many better than him," asserted former CBS musical director and orchestra leader Lud Gluskin.

"He wanted to be his own boss. As a drummer he had too much competition. He didn't like it just being in a band; he wanted to go off on his own. Spike acted like he was doing you a favor if he played for you," stated Gluskin. "His mind wasn't always on his work."

"Krupa *was* in a class by himself," concurred bandleader Harry Sosnik. "There was nobody like that. But Spike was one of the top men. He was very capable and always on the job. He was very professional."

Jones could have been hindered at this stage of his career by what arranger Carl Brandt described as "a mordant sense of humor," which would become more pronounced through the years. "Lud Gluskin had a reputation as a difficult guy to get along with. Not one of nature's noblemen," said Brandt.

"One day in rehearsal, Spike was doing a number; he finished the number and there was a big cymbal crash at the end of it. Lud said, 'Hey, Spike, you're late with that cymbal.' He said, 'I'm not late, Lud. You've just got a slow ear.' (It may have been a pierced ear as well: Gluskin's face adorned a dartboard on Jones' patio.)

By the mid '30s Spike had acquired a penchant for collecting assorted junk—automobile horns, anvils, whistles, sirens, wash basins, alarm clocks, et cetera. He indulged himself in his hobby whenever possible, always on the lookout for odds and ends; the odder the better, especially if they made a noise.

"One night after we played a gig at the Biltmore Hotel, Spike ripped a couple of telephones off the wall and put them under his overcoat," mused Harry Geller. "The wires were trailing out the back as we walked through the lobby. One of the bellhops saw us just before we got to the door; he came up and said something. I picked up the wires and stuffed them in my pocket and said they were part of the acoustic equipment for the drums, and we walked out."

Spike's burgeoning collection filled his little apartment, and soon began to take over his car as well. But the clutter lay fallow until one day in 1934 when he finally formed a novelty band. He chose a name with a familiar ring—Spike Jones and his Five Tacks—and began rehearsing one night a week at Bernstein's Grotto on Spring Street, a block from the Paramount Theatre. The Tacks played a number of gigs in the Los Angeles area, but the combo was short-lived; few of Jones' associates recalled its existence.

In addition to the many bands whose comedy records he was familiar with, Spike had ample opportunity to study—and borrow from—an infinite number of vaudeville acts while working with Rube Wolf at the Paramount. "His stage presence was copied after the deadpan comics," asserted Geller. "They changed the acts at the Paramount every week. That was great schooling for him."

Spike saw such seasoned troupers at the Paramount as Jack Benny, Burns and Allen, Eddie Cantor and George Jessel. Jones appears to have modeled his delivery largely after Benny, but the bandleader's stage persona was an amalgam of many entertainers.

"There was one guy who had a tremendous influence on Spike. He would come out dressed like a clown. He'd chew three packs of gum all at once, and play the xylophone. Occasionally he'd press a button and the xylophone would extend out another octave. He'd hit that note and then it

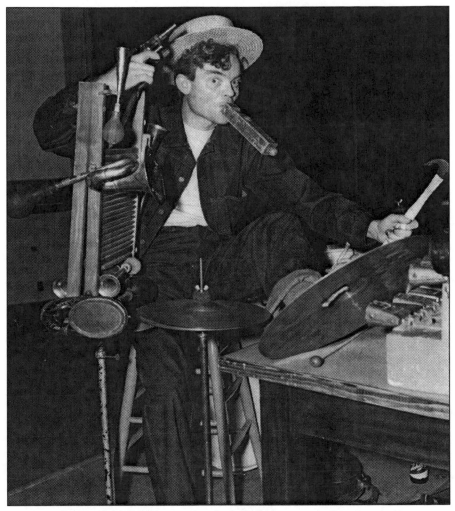

Rhythm in blue jeans: Jones makes a little noise on radio, circa 1942.

would go back in; once in a while he'd take the wad of gum out and stick it on the xylophone pad that moved in and out," recalled Geller.

"There was another act that had a big influence on him, a dog act; not the dogs but the guy who was in charge of them [Al Mardo], who would deadpan throughout the whole thing. Spike would pick up a lot of these mannerisms. He was a great student of things like that."

Jones' style and demeanor also dictated partly from within. "Spike was a very moody guy," observed bandleader Leighton Noble. "He was not your average personality; he was very quiet. He didn't sit around by himself, but he wasn't that outgoing."

In the late '30s Spike commuted to Hollywood studios in a station wagon loaded with all manner of paraphernalia, which looked like a junkyard on wheels. But there was little room for novelty in his record and radio work. While Bing Crosby reportedly called on Spike to "sound on your glockenspiel," Jones was rarely allowed to use anything more unusual on *The Kraft Music Hall,* and only then to back Bob Burns when he played his bazooka, a sort of homemade trombone that looked like a cross between a horn and a gun.

"All we ever did was play soft and sweet to accompany Crosby," Jones recalled. "No cowbells, no gunfire; I never got to use the bass drum at all. One boom and I'd have been fired. Nothing but a discreet rap on the cymbals now and then."

However, he also used singer Margaret Lenhart as a percussion instrument, according to her ex-husband, sound effects man Ray Erlenborn. "The girl singer sat on a little chair beside the drums," said Erlenborn, who later worked on some of Jones' albums and TV shows. "And Spike was the kind of a guy—he used to hit her on the knees with his drumsticks, bang the chair, do stuff like that. She'd come home: 'That son of a gun, he bothers me all the time. I hate to sit in that chair.' "

Such shenanigans aside, things were far too quiet for Jones. "I felt so frustrated I decided to form my own band where I could make as much noise as I wanted," he once said. "We began kidding around, dreaming up screwy arrangements; it was kind of a hobby with me, like some people collect stamps."

The inspiration for the City Slickers varies according to the source. Jones himself gave many different versions over the years. While the band, which would ultimately prove his fame and fortune, had its apparent seeds in the third-generation Five Tacks, the turning point—according to Spike—came during his "soft and sweet" stint with John Scott Trotter on *Kraft.*

"Everything was going along fine [on the show] until someone said he hoped I never hit a wrong note on the chimes I played during Bing's opening," he told more than one interviewer. "It made me conscious of the chimes and, sure enough, the next time I struck one of the bars it was the wrong one.

"If people would roar over an honest mistake I figured they would fracture themselves if I could get unusual instruments, write offbeat arrangements and start pulling gags within an orchestra," he recounted. "That's how it started. A blooper on the chimes."

The versatile Del Porter, composer, arranger, clarinetist and vocalist. (*Skip Craig*)

Veteran radio writer Carroll Carroll also asserted in his autobiography that the idea for the City Slickers was hatched on *Kraft,* for which he was head scribe—albeit under somewhat different circumstances. "When it became clear that [Bob] Burns' bazooka solos had to be protected with suitable background music, John Scott assigned his right-hand man and guitar player, Perry Botkin, to decide what suitable background music for a bazooka solo might be..." recalled Carroll.

"It was Perry and Spike, in collaboration with everyone else in the band, who created the funny arrangements that figured to drown out the baleful blasts of the bazooka. It was these noisy bits of musical goulash, full of percussion, glass crashes, strummed washboards, and pistol shots, that were the inspiration for Spike Jones and his 'musical depreciation hour.'"

Jones himself recited so many stories about the band's beginnings none of them can be taken without the proverbial grain of salt. His favorite anecdote concerned the time he attended a performance of Igor Stravinsky's *Firebird Suite* at the Shrine Auditorium in Los Angeles, danced by the Theodore Kosloff Ballet Company. "Stravinsky had on some new patent leather shoes that night, and every time he would rise up to give a down beat, his shoes would squeak," Spike related in a 1963 radio interview.

"Here would go the violins and *squeak squeak* would go his shoes. He should have worn a pair of sneakers. And the pseudos who went down to see the ballet, they didn't know what they were looking at anyway. They thought, Stravinsky's done it again. New percussive effects. They didn't know what it was, and I was hysterical. I was sitting real close and I could see and hear the shoes. When I left, driving home, I got to thinking if you made planned mistakes in musical arrangements and took the place of regular notes in well-known tunes with sound effects, there might be some fun in it."

The story varied a little with each successive telling. The conductor with the squeaky shoes was not always Stravinsky—on at least one occasion it was Serge Koussevitzky. The setting was most often the ballet, at other times a symphony concert. But it made a good story, and rarely—if ever—was Jones without an audience.

The genesis of the band has also been attributed to other circumstances. "A lot of the guys in the sound effects department at Walt Disney Productions thought Spike got the idea for the City Slickers from them," revealed veteran Disney animator Ward Kimball. "Spike would occasionally come in on an orchestra call, when we were working on a Silly Symphony or a Mickey Mouse cartoon. He came over one day when we were working on what we called the Gadget Band.

"We wanted some screwy music for a gag picture, where we had funny visuals, live action plus cartoon. We played funny things like a bubblelonium, which you'd blow through, and a shoesaphone—where you have a pair of old tennis shoes, and these long mailing tubes of different diameters and lengths; it would act like a marimba. They were all crazy things, all artificially-created sounds which had tonality," mused Kimball.

"We had the largest collection of crazy things for sound effects of any studio in Hollywood. Jim MacDonald, the head of the sound effects department, would go to wrecking yards and bring back all sorts of things. This is where Spike got the idea. It all was planted in his head when he went over there, and he was so fascinated by it…he wanted to see how everything was working," said Kimball. "I didn't know who he was then. He was just a studio musician."

In a less likely scenario, Thurl Ravenscroft—whose distinctive voice was heard on several of Jones' records—claimed his non-instrumental singing group, the Sportsmen Quartet, provided the inspiration for the band. "We used to take old songs and horse 'em up. Spike came to us and said, 'Can I borrow the idea?' We said, 'Sure.' And that was the start of what he did…" asserted Ravenscroft.

Whatever the origin, Spike was not the sole proprietor of the concept for the City Slickers—though he never acknowledged it publicly, or even hinted anyone else was involved. But Del Porter, who sang with The Foursome, was his partner from the outset.

Porter, a native of Oregon, had traveled the Northwest with a number of bands before joining the quartet, which Jones had backed on Decca records. He achieved considerable success with the group, notably in a pair of Broadway shows with Ethel Merman—George and Ira Gershwin's *Girl Crazy* and Cole Porter's *Anything Goes*. The Foursome also went on the road with one of Glenn Miller's early bands and recorded with Red Nichols.

Following the quartet's appearance in the Eleanor Powell movie *Born to Dance,* "I had a long dry spell. Nothing happened," Porter recalled in an interview with archivist Ted Hering. "Finally, I got with Spike. He said, 'Why don't you get a band?' I said, 'Well, maybe I will.' So we got a group of guys together, and we rehearsed like mad—we had some great stuff, some good entertainment."

The Feather Merchants was a six-piece group whose name was suggested by the feathered Tyrolean hats they wore. They patterned themselves after the musical madness of Frank and Milt Britton and Freddie Fisher's Schnickelfritz Band. "We put the two together and took it from there," said drummer Danny Van Allen. In the tradition of Fisher, "we were primarily a dance band and played comedy in between."

A direct forerunner of the Slickers—although much less polished—Porter's group played such novelties as "Water Lou," "Red Wing" and "Siam," which he wrote especially for the Feather Merchants. As versatile as he was prolific, Del could play virtually any instrument. He even concocted a few himself, including a homemade bagpipe which consisted of a tin whistle, attached to a douche bag by means of a rubber hose.

Porter, who had a natural gift for comedy, was inspired by Cole McElroy, with whom he worked in the '20s. "They played dance halls, and they always had comedy numbers. The McElroy band did an awful lot of that. And Del was always the one who put on the crazy uniform or the funny hat," reflected his lifelong friend Raymond M. Johnson, who sang alongside him in the Foursome.

In December 1939, the Merchants auditioned against—and beat out—several bands, including Stan Kenton's, for a job at Sardi's on the Sunset Strip. At the conclusion of their engagement, they held forth at the Santa Rita Hotel in Tucson for several months, where they did a bang-up business; unfortunately, they didn't always get paid.

When they returned to Los Angeles in 1940, they stayed afloat by playing market openings. "Things were tough then, believe me," said Porter. "Every so often, over a loud speaker, they would call out a special, like 10 pounds of potatoes for a nickel. The music would stop—the band would run in and get a nickel's worth of potatoes."

But Jones, who was making $10 a week as manager of the band, had bigger things in mind. "Spike said, 'Why don't we kind of go in together with this thing, and let's see what we can do,'" recalled Porter. "So I said, 'Fine.' That's the way it started. We started rehearsing at my house, and it evolved from the Feather Merchants into the City Slickers.

"We rehearsed at my house several times. Then as the band grew bigger we went up to the Hollywood Cemetery, where there was a little stone building that had a recording studio in it. And we rehearsed in the cemetery."

The precise evolution of this audition-rehearsal band—which consisted of various studio musicians of Del and Spike's acquaintance—remains unclear. "We disbanded the Feather Merchants, then Spike started the Slickers," recalled Danny Van Allen, who became one of three part-time drummers for Jones. "We decided to split up the Merchants because we were working a lot of jobs we weren't getting paid for."

Adding to the confusion surrounding the genesis of the City Slickers to this day is the existence of another Jones-Porter band, concurrent with the Merchants. This group made experimental records for the short-lived Cinematone Corporation under two names, Penny-Funnies and Cinema-Fritzers.

The records, which featured ten songs on each side, were made especially for Cinematone's unusual Penny Phono jukebox. The 12-inch discs began spinning at 20 rpm, increasing to roughly 60 rpm as they played. "They were big records…the closer it got to the center the faster it ran," recalled Porter.

"They were supposed to go into machines for a penny a play. I had a friend in the juke box business up in Portland; I wrote him about it. He

Cinematone Band, circa 1939. In the foreground: Jones (left), banjoist Perry Botkin. The trumpeter is believed to be Frank Wylie. (*Ted Hering*)

said, 'Hell, we can't make any money at a nickel, much less a penny.' So that thing kind of went by the boards."

Because the Penny Phono could not play 78 rpm records, the corporation built its own fully-equipped recording studio. Jones served as music director for the Hollywood-based company, signing Irving Aaronson, Gus Arnheim, Billy Mills and other talents.

Little is known about Jones' own Cinematone recordings. Few of the "penny records" exist today, although several acetate dubs were found in the bandleader's library after his death. Evidence indicates there were at least two recording sessions; the first took place on May 29, 1939, and yielded five songs which appeared on three discs, including "Runnin' Wild" and "Sweet Adeline."

Jones' presence on the first session can only be assumed, as the *accredited* musical director on that date was his friend John Cascales. Since Cascales recorded with his own band (aka the Cinematone Recording Orchestra) for the company earlier that month—and was employing Jones as a sideman at that time—he could well have acted as a front for the untested novelty group.

Carl Grayson, while under contract to Columbia Pictures.
(*Eddie Brandt's Saturday Matinee*)

The band's personnel—according to the contractor's report for an August 1940 session—included future Slickers Del Porter, Perry Botkin, Kingsley Jackson (trombone), Stanley Wrightsman (piano), Frank Wylie (trumpet) and Gene Miller (sax), along with Spike (drummer), Wally Ruth (sax) and George Boujie (bass).

"We had some good men," observed Boujie. "As I recall, it was Spike's group, and he put it together; he was very enterprising. He had some guys in there he could count on to rehearse a lot for him—for nothing, probably—and form this group where they could maybe do a few casual jobs. Which I wasn't interested in, but these other guys he had were.

"Spike had done a lot of professional work, he knew the racket. This was more or less his baby. He had a good brass section. It was small, but it was good. We played on time and got it out; we didn't want to waste too much time on sessions."

Asked to describe the Cinematone band, Boujie ventured, "It was a cross between the Hoosier Hot Shots and the City Slickers." He further related: "Later, Spike wanted to change to string bass, instead of tuba. I was out of the picture by then but he called to ask me about it. I said, 'If I were you, I wouldn't. If you use the string bass, you'll sound too much like the Hoosier Hot Shots.' "

One individual who made a decided difference in the embryonic stages of the band—although he was a member of neither the Feather Merchants nor the Cinematone group—was Carl Grayson.

Grayson was a contract player at Columbia Pictures in the late '30s when he was chosen to replace Roy Rogers in The Sons of the Pioneers. While grooming him for stardom, the studio fixed his nose—wrecking it, as far as he was concerned—and changed his name to "Donald" Grayson, a name he kept when he first joined Del and Spike.

In December 1940, the band was hired for a regular engagement at the Jonathan Club in Los Angeles. The downtown social club, an exclusive businessman's establishment, allowed the group to do their novelty numbers but employed them principally to play for dancing on Thursday and Saturday nights.

The nine-piece Jonathan Club Dance Band, as they were tagged, was led by neither Porter nor Jones. "Carl Grayson had a little following as a bandleader, so we used his name," recalled drummer Danny Van Allen. "He was better known than Del or Spike. He had a reputation as kind of a society band, but he was fading out. That's when Spike picked him up and let him front the band."

While the whole truth about the evolution of the band and the roles played by Porter, Jones and Grayson is unlikely to ever surface, the evidence indicates Porter made a major contribution.

"Spike had something to do with it, but Del was really the leading force in getting the City Slickers started," contended Porter's longtime friend, Ray Johnson. "It was supposed to have been a partnership, but it didn't turn out that way. Spike just took it over and Del was left out in the cold."

Porter's undeserved obscurity today is partly his own fault. "Spike was a slick guy," reflected Porter. "Of course, I didn't care; I didn't want all the trouble of looking for jobs and all that sort of thing. I was too busy creating. I was a lousy salesman, as far as that goes." If he was unhappy Jones usurped leadership of the band, Porter stayed with the group and remained a prime influence on their repertoire.

Making Tracks
The Band's Early Years, 1941–1945

Few people took Spike and Del Porter seriously when they started a band, least of all their fellow musicians. It was nothing more than a spare time proposition, and many of them—who had steady work in radio—departed after a rehearsal or two. Spike himself continued drumming on *Kraft Music Hall* and *Fibber McGee and Molly*, relegating the group to his off-hours.

Porter, who was all talent and no ambition, soon took a backseat to his partner. "Spike Jones Group" was the label credit on the audition records making the rounds early in 1941; however, the outfit continued their Saturday night gig throughout the year billed as Donald Grayson and his Jonathan Club Dance Band.

On March 27, 1941, as Bob Burns did his solo on *Kraft Music Hall*, Spike's cowbells, gunshots and automobile horns were clearly evident in the background for the first time, along with King Jackson's trombone fonks. Despite the distinct City Slicker sound, however, the band is believed to be John Scott Trotter's.

In June, Jones' peculiar percussive effects were again heard loud and clear, within the Billy Mills orchestra, on *Fibber McGee and Molly*. Spike's group was still in its embryonic stage the following month when Robert Redd wrote them into an episode of his NBC situation comedy, *Point Sublime*. The band made their official radio debut that July—alias Duke Daniels and his City Slickers—in a sketch with Cliff Arquette, playing "A Hot Time in the Old Town Tonight."

The origin of the name City Slickers remains a mystery. Del Porter vaguely remembered it was Spike's idea, but was uncertain. Bill Harris, who remained friends with Jones long after their graduation from high school and the Five Tacks, was under the impression actor Don Ameche was involved. "Ameche had a radio show, and Spike was playing on the show. He said something about 'Those city slickers,' and Spike liked that," said Harris.

Pioneer country singer-composer Cindy Walker, who sang on some of the band's "home recording" sessions, claimed she was the one who suggested it to Spike; she credited her song, "Gonna Stomp Them City Slickers Down" (later recorded for Standard Radio Transcription Service), as the source.

The name by which the band became famous may not have been first choice. Ralph "Joe" Wolverton, a guitar player of Spike's acquaintance, had a four-piece novelty band called the Local Yokels. When Spike heard the group was disbanding, he reportedly tried to buy the name and some of the instruments. Wolverton refused to sell the name; he wanted to reserve the right to use it again.

Jones had not officially emerged as the leader when one of the band's test records, or home recordings, found a sympathetic ear at RCA Victor. On the advice of Harry Meyerson, the company's West Coast recording manager, producer Leonard Joy signed the band for a session. The group was assigned to Victor's budget or "lowbrow" label, Bluebird, which was home to such artists as Glenn Miller, Fats Waller and Artie Shaw.

"As I see it, the distinction was that Victor was perceived as somewhat highbrow, whereas Bluebird was more for the masses," observed Dr. Demento. "My guess is that Spike was assigned to Bluebird not because they didn't think he'd sell, but because RCA executives perceived his music as being lowbrow."

On Friday afternoon, August 8, 1941, the band entered Victor studios for the first time. If Jones attached any historical significance to the occasion, his accomplices apparently did not. "It was a lot of fun but it never occurred to me it was going to be anything big," said trumpeter Bruce Hudson, a *Kraft* colleague of Spike's who was hired for the afternoon. "We were freelance musicians who were having a ball doing crazy music."

Del Porter sang the numbers and did the basic arrangements with trombonist King Jackson, who pumped a lot of imagination into the group. Jones may have been the *de facto* leader, but as far as the bandsmen were concerned, it was a collaborative effort. "We were all leaders," asserted Hudson. "We did the thing together, all throwing our ideas in."

When "Behind Those Swinging Doors"/"Red Wing" was issued that October, the label identified the group—for the first time publicly—as

Ready to conquer the world, late 1942 or early 1943. Front row, from left: Frank Leithner (piano), Spike, Del Porter (clarinet), John Stanley (trombone). Back row: Country Washburne (tuba), Don Anderson (trumpet), Carl Grayson (violin), Luther Roundtree (banjo).

Spike Jones and his City Slickers.

"Later," revealed Bruce Hudson, "I heard there was almost litigation between [banjoist] Perry Botkin and Spike. After Spike became famous, Perry said we all owned the thing, because we all did it; he said it wasn't Spike's organization, it belonged to all of us because we got together and made up the arrangements as we went along.

"I'm sure it would not have gone if Spike hadn't been the motivating force. No doubt about it. The only sour apple would have been Perry, who thought we should have a part of the success, which we did not deserve. All we did was play," reflected Hudson.

Carl Grayson continued to front the band at the Jonathan Club, evidently due to contractual agreement, through June of the following year. Not until July 1942 did Spike Jones and his City Slickers make their first public appearance as such; switching to Friday nights, they performed at the elite club for the remainder of the year.

Still primarily a dance band, the group became a little crazier that year, and a lot more like the Slickers of legend, when Spike discovered Grayson had latent talents. Along with an ear for dialects, Carl's bag of tricks included the *glug*, an outrageous noise that emanated from his throat and sounded not unlike someone swallowing their tongue.

"When he joined, we didn't know he had all these attributes, of making the funny sounds. Had no idea," said Del Porter. "But he was indispensable. Whenever you needed a funny sound, Carl had it. Musical saw, anything."

Within a year of their first Victor session, most of the Slickers involved—including Perry Botkin, King Jackson, pianist Stan Wrightsman and bassist Hank Stern—departed for greener pastures. Porter and Grayson were the exceptions. Don Anderson, a colleague of Spike's from *Fibber McGee and Molly*, joined the day after the initial session, becoming the band's first steady trumpet player.

Botkin, who was becoming increasingly busy with radio work, brought in Luther "Red" Roundtree to replace him on banjo. Wrightsman, a first-rate jazz pianist who didn't much care for the Slickers' slam-bang style, opted out soon afterwards; Frank Leithner, who worked *The Eddie Cantor Show* with Spike, took his place. Jackson left to serve in a hitch in the army and was replaced by trombonist John Stanley.

Hank Stern's successor on tuba and string bass, was, like Porter, a man of almost limitless talent. Joe "Country" Washburne first made a name for himself as a top-flight jazz musician in his native Texas, working with the legendary but reclusive pianist Peck Kelley. He later sang and played with Ted Weems, who encouraged him as a songwriter by featuring Washburne on some of his own compositions, including the hit "Oh Mo'nah."

Country, whom Spike knew from Billy Mills' band on *Fibber McGee*, eventually took over most of the arranging duties from Del. In doing so he became a major influence, helping to alter the Slickers' sound from the pleasantly silly cornball style that had gotten them started, to the riotous, all-stops-out madness that made them justifiably famous.

Washburne also brought in another individual who was to become of profound importance to the organization. Ernest "Red" Ingle, his colleague from the Ted Weems band, was more than capable on the saxophone; it was for his comedic talents, however, that he would be most cherished.

Ingle, who as a youngster was coached on violin by the great Aus-

Red Ingle, musical comedian of the first rank. (*Duke Goldstone*)

trian virtuoso Fritz Kreisler, got his first break with jazz entrepreneur Jean Goldkette. In the '30s he did considerable comedy and novelty work with Weems. Even in those days he did not go unnoticed; Perry Como, who sang alongside him in the group, was to remember Red as "one of the most talented men I've ever met."

Employed by the government during the war, Ingle left early in 1943 to take a commission in the Air Force. When he flunked the eye examination, Washburne called and offered a solution to Red's sudden unemployment: "How would you like to work with Spike Jones?"

Ingle joined Spike and the Slickers during a transitional period for the band, a few short months after "Der Fuehrer's Face" had made them instant celebrities. Unlike most of the Slickers he was not hired primarily for his musical skills. Spike made use of Red's comic abilities from the outset, relying heavily on him for the gags and vocal effects that went into the desecration of the songs.

Jones' true genius was to emerge not in the recording studio, but behind the scenes. In the weeks and months following the release of the group's first unqualified success—as avenues once closed to them began springing open—he worked at a feverish pace to ensure the band would not be a one-hit wonder.

His talent for promotion was evident even before "Der Fuehrer" started to climb the charts. He didn't depend on Victor to publicize his efforts; he entrusted the job to the one person he knew he could count on—himself. While in New York ostensibly to do battle with company executives over the use of the raspberry, he ran around to record stores asking for releases by the Slickers—a group with whom most shopkeepers were not yet familiar. Before long, they would not be able to keep his records in stock.

Martin Block was the one who decided to play the anti-Hitler tune repeatedly on his show, but Spike was the one who brought him the record. Although Block had a reputation as an ogre, he was also a power-ful radio personality who could make a bestseller out of anything from cigarettes to reducing tablets.

Jones' instincts were right on the mark; taking the record to Block was not a fluke but a calculated maneuver. In the months ahead, he began to construct a modus operandi that inspired awe in his former associates long after his passing. "He had an idea and he worked his tail off achiev-ing it. I don't think people appreciated the work he put into it," said Dick Webster, who eventually became Spike's manager.

"Spike made it pretty much on his own. He had the assistance of some of his members, but he was always so far ahead of everybody—the publicity people, everyone. He had the mind. He had these people work-ing for him, but he was the genius behind the whole thing."

Within weeks of his newly-found success, Jones hired Del Porter's songwriting partner, Carl Hoefle, as contractor and treasurer; the money was beginning to roll in and he needed someone to handle it. At the same time, he also went into the music publishing business with Porter and Hoefle. The songsmiths, who had a firm called Tune Towne Tunes, appeared to have a good thing going; if there was money to be made from the sale of City Slicker songs as sheet music, Jones wanted to share in the profits.

But all was not well in the record business. When the president of the

Home-grown corn for the Allied Forces, London, 1944. Top: Elsa Nilsson, Del
Porter, Eileen Nilsson, Chick Daugherty, Nick Cochran. Bottom: Herman Crone,
Jones, emcee Ronnie Waldman, Carl Grayson and Red Ingle. (*John Wood*)

American Federation of Musicians demanded recording companies pay a
royalty on every disc pressed, without regard to sales, the industry practically ground to a halt. The ban, which took effect on July 31, 1942, was to
bar the City Slickers from recording studios for more than two years.

Although Jones and company remained almost frenetically active
for the 27-month cessation, the restraining order decreed by James C.
Petrillo nearly put their career on ice. Had it not been for the fortuitous
timing of their unexpected hit, the group would have likely disintegrated;
in any case, the wartime ban on record-making was a cold shower they
could have done without.

The "musical madcaps," as they were being called, found themselves
busier than ever—in spite of Petrillo. In mid-October, the Slickers became the house band on Bob Burns' *Arkansas Traveler*. A few weeks later
they started their own show, *Furlough Fun*, for Gilmore Oil. On week-
ends they visited army camps, in addition to other local gigs.

It was about this time that Spike quit *Kraft Music Hall* and soon
after *Fibber McGee*, so as to devote full time to his own enterprise. In
order to keep things running smoothly, and make certain the machinery
was well-oiled, he now turned the bulk of his energies to marketing the
band. To this end, he replaced himself and his other part-time percus-

sionists with Everett Hoagland's longtime drummer, Beauregard Lee.

Requests for personal appearances began pouring in from all over the country, but Jones was in no hurry. "We could have cleaned up on the basis of one number," he explained. "But we'd have wound up broke. We didn't have enough ideas to fill a show. Then people would have gotten sick of 'Der Fuehrer's Face' and us at the same time."

The Slickers busied themselves with radio and movie work instead. They also made personal appearances at many Southern California high schools, including Spike's alma mater in Long Beach, selling war bonds. The fans got a firsthand look at the group whose records were all the rage; the band got a chance to try out an expanded version of the show they had offered at private clubs.

In July 1943, Spike and company embarked on a nine-week "Meet the People" tour, named for an MGM film they had just completed. The trip took them through the Midwest and out to the East Coast for the first time. They started in Omaha and ended in Cleveland; along the way, they broke house records in Milwaukee and New York.

The band met with an initially cool reception in New England, a harbinger of future tours. "Bostonians sat so tight-lipped and feeble-handed after each number that Spike thought the act there was a fizzle," *Radio Life* reported. "But as soon as the repertoire was completed, Spike and the Slickers were surprised by a tremendous ovation."

Jones augmented the band with Elsa and Eileen Nilsson, a blonde sister duo from Kansas who had sung on his radio show, and other vaudeville acts. In addition to five or six shows a day, the group played for bond rallies and veteran's hospitals, toured factories and otherwise made a spectacle of themselves. To combat their rigorous schedule, they often drank to excess—particularly Carl Grayson.

"Carl would get up in the morning, he'd go to the bottle first thing," recalled banjoist Luther Roundtree, who roomed with him on the tour. "He was so drunk he couldn't get to the theatre half the time; he didn't make half the shows. Spike would say, 'Where's Carl?' I'd say, 'In the hotel. Out.' He said, 'You should have gotten him down here.' I told him, 'The guy's 6'2"— I can't pick him up and carry him down here. I'm not his keeper.'"

Grayson, who claimed alcohol had a positive effect on his asthma, was not the only one who caused problems for Spike. The bandleader found himself in continuous conflict with Roundtree, who didn't want to go on tour in the first place. While Grayson was too important to the

Man with a horn: Country Washburne, circa 1945. (*Skip Craig*)

organization to consider letting go at the time—his inspired performance of "Der Fuehrer's Face" was vital to their success—Roundtree was fired at the end of the trip.

"I have no animosity toward Spike," he reflected. "It wasn't all his fault; it was just as much mine as it was his. I should have been honest with him and told him to get someone else for the tour.

"Spike wanted me to do a stand-up comedy thing. I got sick in Omaha and I wasn't prepared; I couldn't do it. He cut my salary. Then in Kansas City he tried to hire a friend of mine who was a banjo player, to replace me. I didn't say anything. Finally in Cleveland we had an argument; I said, 'The hell with you.' Naturally, he fired me.

"Later I went to his house to apologize. I told him he should make up the salary he didn't pay me on the road. He said okay, but he made me sign a paper stating that I would never ask anything from his estate. He made me go to a lawyer and get the thing drawn up," recalled Roundtree.

Jones drew up a new contract at the end of the cross-country tour, which cost him the services of another Slicker. "I wouldn't sign, and a couple other guys wouldn't either," revealed trumpeter Don Anderson, "because he owned you and your mind and everything else. His contract was all right at the time, except I didn't want it; I could do better freelance. If you had any ideas he owned them, he owned everything. You didn't get any part of anything if it went. You couldn't make any money.

"I got along with Spike fine, but I think he had a hard time later as he started to make it. He told me once, 'Don, if I ever start to get swell-headed, let me know.' Things were starting to pop for him. I don't re-member ever letting him know, but after he got going, he got a little bit that way. I guess you can't help it; everything was happening for him," said Anderson.

Spike also demanded "first call" on the availability of his sidemen, most of whom had other jobs and still considered the band something they did for a lark. Wally Kline stepped into Anderson's shoes and Joe Wolverton—who had refused to sell Spike the name of his group—re-placed Roundtree on banjo and guitar.

Frank Leithner, who worked seemingly every radio show in town, was one of the few Slickers who named his own terms, and got them. He agreed to play piano on *Bob Burns* but refused to go on the road and give up his lucrative freelance work. Carl Hoefle, a mediocre pianist by all accounts, substituted for him on tour. Herman Crone, who worked with many of the big bands, played the local jobs Leithner couldn't handle—much as Charlie LaVere, a frequent '30s studio colleague of Spike's, had done prior to him.

The success of the tour—and the ever-increasing royalties from his records—enabled Spike and his family to move from the distinctly middle class Farmdale Avenue neighborhood of North Hollywood, to a stylish home on Beverly Hills' Roxbury Drive. Jack Benny and Lucille Ball were practically neighbors, situated just a few blocks away. By this time Jones' earning power was so great he hired Benny's brother-in-law, Myrt Blum, to manage his finances.

The City Slickers continued to do their part for the war effort throughout the duration of World War II. In addition to visiting army hospitals, they made special records for the Morale Branch of the Armed Forces; V-Discs, pressed on a plastic compound due to the shortage and

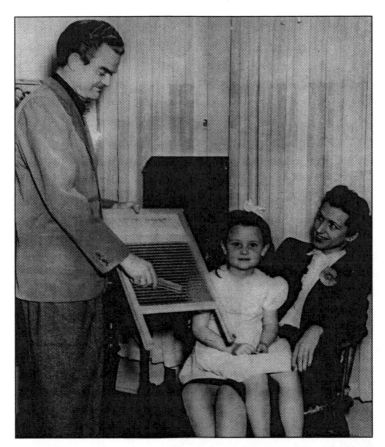

On the home front: The washboard wizard with wife Patricia and daughter Linda.
(*Ted Hering*)

fragility of shellac, were distributed to far-flung military bases.

A pair of the Slickers' Standard Radio transcriptions was reissued on V-Disc, including a once-popular tune called "Cocktails for Two." But neither Spike nor Country Washburne, who did the arrangement, had an inkling of what was to come. Nor did anyone else.

In July 1944, USO-Camp Shows enlisted Spike and his men to entertain U.S. and Allied forces in Europe. Jones took a troupe of twelve on his nine-week jaunt, including ever-dependable Del Porter, anything-but-dependable Carl Grayson and sure-fire laugh-getter Red Ingle.

Dick "Red" Morgan, who had recorded with Benny Goodman and Alvino Rey, joined the band on banjo and guitar. Bandleader Nick Cochran, who billed himself as "King of Cockeyed Songsters," filled in on trumpet, just for the tour. The comely Nilsson Twins assured the group of an enthusiastic audience, while drummer Beau Lee acted as manager of the unit.

The band took a train to New York and waited for transportation overseas. After some delay, they boarded a troop ship—the Aquitania, a converted British liner—bound for Scotland. "Being unescorted, she had to zigzag across the Atlantic to keep from being an easy target for German U-boats. As a result, the crossing took five days," recalled Major Andrew C. Pinchot, an Air Force pilot whose stateroom adjoined the Slickers' quarters.

"Spike and his band went right to work as soon as we set sail, giving three and four performances daily. There were an estimated 7,000 troops aboard," reported Pinchot. "By the time we reached Glasgow, Spike and his group had given 21 performances for the troops. I remarked to Spike that it was some contract he had signed with the USO…He answered, 'Our contract doesn't begin until we reach London. I just wanted to entertain the troops.'"

"Spike was very patriotic," said Luther Roundtree. "He wanted to do something for the war effort. He took them right to the front line where it endangered not only him but everyone involved."

The Luftwaffe arrived in London just hours before the band. On an inbound train the Slickers got their first close-up of the war, six miles out of town. "A buzz bomb had hit the railroad track and bombed it out; we couldn't get in. It was a dark, bleak day. We finally got ahold of the USO, and they sent a couple of buses out and picked us up," recalled Del Porter. "We had buzz bombs like mad then; we had three or four a week while we were there."

Red Ingle and Dick Morgan had a narrow escape one night, as Ingle's son Don recalled. "Dad roomed with Dick and they went out to see Glenn Miller, whom Dick had known since college at Colorado. While they were away from their digs a buzz bomb fell in the park across from their hotel. The blast was hard enough to cause large chunks of ceiling plaster and stone to fall down right on their beds. Had they been in the hotel asleep rather than carousing in some club with Miller and a few others from the Air Force band, they could have been seriously hurt or even killed," stated Ingle. "Dad always said that it was proof that drinking might not kill you—in this case it saved their lives."

The band spent two weeks in England entertaining in hospitals, giving as many as 12 shows a day. At night they partied, eschewing pubs for private clubs with longer hours, while waiting for the green light to continue on to France. Before they left, the City Slickers attended a big bash at an RAF officer's club in London, where they jammed with Miller and his bandsmen all night. It was a party Jones would never forget.

The troupe reached France just after Gen. George S. Patton swept through, as his men were rounding up the retreating Germans. "They were still exploding land mines on the beach," said Porter, whose "Hotcha Cornia" was the most-requested number of the tour. They landed on a beachhead where they gave a show that night, along with Dinah Shore and Edward G. Robinson. An estimated 16,000 men showed up.

Spike and the gang were attached to Ninth Air Corps for the remainder of their sojourn in France, eating and sleeping with GIs. They performed three times a day on landing strips, and gave impromptu concerts in between.

"The band would stop—they'd get someplace and there'd be a few hundred guys sitting by the road. They'd stop and get out and do a number or two for them, jump back in the car and go," said Don Ingle. "There were people out there who were really hurting and in bad shape, and that made the band feel all the more obligated to always be up and do their best to take people's minds off the horror they were going through."

At times they performed no more than a mile from the front lines. "We were sniped at three different times," Jones later reported. "But you get like everyone else over there; you don't go around frightened all the time. You come to accept sort of a fatalistic attitude; you figure if one comes along with your name on it, that's that.

"I ran into a German prisoner; he loaded a piano onto a truck for us. He told us he'd heard our record of 'Der Fuehrer's Face'—then he asked for my autograph. I couldn't help thinking while we were in France, if I should happen to be captured, and the Germans found out I was the fellow who recorded that song, that they might lose their sense of humor."

For once, Jones was apparently on the level: "I remember my dad talking about it," recalled Beau Lee, Jr. "There was a price on their heads from the Nazis."

The band was given $1,000 worth of traveler's checks to cover expenses, but the trip was no vacation. The group was subject to military orders at all times. They were not allowed to keep diaries, nor were they permitted to take cameras, radios, flashlights or electric razors; they were also expected to handle their own luggage. The Slickers' efforts earned each of them $25 a week, except for Spike, who did not draw a salary.

They were asked to submit their scripts for approval, to the special services officer at each base, and forewarned by the USO about "the necessity of seeing that the show is kept clean"—due to recent complaints from the War Department about "indecent material." Nevertheless, their repertoire included a little ditty penned by Foster Carling called "SNAFU," which had been too suggestive for Victor:

> He'll always be a private
> And I don't mean first class
> He wouldn't know his elbow
> From a foxhole in the grass.

The tune was a bit more salacious on the tour than it was when the Slickers sang it on Armed Forces Radio:

> They asked why he brought her
> into the battle zone.
> And he replied, "Cuz I could not
> leave her behind alone."

On arriving in New York at the conclusion of their trip, the band had no place to stay. Hotel rooms were almost impossible to get while the war was on. When Jones called Martin Block and asked him to make an appeal over WNEW for rooms, he got chewed out instead—according to Spike. "Why didn't you tell me about 'Cocktails for Two'?" demanded Block. "What's to tell?" said Spike. "The thing's a smash on transcription," replied the disc jockey.

The war was far from over when they returned home, but RCA Victor was about to come to a cease-fire with the musician's union. Spike wasted little time once the truce was declared; within two weeks the band was back in the studios.

On November 29, 1944, Jones and company recorded "Cocktails" for commercial issue. Within weeks of its release, it was among the hottest-selling records in the country. Their brutal attack on the Sam Coslow-Arthur Johnston song ultimately became Spike's biggest success; to this day, it is synonymous with his name.

Though the tune was to ensure Jones of a high standard of living for years to come, not everyone shared in its success. Coslow, who was less than thrilled at the wreckage of his masterpiece, cried all the way to the bank; the arranger did not. Country Washburne, whose brilliant handiwork forever Spiked "Cocktails," had cause to weep, but not for joy. He had no share in the

Spike and Helen Grayco, around the time of their engagement in 1947.
(*Spike Jones International Fan Club*)

royalties, nor did he receive any acknowledgment for his contribution.

Washburne, who was no longer a regular in the band, continued to arrange for Spike despite the relative anonymity of the task. A modest and unassuming man who failed to assert himself, he had a personality that equipped him to get along well with his employer.

Not long after the release of "Cocktails for Two," when it was obvious that the Slickers were on their way to new heights, Del Porter got into a confrontation with the leader of the band. "Something happened between Spike and Del. It was something personal," ventured Eddie Brandt, who started as a band boy in 1944 and progressed to staff writer. "I don't know what it was but they were never close again. Del never said anything because he wasn't the type that would say anything. It wasn't money, because Spike paid everybody top money."

Porter did confide in his best friend, singer Ray Johnson, who recalled, "When Spike started making all this money, Del went to him and said, 'Where do I come in? What's my picture in this contract?' Spike said, 'What contract?' So Del just quit. That's what he told me," said

Johnson. "I guess they had an agreement that it would be a 50-50 deal. There was nothing signed, apparently, but it was a partnership."

Whatever happened, Porter was not particularly bitter about it in later years. "Del was a very gullible person," said Zep Meissner, who joined the band on clarinet in 1944. "Spike was a businessman, and that's where Del lacked; he was a horrible businessman."

"Del was an easy-going guy," noted Johnson. "Nothing seemed to ruffle him. He was even-tempered, to his own detriment. He never asserted himself as much as he should have."

Porter was not the only partner Jones lost in 1945. He and his wife, Pat, were separated that January. They got back together in August, but it was to be a short-lived reconciliation.

That same month, the band played a benefit on an island off the California coast. "Spike needed a girl to go over to Catalina with us," recalled Zep Meissner. "I said, 'I know a gal who looks good but can't sing.'" Enter Helen Constance Greco, a 20-year-old bleached blonde from Tacoma, Washington, who had appeared on local radio shows and toured with Stan Kenton.

Greco (soon to change her name to Grayco) was singing with Hal McIntyre's orchestra at the Hollywood Palladium when Meissner spotted her and tipped off his boss. "Spike came in with his manager one night and he needed somebody to tour with him," she recalled. "He asked me if I would consider singing with his group and going on a tour of the West Coast. At the time, I thought, 'My God, is he kidding?' I said, 'I'm a straight singer, I don't do any comedy.' He said, 'That's exactly what we want. I want a direct contrast to everything else we do, and I think you'd be very good for it.'"

Helen, an ardent fan of Spike's music—as was her mother—"half expected to find him swinging from a chandelier waving a string of cowbells" when she first met Jones. She quickly found herself attracted to the quiet, straight-faced bandleader but realized "there was a wall of business between us a mile high…He was interested in me solely as an investment," she mused in a magazine article.

Some time went by before Spike suddenly asked her out, for an evening at the Pump Room in Chicago—and made it clear that things were no longer "strictly business" between them. Their courtship gave Zep Meissner cause to regret he had recommended the songstress to Jones. "Pat was a beautiful person," he observed. "If I'd known I was going to break up Spike's marriage, I'd never have introduced him to Helen."

Jones' first marriage, however, was on thin ice long before the divorce; he had dated both the Nilsson Twins, and had a fling with Miriam LaVelle, a dancer in the show. "Pat was a doll when he met her, but he outgrew her," stated writer Eddie Brandt. "Spike became a celebrity, and he went on. He was not a handsome guy, and before he became successful, he probably didn't have every girl throwing herself at him. Helen came on the trip to Catalina; she sang that one time, that was it. He flipped over her."

According to those who knew them both, there was a difference of night and day between Pat and Helen. "Patty was not the kind of person of flamboyance a guy like Spike would have married," observed her close friend, Harriet Geller. "But it lasted for a long time. They were a strange combination, because Spike's whole world was in his head. Patty was too good for Spike; she was a perfect lady. He really gave her a bad time."

It has been argued that Jones' marital difficulties are of little consequence to the overall picture, given his achievements. "We all have our weaknesses, and we're all human beings," observed Earl Bennett, who spent several years in Jones' employ under the guise of Sir Frederick Gas. "I think what people should know is what Spike accomplished in spite of the fact that he was a human being beset with all these ordinary problems…when you overcome all that, and still get done what Spike did…he was a fantastic producer."

Vaudeville Days
The Theater Tours, 1944–1946

Radio broadcasts and record dates, augmented by occasional movie work, kept Spike Jones and his City Slickers hopping in the early years. But once the 1943 cross-country tour had proven their drawing power as a live attraction, the band was never busy enough for their irrepressible leader.

Prior to the USO tour and as soon as possible on their return home, the group traveled to San Francisco and the Bay Area. Thereafter, whenever they could break away, Spike and the boys played towns and cities up and down the California coast. In addition to performing the offbeat repertoire they had made their own they doubled as a dance band; the average club date consisted of two sets of dance music and a comedy show in between.

The Slickers continued to play movie theatres throughout the mid-'40s, as they had on their initial nine-week tour. The group was then much in demand as a last vestige of vaudeville. But it was ersatz vaudeville; the genuine article had been dead for more than a decade. They shared the bill not so much with variety acts—though there were a few—as with motion pictures.

In between feature films, they did a one-hour show; the alternating picture was the same throughout the day, but a number of people invariably spent the entire day at the theatre; after all, the movie simply gave them a chance to "rest" between City Slicker shows, as a disc jockey observed.

The troupe was aided and abetted in early live performances by the Black Brothers, a duo of baggy pants comics who did a tumbling act; Low, Hite and Stanley, a "pyramid of comedy" consisting of a midget, a giant and a medium-sized man in the middle; "girl singer" Lillian Long; the invariable tap dancer; and a harpist who smoked a cigar while knitting a serape—and condescended to playing the occasional note.

THE BOX-OFFICE SURPRISE OF 1943!

ORPHEUM, Omaha
$32,000

TOWER, Kansas City
$13,000

ORIENTAL, Chicago
$28,000

LOEW'S STATE, New York
$37,800
(Including the biggest
Sunday in the State's
history!)

RKO, Boston
$32,000

PARAMOUNT,
Hammond, Ind.
(One nite)
$3,600
(House Record!)

RIVERSIDE, Milwaukee
$22,000
(House Record!)

Management:
MELVILLE A. SHAUER AGENCY
9120 SUNSET BOULEVARD, HOLLYWOOD

Personal Management:
NATIONAL ARTISTS' SERVICE
IRVING GREENWALD · JUNE BUNDY · CARL HOEFFLE

PERSONAL APPEARANCES:
SPIKE JONES and his CITY SLICKERS hit top grosses in every theatre played on a coast-to-coast tour.
READ 'EM AND LEAP!

RADIO:
SPIKE JONES and his CITY SLICKERS start second year for Lifebuoy with Bob Burns over NBC October 7th and begin second year for Gilmore Oil on NBC October 8th.

PICTURES:
SPIKE JONES and his CITY SLICKERS featured in "MEET THE PEOPLE" soon to be released by Metro-Goldwyn-Mayer and "THANK YOUR LUCKY STARS" soon to be released by Warner Bros.

RECORDS:
SPIKE JONES and his CITY SLICKERS give you VICTOR BLUEBIRD hits including: CLINK, CLINK, ANOTHER DRINK · PASS THE BISCUITS, MIRANDY SIAM · BEHIND THE SWINGING DOORS · DER FUEHRER'S FACE · SHIEK OF ARABY · HOTCHA CORNYA:

BOND SELLING:
SPIKE JONES and his CITY SLICKERS sold over $3,500,000 in War Bonds and Stamps in nine appearances in Southern California high schools.

The City Slickers' 1943 "Meet the People" tour proves their drawing power.

"We always carried acts that were paid by Spike," recalled writer Eddie Brandt. "The Black Brothers were one of the first acts he had; they were two old vaudeville guys. Besides doing their own act, Spike would work them into the show. We had to get acts that would work with us; with Spike, you were stuck on stage the whole hour."

Singer-impressionist Judie Manners was an integral part of the show. The wide-mouthed, rubber-faced soprano, who struggled through "The Glow-Worm" while Red Ingle did his best to make a shambles of the number, held her own amid seasoned company. "Ingle loved her, because Manners was a real old-time pro although she was young," said Brandt.

Carl Grayson was a walking warehouse of funny sounds and Del Porter a reservoir of zany ideas, but Ingle was the one true comic in the group in those days. "There was nobody in the band as funny as Red," contended Zep Meissner. "Guys like him were funny in themselves, they didn't need material."

When Ingle stepped out from behind his tenor sax, the noise level increased audibly. "The stage shows became more active—or more violent—when Dad came on the band," said his son, Don Ingle, himself a musician. "He had basically a vaudevillian's approach to musical sight gags—the facial things, the body motions, the running gags; shooting the arrow off in the wings, with a midget running back on with an arrow pinned to the seat of his pants."

Red's big number—and one of the show's highlights—was Country Washburne's disarrangement of the Gus Kahn-Neil Morét standard, "Chloe." The band would open with a sequence from "The William Tell Overture," then Ingle would bounce onstage, lantern in hand, adorned in a leopard skin or nightgown and cap, fright wig and dilapidated combat boots. His high-pitched, operatic "Chhhlo-o-o-o-eee!" ("Where are you, ya old bat?!") and his scramble to a makeshift outhouse ("I gotta go!") brought shrieks of appreciative laughter.

Ingle's biggest competition for applause was 6-foot, 250-pound George Rock, a genteel trumpeter with a talent to match his size. Rock was playing in Freddie Fisher's Schnickelfritz Band at a popular Hollywood watering hole when Spike invited him to join the City Slickers in 1944; before long, his virtuoso trumpeting—and his talent for mimicking children—made him the most valuable musician in the ensemble.

Rock's innovative technique was not wholly appreciated by the early members of the group. "He kind of spoiled the flavor of the band, as far as myself and several of the old-timers in it were concerned, because he played so many notes," asserted Del Porter. "You never knew where the melody was." But Rock was to become the mainstay of the group, remaining 16 years. His services were indispensable, and Jones paid him accordingly.

"Spike could hire all the trumpet players he wanted, but none of them could play like George," declared Eddie Brandt. "He had that big fat tone and he could bend all the notes. Nobody could do what he did; he was unbelievable. He had the Slicker style, and Spike knew he had the style, so he took Rock away from Fisher.

"Freddie Fisher never forgave Spike. But he couldn't do anything for Rock. He was going no place, doing hillbilly movies at Republic. Low class comedy—blacked-out teeth. But Spike had big ideas.

"George was the only one you couldn't do a show without. We could not have played without him," stressed Brandt. "When you've got a trumpet, a trombone, a clarinet and a sax, and a trumpet's the lead, what do you do? I'd hate to hear a sax playing George's part."

Rock had other tricks up his sleeve. "George was a showstopper, all across the country and back. They'd turn all the lights out, just a spotlight on his face, and this silly hat. He'd start singing in this high falsetto voice, like a little girl. Then they'd spread the light, and here's this great big guy, and this tiny squeaky voice coming out of him. It would just break the people up. And he'd have to start five, six or seven times before he'd finally get into the song," said Five Tacks alumnus Herschell Ratliff, who joined the band on tuba in 1944.

The band was a hugely popular attraction in the mid- '40s, although they had yet to reach their peak. "We broke all house records for the Strand Theatre in New York, every theatre we played—they were lined up at 8 o'clock in the morning to hear the Spike Jones band," recalled bassist Candy Hall. Not every venue was appropriate for the group, however: "We worked a big stadium in New York one time; I guess we looked like fleas down there. About the only big laugh we got was the one where the midget ran between my legs," said Hall. "We packed the place, but there was too much going on—the stadium was no place for the show."

Regardless of where they performed, the gig was no picnic. "People don't understand this vaudeville thing. They don't realize what a tough job it was," stressed George Rock. "We would maybe do our first show at 11 o'clock in the morning in the vaudeville house, and we'd do six shows during the day. Sometimes they would cut the movie that was opposite us and they [the characters] would be talking about a murder and you didn't see it happen; they kept cutting the film to let us put in more shows and less time in between shows.

"Once we had to do six shows in Detroit then go across the river about 4 o'clock in the morning and do a benefit show for B'nai B'rith in Windsor, Ontario, then be back at 11 o'clock in the morning to do our first show. That was rough. We would do weeks and weeks of this stuff with no rest in between at all."

Jones' business savvy was by this time obvious to the members of his group, who were sometimes called upon to assist him. Beau Lee, who alternated on drums with Spike, doubled as a manager of sorts. He traveled ahead of the band making accommodations, joining the show wherever feasible. While Jones took his turn at the drums, Lee would be out front counting the house, to keep the management honest.

"You've got to be on your toes about checking the gate; you don't let people get away with anything if you can help it," said Beatrice Lee, the musician's widow. "A lot of little odds and ends have to be taken care of—you've got to see about the pit band and the electricians, and make sure

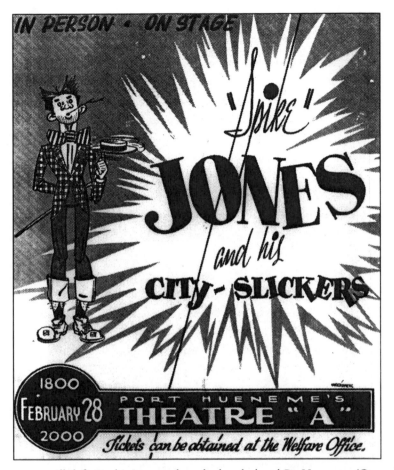

Jones was still defining his image when the band played Pt. Hueneme (Oxnard), California, circa 1945. (*Dr. Horatio Q. Birdbath*)

all those things are handled. Spike knew Beau had been in vaudeville, and he probably thought Beau would be able to handle it well." So well it soon became Lee's full-time job.

Part of the job was making sure the bandsmen got to the theatre on time, and were sober enough to play the show—including the boss. "Spike was a big drinker then. He drank a fifth during the show; he had a valet who stood on the side with a whole glass of bourbon for him," recalled Eddie Brandt. "When I joined him, the whole band was a drinking band. But Spike put up with everybody else because he was drinking too."

"Talk about hangovers. They were one of the hardest-drinking bands I ever saw," mused Tommy Pederson, who played trombone on "The Jones Laughing Record." "Everybody was drunk all the time. I don't know how they got anything done."

Jones and his troupe had already been nicknamed The Band That Plays for Fun by then—perhaps in part because of their elbow-bending recreation—but their humor was comparatively tame in those days. "On occasion, one of the guys rolled up a newspaper and hit the other one over the head, but that sort of thing was very rare. Most of the comedy relied on sound then, more than it did on the visual," said Hersh Ratliff.

"Spike told us when we went on the stage, 'I don't want to see any-body laugh. This is strictly serious. We're trying our darndest to play some-thing beautiful—but things go wrong.' He said, 'If you're trying to make it funny, it won't be funny.' That was his philosophy. The band sounded beautiful, but every once in a while something would jangle or get lost; that made it funny."

By 1945 the City Slickers' style had begun to evolve from slightly silly to full-blown crazy. Under the guidance of their leader—a longtime Marx Brothers fan—all traces of subtlety vanished. "I couldn't under-stand it when Spike went from the sophisticated type of comedy to the obvious, slapstick stuff like Mack Sennett," stated Ratliff. Nevertheless, he recalled an incident which would appear to mark the transition.

"We were out at the big army hospital in Washington, D.C. They put a whole bunch of guys up in front, basket cases—no arms, no legs; all of 'em wanted to die. The psychologist came over and said to us, 'Look, do something. These guys, we can't break 'em. They just want to die.' We all got together and we put on the funniest show," he remembered.

"We practically tore the stage apart," said Ratliff. "We kicked holes in the drums, knocked the legs off the piano. We looked down at those guys and the tears were rolling down their faces, they were just crying. We had to ditch out; they wanted to give us their ration cards and everything, they were so thankful. What medicine and all those doctors couldn't do, that crazy band did. We didn't plan anything; we improvised the whole show. We broke those guys down and they were laughing like mad."

Inevitably, the Slickers soon became as visually outrageous as their music suggested. Decked out in garish checks and plaids of their choice, with color-coordinated shirts and ties, black derbies and high-button shoes, their very appearance was every bit as loud and ludicrous as their music.

Although Jones left most of the comedy up to his associates, he had to have the wildest wardrobe of all. Ernie Tarzia, who kept him sharply attired offstage, created a striking checkerboard pattern which soon be-

Pausing for refreshment in Milwaukee, circa 1945. From left, George Rock, Judie Manners, Giggie Royse, Mary Jane Barton, Dick Morgan, Spike, Herman Crone, Red Ingle, Mavis Mims, Carl Grayson and Jones' valet, Scotty. (*Warren Dexter*)

came the bandleader's trademark. Spike eventually had over a dozen such suits made at $300-500 apiece—blue and orange, black and chartreuse, red and blue, blue and white, and equally gaudy combinations. He changed costume four or five times a night.

The makeup of the band was in a state of constant turnover during the mid-'40s. Among the short-term sidemen Spike hired in this period were trombonist Harry "Chick" Daugherty, who seldom drew a sober breath during his tenure; Gilbert "Giggie" Royse and Ormond Downes, who alternated on drums; Dick Peterson, who succeeded them; singer-saxophonist Eugene Walla, alias Ding Bell; clarinetist Bob Poland and bassist Candy Hall, both of whom were also part of Jones' short-lived Other Orchestra.

"Spike would hire a musician and give him two weeks to learn the book, to be able to play the show—and if they couldn't play it by then he'd let 'em go," observed Bill King, a juggler who was hired for three days and stayed with Jones for 13 years. "The book was kind of hard to learn; if you couldn't play his stuff, you just couldn't play it, that's all there is to it."

When Kaye Ballard auditioned for Jones in Cleveland, he decided the teenaged singer-comedienne had great potential, despite her inexperience; he signed her to a seven-year contract and began grooming her for stardom. In less than a year, however, she made a sudden, unplanned exit

Trumpeter George Rock dominated the City Slickers after "the drinking band" departed.

from the band.

"Kaye was a natural talent. She was so *funny*—and she didn't have any real material yet, just a bunch of jokes and imitations. Spike had big hopes for her. He was having her coached; he had Kay Thompson, who wrote for Judy Garland, writing her material," recalled Eddie Brandt. "When we got to Loew's State in New York, she just killed 'em. She tore the joint down. And the agents all grabbed her, 'cause she was so hot.

"They looked up her contract and found out she was only 17 when she signed it. Spike didn't know that. We finished at that theatre—she left him, *boom!* Kaye always regretted what happened, but she would've never gone any place. She shouldn't have done it. But she didn't know; she was very naïve and very young."

The entertainer went on to a successful career, but Jones never spoke to her again. "We were sitting in a restaurant once in Chicago," mused Brandt, "and [columnist] Irv Kupcinet came up to him and said, 'How is Kaye Ballard?' Spike said, 'Did you ever have cancer?' "

Many of the auxiliary talents who joined the troupe in those days lasted longer than the musicians. Bird and animal imitator Purves Pullen—or Whistlin' Pullen, as he was known during his stint with Ben Bernie—traveled with Jones for five years. He was first ordained a doctor of ornithology by Spike and rechristened Dr. Horatio Q. Birdbath. When asked what the "Q" was for, Jones replied, "It's going to stand for Quinine, because you're hard to take."

Veteran stage and film actress Aileen Carlyle was brought in to replace the original "Glow-Worm" singer, Judie Manners. Carlyle was equally adept at comedy, but unlike her short, slender predecessor, the red-headed soprano was round and heavy set, establishing a precedent for those who followed in the role—a succession of women of whom George Rock noted, "They were all fat and sang high."

Jones' stable also included giant J. Lockard Martin, alias Junior; dwarf Frankie Little; acrobatic dancer Betty Jo Huston ("The Human Cartwheel"), who married George Rock; showgirl Mavis Mims; and tap dancer Dorese Midgley. "Spike auditioned everyone. He was always open; he always found time to look at someone," noted Eddie Brandt.

"Spike made a profession out of finding comics, and he had a great supply of them," said Ish Kabibble, the trumpet-playing comedian whose real name was Merwyn Bogue. "Spike made me an offer to quit Kay Kyser and come with him. I thought his band was very funny. But I was a Kyser man; I refused to leave. He said, more laughing than anything else, 'If you don't come with me, I'll have to get somebody that'll imitate you.' And I said, 'Go ahead.' "

Candy Candido, who played string bass with Ted Fio Rito and was prized for a trick voice that ranged from prissy falsetto to gravelly bass, was also approached by Jones. But the bandleader couldn't match the $750 a week Candido was able to command from Jimmy Durante.

While Spike was ever on the lookout for new talent, he didn't always know it when he saw it. "I went backstage when he was at the Oriental Theater in Chicago, and asked for a job," recalled Frankie Little, a former

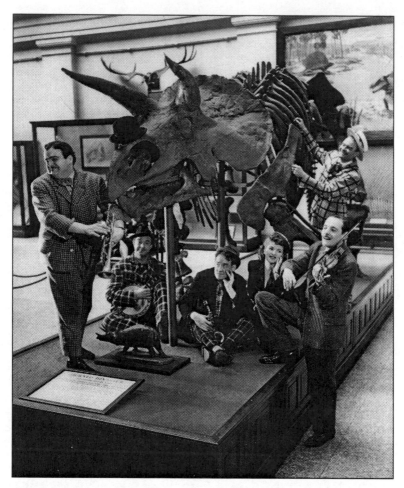

The band that set music back 10,000 years: George Rock, Dick Morgan,
Red Ingle, Judie Manners, Carl Grayson and Spike cut up with a captive
audience, circa 1945. (*Ted Hering*)

circus clown. "He didn't want me. Then Red Ingle saw me and he said,
'Jesus, I could use you.' He shot a bow offstage in 'Chloe' and I came out
screaming, with a arrow shoved in my back."

Ingle's slings and arrows never missed their target, although they were
not always part of the act. "Among the guys, he'd do a lot of cute practical
jokes, sometimes bordering a little bit on the blue," recalled Don Ingle.
"One time, Kaye Ballard was out there doing her 'Dear Mr. Gable' number, the imitation she did of Judy Garland. The next number up was 'Chloe.'

"Dad would wear G.I. shoes with the heels off and this baggy-
crotched leopard skin; the crotch was down below the knees. He was

waiting, getting ready to go on—and he was mooning the band from the wings. The audience couldn't see it, but the guys in the band were all cracking up; they were having a hard time trying to keep a straight face."

The face of the band changed radically in 1946. It was a pivotal year in Jones' life and career, a time of dramatic personal and professional change and upheaval. His first wife, Pat, would divorce him that fall, owing to his blossoming romance with singer Helen Grayco. His romance with the public was also blossoming; his records were making him more in demand than ever, with the result that his tour schedule was growing rapidly. It was at this point he realized he could no longer indulge in the heavy drinking he and the Slickers had enjoyed since the early days.

"Spike had a personality change," asserted Don Ingle. "Things changed after he started going with Helen. He used to be one of the guys, until he got religion and stopped drinking, and decided he was going to be a businessman first. He started losing a lot of his best talent after that."

Beau Lee, who had strongly advised Jones to quit drinking, ostensibly left the band about that time due to a serious illness. But he also had a falling out with Jones. "No matter whether my dad was right or wrong, he was always right," acknowledged Beau Lee, Jr. "Beau was always right, and Spike was just about always right also," added Beatrice Lee. "They were both very dominant personalities and sometimes they clashed. And sparks would fly. After Helen came into the picture, the friendship seemed to deteriorate. I know Beau really didn't approve of Helen, and maybe they had words about that."

Spike had unpleasant exchanges with many of his sidemen, whose drinking habits he couldn't tolerate once he quit the bottle himself. Carl Grayson was among the first to be cut from the roster. Some of Jones' associates were surprised at the move; others felt he had been tolerant of Grayson's excessive boozing for far too long.

"If I'd have been the bandleader, I would not have taken what Spike did from Carl," said Zep Meissner. "With the other guys, the public didn't know it, but when Carl was drunk you could really tell—which was about 90% of the time."

"Carl was the most lovable sweetheart of a man who ever lived. I didn't understand why Spike fired him until I had my own band," observed Eddie Brandt. "But Grayson was a key man. When you're making $10,000 a night in theatres and nightclubs and you've got a guy you're depending on—if the guy doesn't show up, you're through. No wonder

The crowd in front of the RKO Golden Gate Theatre in San Francisco attests to the band's popularity as a vaudeville attraction. (*Warren Dexter*)

Spike fired him."

It was with genuine reluctance that Jones dismissed Grayson, however, given the vital role he had played in the bandeader's success. "Spike was real concerned about it," noted his longtime friend, Gordon Schroeder. "He would confide in me. He said, 'I hate like heck to let Carl go, but I can't take a chance on him.' "

Grayson never worked again, apart from an RCA session for Spike and a brief stint with Brandt's band. An irredeemable alcoholic, he was reduced to panhandling in his last days; at his premature death, three people attended his funeral.

Once Grayson left the group, Jones wanted nothing to do with him. Spike had grandiose plans, and his hard-drinking one-time star did not fit into them. Nor did anyone else he could not depend on. After three years of what amounted to little more than a glorified vaudeville show, he decided to shoot for the big time.

On the Road
The Musical Depreciation Revue, 1946–1950

The Road was a fact of life for denizens of the big band era, moving from one town to the next by whatever haphazard means was available. Hours were fatiguing, work was arduous, meals erratic and sleep uncertain. Traveling with a band was no life. But for a dynamo who did things bigger and better than the competition—and delighted in the meticulous planning that gave other bandleaders headaches—the road was a grand canvas. Spike Jones thrived on it.

"Harry James was the same way; he felt the road was the thing. They both loved the road," said trombonist Robert Robinson. "It was fun, but it was a lot of hard work. We were going day and night. There was no such thing as time off."

Late in 1946, Spike launched a two-hour extravaganza called *The Musical Depreciation Revue*. While he had high hopes for his new enterprise, not all of his associates shared them. "I remember the first time he told me about it," said George Rock. "I thought, 'Boy, that's going to be a drag, doing a two-hour show.'

"The idea didn't impress me at all. I thought he was going to blow it. I didn't think it was going to go over because movie theatres had been so phenomenal, the reception and the crowds. What more do you want? But Spike undoubtedly figured he could make more money—which was out of my realm. I didn't care, as long as I got my check."

The new *Revue*—a combination concert-variety show that threatened to erupt into a three-ring circus, and sometimes did—was showmanship on a grand scale. The venue varied, from opera house to baseball stadium to fairground, but every city and town in the United States and Canada with a stage big enough to accommodate the fruit of Jones' unfettered imagination—and an auditorium big enough to house the fans—was a potential stop on the itinerary.

95

Up to this point Jones had gotten by with a haphazard system of management, selecting various members of the band to assist him in scheduling the trips and making the concomitant arrangements. But the logistics of putting together tours that would take them on the road for five and six months at a time were more than he or anyone in his employ could handle.

"Spike had a hard time finding a good agent," said Del Porter. "Mel Shauer Agency tried to handle us at first, but they just got no place. They got us little things, but nothing big. Beau Lee wasn't a real agent; he didn't have a license." The situation improved substantially after Jones turned the reins over to Ralph Wonders of General Artists Corporation, but not enough to keep pace with his drive for success. He wanted more control over his burgeoning empire.

The wheels were ever turning. First, Jones coaxed Wonders away from GAC with an offer he couldn't refuse, including a piece of the action. Wonders had been head of CBS' Artists Bureau under William Paley before he became West Coast vice president of GAC; he had the kind of organizational skills Spike needed to literally get his show on the road, and keep it running smoothly. They promptly incorporated under the name Arena Stars, as a tax shelter, then made a deal with Music Corporation of America to handle the bookings.

While Jones oversaw all facets of his mad monarchy, he focused his talents on what he did best. "Spike didn't want to be bothered with the basics; he only wanted to be bothered by the artistic end," said Dick Webster, who worked alongside Ralph Wonders at Arena Stars. "Wonders and I took care of contracts, personnel, accommodations, and transportation. We did a little booking, but we had no license; contractually it was done by MCA. It was our duty to make sure he played the right spots and got the right amount of money, and dictate to MCA what we needed."

Business Administration, which handled the financial aspect of Spike's operation—as they did for many star clients—advised him where to invest his money and where to spend it. "They were not in an advisory capacity as to 'record this' or 'play here'—that was our job," explained Webster. "They made up the payroll; I counted the money."

Despite who did what, there was never any question as to who ran the show. "Generally the top talents don't have much business acumen, but Spike did," affirmed saxophonist Eddie Metcalfe. "Ralph Wonders was a very sharp man, but I think Spike was probably five blocks ahead of him all the time."

Spike and Ralph Wonders, a combination that hit the jackpot.
(*Spike Jones International Fan Club*)

"Spike was a very astute businessman," concurred juggler Bill King. "One time Spike and Ralph were having an argument about something. And Spike finally said, 'Well, Ralph, put your name on the marquee and see how many people come in here.'"

The initial one-month tryout of the *Revue,* which opened in Fargo, North Dakota, in November 1946, was the curtain call for the then-current Slickers. It was the beginning of a new phase in Spike's career, but the end of the road for most of the sidemen who made the trip. He was fed up with the "drinking band," and they with him.

Red Ingle left of his own accord about the time Jones cleaned house. While he had grown tired of the road, it was ultimately a matter of finances—and principles—which caused him to leave. "They were doing an awful lot of traveling and Dad was going to give notice and do some studio work," said Don Ingle. "Spike said, 'No, no, we've got a tour and we've got to have you.' It turned out there was a rider on the contract, that they had to produce Red.

"Spike said, 'I'll tell you what, you go out and make the tour, and when you get back we'll give you an increase in salary, and we'll also give you this lump bonus,' which was quite a few thousand dollars. When Dad got back, Spike had forgotten all about it, didn't remember ever saying it," asserted Ingle's son. "My father was a very trusting person; he wasn't the greatest businessman. That's the major reason Dad left."

Following his departure from the City Slickers, Ingle went on to start his own novelty band in association with Country Washburne, and enjoyed a success that surprised even him; his first single, "Tim-Tayshun," reportedly sold over three million copies.

Banjoist Dick Morgan, a reformed drinker, and George Rock, a tee-totaler from the outset, were the only seasoned troupers to remain in the group. Clarinetist Mickey Katz, who had been brought in earlier that year to replace Carl Grayson—and prided himself on staying sober in a group full of *shikkers*—also survived the purge. Together with drummer Joe Siracusa and saxophonist Dick Gardner, both of whom joined just prior to the tour, they formed the core of a new band. Jones soon added Roger Donley on tuba, Paul Leu on piano, Merle Howard on sax and Robbie Robinson (to be replaced shortly by Joe Colvin) on trombone.

"George Rock was the fulcrum, musically, of the band," observed Joe Siracusa. "Before I joined, it was kind of a dixieland, almost a polka-type feeling. But when I got in the band, George inspired me so much with his playing... he'd set the mood and the tempo, and we all just kind of followed him. We started a whole new style for Spike, created on what George was doing."

Winstead "Doodles" Weaver, a 33-year-old funster who had appeared in two Broadway revues and dozens of films—including *Topper* and *A Yank at Oxford*—was hired to head the laugh department after Spike caught his act at the Pirate's Den nightclub in Los Angeles. It was a perceptive move on Jones' part. In addition to his mile-a-minute stand-up routines and a gift for pantomime, Weaver generally behaved like a fugitive from a nut house.

The *Revue* "fit right down my alley," observed Weaver. "Spike had asked me to join him before, but I didn't like vaudeville, doing four or five shows a day. I didn't want to go with him because it was too much work. There's no sense doing four shows a day when you can do one."

The comedian was notorious for his antics as an undergraduate at

Licorice shtick: master clarinetist and funnyman Mickey Katz. (*Warren Dexter*)

Stanford University, as a result of which he had his own following. His fellow alumni were ever faithful. "Doodles was a killer," said Mickey Katz. "He used to put on these funny little goggles that lit up. We went into Hutchinson, Kansas, and there were 40 guys in the first two rows with the lighted goggles—barking—just to greet him. He was a riot."

Weaver's *piece de resistance* was a pun-filled horse race routine ("It's girdle in the stretch...") he had done in nightclubs for several years before he joined Spike. "I had a four-piece band, and we'd do take-offs," he noted. "The horse race was an imitation of an announcer named Joe Hernandez, who had this droning voice: 'Rrround the outside...'" The sketch became a classic; the inevitable winner of the race—a pathetic nag called Feetlebaum—emerged a household word.

Mickey Katz (left) shares the mic with Red Ingle on a 1946 tour. (*Skip Craig*)

Ralph Wonders and Dick Webster arranged first-class transportation for the ever-growing cast of Jones' traveling carnival. While other bands with whom they crossed paths, like Jimmy Dorsey's, traveled by bus, Spike leased two Pullmans and a 70-foot baggage car. Having his own private train was the only logical solution to the potential headaches which could arise on months-long tours of one-night stands. Jones' unusual mode of transport was not without precedent; Paul Whiteman's band had toured in a pair of Pullman cars during the 1920s.

"The conditions under which we traveled were ideal," said Joe Siracusa. "After the show at night, we would go to our berth and we would have a good night's rest, and wake up at our next destination. Normally, it meant not carrying bags into hotels, checking in and out of hotels, plenty of time to look for a decent restaurant, stretch our legs... for a musician, they were the best possible conditions under which we could travel."

There were lots of restless nights, however. "On those one-night stands, it was nothing for Spike to shake me awake at 3 or 4 o'clock in the morning, 'cause he couldn't sleep," recalled staff writer Eddie Maxwell, who traveled with the band. "We'd go into the men's lavatory where there was a light on all night, and we'd work. Siracusa had a berth near him and so did I. If Spike couldn't sleep, we couldn't sleep. We took it in stride; that was our job.

"We used to play poker in the men's lav too, because that was the biggest room there was. If we wanted to stay up and kibitz or do something constructive, that's where we went. We'd get the porter to bring in folding chairs," said Maxwell. "Any time there was a poker game, Helen was wide awake. She was a good poker player; she won plenty. Nobody had to let her win in order to keep their jobs."

In addition to solving the not inconsiderable problem of accommodations, the train also allowed Spike to take his own stagehands and electricians, as well as eight tons of props. He also hauled his own lighting equipment and speaker system. Things could go wrong—and sometimes did—but rarely did he or Wonders take anything for granted. Upon arrival in any town, their requirements were few: 15 wooden back chairs, one grand piano in perfect concert pitch and three eggs per performance.

Despite the staggering number of props and instruments they carried, the Slickers were always in search of more. "No matter where we stopped, the guys in the band would all get off the train and go into town, and they'd look in the junkyards and the pawnshops for things they might make music with," said singer Eileen Gallagher. "They wanted to make music with things that were really extraordinary."

The group also went looking for showers, which they didn't have on the train. While the bandsmen often went to the YMCA or rented a hotel room so they could all clean up, they were sometimes forced to do without. "On one tour we were unable to take baths for 41 days," charged Mickey Katz. "We lived like animals on that train. We almost froze to death one night because there was no heat."

Hotels accommodated recreation as well as personal hygiene. "We actually played football in a hotel room in St. Louis," chuckled Eddie Maxwell. "It was one of those things that just happened. I threw something to save myself from walking over to hand it to somebody. They threw it to somebody else, and then—first thing you know, we were tackling each other. There must have been at least 18 of us."

Portrait of the artist as a rising star: Winstead "Doodles" Weaver. (*Ted Hering*)

Traveling the country with a 44-piece troupe appealed to the show-man in Jones and the businessman as well. It wasn't long before he discovered The Road was literally the road to riches. To their dismay, the cast found themselves breaking endurance records as well as attendance records. Even before the *Revue* officially opened, at San Francisco's Curran Theatre on July 31, 1947, they had established a precedent for durability: 139 consecutive shows in 139 cities.

"It's the old vaudeville joke, but many times we didn't know what town we were in," asserted Joe Siracusa. "We played places where they hadn't had a train in 20 years. Almost as a gag one time, Spike said, 'Thank you, ladies and gentlemen. It's a pleasure to be here in…' And he couldn't think of the name of the town. It became part of the routine."

Despite the working conditions, many felt Jones was reasonably generous when it came to salaries; others found him unstintingly cheap. "Spike never paid the musicians a helluva lot. He paid them as little as he could pay 'em," noted Bill King. "But I was never in that class, so I never had those problems with Spike. I was getting $350 a week when everybody else was getting $125 or $175, so I did very well. I kept the same salary for 13 years.

"A lot of those guys were only getting $125 a week, and they couldn't keep a house up in California and go on the tour and come back and make it up. I don't think Spike was paying those guys enough money to make it work," said King. " A lot of the musicians wouldn't stay because the job just didn't pay enough, and $125 a week back in those days was a pretty damn good salary for a musician."

Mickey Katz, who did comedy bits in addition to his clarinet solos and helped conduct the show, never felt Jones paid him what he was worth. "I once said to him, 'Spike, in your tax bracket you could give me a raise of $500 a week, and it wouldn't cost you $100.' He said, 'I know, but I don't want to spend the $100.' We knocked our friggin' brains out in Washington, D.C., one time, doing six shows a day," reflected Katz. "Spike said, 'You'll all get a big bonus for this.' We each got a $18.75 war bond. He made $80,000 that week.

"Spike didn't pay big money because he didn't have to. Everybody wanted to play with him. I wanted to up to a certain point, and after that it wasn't enough," said Katz. "I was more serious than a lot of the fellas in the band. I had a good family life; I didn't want to be on the road all the time. I was looking to better myself and unfortunately you couldn't with a band because the leaders were out for themselves."

Before Katz left the group to record his own song parodies for RCA and Capitol, with a comedy-klezmer band he called the Kosher Jammers, he recommended the services of a young entertainer from his hometown. Freddy Morgan auditioned over the telephone from a nightclub in Florida; he was hired for four weeks and stayed 11 years.

"I did some imitations of Edward G. Robinson and barking dogs and sang in Japanese dialect. People sitting at the bar near the phone thought I had gone off my rocker," recalled Morgan, who adopted the goofy haircut of Ish Kabbible (or his prototype, Moe Howard) and eventually became the top banana in the bunch—a role Katz himself had sought.

At 36, Morgan was already a show business veteran when he joined Jones in 1947; he had played New York's legendary Palace Theatre when barely out of his teens. Spike hired the amiable banjo player without realizing he was a skilled comedian as well; within a month, he discovered Freddy's impeccable timing and his gift for dialects.

Morgan was an original whose talents were innate. "I don't think he copied anybody," observed his widow, Carolyn Livingston. "According to his mother, Freddy carried on the same way in school. He was always being called to the principal's office for making faces or doing something. I think he was a natural born idiot," she said affectionately.

Earl Bennett, who joined the band shortly after Morgan, was a monologist with a novelty all his own. Inspired by "a village idiot named Topsy" from his youth in Liberty, Missouri, he rubbed two tree branches together to simulate a violin—or a Sadivarius, as he called it—accompanied by a squeal made by playing a reed through the crack in his teeth. Jones renamed the young comic Sir Frederick Gas, a moniker he had already used as a gag credit on record labels. The belches attributed to Gas, however, were actually supplied by George Rock.

In a break from the Slicker uniform, Bennett's tramp costume gave way to a tuxedo with baggy pants; at Spike's bidding, he also copied the finger-in-the-light-socket hairstyle of radio's famed "Mad Russian," comedian Bert Gordon. "Spike wanted the hair to get wilder and wilder, and of course I went along with it, because it was job security. But after a while it became a terrible burden. I hated it," said Bennett. "One time I was so tired I went to sleep in a barber chair; the guy gave me a real honest to God haircut. And Jones chewed me out. He said, 'Would Jimmy Durante get his nose fixed?!' "

Bennett had honed his talents in shorter-haired days as an entertainer during a stint in the army. At 28 he was younger and less seasoned than Freddy Morgan or Doodles Weaver, but he had knocked around Hollywood—and been knocked around—for a while; he would soon prove a valuable addition to the troupe, whose ear for dialects was as keen as Morgan's.

The comedians became friendly competitors. "We were on the bus, and to keep from being bored to death we'd do all kinds of things," recalled Bennett. "So I was taking a crack at imitating Peter Lorre, and Freddy was taking a crack at it—I think Freddy felt he had that sewed up. Somebody in the back of the bus says, 'Gas does a good impression of Lorre.' And I heard Freddy say, 'Jesus Christ, I hope not.' I won, but at the end of this [singing

Hey, Mr. Banjo: Comedian Freddy Morgan in his pre-City Slicker days. (*Skip Craig*)

"My Old Flame"]—night after night after night on stage—I felt like my throat was bleeding. I said, 'I wished Freddy had won this thing.'

"At that time, when Freddy first came with the show, he had a little problem finding his niche. He finally became the funniest, and the very best part of the show—in the beginning, he was doing bits that were all right, but they weren't the masterpieces he created later," said Bennett. "Working with Freddy was the richest experience I ever had on stage. I didn't mind being a straight man for him. His timing, and his reactions... to me, he was pure, rich, wonderful talent."

While the personnel had pretty much stabilized by 1947, Spike was always ready to make room for new talent—regardless of where he found it. Dick Gardner heard Jack Golly playing jazz clarinet in Chicago's Brass Rail; singer-saxophonist Eddie Metcalfe, who supplanted Merle Howard, was discovered on a California golf course. Bill DePew, who played alto sax with Benny Goodman, replaced Golly after two years at Metcalfe's prompting.

To further ensure there was never a dull moment in *The Musical Depreciation Revue,* Jones brought in Gladis and Gloria Gardner, a teen-aged dancing duo who replaced the Nilsson Twins as Slickerettes; Bob Perry and Paulette Paul, a trampoline act who billed themselves as Paul and Paulette; juggler Lottie Brunn; a succession of vocalists, including Irving "Paul" Judson and Dick Baldwin; and a number of tap dancers and roller skating acts.

On rare occasions in large venues, like the historic Curran Theatre in San Francisco and the Lyceum in Minneapolis, Spike hung an elaborate curtain with neon lights, made at his bidding by cartoonist Milt Gross. "The curtain worked with the overture played by the pit band," recalled Earl Bennett. "It was very complex and cost a lot of money. It blew bubbles, and people stuck their tongues out; all these strange things happened. The guys were climbing up and down ladders to operate all this stuff. Nobody ever had an opening curtain like this; it made a damned interesting show."

Surrounded by all manner of noise-making props and other para-phernalia, the Slickers generally opened the *Revue* with a frenetic rendi-tion of "Der Fuehrer's Face" or "That Old Black Magic." Then the Slickerettes or the Saliva Sisters—"the spittin' image of each other"—welcomed the audience with an introduction penned by Mickey Katz:

Howdy, friends, we ask you please
to pardon this intrusion.
We just came out to tell you
'bout this musical confusion.
Guns will pop, bells will ring,
but don't you be afraid.
There'll be an intermission
for refreshments and first aid.
You'll hear some funny noises
and some most unusual tones,
but whadya expect—Stokowski? —
when you came to hear Spike Jones.

The performers varied from one tour to the next, but there was little change in the content of the show. When "Glow-Worm" singer Aileen

Sir Frederick to you: Earl Bennett stifles a belch.

Carlyle tired of having doves shot out of her hat, she was replaced by Ina Souez. The renowned prima donna, who had conquered Europe in her prime, was down on her luck when Jones offered her the job. "I grabbed it," Souez later recalled. "No matter what I thought about my career, Spike was offering me some real money, and it turned out to be the most wonderful experience I ever had."

Harpist Charlotte Tinsley, who recorded and played Los Angeles area gigs with Spike, was too busy to travel; she also refused to smoke the cigars that came with the job. Nancy McDonald, Betsy Mills and Helen Kramer took her place behind the knitting needles on the road, continuing work on the endless serape.

Dick Morgan, who inherited "The Glow-Worm" and "Liebestraum" when Red Ingle called it quits, became better known for his own contributions—and his rubbery countenance, for which he was affectionately nicknamed Icky Face. A skilled purveyor of barnyard sounds, Morgan has been credited with the idea for the nutty *cackle chorus* on "Holiday for Strings," which featured himself and Carl Grayson (later Dr. Horatio Q. Birdbath) in coxcombs and tail feathers, strutting and squawking in time to the music.

Doodles Weaver picked up "Chloe" from Ingle—which he did in a raccoon coat and beaver cap—and donned a grass skirt for "Hawaiian War Chant." He won more applause with original routines, including his one-man baseball team pantomime, performed to the accompaniment of "Take Me Out to the Ballgame."

At the hub of the chaotic goings-on was Spike himself, manipulating an ensemble of homemade instruments he affectionately called "the heap." The contraption consisted of locomotive and police whistles, sleigh bells, beer bottles, a brake drum, a gong, an oversized telephone, a Greyhound bus horn, artificial hands and other necessary props. Suspended across the top was a string of markers, of the pool hall variety—when a gag went over well, he'd mark it.

Jones, who sometimes accompanied his harpist on the latrinophone—a toilet seat strung with wire—got some of his best laughs by choosing the unlikeliest of batons. He conducted the band with a .38 caliber pistol, a mop, an umbrella, a nightstick, and frequently a toilet plunger. He once chastised a disc jockey for claiming he used a whip. "That's sheer libel," he declared. "A whip—the very idea. Everyone knows I use a blackjack."

For the most part, Jones left the comedy in the capable hands of his cast and emceed the show. "You couldn't call Spike a performer in the true sense of the word, but he was the catalyst. He knew how to take talent and organize it and bring out the best in everybody," said drummer Joe Siracusa.

"Doodles is a good example. We took his stand-up nightclub act and made it a production. Spike and I went down to Paramount Pictures and ran through a lot of old films; we picked out footage of old accidents, planes going through barns, et cetera, and compiled a film we projected on screen while Doodles did his Feetlebaum [horse race] act. Then we played 'The William Tell Overture' behind him." For good measure they shot new footage of an old sway-backed mule, which they cut to every time Weaver intoned, "...and Fee-tle-baum."

"Spike did the same thing with Earl Bennett," Siracusa pointed out. "Earl would do this act, playing the twig like a violin, and we set it up with a full orchestra introduction, in a spotlight, the whole bit. He took these acts and presented them in the most productive, showbiz way. Everything was production with Spike; he was a genius at that.

"When Earl first came to the show, we didn't know what he did; we hadn't seen him perform. We never saw his complete act, until the first night of our tour. We were out in a ballpark in Phoenix or Tucson. He came out and did the bit with the twig, and a monologue. He broke us up," said Siracusa. "George Rock couldn't stop laughing. Doodles came out and took his hat and threw it at Earl, and said, 'That's for being funnier than me!' Spike kept that moment for the band, so the band could react, and get the most out of us. He was a true showman, not only to the audience, but to the people in the band."

Ventured Eddie Maxwell: "I think the word that describes Spike—without negative connotations—he was an opportunist, in that he recognized the potential in a person or a piece of material. I don't mean that in a negative way at all."

The Musical Depreciation Revue promised audiences two hours or more worth of sheer lunacy, and never failed to deliver. Pint-sized Frankie Little pulled a rope across the stage, reappearing at the other end of it. Doc Birdbath gave the *band* a bath, pouring water on them from a prop horn. A headless corpse fell from a box seat. Pigs slid down chutes and snakes sprang from the trombone.

George Rock, as an unwed mother-to-be, sang a tale of woe in high falsetto. A saber-wielding Dick Morgan ran past, in hot pursuit of a curvaceous showgirl; half a man (Little in Morgan's pants) returned, chased by the girl with the sword. Pigeons flew out of Roger Donley's tuba; Joe Colvin's pants went up and down in sync with his trombone fonks.

The show was often as surreal as a Salvador Dali painting. "I would sing 'Some enchanted evening, you may see a stranger,' and these two guys would come walking out with hats on top of their shoulders; they'd take off their hats and bow to each other, no heads. Spike liked to have strange things happen," recalled vocalist-saxophonist Bernie Jones, who replaced Eddie Metcalfe. "As long as it didn't hurt the show, he got a kick out of things like that."

Even the serious moments in the show were anything but. "Although I sang straight vocals, there was a lot of hell raised behind me," said

Spike interviews Aileen Carlyle as an intro to "The Glow Worm" routine. (*Skip Craig*)

Metcalfe. "When you have George Rock spitting in your face, on one side, and Dick Morgan making faces at you on the other, it isn't easy.

"Helen Grayco's spot was the only thing that wasn't funny. Some people felt it should have been a fun show all the way—but she brought kind of a sobering influence to it with the numbers she did, the torchy kind of songs. The show would decelerate, if that's the word. Then we'd pick right up again with Doodles or somebody like that to get it back into the fun mood again," noted Metcalfe.

"The only time I ever got nervous was playing behind Helen," noted Joe Siracusa. "I didn't know what to play behind her, and I was very self-conscious about it. Slicker stuff I never worried, I didn't even think about it. But playing behind her, everybody was nervous, even Spike. He was a nervous wreck."

Despite the onstage apprehension, Helen's numbers provided a breather for the audience, and also gave the Slickers a much-needed chance to catch up with the pace of the show. "I played second pistol," explained Metcalfe. "My job was to reload when Helen was singing or some other act was on, because Spike couldn't do it fast enough. We each had a brace of pistols; I had three under my stand and Spike had two in the tray under his cowbells. I had to keep them loaded [with blanks] all the time."

If the show resembled the hit Broadway revue, *Hellzapoppin,* it was no accident. Jones was a big fan of vaudeville comics John "Ole" Olsen and Harold "Chic" Johnson and borrowed unhesitantly from their popular conglomeration of zany routines and sight gags. When Spike fired his pistol in the air, a flock of dead ducks rained down, followed by a lone duck on a parachute. Two decades earlier, when Johnson shot down a chicken, Olsen would quip, "It's a good thing cows don't fly!"—only to have a cow come crashing down.

But where *Hellzapoppin* was truly unpredictable (the show being different every night) and equally chaotic backstage, the *Revue* only appeared that way. "The thing that seemed so crazy on the stage was intensely worked out. It looked like bedlam but...it was organized bedlam," said manager Dick Webster.

An excerpt from the script for the show's opening number – as performed at the Riviera Hotel in Las Vegas—illustrates just how precise the planning was:

BAND PLAYS 2 BARS "SABRE DANCE" MELODY. DOWN-BEAT 3RD BAR, SPIKE SHOOTS PING PONG BALL OUT OF GUITAR WHICH HITS PETER JAMES ON CHEEK. FREDDY [MORGAN] MAKES NOISE WITH PNEUMATIC DRILL ON 2ND BEAT OF 3RD BAR. BILLY BARTY HITS FRYING PAN WITH SPOON ON DOWNBEAT OF 4TH BAR. ON 2ND BEAT OF 4TH BAR, PETER JAMES BREAKS EGG INTO FRYING PAN. RAY HEATH MAKES A TROMBONE GLISSANDO PULLING HIS PANTS UP ON 2ND BEAT OF 5TH BAR, AND 2ND BEAT OF 6TH BAR.

"Things got pretty wild sometimes, but it was very well rehearsed. Spike was a perfectionist; he was pretty intense about everything. He worked for his success," stressed Webster. "He wanted perfection and he usually got it—he was a glutton on rehearsals."

Dick Morgan reprises "The Glow Worm" with Ina Souez.

Even his wife was not spared in the bandleader's relentless drive for perfection. "He was very hard on me at times," Helen Grayco recalled. "If I were performing one night, and he didn't like the sound, or he didn't like the lighting, or he didn't particularly like my performance, that's when our relationship went from boss to singer, rather than husband and wife or boyfriend and girlfriend," she observed. "He was a tough taskmaster, there's no question about it."

Perfection aside, the show was just outrageous enough that when things didn't go as planned, the audience was unaware of the fact. At times one of the Slickers would purposely hand Spike the wrong prop. On one occasion he was supposed to aim a seltzer bottle at somebody; instead, they handed him a gun. It happened so fast, he pulled the trigger without thinking. It was a real gun, but fortunately it produced a flag instead of a bullet.

He was not always so lucky. "Spike shot himself in the hand once," remembered Earl Bennett. "He got powder burns. He went running off the stage during a show. Even though it was a blank, just that wadding could put your eye out. I'm sure it stung like hell."

Jones often felt the sting of backstage jokes. "We really fixed him one time," revealed Hersch Ratliff. "In 'Chloe,' when the girl sang '...night shades falling,' he was supposed to pick up this big washtub and dump it out on the floor. So the guys nailed the tub to the floor. When we came to that part in the song, Spike reached over to lift this thing up, and of course it was nailed down. He yanked, and he yanked, and he finally yanked it free but he tore the floorboard loose. It upset his drums, and the bass drum rolled down into the orchestra pit."

The bandleader himself was the perpetrator in one incident, which took place in Wheeling, West Virginia. As Helen Grayco recalled it, "The theatre was over a fish market... the silliest shaped theatre I had ever seen. It struck me so funny that I broke right in the middle of my number and began to laugh. The audience began to laugh too. This gave Spike an idea..."

According to band members, the resulting horseplay was due to a lover's quarrel. "Spike and Helen were having an argument. It was cold there and she had on a low-back dress," mused trombonist Robbie Robinson. "Spike had a bottle of seltzer water, and when she got through singing he let her have it with that ice cold water. The people thought it was part of the show."

The incident was "a real departure—they didn't talk for a couple of days," noted Joe Siracusa. "The standard gag in the band was that Helen would do something to make Spike unhappy; Spike would take it out on Ralph Wonders; Ralph would take it out on the band; we'd take it out on the band boy; and the band boy would go downstairs and kick the pig we used to carry with us. We used to joke about it—that was the protocol of the band. Who else would you pick on?"

Backstage disharmony aside, Jones rarely allowed himself the liberty of the seltzer stunt. While he wanted the feeling of utter chaos at all times, the *Revue* was planned well in advance, and timed to the split second. "It was a monotonous job because you were never allowed to do anything in the way of improvising in a tune," contended Joe Wolverton, who rejoined the band briefly in 1946. "I took a guitar along on one trip and I was doing a little improvising. The guys liked it, but Spike didn't; it didn't belong in there.

Everything we ever played was played exactly the same way every time."

The monotony sometimes inspired Jones' associates to alter the routine, especially after he reorganized the band and the *Revue* got going full steam. "I was always pulling gags," attested Siracusa. "When you do the same show every night for 105 nights, you have to improvise to get that feeling of spontaneity. A lot of gags we did just to keep the guys happy, keep 'em laughing. I felt if I could help the guys laugh and relax, it would make for a happier group."

"The tricks we'd play on those guys during the show..." mused clarinetist Jack Golly. "Dick Gardner was a real nervous little guy; Doodles and I used to try and think of everything we could do to harass the guy, because he was so funny and nervous. He played a fiddle solo. He'd get up and play the damn thing, then he'd come back, and he was so careful where he put this fiddle because it was very valuable to him.

"Doodles and I went out and got one in a hock shop—one night there was a blackout, and we put this old fiddle in Gardner's seat. When I say blackout, it was black; you couldn't see a thing," said Golly. "Right after the blackout, Gardner comes back from the microphone—he had a bit up there—and he sits down, and sits on this fiddle. And you could hear it go *crrruuunch*. And Gardner says, 'Oh, my God!' Spike came running out, 'What happened? What happened?' 'Gardner just sat on his fiddle.' And Gardner's holding this thing up; the whole band is dying laughing."

The band also had a hard time keeping its composure one night in Hutchinson, Kansas. "There were about 20 or 30 girls in the two front rows," said Doodles Weaver. "They had seen the show before, and they knew the lights went out during 'Hawaiian War Chant.' Just the fluorescent lights were on.

"By this time they'd made themselves very well known, laughing and everything. When the stage went dark for 'War Chant,' all the girls took these lights—they had these little lights that used to go off and on—and they put them in their bosoms. It was a funny gag, particularly for 1947; it was risqué then. It was a panic and Spike went into hysterics, as did the entire band."

Bill King took advantage of a prop cello and an onstage tub of water (which Doc Birdbath used to fill his tuba) to liven up many a dull evening. "The plug in the end of the cello bow that held the strings eventually came out; it would hold about half a thimbleful of water. I could put that cello bow down in the tub, and fill that little hole," recalled King.

"There would be some old stagehand sitting on the stage eight or ten feet away, watching the show, and I could splatter him good—I could pick somebody out and just nail 'em. I'd drive 'em crazy; they never did figure out where that damn water was coming from." The audience wasn't safe either: "You'd get a gal sitting close to the stage in a low cut gown and I could just drop 'em right in there."

While he enjoyed the occasional surprise engineered by one of his bandsmen, Jones preferred to know what was going to occur, and when. But the City Slickers liked to cultivate the idea that anything could happen, offstage as well as on. "We called the Spike Jones train 'a whorehouse on wheels,' " claimed Doc Birdbath. "There was nothing really going on, but it was the idea, with all the gals on board, and the men away from their wives."

Other members of the band gave some credence to the suggestion, however, that not all the action took place on stage. "We were all lonesome and horny," confided one City Slicker. "It was convenient. We were living together on the train. It was fertile ground; we were sleeping in the same cars."

"Most of the guys didn't cheat," asserted Bill King. "Most of them were happily married, and you really didn't have much time. When we were on one-nighters, you'd have to be at the train usually by midnight or one o'clock to go to the next town. Some of the guys did—there was a trampoline act with us, he could pick up women real quick; he used to bring 'em on the train once in a while."

"One of the young guys in the band considered himself quite a lover," reported Eve Whitney, a one-time showgirl then married to staff writer Eddie Maxwell. "Every town they hit, he always bragged about his conquests, and everybody started laying odds as to whether he was going to score or not. We arrived in Chicago, we're sitting around kibitizing and he says, 'Wow! Did you see that doll in the drugstore?' She was a very pretty young girl. He says, 'Fair game for me. Before we leave here...' They started making bets. It really ticked me off, 'cause he was supposedly a married man. Apparently the girl's mother had told her about musicians; she wasn't having any part of him. But he kept saying, 'I'm going to score, you watch.'

"The last day there, he comes down, he says, 'She's asked me to meet her when her shift is over at ten o'clock, in the drugstore. Put your money up, you guys; this is it.' That night about 9:30, I go down; sure enough, there's the guy sitting at the counter with this successful leer on his face," recalled Whitney. "I had my 15-month-old daughter Casey with me, so I

gather her up and walk into the drugstore. And before he can say anything, I throw my daughter in his arms and say, 'I'm sick and tired of being stuck with her. Supposing you look after her for a change!' And I walked out. And he started screaming, 'Wait a minute!' He never made it with the girl. He could never convince her. He was so mad, he wanted to kill me."

The things that happened on the road were not as wild as the stage show itself, once the drinkers were gone, and "the milkshake band" took their place. For one reason, the Slickers were pressed into a maternal role, with the addition of the 17-year-old Gardner Twins to the organization. "They kind of mothered us," mused Gloria Gardner. "We were absolutely wide-eyed and just scared to death. But they were the nicest bunch of people we ever knew. It becomes a family—we were the kids, and they knew it. They were very responsible and actually took care of us."

The attractive and energetic teenagers, whom Spike nicknamed The Mice because of their blonde hair and light complexions, were initially left alone by the men—until trombonist Joe Colvin joined the band. "When my sister Gladis met Joe, it was one of those things—they fell in love instantly," said Gloria. "Spike told Joe, 'Stay away from her, she's not even 18 years old.' Gladis was allowed to see Joe after she turned 18. It was love at first sight, and it stayed that way…"

The bandsmen *could* be just as crazy offstage as on, but they were usually restrained by a measure of common sense—Spike's, if not their own. "He told me in no uncertain terms, with this new family-type show, he wanted the kind of guys he could take any place without being ashamed of them," observed Siracusa. "It was very important to him, how we appeared in public. When your career is at stake, your values change.

"No drinking allowed: this was the image Spike wanted, and the type of men he wanted to be associated with," said Siracusa. "Doodles was the exception; he was kind of a kook." Even Weaver, the only member of the cast who regularly hit the bottle, often went on a health kick between binges. After a brief diet of strawberry soda and YMCA workouts, however, he would get smashed again.

One night in Chicago, Weaver went out on the town and got into trouble. "After one of the shows, I felt particularly good. I had some friends in town, they had a party, I drank a little too much and I stopped at one of those places," he recalled. "A couple of guys followed me…they jumped me and hit me with a blackjack and knocked me down. Which they do in Chicago—it's called mugging.

"I made a mistake; when I went down, I got up again. So I had a tussle with these guys. They took some money out of my wallet, and they took my watch. I can imagine what those two guys thought—they were professional hoodlums—I had to think they laughed about it, because it was a Mickey Mouse watch. They probably expected to see a $10,000 watch. It was $1.98 watch; their blackjack cost more than that."

Weaver might as well have sent out an engraved invitation. "He got loaded in a bar around the corner from the Studebaker Theatre, and he had a big yellow diamond—it was so flawed it couldn't have been a $1,000 stone, but he would brag about this big diamond. And the way he talked about the watch you could get convinced this was a very valuable watch he had on, this Mickey Mouse watch," said Earl Bennett.

"I don't know what the truth of it was, but Doodles was pretty good at dramatics," observed George Rock. But Bill King remembered, "Doodles got the hell beat out of him. He was in bad shape, but he went ahead and did his act and everything. 'Course when he put on some of those crazy wigs, he didn't look bad with a black-eye anyhow."

Bennett added: "He did the next show in Milwaukee with his head swathed in bandages, and a big derby to try to cover it. That was the only time Weaver got mugged; getting drunk happened too often."

The other big drinker in the organization, ironically, was Arena Stars' president, Ralph Wonders. One day he was trying to light a cigar and burned his nose, ending up in the hospital. On another occasion he went out boozing with a stagehand, and landed in jail; Spike had to bail them out the next morning before he could leave town. Jones—who fired a newly-hired saxophonist for missing a cue on his second night—had made it clear he would no longer tolerate such excess. But Wonders could be depended on to get the job done in spite of his drinking habits, and gradually tapered off.

"You didn't come on the stage drunk," stressed Gloria Gardner. "I remember the time Ding Bell [Eugene Walla] didn't show up. Dick Gardner rushed down and did his part. Ding came staggering in—the show had been on about 15 minutes—Spike picked up this whole rack of saxophones and stuff and just flung 'em straight at him, right across the stage. The audience thought it was part of the act. Scared the hell out of me," said Gloria.

"Spike was very reliable as far as being there when he was supposed to be, and he expected the same from his men," said Dick Webster. "It was a wild bunch of characters; even offstage they were pretty nutty. I think George

Rock and I were the only sane people. We picked each other to room to-gether; he and I thought everybody else was crazy."

Even the band's star trumpet player had his idiosyncrasies, however. Rock, a descendent of Daniel Boone, was a collector of antique firearms and an expert marksman; on long train rides, when it took all day to reach the next town on their itinerary, he would amuse himself by using telephone poles for target practice.

"One time George and Joe Colvin were riding in Joe's convertible, I think coming back to L.A. from San Francisco," stated Earl Bennett. "I don't know what precipitated it, but Joe said something to George which became a challenge, and Joe said, 'You wouldn't do that.' Rock said, 'Like hell I wouldn't.' And he shot the gun right out through the canvas top of Colvin's car. He couldn't resist something like that."

But nobody could challenge Weaver for his wacky inventiveness, on or offstage. "Doodles was the character of all time," attested Eddie Max-well. "It might have been against his religion to have suitcases; he would travel with shopping bags, the big ones with the loops." Added Joe Siracusa: "That was classy, because other times he would just take a pair of pants, tie the legs together, and stuff the clothes inside." The shenanigans con-tinued unabated through five seasons on the road.

Siracusa, who had a penchant for zany ideas himself, designed back-drops and created new instruments when he wasn't behind the drums. Dick Gardner, who served as the band's librarian and copyist, could play the clarinet while standing on his head—an ability that did not go unno-ticed by Spike.

But almost every member of the band was multi-talented. Earl Bennett, who had studied art with famed muralist Thomas Hart Benton, was a painter and sculptor whose abilities often came in handy, building props for the show. Freddy Morgan turned out to be a more than capable writer of songs and comedy sketches, to Jones' surprise. Pianist Paul Leu's abilities as an arranger were put to equally good use.

While Spike discovered hidden talent in many of his City Slickers, he knew precisely what he was getting when he added Edward F. Cline to the payroll. The veteran film director, who began his career with Mack Sennett, collaborated with Buster Keaton on a series of highly regarded silent shorts in the 1920s; he reached his zenith with W.C. Fields in the early '40s, with *The Bank Dick* and *Never Give a Sucker an Even Break.*

Cline was at the end of his film career when Jones hired him, circa 1949, as a combination gag man, gofer, sounding board—and scapegoat. "He would contribute, but he was a whipping post. Anything that would go wrong, Spike would take it out on him," observed Eddie Brandt.

"He would run and get sandwiches; he was a coffee boy. Spike probably got a lot of things from him when we weren't there, things we thought were Spike's—he'd throw it out at the meeting and we thought it was coming from him. Spike kept it hidden that Cline had done the Keaton and Fields films. But he was the greatest, and that's why Spike had him around," said Brandt.

"If Spike needed an answer, Eddie Cline would give it to him," echoed comedian Billy Barty, who toured with Jones for several years. "He was in on everything. Always in the background. The silent man who knew all. Always looking, always listening, but never speaking. Only through Spike."

Jones, who excelled in his ability to recognize talent in other people, demonstrated his own talents most effectively when few people had their eye on him. Onstage, he was the guy in the crazy suit who introduced the acts and manipulated the gadgets; offstage, he was a clear-headed promotional wizard whose keen attention to trends and demographics resulted in packed houses throughout North America.

He invested more time and energy on public relations than all other facets of his operation. Spike spent $10,000 a year on promotion and got every penny's worth; he also received thousands of dollars worth of free advertising by writing gag letters to newspaper columnists, who dutifully printed them. "After traveling 26,000 miles, visiting 125 cities and playing to more than 1,000,000 people in the last 11 months, we feel we deserve a rest," ran a typical letter. "So anyone wishing to see the revue during the next three months will have to go to the All American Van & Storage."

"He used to say, 'Think of something I can do I'll get sued for,' so he could get his name in the papers," revealed Bernie Jones. "He'd always like to have a lawsuit going, where he'd get his name around a lot."

A national syndicate could not have outdone the bandleader; it took four clipping services to Keep Up With Jones. He put his name before the public in every conceivable way—banners, placards, handbills, product tie-ins, radio spots, contests and giveaways announced his arrival weeks ahead of the tour. He even had his own supermarket, which he milked for all it was worth.

Dr. Horatio Q. Birdbath (left) breaks up Dick Morgan during a rendition of
the cackle chorus. (*Skip Craig*)

Spike had everything down to a science. If the auditorium seated
2,500 or more, they did one two-and-a-half-hour show; if it was a 2,000-
seat hall, they put on two two-hour shows. He was nothing if not meticulous. From the outset of the *Revue,* he paid strict attention to the details
which eluded others. The information necessary to grease the wheels and
keep the receipts rolling in at the box office was ever at his fingertips.

At Jones' bidding, Doc Birdbath kept an exploitation sheet at every
stop along the way, noting the name of the promoter and the manager; the
scaling of the house, the seating capacity, the rental price; the size and condition of the stage; lighting equipment, switchboards, voltage, microphones;
dressing rooms; transfer companies for baggage; weather condition and

population; local newspapers and radio stations; local RCA distributor and contact man.

Birdbath found himself getting off the train at 7 a.m. while everyone else was still asleep, calling on columnists and disk jockeys. He made countless promotional appearances, flanked by the shortest and tallest members of the band—Frankie Little, who stood 48 inches high and weighed in at 100 pounds, and Junior Martin, who measured 7 feet, 7 inches and wore size 18 shoes.

Little didn't mind clowning, but he wanted respect; he was no sideshow freak. He sold programs in the lobby with Martin, but sometimes drew the line at walking down the street with him—"I don't want to look conspicuous," observed Frankie. Junior, every inch the gentle giant, was more obliging; he didn't mind the constant jokes about his size. "We always try to get adjoining rooms for him," Spike would tell reporters. "Nobody ever has a bed to fit him so he usually doesn't get any sleep from the waist down."

Martin and especially Little were beloved by their co-workers, who accepted them as peers, if not at eye level. "It's so funny how you get used to people around you and you take them for granted," mused Eileen Gallagher, the 220-pound soprano who replaced Ina Souez. "Locks Martin and Frankie Little and I used to pal around together. One day, we were walking down the street, and people were coming toward us, and they all started talking and looking at us and pointing.

"I looked at Locks and Frankie and I said, "What the hell is the matter with those people?' Locks said, 'C'mere.' He took us, and we stood in this store window, and naturally, I could see the three of us together—no wonder they looked at us so strangely. To me, there was nothing unusual; they were my friends, and my people I was with every day," said Gallagher. "But I realized to other people who never saw us before, we were quite a surprise. I said, 'They probably think the circus is in town.'"

Armed with an endless supply of Spike Jones Bubble Gum made by Fleers, Birdbath, Little and Martin staged bubble gum-blowing contests at every major stop on the itinerary. No promotional stunt was too outrageous for Jones, so long as it caught the attention of the public. In Chicago, the band paraded down the street on behalf of the March of Dimes, bundled up in ragged raccoon coats; in San Francisco, they donned their union suits to march from the Curran Theatre to the Palace Hotel, where the American Federation of Musicians was holding their annual convention.

Such stunts were all in a day's work. As a result, disc jockeys throughout the country could be relied upon to plug the *Revue*, along with the latest records, for all they were worth. "One of the things that endeared us to them," observed Eddie Maxwell, "was that we'd come in with a prepared script for the interview, and always give the disc jockey the laugh lines, so he'd wind up getting laughs and being a comic."

Knowing full well Doodles Weaver could reduce an interview program to utter chaos within moments of arrival, Spike and the deejays made sure he had no shortage of opportunities. The nation's disc jockeys, whom Jones initially courted to give record sales a boost, ultimately proved to be some of the biggest fanatics among his fans. They often staged their own stunts without any prodding from Spike—or any warning to him.

Ray Starr and Erling Jorgensen welcomed him to Waterloo, Iowa, in their own fashion. They not only plugged the upcoming show by playing his records, they also ran their own spots with excerpts from the discs: "KAYX in Waterloo. *'Where are you, ya old bat?!'* The time is 2:15." When Spike arrived they met him at the depot, accompanied by a buck-toothed, cigar-smoking Chloe in high heels and a red fright wig.

The mayor of Auburn, Maine, showed his admiration for the City Slickers by naming them honorary dog catchers. Another fan was Beverly Osborne, who owned the Chicken in the Rough restaurant franchises. "He was a Spike Jones freak, a groupie," said Eddie Metcalfe. "He thought it was a great outfit. He used to meet us at the train station in Oklahoma City with fire engines and hook-and-ladders, and we'd ride to the hotel, or to the hall where we were going to play. Then he'd entertain us that night after the show."

Jones occasionally rewarded his friends and fans by inviting them to sit in with the band. During the Indianapolis 500 in 1946—in which he sponsored a race car built by his friend, Gordon Schroeder—Jones found himself in a playful mood one night, while playing the biggest theatre in town.

"He broke all house records for attendance at the Circle Theatre," recalled Schroeder. "I stopped by one night and went in the dressing room. Spike said, 'We go on in five minutes. Do you want to go on with us?' I said, 'Sure, why not?' He grabs a chair and puts it right in the middle of the stage. Red Ingle had an old beat-up stovepipe hat like Abraham Lincoln; he said, 'Here, put this on.' Spike brought me out a newspaper. I said, 'What do you want me to do?' He said, 'Just sit there and read the paper.' I sat there and read the paper during the whole show.

"Spike would do things like that," said Schroeder. "One night in San Francisco, some little guy who was in the Merchant Marines—a miniature man, not a midget—came to the stage door. He'd met Spike in Catalina; he was a sharp-looking little guy who'd worked in the Ice Capades. Helen Grayco was onstage. Spike said, 'You want to do something in this number, to get back in show business?' He said, 'Sure.' Spike had him go out—Grayco didn't know he was there—she was singing this real sexy song about 'My Man,' and this little guy came running across the stage and grabbed her around the knees, broke her up."

Honorary Slickers who occasionally traveled with the troupe included *Houston Press* columnist Paul Hochuli and *American Magazine* writer Tom Bernard, who treated their readers to accounts of life on the road. "In another week or so I should be able to struggle from my oxygen tent and out of my bandages, and renew, at least physically, my previous peaceful existence... My mental future, however, is in doubt," Bernard told his readers. "As my psychiatrist said, 'Any jerk who undertakes such an assignment without previous conditioning deserves nothing more than a prolonged incarceration in a booby hatch.'"

When Jones played Chicago's Civic Opera House in 1949, he put cartoonist Chester Gould in the lineup with an old beat-up trombone; Gould reciprocated by adding "Spike Dyke and his Musical Nuts" to the cast of his *Dick Tracy* comic strip, involving them in a murder mystery. Hank Ketchum and Al Capp paid Jones similar tributes a few years later, making reference to him in their respective *Dennis the Menace* and *Lil' Abner* strips.

Further vindication of the bandleader's popularity came in the form of box office receipts, the ultimate barometer. By the late 1940s, Arena Stars was grossing well over a million dollars a year—at a time when the best seat in the house could be had for $3, regardless of where they played. Spike got additional mileage from the system he set up by representing Roy Rogers, comedy duo Homer and Jethro, bandleader Spade Cooley, the Sons of the Pioneers and others who played the same circuit.

While the gigs almost always went according to plan, there were a few missteps along the way. When the band opened a four-week engagement at Slapsy Maxie's nightclub in Hollywood, in November 1948, *Variety* reported, "anything can be expected to happen—and undoubtedly will." Jones had been guaranteed $10,500 a week, but when the owners' check bounced at the end of the first week, the unexpected happened—the musicians' union ordered him to walk out on a capacity crowd.

Jones and his confederates gather in front of San Francisco's Curran Theater in their Sunday best. From left: Junior Martin, Dick Morgan, Roger Donley (partly hidden), George Rock, Evelyn Lunning, Paul Leu (partly hidden behind her), Eddie Metcalfe, Joe Siracusa (with drum), Spike, Jack Golly, Dick Gardner (partly hidden), Joe Colvin, Betty Phares, Earl Bennett, Frankie Little and Bill King (with bowling pins).

"Spike didn't get the money he wanted, and that was it," conceded Gloria Gardner. "We walked out in the *middle* of the show, on a Saturday night. My sister Gladis and I were ready to go out and open the second half. I said, 'We're walking out with the people sitting there?!' Spike said, 'Yeah, we're walking out of here.' So we did. We closed Slapsy Maxie's flatter than a pancake."

"That was a wild incident," said Joe Siracusa. "Ralph Wonders gave us the sign from the audience: 'Cut the show.' Spike was anticipating what was going to happen. As far as I can remember, we went back and finished the engagement, after the dispute was settled."

"There were a couple of hundred furious people when he failed to play his second show," club owners Charlie and Sy Devore told the press. But they didn't hold a grudge against Jones: "It is just the case of a very great artist…listening to a lot of bad advice."

The walkout sounded a discordant note rarely heard in the glory days of Spike's romance with the public. By contrast, the highlight of Jones' years on the road—and the finest hour for many of those who worked with him—took place March 6, 1948, at the Hotel Statler in Washington, D.C. At the request of President Harry S. Truman, Jones and company performed at the 25th annual dinner of the White House Correspondents' Association.

Virgin Islands Vertigo was pre-tested: Doodles Weaver pitched his baseball sketch and Freddy Morgan masqueraded as Stalin. Helen Grayco sang the usual torch song and Dick Gardner did his violin solo. George Rock donned his Little Lord Fauntleroy outfit to sing "Blowing Bubble Gum"; Dick Morgan and Doc Birdbath clucked the cackle chorus and did their "Sheik of Araby" levitation routine.

At intermission, the Slickers were joined by a surprise guest—the President's daughter, Margaret, who had kept her appearance a secret from Truman for months. "We didn't know who it was going to be," recalled Joe Siracusa. "Spike just told us, 'When the guest artist appears, no fooling around.' Earl Bennett concurred: "We were told, 'You sit still, you don't cross your legs, you don't look at each other; you just sit there like a church choir.'"

The Slickers were in for a bigger surprise than they knew. "We expected Margaret to be pretty lousy, from all the publicity," said Bennett. "She sang a 17th century shepherd's song, in a dissident and off-key manner, and we were all cringing and waiting for this agonizing performance to be over. And just toward the end—it was too well-timed to be that accidental—her accompanist reached for the music, and missed it. Then he made a mad grab at the music, and it all went flying all over that end of the stage, and he starts playing the wrong notes—and she wound up finishing her song on a terrible sour note.

"The White House correspondents gave her a standing ovation. I was offended by that because it was a bad performance, and she didn't rate a standing ovation. It didn't dawn on me, until many years later, that she'd out-funnied us—it was all planned, the guy missing the music, her singing the sour note. The correspondents were sharp enough to get it. I was so naïve," admitted Bennett, "to think we were the only ones who could put a musical joke on stage; I couldn't associate her pulling a prank, being the President's daughter."

Siracusa remembered the occasion as "a tense and exciting experience. There were literally guys behind the potted palms, like you see in the mov-

A rare moment off the road: Helen, Spike, Leslie and Spike Jr. in the bandleader's
Jaguar, in front of the family's Beverly Hills mansion. 1954.

ies," he mused. "Imagine the situation—we're using gunshots in the show,
and there's a President sitting out there. *They* loaded Spike's guns, of course.
We were all nervous. Spike had a special suit made—white with gold braid.
He almost couldn't put it on, he was so nervous."

"Spike was very uptight," asserted Bennett. "There were Secret Service brass assigned to watch practically everybody in the band for three or
four days before we did the show. Weaver spotted the agents, and we
made great sport of this by punching a hole in the newspaper and watching the Secret Service men in the lobby of the hotel."

The game was a disguised effort to alleviate tension. "No matter
how much you try and rationalize it, we were tense," said Siracusa. "We
were playing for the President! How do you top an experience like that?
Where do you go from there, after being chosen the outstanding American talent of the year?"

Though Spike never topped the event in the course of his career, he
had occasion to be equally ecstatic—and equally nervous—at his wedding that summer. Spike and Helen were married in a brief service at the
Beverly Hills Hotel on July 18, 1948, seven months after their engagement—and nine months after his divorce from Pat became final.

Helen, who came from a big Italian family, had been on the road

with the band long enough to know what kind of ceremony to expect—
"a quick, quiet trip to the nearest Justice of the Peace." But Spike decided
she deserved nothing less than a real wedding with white orchids and
champagne. He even took time out for a honeymoon in Honolulu.

Before long, Spike and Helen moved into a big Colonial-style home
in Beverly Hills, a quarter of a mile below the Sunset Strip. They immediately added on an office and a lanai. Ten months and a day after their
wedding, the first addition to their long-planned family arrived; Spike Jr.
(originally nicknamed "Tack") was followed two years later by Leslie Ann.

On or off stage, Jones relished a good joke. The unsuspecting visitor
to 708 North Oakhurst Drive—which his associates dubbed Mt. Vernon—
was in for an ample dose of his humor. For openers, the welcome mat
read STOKOWSKI. On the walls of his den hung laughable examples of fine
art, painted by Earl Bennett—"Whistler's Mother" clutching a racing form,
a cross-eyed "Mona Lisa" and "Blue Boy" in tennis shoes, with Spike's
face. The latter was signed Sir Fredric *Gasborough*.

At home, as on the road, Jones promoted the image of himself as a
zany with zest and abandon. Although he did not remove the fish from
his aquarium and substitute a shark for the benefit of a TV crew—as once
reported in the newspaper—a rubber octopus did surface in the family
swimming pool.

On one occasion Jones got a traffic ticket for driving around with a
plastic mask on, which made it appear his head was on backwards. A
variation was the "headless driver" stunt he staged to help the police department call attention to reckless driving. "He could make a joke out of
anything," affirmed his friend, Gordon Schroeder.

Spike lived in the office and the den of his $65,000 mansion when
he was home—sleeping days, working nights—but he was often out of
town. As long as he could fill an auditorium, he was not about to quit the
road. He couldn't disappoint his public, nor turn his back on the money;
by 1950 he was earning, and sometimes spending, an annual income well
in excess of $200,000.

But the lifestyle he had grown accustomed to did not come cheap.
His allegiance to his public dictated a punishing schedule, keeping him
on the move as much as 10 months of the year. Helen eventually tired of
traveling with the band and began staying home with the family, but
Spike continued making the tours. He seldom saw his children while
they were growing up.

The demands of being on tour resulted in "a lot of marital disasters," acknowledged Earl Bennett. Although the Slickers brought their wives and children up to Las Vegas or Lake Tahoe to be with them at the beginning of a season, anything resembling a normal family life was out of the question.

"The road wasn't for everybody," conceded George Rock, whose marriage to dancer Betty Jo Huston was one of many casualties. "We always had quite a bit of time at home, but it didn't really justify the other times when we were gone. I did love my family; it was a drag to be away from them. I didn't think about it so much at the time, because I was able to give them everything they wanted. Later, in retrospect, you try to balance it and see if it was worth it."

The sacrifices were great, but Jones and his fellow troupers did not go unrewarded. "We had a lot of fun, we made a lot of money, we went to the best restaurants," recalled Doodles Weaver. "The people treated us like kings. They'd meet us at the train and take us around in their cars; they'd have a big dinner for us after the show. They'd be looking forward for two or three months each time to our visit. They couldn't do enough for us."

"Hundreds of people would come up after the show," reported Doc Birdbath. "They'd say, 'This two hours of fun has released me and made me a new person. The laughter and the fun and the happiness we got with what you did, will last us the rest of our lives. Thank you for being here.' And that's all Spike wanted to hear—that it made people happy."

Hot Wax
Victor Records & Standard Transcriptions, 1941–1955

The record industry did not provide Spike Jones with the most elaborate showcase for his fertile imagination, but it launched him on his spectacular career and promoted his endeavors in all other media. Records were his best advertisement, the least ephemeral form of popular culture on which the maestro left his distinct and indelible mark.

Jones made the rounds of record companies for several months before RCA Victor Corporation offered him a contract in 1941. Asked for details in later years, he claimed Decca, Columbia and Victor had drawn straws for the privilege of signing the band—and Victor drew the shortest.

As usual, the bandleader was only too happy to camouflage the truth with a joke. What he never made public was the fact that he had pulled off a bit of a coup. "Spike talked [Artists & Repertoire representative] Harry Meyerson into doing a date," revealed one of Meyerson's successors, Walter Heebner, who supervised many of Jones' RCA sessions later in the decade.

"In those days, the record business was just coming out of a big slump. Most of the activity was controlled by New York. The brass didn't want Meyerson going ahead, doing dates on his own; Harry was not supposed to do a date of his own volition and set up a budget and so forth. So he just went ahead and did it, and I'm glad he did," said Heebner, noting that Meyerson would have had to get the approval of Leonard Joy, "chief boss in New York," before he could sign Jones.

"I was in the sales department in Camden, New Jersey, at the time we got the test pressings of the first date Spike did. And I fell off my chair, I thought they were funny as hell. We all cracked up," recalled Heebner. "Leonard was told by us guys in Camden to go ahead and pursue this Spike Jones."

The firm that courted the untamed music maker, one of the oldest and most successful companies in the industry, had almost dropped out of the disc business a decade earlier. Instead, Victor's record operation survived the Depression by introducing a group of lower-priced labels, the most successful of which—Bluebird—was assigned to the fledgling novelty band.

The makeshift ensemble soon to become known as the City Slickers chose an odd batch of tunes to wax for their initial three-hour session: "Red Wing"—the 1907 tune about a lovesick Indian maiden—"Barstool Cowboy from Old Barstow," Fleming Allan's "Behind Those Swinging Doors" and "The Covered Wagon Rolled Right Along."

While the music they made was hardly sophisticated, Jones' crew was anything but motley. The bandsmen whose presence earned them $40 apiece on that historic August day in 1941—Del Porter (clarinet, ocarina, vocals), King Jackson (trombone), Bruce Hudson (trumpet, slide whistle), Stan Wrightsman (piano), Hank Stern (tuba) and Perry Botkin (banjo)—were among the best in Hollywood.

The earliest recordings by the band featured a pastiche of musical styles—washboard band, honky-tonk, ragtime, traditional jazz. "Swinging Doors"—the top side of the first release—was a typical saloon song done in the old music hall style, featuring Wrightsman at the keyboard. "Covered Wagon," dominated by Hudson and Botkin, had more of a Dixieland favor.

Though Jones was to revolutionize the field of comedy music the following year, it would appear Victor had little notion of what the Slickers were about. The first record was issued without fanfare, the A side described as a "Waltz" in their monthly bulletin and the flip side, "Red Wing," as a "Bright Two-Step."

However, according to Dr. Demento, "Only Spike Jones ever had anything designated as a 'Bright Two-Step.' For that matter, only Spike had anything designated as a 'Bright' anything. Couple this with the fact that the two-step was an extremely archaic form of dancing by 1941, and you see that Victor/Bluebird was clearly injecting a touch of humor into Spike's labeling."

The all-but-forgotten discs recorded for Standard Radio Transcription Services, Inc.—beginning late in 1941—were substantially different from the sides the Slickers did for Victor in the same period. Although they occasionally chose the same tunes, the majority of the transcriptions were much less overtly comic in instrumentation and arrangement.

The Standards, recorded on lacquer-coated aluminum or glass and pressed on 16" vinyl discs which turned at 33 rpm, were leased to radio stations to air at their convenience. The sessions were more frequent, and more productive, than the Victor dates; ten numbers were done in a Standard session, as opposed to the average four for RCA.

The transcriptions, many of which were cut at NBC, required a no-nonsense recording atmosphere. Each side contained four or five tunes; once they began recording a side, the artists had to get everything right on the first take, or start the side over again. While their performances were by necessity more inhibited than those for RCA, the band was allowed a greater latitude in their choice of material—which ranged from "You're a Sap, Mister Jap" and the patriotic "Yankee Doodler," to "Horsie, Keep Your Tail Up" and "Never Hit Your Grandma With a Shovel."

"Your Morning Feature," a then-risqué soap opera parody (also known as "Virgin Mary Sturgeon"), was sent to disc jockeys by Spike as a *Standirt* Production. The culprits behind the disc—intended strictly for the deejays' own amusement —were identified only as The Country Dodgers.

The earliest Standards featured vocalist Cindy Walker singing many of her own compositions, including "Barstool Cowboy," backed by the Slickers. King Jackson got the opportunity to use his pleasant down-home Texas drawl ("Dodging a Gal from Dodge City"), rarely heard on 78s; he and Porter displayed their versatility by providing the arrangements for both the transcriptions and the commercial records.

The second Victor session, held in January 1942, yielded nothing especially crazy. "Pack Up Your Troubles" featured a delightful ocarina solo by Porter; "Clink Clink, Another Drink," another barroom ballad, spotlighted Botkin on the banjo. "Beautiful Eggs," a song about a farmer's daughter sung by Del, threatened to break the pattern with its sly wordplay:

> Oh, beautiful eggs.
> She has such beautiful eggs.
> They're gorgeous; they take the prize.
> Everyone buys. Even henpecked husbands
> say they're just the right size.

The Alfred Bryan-Herman Paley song—relatively innocent by today's standards—was well-received in public performance, but too risqué for Victor's sales department. "I thought they were being very stodgy, but I did not prevail," said Walt Heebner. It was the first of many to be with-held from release—an unfortunate and undeserved fate for one of the band's better Bluebird recordings.

"Siam," which the group waxed that April, featured Carl Grayson's melodious voice (and his throat glug) for the first time, but made only mild use of the effect. "Little Bo Peep Has Lost Her Jeep" was far more clever instrumentally than any of their preceding tunes. Featured were clanking cowbells, bristling sand blocks, a full complement of honks, fonks and beeps and a crashing automobile.

While the Slickers were hired for their musicianship, between them they could do just about anything in terms of vocal effects—snorts, hic-cups, gurgles, glugs, croaks, screeches, et cetera.

Spike seldom went outside his own organization for human or instru-mental effects. He did bring in an extra trombonist for the first Victor ses-sion—not to augment King Jackson, whose trombone fonks were incompa-rable, but to belch on "Swinging Doors." Jimmy Thomasson (an occasional sub for Jackson) wasn't in the same class as a musician, but he could belch a perfect E flat; this trick earned him $30 for three belches, at $10 apiece.

Rarely would Jones seek out a Hollywood talent. Mel Blanc, then toiling anonymously at Warner Bros. as the voice of Bugs Bunny, was hired to slur and hiccup his way through the chorus of "Clink Clink"—but he was an old friend of Porter's, and an exception to the rule.

Despite the fact that movie character actor Billy Gilbert had elevated the sneeze to an art form, Spike never called on his abilities; Frank Leithner took care of Jones' every need in that department. "Boy, could he sneeze—any time he wanted," marveled Don Anderson. "We were doing this show at the Pasadena Civic Auditorium one time. Frank got up and did this big sneeze and hung a goober right on the microphone."

By mid-1942, the City Slicker style was beginning to mature, due in part to the shifting of personnel. The reorganized Slickers—Jones, Por-ter, Jackson, Grayson (violin), Don Anderson (trumpet), Frank Leithner (piano), Country Washburne (tuba) and Luther Roundtree (banjo) pro-duced a somewhat zanier and more full-bodied sound than the original group.

Other influences began to modify the band's sound, too. Chief among them was the raucous tempo of klezmer music, which had flourished in the cabarets of Eastern Europe and migrated to America on the horns of itinerant musicians—and soon manifested itself in everything from Betty

An advertisement from *The Billboard Music Year Book*, 1943. (*Steve LaVere*)

Boop soundtracks to George Gershwin compositions.

The corn still took precedence at this stage. "Hotcha Cornia (Black Eyes)," recorded in July 1942, came as close to defining the style as anything ever harvested on wax. Jones—manipulating pistol, Klaxon horns, sand blocks, and xylophone with remarkable dexterity—laid waste to the classic Russian folk tune "Ortchi-Tchornia (Dark Eyes)" with irreverent zest.

"Der Fuehrer's Face," which was to finally alter the Slickers' mediocre track record in the sales department, was recorded during the same session. The first take was identical to the Standard transcription—although not quite as stiff in performance—which saluted Hitler with only a mildly sarcastic fonk. It was the second take that made history.

A few months earlier there had been "little reaction" to the raspberry on Teddy Powell's rendition of "Serenade to a Maid"—which sounded more like an expulsion of gas than the toy razzer used by Jones. But the Slickers' target was greater. "Spike told us he had it on good authority that Hitler heard the record—it was such a big hit, he must've heard it—and it made him furious," said Luther Roundtree. "That tickled all of us." More than a decade later Jones was still boasting, "I was number seven on Hitler's list."

While Germany's *Führer* menaced the globe at large, the czar of the musicians' union intimidated the entertainment world. James Petrillo's master plan—to annihilate the record industry—was as moronic as Hitler's, in its own small-minded way. Their machinations had been foreshadowed equally far in advance.

The pugnacious, roughhewn ex-trumpet player who headed the American Federation of Musicians had declared vehement opposition to recordings throughout the '30s. Years before his mid-1942 decree, Petrillo had imposed a similar ban on members of the Chicago union, in an attempt to end the threat to their livelihood—as he perceived it—brought about by canned music.

Petrillo averred that musicians were impairing their own employment opportunities by making records. His real target, however, was the radio industry, which denounced and reviled him for his actions. The controversial decree, which was strongly opposed by the networks, kept the Slickers from capitalizing on their unexpected hit; fortunately, it did not interfere with radio work, live performances and V-Discs. The action did, however, cost AFM members an estimated $7 million in lost wages.

Spike's ascension in the music world, meanwhile, was marked not only by a gold record, but the acquisition of a title he would become identified with for years to come. *Down Beat's* annual "King of Corn" award was a derogatory honor when Jones first set out to take the crown away from Guy Lombardo—but if Benny Goodman could be King of Swing, he figured he could be King of Corn. Beginning in 1943 he reigned 10 years as the undisputed champ, until the title was retired; the label became a liability, however, long before it was dropped.

In mid-1944—by which time he was promoting himself as "the dandruff in long hair music"—Jones announced plans for an Album of Musical Depreciation containing "songs you'd like to forget," to be recorded when the war was over. The shortage of raw materials was given as the reason for the delay. "Priorities have me licked," he explained to the press. "I can't get enough washboards, auto radiators, cowbells, and other such instruments to do the big, unsymphonic numbers I want in the album."

"Cocktails for Two" was but one of 20 numbers recorded for Standard Radio Transcription Services in July 1944, shortly before the band's USO tour. Many of the tunes were highly amusing—including such long-forgotten selections as "Down by the O-Hi-O," "Paddlin' Madelin Home" and "He Broke My Heart in Three Places"—but they were instrumentally tame by comparison with Country Washburne's wild interpretation of the decade-old hit.

The song—reportedly waxed at the suggestion of Lena Horne—started out as "soft and sweet" as anything Jones ever backed Bing Crosby on, with a choir of angelic voices setting the tone. "The first 30 seconds, you'd think you were listening to Fred Waring and his Pennsylvanians," reflected Eddie Brandt. "And all of a sudden, all hell breaks loose. The overly sentimental and overly conservative style of people like Waring was blown all over creation."

The romantic mood was quickly mutilated beyond repair: the stillness of a secluded rendezvous shattered by police whistles and gunshots; a quiet avenue congested with traffic; a refreshing cigarette choking the lungs; a tangy cocktail producing an incurable case of hiccups. Written by Sam Coslow and Arthur Johnston in 1934 to celebrate the repeal of prohibition, the song appropriately helped the City Slickers celebrate the end of the record ban.

Due in part to a huge backlog of recordings and an acute shortage of raw materials, the recording industry took their time in settling the dispute—which the U.S. Senate, the Department of Justice and even Presi-

Double your pleasure, double your fun: Eileen (left) and Elsa Nilsson crown Spike
"King of Corn" on behalf of *Down Beat,* 1944.

dent Franklin D. Roosevelt had failed to resolve. While Decca capitu-
lated to AFM's demands for fees toward an unemployment fund in 1943,
Columbia and Victor procrastinated another year, until they could no
longer afford their convictions—as Jascha Heifetz reminded them when
he ended his long contract with RCA and signed with Decca.

The resolution was a happy one for Jones and Victor. So popular was
the commercial version of "Cocktails for Two," recorded late in 1944, RCA
manufactured 150,000 special pressings for jukebox use with the tune on
both sides—when one side wore out, the other could be played. The record
reached No. 4 on *Billboard's* Hit Parade and stayed on the charts for eight
weeks.

Although the bandsmen had no idea the record would become the hit it did, "they knew it was good," affirmed bassist Herschell Ratliff. "It was a good number to start with. We wanted to keep it in pretty good taste; we didn't want to destroy the original idea that this was a fine piece of music. I think the comedy enriched it instead of tearing it down."

Sam Coslow could not have agreed less. "I hated it, and thought it was in the worst possible taste, desecrating what I felt was one of my most beautiful songs," reflected the composer in his autobiography. "The blow was somewhat softened over the next few years when I received royalties for the sale of two million records of Spike's version...[but] I think I still would have preferred Spike not to have made that record."

Jones' interpretation of "Holiday for Strings," which had its debut on *The Bob Burns Show* that spring and was recorded the same day as "Cocktails," garnered an entirely different reaction from its creator. But the bandleader had some anxious moments when he was unable to contact David Rose prior to the first broadcast.

As Spike recalled: "I debated with my business manager, with the members of my band and with friends. What should I do—play it without Dave's consent or hold it up? Well, the show was all rehearsed, timed and set, so there seemed to be nothing to do but go ahead. So, we played our version and I went home after the show feeling like a dirty dog." He needn't have worried. Rose called as Spike was climbing into bed, to report he'd heard the number on his car radio; he was ecstatic about it.

With the ban rescinded, the Slickers got the chance to finally record many of the standards in their repertoire. Their mutilations of "Chloe" and "That Old Black Magic"—by then old favorites from the band's radio broadcasts and personal appearances—fared better than others. Neither was as funny on disc as in live performance, but that didn't dampen sales; Red Ingle's rendition of "Chloe" spent four weeks in the Top Ten, resulting in the band's third gold record.

Their continued success was the result of careful planning. "They used to have these idea conferences at Spike's," recalled Don Ingle. "They put down a couple of jugs of sour mash whiskey, ice cubes and glasses and sketch pads. Everybody sat and kicked around ideas, Country Washburne and my dad and Spike and Del Porter and maybe Carl Hoefle. Spike would contribute ideas, but he would encourage them to brainstorm it. And of course the bourbon—by the time they'd had a few slugs, the ideas began to flow and get a little wilder, and they'd start laughing and kick things around.

"A lot of the sight gags and the sound gags were Dad's. I would probably be accused of being prejudiced, but he was a very prolific sound effects department," said Ingle. "They would dissect it by word, by line, where a pistol shot should come in for effect, a piece of broken glass. They would have one of these meetings, they'd go for four hours. At the end of that time, they might have one or two tunes sort of outlined as to possible effects on them. Country would then build the arrangement."

The rhapsodic "You Always Hurt the One You Love"—a Doris Fisher-Allan Roberts composition which earned a gold record for the Mills Brothers—sounded like an audio interpretation of a Rube Goldberg cartoon after Spike and his gang attacked it during one such session. In an uproarious burlesque of the Ink Spots, Carl Grayson mimicked the group's lead tenor, Bill Kenny, and then turned things over to Red Ingle—who mocked the Spots' bass singer, Orville "Hoppy" Jones, with an ad-lib interlude.

In the fall of 1945, Spike began work on a Christmas present for his daughter, Linda. Tchaikovsky's "Nutcracker Suite" was not only his most ambitious project to date, but a complete departure from everything that preceded it. What better gift for a six-year-old than a classic storybook tale—chock-full of sugar plum fairies, lemon drop moons and dancing lollipops—as told by her favorite bandleader?

The City Slickers—George Rock on trumpet; Ingle on clarinet, sax and violin; Zep Meissner on clarinet and sax; Dick Morgan on guitar; Grayson on violin; Washburne on bass; Chick Daugherty on trombone; Herm Crone on piano; Ormond Downes on drums —were given an unprecedented opportunity to demonstrate their skill. With dazzling versatility, they imitated everything from a full-scale symphony orchestra to a rowdy dixieland band.

Augmented for the occasion by Jack Marsh (bassoon), Phillip Shuken and Luella Howard (flute) and Mary Jane Barton (harp)—with special lyrics by Washburne and Foster Carling—Spike and his bandsmen brought the composer's fantasy world to life with a technical virtuosity few had thought possible.

They also made it funny. The by-now-familiar sound effects—sneezes, cowbells, howls, fonks, creaking doors and Chinese gongs—were carefully worked into the orchestrations, however; not even the gunshots were intrusive. While the resulting album was nothing short of a masterpiece, his daughter was unimpressed.

All in a day's work: Spike signs autographs for his loyal fans. (*Ted Hering*)

"I was told my dad really did 'Nutcracker' for me, and he was very disappointed I didn't care about it. I think he overestimated my taste level at six; I was never into fantasy," stated Linda Jones. "I guess my dad thought I would love it, and I didn't. I realize the beauty of it now; I think it's magnificent."

"Hawaiian War Chant" was arguably the most memorable tune of Jones' 1946 output. The bandleader's savage parody of the song, made popular by Tommy Dorsey, was highlighted by Carl Grayson's deep-throat glugs—one of the principal elements in the success of "Cocktails"—and Dick Morgan's steel guitar.

George Rock recalled the number for other reasons. "The recording sessions were pretty cut and dried. The only one I remember that was different," said Rock, "was when we had a party at Spike's house, and we were to go down to RCA and record after the party. 'War Chant' was one of the numbers we were supposed to do. Everybody was...not everybody, but there were enough of us stoned that we couldn't get it recorded; we had to come back the next morning and do it. We had to just call off the session."

"War Chant" was the last recording Grayson made before his dismissal from the band. While Jones was hard put to replace his overall talent, he was not short of supply when it came to glugs. Mickey Katz was an expert glugger—faster than Grayson, and just as funny—as he proved on his nutty rendition of "Jones Polka" that year. Doc Birdbath and Joe Siracusa were more than capable, and Spike was no slouch himself in that department. "But nobody could do a 'wet' glug like Grayson," asserted Eddie Brandt.

Throughout the course of his career, Jones was ever restless and dissatisfied. "He could never lose the image of the City Slickers," said Brandt. "He had a good knowledge of all music, including the classics—he knew all that type of stuff. But he could never change his image, no matter what he did."

When Jones put together a black-tie orchestra in 1946, for a seven-week engagement at the Trocadero—a popular night spot on Hollywood's Sunset Strip—he told the press, "I am fed, gorged, stuffed and bloated with being called the King of Corn. It takes crack musicianship to be a City Slicker," he insisted. "Maybe my new band will change the minds of a lot of morons who vote for us in *Down Beat*'s poll year after year."

Spike could produce a big band sound as clean and crisp as anyone else and he turned out some shining examples of it on Standard transcriptions during that time, such as "When Yuba Plays the Rumba on the Tuba." But his so-called Other Orchestra, which shared the bill with the City Slickers, was a dismal flop. "No funny stuff, just beautiful music," Katz recalled of the Trocadero stint. "And do you know what the crowds who came in said? 'What kind of crap is this? If we want a symphony, we'll go to Hollywood Bowl.' "

Howard Hughes, an unabashed fan of the City Slickers, was a regular at the Trocadero during Jones' engagement—tennis shoes and all. However, the eccentric industrialist stayed only for the Slickers' portion of the program, avoiding the Other Orchestra like a harmonic plague.

Thirty of the finest musicians in Los Angeles—including seven violinists, two viola players and a cellist—could not convince the public Spike was on the level. The experiment cost Jones $30,000. "I guess he was trying to get rid of some money instead of giving it to the government," ventured trombonist Eddie Kusby, who was featured on "Lassus' Trombone."

Rimsky-Korsakoff's "Flight of the Bumblebee" took a turbulent ride through Slicker territory, shortly after the Trocadero engagement. It was reborn as "The Jones Laughing Record," with Frank Leithner impersonating a Sneezaphone and trombonist Tommy Pederson mimicking a bumblebee—interspersed with boisterous laughter.

"Spike had all these poor guys up there laughing—all these laughers I'd seen in the movies. After about the third take, their voices were all gone. And my tongue was about shot anyway," recalled Pederson, who arrived at the session with a hangover. The number (a take-off on the popular "Okeh Laughing Record" of 1922) was decidedly offbeat, but more along the lines of what the public expected from Jones that year, instead of "beautiful music."

Jones' version of the evergreen "Laura" was not at all what composer David Raksin expected. "It was too tame," lamented Raksin. "When Spike asked how I liked it, I said, 'I was hoping you'd *do* something to it.' It was fun, but it should've been a lot more vulgar. He had the ability to take something and really tear it up."

Apart from "Love in Bloom" and "By the Beautiful Sea"—which most of Spike's fans missed—there was little of the typical City Slicker sound etched on record in 1947. Doc Birdbath joined forces with the Saliva Sisters and the Barefooted Pennsylvanians (or so the label stated) to mutilate the former, a tune popularized by Bing Crosby. The latter might have—and should have—been an equally big hit, with its jazzy overture, comic interludes and quaint lyrics by Harold Atteridge:

> When each wave comes a rollin' in
> We will sink or swim
> And we'll float and fool around the water.
> Over and under and then up for air
> Pa is rich, ma is rich, so now what do we care?

When people started complaining that a line in the World War I era song sounded like "And we'll float and *feel* around the water"—or something even more salacious—the record was quickly pulled from circulation. The offending line was inaudible to many of Jones' fans who heard the commercial release. But there were apparently two versions: "I could never hear it," said disc jockey Jim Hawthorne, "but you could sure hear it on the acetate Spike brought me. He said, 'Don't ever play this on the air.' It was very clear, no question about it; you could hear it as loud as anything. I said, 'I can't leave this at the station.' "

Jones' records were a staple of Hawthorne's zany show on KXLA,

Jones (atop Frankie Little) makes American Federation of Musicians president
James Petrillo an honorary City Slicker. Among band members attired in their "union"
suits are Joe Colvin, Eddie Metcalfe, Bill King, George Rock and
Earl Bennett. San Francisco, 1949. (*Ted Hering*)

Los Angeles. "I'd play his stuff constantly. He'd rush the acetates over to
me," said the influential deejay, who went solely by his surname. "They
[artists and song pluggers] knew they'd get a play from me if they brought
me something nobody else had. They'd give it to me first, knowing if I
played it, the next day it would be on the stands; the stores wouldn't dare
not put it out."

Even Dinah Shore sounded like Spike Jones when Hawthorne got
done with her: "I'd play my records backwards. I would play 'em the
wrong speed; I would put in my own sound effects. But I wouldn't play
'em straight."

Jones and company wouldn't—or couldn't—play it straight either, but recorded little of the familiar in 1947. One of the most enduring numbers to emerge from the many he cut that year was Doodles Weaver's horse race routine, which Spike combined with Rossini's "William Tell Overture" at the suggestion of A&R man Walt Heebner.

"The Man on the Flying Trapeze" immortalized more of Weaver's stream-of-consciousness nonsense on disc, while "None But the Lonely Heart" featured Spike and Helen—newly engaged—mocking soap opera. "Ill Barkio," a duet between a soprano (Ina Souez) and a barking dog (Doc Birdbath), was held back for over three years. Two of the more amusing numbers would not see the light of day for almost 50 years: Mickey Katz's "I Wuv a Wabbit," sung by Arthur Q. Bryan (the voice of Elmer Fudd), and "My Cornet," which showcased George Rock's versatility on the instrument.

Record buyers missed out on far more when James C. Petrillo— whom historian Sigmund Spaeth called "music's greatest enemy"—again declared war on the record industry at year's end. After the resolution of the 1942-44 ban, he had avowed, "If…the companies fail to change [their past course], the AFM will not hesitate to break off relations and leave them to die by their own nefarious schemes."

This time the all-powerful union president targeted juke joints and disc jockey shows which depended on recorded music, citing the unemployment that resulted from their extensive use of records. Petrillo's declaration that there would never be any recording of any kind again wasn't taken too seriously, due to similar statements in the past, but record companies once more built up huge backlogs of material.

Between October and December of 1947 Jones hurriedly recorded thirteen numbers, plus another children's album—"basically everything we could get our hands on," said George Rock—in anticipation of the forthcoming ban.

"Petrillo's intentions were good. I just don't think he took the right approach," mused Joe Siracusa. "We were all working, making a living; we had no gripes about it. But it made us work our butts off, trying to get all those records made."

Most of the eleventh-hour recordings were cut in Chicago because the group was on tour in the Midwest. Two of the maestro's all-time best, and one of his worst, resulted from the industry-wide beat-the-ban strategy.

Jones cheerfully added insult to injury when he found another hit from the prolific pen of Sam Coslow and Arthur Johnston as ripe for parody as "Cocktails for Two." At the suggestion of Eddie Brandt, Spike gave "My Old Flame" a musical hotfoot. First, he had Paul Judson sing the romantic ballad as written, followed by a five-alarm instrumental with sirens blazing; then Paul Frees, the young impressionist who had mimicked various movie stars on "Pop Corn Sack" earlier that year, was brought in to sing the reprise.

"Originally Spike just wanted me to do it as Peter Lorre," revealed Frees. "All he was going to have me do were the straight lyrics, as Lorre. He didn't tell me how to do it—it just was a matter of coordinating me with the music. During rehearsal I started ad-libbing. He liked what I did, so we used a lot of it. I also ad-libbed a few additional lines during the session."

> My old flame, my…my new lovers all seem so tame —
> *They…they won't even let me strangle them…*
> I…I've met so many who have fascinating ways
> a fascinating gaze in their eyes—
> that eye that kept winking and blinking at other men,
> it was…I was…
> Some who took me up to the skies.

"I'm in and out in half an hour when I do a recording," observed Frees, who did many with Jones over the years. "But I would work several hours with Spike, or maybe half a day. He was very picky. He knew exactly what he wanted and how he wanted it—and he worked until he got it. He was very much the perfectionist."

Don Gardner's "All I Want for Christmas (My Two Front Teeth)" very nearly did not get recorded. The song destined to become a holiday perennial—written for an elementary school Christmas pageant on Long Island, New York—had been rejected all over town by the time it made its way to Jones. By then it was almost December—too late to get it out in time for Christmas. But with the threat of the record ban for an indefinite period, he recorded it nonetheless.

According to George Rock, the selection was more of an impulse than anything else. "Somebody saw it laying on the piano. They said, 'This would make a good tune for you. Let's give it a shot,' " recalled Rock, who won wide renown as the gleeful child who whistled through

Spike and Helen discuss the "Charleston" album with an RCA sales rep.
(*Spike Jones International Fan Club*)

the gap in his teeth. "We just picked it up and recorded it. The first take was the way I did it onstage…with a *phbbt!* for the 's.' It would not record correctly. I tried then the whistling, which recorded well whereas the raspberry would not work."

However, Eddie Brandt remembered, "The tune was brought to me. I didn't pay any attention; I just gave it to Spike. Then Freddy Morgan and I had to rewrite the tune [uncredited] because there was nothing to it. Freddy and I wrote a big long verse, we wrote another bridge, we wrote an ending and everything."

When the record was finally issued, a year later, the extra effort paid off; within six weeks, it reportedly sold 1.3 million copies. "In the beginning, it wasn't a song anybody could do," said Brandt. "It was perfect for Spike because he had George. After the song was a hit, everybody did it." The record-buying public deluged Rock with some rather unusual fan mail—thousands of teeth, a pair at a time, in response to his plea.

Brandt and Morgan collected handsome royalty checks for co-writing the seldom-played song on the flip side, "Happy New Year." Observed Brandt: "Spike gave us the tune on the back for working on 'My Two Front Teeth'—we couldn't get any royalties on that because the guy [Don Gardner] already had it published. Freddy and I made over $7,000 the first year."

Jones' attempts to fairly compensate the writers for their efforts, however, caused discontent within the band. Mused Bill King: "There was great animosity between George and Freddy. George was really pissed off at Freddy making so much money on that thing, a song nobody ever heard; George was the voice on 'Two Front Teeth' and all he got was the recording fee, $150 or whatever. Finally the animosity got so great Spike gave George a royalty too."

The most complex project the band recorded at RCA's Chicago studios that December was a children's album written by animator Frank Tashlin. "How the Circus Learned to Smile," despite Joe Siracusa's clever sound effects and Doc Birdbath's animal impressions, was as banal as anything Jones or Tashlin —about to make a name for himself as a screenwriter-director—ever produced.

Spike apparently hoped he had another "Nutcracker Suite," but the Slickers knew better. "We called it 'How the Circus Learned to Smell,' " claimed Birdbath.

The music industry learned to smile again when public pressure, imported records, increased production of bootlegs and the threat of Congressional action helped to resolve the latest cessation on the manufacture of discs. With the ban lifted after 12 months, the Slickers were back in harness early in 1949. Spike had made a tongue-in-cheek promise to his fans on "Happy New Year" that things would be different:

> In this coming year I'm gonna be discreet
> Have the Slickers playing music soft and sweet
> I resolve to treat Tchaikovsky tenderly
> And set his Second Movement off with TNT.

The band got off to a slow start with a few predictably silly numbers, but came back in full force with some of their best material in years—and some highly entertaining departures from the norm.

"Dance of the Hours" presented the band at its best, in a brilliant rearrangement of the music from Ponchielli's opera La Gioconda. Charlotte Tinsley opened with a lilting harp solo, accompanied by flutist Phillip

Ace in the hole: songwriter Eddie Maxwell. (*Casey Clair*)

Shuken. The Slickers—George Rock (trumpet), Joe Colvin (trombone), Jack Golly (clarinet), Dick Gardner and Eddie Metcalfe (sax), Joe Siracusa (drums), Roger Donley (tuba), Paul Leu (piano), Dick Morgan and Freddy Morgan (banjo) and an unidentified pistol wielder—shone as brightly as ever.

The time-honored composition sounded like music appreciation day at a lunatic asylum by the time the band got done with it—at which point Doodles Weaver, "direct from the press box at Indianapolis," took over the microphone. The ensuing race, narrated at lightning speed, came to an appropriately smashing finale. The winner—who else?—Feetlebaum.

Completely reorganized since the high watermark of "Nutcracker Suite" and the Other Orchestra fiasco, the band pulled out all the stops on "Dance of the Hours" and the selections that followed. "Riders in the Sky," recorded the same day, boasted a wonderfully zany instrumental but opened more ears with its lyrics.

Dick Morgan (alias I.W. Harper) gave forth in his best "whiskey tenor," partnered by Earl Bennett (alias Sir Frederick Gas) as his Yiddish-accented pardner. When they introduced their rendition on Jones' radio program the closing verse did not exactly flatter the singing bandleader who made it popular:

> When Johnny comes marching home again, hooray, hooray.
> He'll make the guy who wrote this song pay, and pay.
> 'Cause all we hear is "Ghost Riders" sung by Vaughn Monroe.
> I can do without his singing—but I wish I had his dough.

Monroe, who epitomized the sappy pop music Jones loved to desecrate, was often the butt of Spike's jokes. He took most of Jones' derisive remarks in stride, but decided the funster had gone too far this time.

"Vaughn was a very nice fellow, but he was like a big baby. He never graduated from the adolescent stage; he thought the record was a *real* slap at him. And it actually wasn't. It's a laugh," said Walt Heebner, who sensed there would be a problem at the outset. "When I heard it, I said, 'Spike, you better get ready to put another ending on there.' Sure enough, we had to do it."

"Monroe hit the ceiling," recalled Earl Bennett, who admitted to being "the guy who came up with the idea that got the record in trouble. Monroe got with Stan Jones, who wrote the song, and convinced him to get pretty angry about it. I pointed out to Stan, 'What do you care? You get more money every time we sell a record.' He said, 'Yeah, that's right.' But it was a little late for that, because it got yanked."

RCA released an alternate take with the offending line omitted; in its place, Morgan yodeled, "Yippie-i-yay..."—interrupted by a gunshot, followed by a moan. The limited pressing of the objectionable version became an instant collector's item in West Coast record shops.

"We always tried to start little feuds with Monroe and everybody, to get publicity," observed Eddie Brandt. "We couldn't do Irving Berlin in those days, Rodgers and Hart, Rodgers and Hammerstein, Cole Porter. Spike always wanted to do 'Begin the Beguine' but Porter wouldn't allow it. We couldn't do a lot of the classics. The writers were big; they had complete control. Now the songs are in catalogs, the writers are dead and nobody gives a damn about anything."

Deceased composers raised considerably less fuss, and Jones took every opportunity to "decompose"—as he put it—the cherished works of those who had gone to their final resting place. Offenbach, Liszt, Brahms and Bizet were among those to suffer indignities at the hands of the maestro that year, not only because they were dead but because classical music was then at the apex of its popularity.

"Morpheus"—a pastiche of themes from "Orpheus in the Underworld," concocted by Eddie Maxwell—began innocently enough, with Freddy Morgan warbling a lá Maurice Chevalier. It quickly descended into a hell-raising cacophony that might well have stirred Offenbach in his grave.

The Slickers gave it everything they had, with a full complement of honks, clanks, screams, whistles, sneezes and gunshots. The star performer, however, was Carl Grayson, brought back just for the occasion. In spite of his drinking problem, a talent was a talent was a talent—and no one else could glug to the tune of the "Can Can" without choking on his tongue.

Among the more complicated and most outrageous numbers of the period was "Rhapsody from Hunger(y)," which began life as "A Goose to the Ballet Russe." A musical goulash—incorporating Liszt's "Hungarian Rhapsody No. 2" and Brahms' "Hungarian Dance No. 5"—it started out soft and sweet, as per Spike's New Year's resolution. True to form, it soon erupted into a glorious free-for-all. From banjo concerto and cackle chorus, to horn sonata and auto collision—by way of some sizzling hot jazz—it proved what Spike had always maintained: it took genuine musicianship to be a City Slicker.

If the Slickers sounded like they were having fun at the same time, make no mistake about it—they were. "The gentleman in charge at Victor once got upset with me because I was fooling around at the session like we did onstage," said Joe Siracusa. "That's the way we were. We were a bunch of guys playing happy music. They wanted us to be more serious. I said, 'This is the way we are.' The music had the same vitality, the same feeling on record that we had on the stage. It had to, in order to be successful."

During the two consecutive sessions in which he recorded "Morpheus" and "Rhapsody," Jones assassinated the opera "Carmen." His chief accomplices, Jay Sommers and Eddie Brandt, put Bizet's hot-blooded gypsy girl ("Messy Soprano" Eileen Gallagher) to work in a bubble gum factory; they gave her a three-eyed lover who preferred throwing the bull to pitching woo, and a suitor with over-starched undershorts.

The parody, which Jones had done earlier that year on his radio program, was the subject of serious disagreement between the bandleader and A&R man Walt Heebner. "I told him I didn't believe that was the sort of stuff that would sell records," said Heebner. "I told him he was making a very bad mistake. Matter of fact, I told him *he* was not funny, his music was funny."

The material Jones recorded for RCA was primarily his own decision. "He'd come in on the basis of an idea, and they'd run it down and talk it over," recalled Heebner. "The band never came in with everything worked out. Spike was open to suggestion at all times." Heebner would veto Jones' ideas "if they didn't make too much sense. But I was not a dictator. He was the talent; I was only the supposed commercial producer.

"Spike was a damned good artist; we never had any trouble. The only difficulty we had was with 'Carmen.' I thought that stunk. And told him so. It was material for radio, because you hear it once and it's gone. With a record, you want to play the record over again," reflected Heebner. "After that one, which I believe was pretty much of a bomb compared to his other sales, he realized what I had told him—and it wasn't only my thought—was correct."

Eileen Gallagher concurred. "I wasn't too crazy about it, either. It was okay, but it just didn't have the pizazz of the other things Spike had done, like 'Cocktails for Two' and 'Holiday for Strings.' It didn't have as much nonsense and as much impact as those things," she said. "And I wasn't all that great; I certainly didn't do much for it."

Half a century later, however, Spike Jones Jr. would cite "Carmen Murdered!" (aka "Spike Jones Murders Carmen") as his favorite of all his father's recordings. "It's just masterful," he told a disc jockey. "Every time I hear it…it's phenomenal how it's choreographed and put together. And the fact that it was done live without any overdubs adds even more intrigue to it."

Jones Sr., a man of much intrigue if not mystery, apparently fancied himself as a writer. In fact, he wrote his name on virtually everything the band recorded during this period; he listed himself as co-author on "Carmen Murdered!" and sole arranger on "Rhapsody from Hunger(y)." He further perpetuated the image of himself as a prolific composer by establishing a pair of music publishing companies and applying for membership in ASCAP.

"Spike put his name on lots of arrangements he didn't write—just like other bandleaders. He wanted to get the credit," reflected Joe Siracusa. "Even if he didn't write the stuff himself, he inspired the writers. So many basic ideas really were Spike's. Not all the ideas came from writers. I might be wrong, but I'd say 75% of the original ideas started with him, were inspired by him."

"If Spike sat in and worked with you on an idea, he got a share," explained Eddie Brandt. "But he didn't get any royalties on 'Carmen'— Jay Sommers wouldn't go for it. Spike wanted a third; he sat in on a lot of sessions and threw ideas here and there. 'Carmen' was his idea, but Jay didn't work that way. He wouldn't go for cutting Spike in. If Spike came up with nothing but the title, when you finished he was a third," said Brandt.

The nature of authorship is a complicated issue, however. "Spike *was* entitled to royalties on a lot of stuff because it was his idea; he didn't take a credit unless he actually contributed something," said Brandt. "He was basically an idea man, a good producer and a good editor—the most important damn thing in the world. As a writer, your whole fate is in the hands of the editor; if he's lousy, you're through."

While pianist Paul Leu was considered by many of his fellow Slickers to be the one responsible for most of the arrangements during the late '40s, Brandt contended, "We *all* did every arrangement. We all sat down and outlined how to do a song, what to put in the background. The 'arrangers' were just the guys who could physically write it out."

Producer-director Bud Yorkin, a longtime friend of Jones', repudiated assertions that the bandleader took a backseat. "Basically, I think Spike did the arrangements," he said. "It was a collaboration, yes, but it was him sitting there saying, 'I want a gunshot here...let's do a gag here...we need a gag there...' He was a man of his own destiny with that."

"Spike Jones Plays the Charleston"—the album that followed "Carmen"—was a departure from everything Jones had recorded up to that point, in more ways than one. The Other Orchestra had been heavily augmented with outsiders, but the City Slickers were at its core; only three of the musicians on the "Charleston" sessions were regulars.

"Spike was very considerate," noted Joe Siracusa. "He called and said, 'How are you on playing Charleston stuff?' I said, 'I don't know, I've never done it.' He said, 'It was my thought to get guys who've played it authentically.' I'd have done the same thing—get guys best qualified."

King Jackson, who had joined Red Nichols since leaving the Slickers,

Henry D. Haynes (right) and Kenneth C. Burns, alias Homer and Jethro,
about the time they recorded "Pal-Yat-Chee."

dominated the album on lead trombone, with Arthur Rando (clarinet),
Lou Singer (xylophone), John Cyr (drums) and Arthur Most (second trombone) giving the numbers a bona fide Jazz Age sound. George Rock, Paul
Leu and Freddy Morgan rounded out the orchestra; Del Porter returned to
contribute vocals, which were credited to "Gil Bert and Sully Van."

An excellent recreation of the flapper era—in full swing during Spike's
high school days—the album also cashed in on a national resurgence of
interest in the '20s dance craze. Eddie Maxwell's snappy "Charlestono-Mio,"
based on "O Sole Mio," became part of the Slickers' standard repertoire.

Although Jones was never again to equal the overall quality of his
1949 work, he continued to make some highly entertaining records. His
output became more and more erratic, however, as the years wore on.
There were times when he knew exactly what he was doing, and other
times when he floundered.

It was in the promotional department, once more, that he truly excelled. The later records often were not up to par—many were awful—
but when it came time to get the word out, Spike always outdid himself.
"One time I said to him, 'Gee, I'd like to get a few of your albums to take

back to Indianapolis and play over the public address system," recalled Gordon Schroeder, whose race cars Jones enthusiastically sponsored. "The next day, a truck drove up—there must've been hundreds of records."

The bandleader kept meticulous mailing lists of 6,000 disc jockeys, newspaper columnists and distributors he could rely on for a plug or a little extra push. "Spike had a book the size of the Manhattan telephone directory with almost everybody he'd ever met in the world, and when he came into a town, he'd pull out the pages that were applicable to that town," said New York-based publicist Buddy Basch, who started handling Jones' account in 1950. "When he showed me the book I almost died. It must have weighed about ten pounds; he had every station, including Elephant's Breath, Montana."

Jones kept a disc jockey contact man on salary in Hollywood, New York and Chicago; he sent the deejays cases of Scotch, kept track of their birthdays and sent regards to their mothers. Basch marveled: "He'd call up and say, 'Hello, Fred, how's Ann? Has Jimmy gotten over his hay fever? I'm sorry to hear about your uncle's toenail problem...' This went on forever."

"He sat all night long calling disc jockeys, whenever we had an album come out," concurred Eddie Brandt. "Even in those days, his phone bill must have been $1,000 a month. He and I would sit there the whole night and write the newsletter, then he'd have it copied and sent out. Or he might send a nude gal delivering the thing."

"I'd make these late night trips to disc jockeys in Chicago and places like that with Spike," said Earl Bennett, "but I don't think the disc jockey was all that thrilled I was there. I didn't have a lot to contribute. I think he was more pleased with the bottle of booze Spike brought along."

Jones and company also wrote to radio stations at every opportunity. Recalled Eddie Maxwell: "One of the things we used to do, the rest of the squad and me—on the one-night stands, when we knew where we were going to be a few days ahead—we would write post cards, and disguise our writing so each of us could write six or seven cards, requesting Spike Jones recordings."

Buddy Basch quickly proved he had the energy—and a sense of humor—equal to the task of promoting Jones' efforts. "Every time he had a record come out, I'd do some tie-in with somebody," stated Basch. "One time, he had a record called 'Yes, We Have No Bananas.' Spike was coming to New York—I thought it would be really swell if we did something *big*. I got an outfit like the American Fruit Company or the Banana Council, to provide us with a railroad flatcar full of bananas. And I had it towed into Grand Central Station; we knew what track he was coming in on. I had everybody down there, the networks, the television people, the newsreels...

"I had a showgirl [Toni Carroll] dressed up in a Mexican outfit with a skimpy skirt, and she was Chiquita Banana. When Spike got off the train, we grabbed him. Most of the time I didn't surprise him, but I wanted to see the look on his face when this beautiful girl came over and gave him a big kiss...and then led him over to a flatcar full of bananas. He and the girl and ten tons of bananas—it broke all over—I got the front page of the *New York Daily News*. It said, 'Yes, We Have No Bananas—Spike Jones Sure Has 'Em.' "

Jones kept Basch informed, but left him to his own devices. "He might say to me, 'I want to promote this record.' But he didn't give me a definite direction; it was up to me, what to do and how to do it. He'd say, 'Line up some stuff.' That was about as much direction as I would get," noted the publicist.

"He was very imaginative, and very appreciative of anything you did that was right out of left field. I don't think anything was too crazy for him," said Basch. Indeed, Jones would probably have unleashed a bull in a china shop if he thought it would sell records—if Fred Waring hadn't beat him to it.

Two years after the banana stunt, Basch hired actress Barbara Nichols—a former stripper—to promote Jones' "I Saw Mommy Kissing Santa Claus." Recalled the press agent: "I dressed Nichols in a Santa suit—a red hat, skimpy skirt, kind of hanging out at the top. She went around Christmas time kissing disc jockeys and giving them the record. To say we got air play hardly covered it."

Spike tried to line up a similar gag with another buxom young blonde named Marilyn Monroe, but it fell through. "Six months ago it would have been a cinch," he regretted. "She's getting to be a big deal and isn't putting her lips on just anything any more."

Jones and Victor spared no effort on "Mommy, Won't You Buy a Baby Brother?" in 1950, in an attempt to duplicate the success of "My Two Front Teeth." In addition to the usual promotion, RCA bought almost $30,000 worth of newspaper ads.

"I don't believe any record company has ever spent a similar amount of money on one record. We should know in the next week or so if we have another million seller," sales manager L.W. Kanaga informed Jones in a letter. "We pushed all other records aside in this week's release because of the importance of this record to you and to us."

For his part, Spike paraded down Hollywood Boulevard in his long underwear distributing 5,000 balloons—accompanied by City Slickers, majorettes and a midget in an over-sized baby buggy—and adopted a Polish war orphan in Europe through the foster parents plan. "Now if the public doesn't buy it, it's just because they eat their young," he quipped. But the disc fell far short of the mark, despite the ballyhoo.

Two of Jones' best 1950 recordings were noteworthy for the vocal interpretations and the problems they caused—which did more to publicize them than his own promotional efforts. "Chinese Mule Train" provided Freddy Morgan one of his finest moments, skewering Frankie Laine in a patois so authentic it was almost incomprehensible at times. But dialect humor was beginning to fade from vogue; a number of Chinese organizations complained about the parody.

"The original plan for the recording was to open with authentic Chinese singers and musicians," noted archivist Ted Hering, recalling a conversation he had with Morgan. "When the group Spike hired found out the nature of the record, they walked off the job. Freddy was called upon to ad-lib some pseudo Chinese lyrics instead."

When Jones playfully took "Tennessee Waltz" from the Appalachians and transplanted it to the Bronx, a storm of protest resulted. Sara Berner (telephone operator Mabel Flapsaddle on *The Jack Benny Show*) and Earl Bennett sang the Patti Page hit in heavy Yiddish accents, provoking howls of indignation moreso than laughter. *Billboard* called it "a lapse in good taste"; Chicago and New York radio stations shelved the record when they received vehement letters of objection.

"Sara Berner and I were both proud of the record, and the Jewish community just wouldn't accept it," said Bennett. "I can understand that. But Sara, who was Jewish, thought it was very funny. Everybody at the session thought we had a good record. The Anti-Defamation League didn't think it was respectful."

"Spike was very annoyed. The Jewish critics panned it, and that really hurt him," asserted Bernie Jones. "It made Spike angry because he said people like Mickey Katz could get away with these things, but when he did one they put it down. He was angry they'd jump on him because he wasn't Jewish." It was the Jewish editor of *Weekly Variety*, however, who blasted Katz for a parody "defiling" the legend of Davy Crockett.

Only the purists were upset with Jones' burlesque on *I Pagliacci*. But if Leoncavallo would "cry in his beer" over the movies' use of his opera—

as film critic Pare Lorentz once suggested—he would probably have
drowned himself in drink had he been around to witness the devastation
wrought by Eddie Maxwell's pen.

"Pal-Yat-Chee" gave Arena Stars clients Homer and Jethro an unparalleled vehicle for their homespun humor, and a huge target—"a fat
guy in a clown suit." Maxwell, whose clever words had danced on the
tongues of Abbott and Costello, Danny Thomas and Mel Blanc before
he joined Jones' organization, let all the air out with his lyrics:

> An' he sang about a lady
> Who weighed two hunnered an' eighty
> When she takes a powder
> He just starts chirpin' louder
> An' he don' do a goldern thing
> 'cept to stand up there an' sing.

> When we listen to PAL-YAT-CHEE,
> We get itchy an' scratchy,
> This shore is top corn
> So we go an' buy some popcorn.

Though the parody was as funny as anything Homer Haynes and
Jethro Burns ever did, not everyone was amused. Recalled Burns: "We
cut the record in Chicago; they hired a guy from the opera company
[John Halloran] to come in and sing the tenor part, but they neglected to
tell him it wouldn't be a legit-type record. The guy comes in, and he's got
on a homburg hat and a cane and a scarf, very formal. He walks in the
studio and he sees the City Slickers all set up, and he just about went into
shock."

RCA also apparently had little regard for "Pal-Yat-Chee." It sat on
the shelf for over three years, before it was finally issued as the B-side of
Spike's decidedly inferior take-off on Jack Webb's police drama, "Dragnet." A second number combining the talents of the Slickers and the
hillbilly comedy duo—"Fiddle Faddle" by Boston Pops' composer Leroy
Anderson, as reworked by Eddie Maxwell—was recorded the same day
but issued only as a gift premium.

Jones found only one number in 1951 worthy of his reputation for
parody. "Alto, Baritone and Bass," which poked fun at the overdubbing

techniques of guitarist Les Paul, was another brainchild of Maxwell's. "I wrote all the words and did all the voices," he noted. "That was one of the most difficult things I ever had to do, 'cause I had the earphones on; I had to listen to the band, and I had to harmonize with myself. It's a good thing I was a genius at the time," quipped Maxwell. The record did not see the light of day for more than two decades.

A year of virtual inactivity in the studios was followed in 1952 by a year of departure, during which Jones demonstrated once more just how versatile he could be. The year's output—prodigious by any standards—was highlighted by "Bottoms Up," a smorgasbord of polkas with an international flavor.

While many projects had their gestation in Spike's fertile brain, the polka album grew out of a song by Freddy Morgan and Bernie Jones ("A Din Skal, A Min Skal"), who wrote it simply to alleviate boredom on the train between one-nighters. Bassist Roger Donley and trombonist Joe Colvin, who often blended into the background, stood out on instrumental. Morgan alternated on lead vocal with Del Porter; they were backed by the Mellomen, a popular quartet led by Thurl Ravenscroft.

Jones further puzzled fans that year by organizing a new group, the Country Cousins, to play legitimate "hillbilly music." The selections and the arrangements—of such tunes as "Down South," "I've Turned a Gadabout" and "Hotter Than a Pistol"—strayed far from familiar territory.

"Spike used the best country and western musicians in the business," said Joe Siracusa, who played drums on the sessions, alongside Cliffie Stone on bass; Speedy West, Jimmy Bryant and Eddie Kirk on guitar; Marvin Ash on piano and George Rock on trumpet.

"I was very surprised when Spike wanted to go into country and western. I was thrilled to death when he called," reflected Cliffie Stone. "I thought, 'What am I going to do with this guy?' He said, 'I've seen you play bass on your television show. Would you do that for me?' I said, 'I'd be honored.' I played the slap bass; he was really fond of it, because it was incorporating an old dixieland effect into that new—whatever you call it—thing he was doing. This was done tongue-in-cheek, poking fun at country and western.

"We had a long conversation on the phone about country and western, how sales were, how it was growing, all of those things. I think Spike did country because he wanted sales. I don't think he would've gone into country for a creative release, such as you might go into the classics or big band sounds," observed Stone. "It was purely a commercial venture. He wasn't trying to prove anything," concurred Siracusa.

Jones admitted that "the Country Cousins got me back on the juke-boxes again," but asserted that his reason for "branching out" was neither artistic nor monetary. "It was strictly in self-defense, because some of the so-called pretty records these days are almost as funny as 'Chloe,' " he noted, pointing out that Patti Page had a barking dog on her latest re-lease. "What I am supposed to do? Pretty soon they'll call [André] Kostelanetz a novelty orchestra...aren't there any straightmen left?"

Spike returned to parody in 1953 but was plagued again by censor-ship trouble. His lampoon of the Patti Page hit, "I Went to Your Wed-ding," was banned on WHDH in Boston due to objectionable lyrics—and Earl Bennett's well-timed giggles:

> You tripped down the aisle
> fell flat on your [*giggle*] smile
> Your father was loaded too...[*giggle*]
> He dragged your bouquet the rest of the way
> and then [*giggle*] he went back
> and dragged you [*giggle*]

Spike took umbrage at the ban. "How in anyone's wildest imagina-tion this could be construed to be risqué, I really don't know and I can only say that the other 1,983 radio stations in the U.S. see nothing cen-sorable about it either," he wrote station manager George Perkins in an open letter in *Billboard*. "Of course, George, if you smile with anything but your face, that's your own business; this is a free country."

Pointing out that children made up a large percentage of his audience, Jones declared, "I would not ever intentionally make a risqué record if for no other reason than that I happen to be the father of a three-and-a-half-year-old boy, Spike Jr., and an 18 months old daughter, Leslie Ann. They like music too, George, even mine." While the bandleader was publicly outraged, "I think he was delighted we got banned in Boston," said Earl Bennett. "In those days it was a joke, get your book banned in Boston and then you're a hit."

Jones woke Bennett "at some weird godawful hour of the morn-ing"—on the train, while on tour—and asked for his input on the letter. The comedian replied, "Just write him and tell him you're in the business

An album recorded circa 1953, but never released. (*Ted Hering*)

of making phonograph records, not pornograph records."

Bennett recalled: "Spike looked at me for a minute and said, 'What does that mean?' I said, 'It's a play on the word pornography.' He said, 'What's that?' The guy didn't know the meaning of the word; he'd never encountered it."

Jones occasionally ventured into off-color material over the years, but he was a family man and *The Musical Depreciation Revue* was a "family-type show." He was proud of that fact, and strictly adhered to self-imposed guidelines. But he was also a man of many contradictions.

When Bernie Jones caused a commotion one night by passing around a sketch of a well-proportioned naked woman—that unfolded to reveal male genitalia—his boss requested half a dozen copies, to send

Jones directs the St. Mary Magdalen Children's Choir for "Where Did My Snowman Go?" in this rare behind-the-scenes photo. RCA, 1953. (*Harry Geller*)

to comedian Jerry Lewis and other pals. "Spike liked things like that," said the artist. "Not as far as the public was concerned—but he was one of the boys."

Spike was doubtless sincere in his reply to the WHDH station manager. But what he *meant* was, he would never make such a record for commercial issue. His 1952 Christmas release, "I Saw Mommy Kissing Santa Claus," would not have offended anyone, but the second take—with alternate lyrics by Freddy Morgan—was another story altogether.

"We recorded all the background with the choir and everything, then they were excused; they went home and we did it as 'I Saw Mommy *Screwing* Santa Claus,' " divulged George Rock, who used his usual kiddie voice, as gleeful and exuberant as ever.

"It came on the spur of the moment. We locked the door. Then Helen came by to pick Spike up; she couldn't figure out why wouldn't we let her in," recalled Joe Siracusa. "Spike wouldn't even let her in the door, didn't want her to hear it," chorused Rock. "He didn't want anybody to hear it."

What possessed Jones to do it? "I suppose it sounded like a good idea," said Rock. "Spike had a jaundiced eye after he attained the kind of success he did," observed Harry Geller, who produced the session. "He thought the whole thing was one big laugh. There was nothing unusual behind it; that still goes on."

Although engineers in the booth made acetates of "Screwing Santa" for themselves, news of its existence did not travel far; it might well have destroyed the bandleader's reputation if it had. But the records Jones turned out for public consumption from 1953-55—most of them done with children in mind—did little to enhance it. While his own children undoubtedly influenced such decisions, his choice of material could not have been worse. The uninspired arrangements did not help matters.

"I Just Love My Mommy," "Santa Brought Me Choo Choo Trains" and too many others had the same blandness—and the same condescending tone toward small fry that had warped "How the Circus Learned to Smile," which at least had the virtue of a funny instrumental.

"Where Did My Snowman Go?" and "I Want Eddie Fisher for Christmas" were not only patronizing; they had the additional liability of Linda Strangis' raspy, whiney voice. However, she was the bandleader's niece. Jones' reprise of "Three Little Fishes," the novelty made famous by Kay Kyser in 1939, was a further sign of desperation—yet one more indication he was running out of creative fuel.

"Winter," with its whimsical lyrics (dating from 1910) and delightful barbershop quartet treatment by the Mellomen, was a gem—and a rare excursion from kiddie material during that period. "Lulu Had a Baby," a cute little novelty that would have gotten lost in the shuffle a few years earlier, was another stand-out then.

"Japanese Skokiaan," an attempt by Freddy Morgan to repeat the success of "Chinese Mule Train," paled by comparison. However, it prompted one of the most outrageous stunts ever pulled on Jones' behalf. Disc jockey Bill Stewart played an acetate 56 consecutive times on El Paso station KELP, for three hours straight, causing the switchboard to jam up for most of the day. The deejay, who acted on his own, admonished Spike in a follow-up letter, "For Christ's sake...hurry up and buy a radio station so we can start doing some really goofy things."

Jones' long and prolific association with RCA Victor—which produced some 136 selections and at least four gold records—ended more with a whimper than a bang.

The bandleader fought a lengthy battle with A&R department heads over the type of material he wanted to record, like "Music for Leasebreakers: A Study in Low Fidelity" (the album which eventually became "Dinner Music for People Who Aren't Very Hungry") and "Christmas Story," a narrative sent in unsolicited by an Illinois newspaperman. After enduring a continual lack of cooperation, Jones and the record label came to a parting of the ways in the fall of 1955.

Spike never commented publicly on the dissolution, but four years later, in a radio interview with Chicago area disc jockey Eddie Cuda, he gave some indication of how he felt.

"I recorded for Victor at one time," joked Cuda. "Victor Dumbrowsky—he had a tape machine in his basement."

"I wish I'd have been with him instead of the other Victor," replied Jones. "I was an RCA Victim for 15 years."

The bandleader's retort amazed one former associate. "I'm surprised he would say a thing like that. RCA bent over backwards," observed Walt Heebner, who left the company in 1950. "Spike owed an awful lot of his success to me...and the guy that preceded me, Harry Meyerson. He may have been a little pissed off at me when I told him he wasn't funny, his music was funny, but I think he was the sort of guy that would understand that that was right."

Vantage Point: George Rock
Trumper, 1944–1960

The whole family was musically inclined. My aunt taught music; my father sang. The only time I ever practiced my horn—my father would try to get me to go out and work in the garden or mow the yard or something—and that was my standard excuse, I couldn't because I had to work on the horn. I started when I was 14 or 15.

I went professional around 1939. A band came through my home-town to play the fair. They were rained out the first night so they met at a local hangout downtown and had a semi-jam session. I was the local musical hero so they all insisted I go home and get my horn. I came down and sat in with them and they offered me a job. It was kind of a starvation job but it got my foot in the door.

After that I worked with a band in a little gambling club, then I traveled with a Mickey Mouse-type band. Then I was with Freddie Fisher about three and a half years. That's how I ended up in Hollywood, with Fisher. We came to the Coast and worked the Radio Room at Sunset and Vine—right across the street from NBC. Spike was doing *Bob Burns* and *Furlough Fun*; the guys would come over there and get a drink in between rehearsals and listen to our band. Fisher's band really was a kind of fore-runner of Spike's; we played a semi-dixieland type music but a lot of novelty songs.

One day Spike's regular trumpet player [Wally Kline] got sick on the day of the Burns show. They called and asked if I could do it as a quick sub. I did the Burns show on Thursday, then on Friday I did *Furlough Fun*. That was my first stint with the band. Spike was about to leave on a USO tour. I had already quit Fisher to go with him but the union wouldn't let me leave town; I worked with Charlie Barnet while Spike was gone, then I joined when they got back.

Spike gave me a seven-year contract, and after the first couple weeks he tore up the contract and doubled my salary. First I got $200 a week, then it went up to $400. He was always very good to me in that respect; I didn't have to ask for anything. He really paid me for my efforts.

At the end of a tour, they always gave notice to everybody in the show. The first time I got my notice, Spike came around and started talking to me about something we were going to do and I said, "You just fired me." He said, "They didn't mean you." I said, "Well, I got a piece of paper that said I was fired." He said, "We just have to do that for legal reasons." From then on, I didn't pay much attention when he fired me; he did it every tour. I got paid regardless, whether we worked or not...

When I joined the band just about all of them except me were what I would call heavy drinkers. It was pretty tough in the theater days because you had the first show at noon or shortly thereafter; they would come in with hangovers and some of them were still pretty well drunk. But they were always capable of doing their job.

Carl Grayson occasionally had some problems. He was a very sweet guy; he was quite mild-mannered and meek and inoffensive in every respect. He was a great musical talent. I often wonder how good he would have been had he not been so addicted to alcohol. I probably never saw him sober. When Spike quit drinking he became a lot more sensitive about someone else's drinking; when he was drinking, he didn't care what went on, so long as you made the job.

The show was hard work, and lots of times you didn't feel like doing it. You'd have the flu or something and nobody cared; you still had to come out and do the show. When my father died I wasn't able to go home because I had to stay with the band. I don't mean to sound egotistical, but had I left they'd have had to shut down until I came back. They couldn't call and have someone come in and play my part while I was gone...

The show looked improvised but it was all strictly routine. Spike's introductions would sound very ad-libbed many times but they never were; they were always scripted. When I first joined him he was a very poor emcee, but over a period of years he became a lot more polished. He took lessons, in fact, in elocution. He took some kind of a lesson even on signing his name to get a distinguished signature for autographs. He had everything down to a science.

A pair of gun collectors compare notes. (*George Rock*)

Spike would adhere strictly to teachings and rely only on what he could do. He wouldn't extend himself; he didn't try to tell jokes. Spike didn't want to be funny; he hired other people for that purpose. He wanted to be the businessman and make the money, which he did.

With the business you're a night person, and Spike just extended it. He was almost a workaholic too, which I would imagine is necessary. He *lived* the work and the show; he was constantly working on it. You'd never see him enjoying himself, playing cards or anything.

His spare time was always spent working on something new. Not that he was "on stage" like some pseudo-comics are but his mind was always clickin' away. Even if he was sitting and eating a meal, usually the writers would be there with him, and they'd be talking about some skit or how to change some bit or add something new.

Spike was very strict in adhering to the fact that this was a family type show, and nothing would be done that would offend anybody. The closest he ever came was this little thing I did on "Mairzy Doats" the first couple of years. I went, "Mairzy *phbbt!* Doats *phbbt!* and little lambs that *phbbt!...*" We'd occasionally get a few objections to the raspberries from the straight-laced people in Boston. For some reason Spike didn't think that should be offensive to anybody, and staunchly defended it.

Spike had the last say on writing, but he always had writers. Our radio producer, Joe Bigelow, was a writer for Milton Berle during the *Texaco Star Theater* days; he always said Berle used to rule the script session with "an iron head." It never got to that with Spike because he was always receptive to any ideas. He'd listen to someone and do what they thought was best.

Our writers traveled with us constantly. A few times Spike asked me to sit in on the writing sessions; I hated it. I honestly tried to do things to get out of it, and sure enough, pretty soon I wasn't asked. They would go all night. We would work until 11 p.m. or midnight, and then these guys would go until 4 o'clock in the morning on the writing session. I didn't want any of that. None of the band would have been in on the sessions, except Freddy Morgan and maybe the current piano player...

Freddy wasn't basically a musician; he was a comedian and a writer. During our show, in one of Helen's numbers, there was a four-bar trombone solo—the only solo Joe Colvin got to play the whole night that really featured him. He sat next to Freddy on the stage. And Freddy's playing interfered so much with his playing (in his mind), that Joe would pay Freddy a dollar to lay out during his little trombone solo.

Every night, Joe would lay his dollar on Freddy's stand, and Freddy would lay out. Then immediately after the solo—*planka planka plank*—he'd start in again. If Joe didn't give him the buck, Freddy would play right through the solo on banjo.

I remember Freddy saying he would do anything for a laugh. He didn't care what it was, so long as he got a laugh. When we were at Slapsy Maxie's in Hollywood, there was a scene where Freddy got hit in the face with a pie, which still is a funny bit. And one time Freddy almost literally cried for an hour because somebody put something in the pie that burned his eyes. It was at that time he said he'd do anything for a laugh, but he didn't want to be injured physically in any way.

When we were working the Curran Theatre in San Francisco, Bill King, the juggler, would come running out on stage. We had a pit band; there was an upright piano in the pit. He stepped out on this piano, and he upset it—I think he jumped back on stage, but the piano tipped over and demolished four or five instruments. The audience laughed like hell;

"What rhymes with Tchaikovsky?" Earl Bennett, George Rock and Doodles Weaver help Spike ponder the question. (*Eddie Brandt's Saturday Matinee*)

they thought it was part of the show. The guys came back in to play the intermission music, and here were their instruments mangled...

Spike was probably the most caustic person I've ever known. If he didn't like someone or someone offended him, he could really get salty. But I was with him 16 years, and only twice in all that time did we ever have anything even resembling words.

One morning we were rehearsing a radio show. Both of us were dead tired, we'd had no sleep. He used to all the time facetiously remark about himself, "There's nothing worse than a reformed drunk." I thought I was being funny, and I said the same thing, *to him*. And he took offense.

He said something about somebody's drunkenness, and I said what he had always said. That morning it wasn't funny. Any other time he probably would have laughed. He said something to the effect, "Boy, if other people could kick their bad habits as well as I did mine..." I said, "You're sure right about that." I figured I'd better shut up.

Another time we were playing the Great Northern Theatre in Chicago. The pit band was very friendly; I was good friends with several of them, especially the lead trumpet player. And he cacked some note. They were playing the overture and we were standing on the stage waiting for the curtain to go up, and this guy really flubbed. And I hollered "Whoops!" For some reason, Spike took offense.

I don't think he said anything, but we started playing and he hollered "Whoops!" at me, and he screwed something up, and I hollered back at him. I thought we were really going to get into it. We were like two little kids yelling at each other. Finally I thought, "Gee, that's stupid," and just quit. That was as close as we ever came to getting into any problems. He was always very good to me in every respect...

You had to do things to keep from going crazy. We used to have poker games all night in the men's room of SJ-1, one of the Pullmans we had, and Doodles Weaver would always be drunk. Frankie Little was objecting because Doodles was betting stupidly—according to Frankie—"just throwing money away." Doodles said, "I'll show you throwing money away," and he went and flushed a ten dollar bill down the toilet. Frankie was going to stop the train. He couldn't believe anybody would just throw $10 away like that.

Frankie was a dear little guy. There was a funny dude. He was just illiterate enough that he would say things like, "I saw a great movie picture today—John Wayne in *Two Jima*." Priceless. Doodles was going to write a book; he called them "Frankieisms."

I roomed with Frankie in a hotel in Canada. We went to bed at one or two in the morning. At daybreak I heard this horrendous noise down below in the street, cars—like in the movies—*Bang! Crash!* And the horns! I woke up and there in the window—stark naked, facing the front—Frankie is standing on the radiator, trying to pull the shade down. People are looking up at this, running into each other—you can imagine what a scene that must have been.

I never did let on that I'd seen that. I didn't dare get up and help him; he'd have killed me. He didn't realize the shade wasn't down when we went to bed. The sun came up and it was probably right in his eyes. How the hell would a dwarf pull the shade down, except to stand on the sill and reach up?

Then we had a midget in Hawaii [Tony Boris] who looked like he was ninety years old; he always smoked cigars. In "Laura," he was in the pair of pants—just a pair of pants came running across stage. He was always afraid he was going to miss his cue. We'd look over and he'd be sitting in the wings, in the pants, with the fly open, with a cigar—waiting for his cue. Just a pair of trousers smoking a cigar.

Radio Days
Band on the Air, 1941–1955

Above and beyond all other media, it was radio that allowed Spike Jones to carry out his unprecedented assault on popular music. Without the miracle of broadcasting, and a like-minded anarchist in the person of WNEW disc jockey Martin Block, the manner in which Jones burst upon the scene and took hold of the public's fancy would scarcely have been possible.

Radio in its heyday was far more than television without pictures. It was a live medium that permitted the listener to participate by using the imagination to set the stage and design the costumes—and allowed one determined music maker to promote and market his offbeat product to a vast audience who could visualize his band in action. A gang of musical hooligans who could be heard but not seen was more fun to imagine, in the years before TV obliterated the creative interaction between audience and performer.

"Radio was such a different medium, but we approached it almost like it was the stage," asserted Earl Bennett. There was a lot of pressure, however, "because it was a one-shot thing. You had to get it right and make it funny, 'cause if you died on the air you died; there was nothing to save it."

The indefatigable leader of the City Slickers had logged perhaps 500 hours on America's airwaves by the time his group became the house band on CBS' *Arkansas Traveler*, on Oct. 21, 1942. Twelve days later their own show, *Furlough Fun*, premiered on NBC's West Coast stations. Though there was nothing remarkable about either show—at the time, or in retrospect—Spike and company did double duty for two seasons, appearing on both programs through June 1944.

Arkansas Traveler, which moved to NBC early in 1943 as *The Bob Burns Show*, was a comedy-variety show built around the philosophical hillbilly image "Bazooka" Burns had cultivated on *Kraft Music Hall*. Jones'

171

cowbells were right in tune. The program was broadcast live to the East Coast in the afternoon, followed by a later show for the West—a common practice before the advent of tape.

The typical program consisted of a homespun Burns monologue, a Slicker rendition, a Lifebuoy commercial by the silver-tongued Dick Lane, a comedy skit, a dialogue with "Cousin Luther" (banjoist Luther Roundtree) and a public service announcement for war bonds or fat recycling. Burns' incessant jokes about the war were as predictable as the commercials, but any joke about the enemy—no matter how feeble—was greeted with appreciative laughter.

Rehearsals for the show were less predictable, at least when a new number was being introduced. "Spike had decided to use harp on 'Holiday for Strings.' It was the first time he had ever used harp and none of his arrangers had ever written for the instrument. So they needed someone who could improvise a harp part from a guitar chord sheet," recalled Charlotte Tinsley. "When I went to the rehearsal, they gave me a sheet of music which just said 'ad-lib' all over it."

Furlough Fun gave the individual members of the band a chance to shine. Beau Lee, a more than capable vocalist, was frequently called out from behind the drums to sing such songs as "I Want a Girl (Just Like the Girl That Married Dear Old Dad)." Country Washburne sang his own "One Dozen Roses" and other numbers; Del Porter and the Nilsson Twins were heard regularly. Herman Crone did many of the arrangements.

Jones, who left the master of ceremonies job to "femmcee" Beryl Wallace and the comedy to George Riley, made little attempt to turn the spotlight on himself. Wallace, a beauteous Earl Carroll showgirl, interviewed servicemen who had seen active duty; a cash prize would be awarded to the winner of a quiz, such as "How many raspberries were there in 'Der Fuehrer's Face'?"

The Slickers made frequent guest appearances on *Kraft Music Hall* and other programs during the war. They were often part of the line-up on *Command Performance*, recorded at CBS for Armed Forces Radio Service. The shows—which they performed gratis for the war effort, along with Hollywood's most popular entertainers—were never heard by the general public. "Those were the biggest thing we ever did," recalled writer Eddie Brandt. "Five hundred celebrities tripping over each other."

The Slickers held their own amidst the top talent in town. "Jimmy Durante loved the band," said Hersh Ratliff. "He'd come over and crack his jokes to see if they would go over. 'If I can make you guys laugh,' he

John Stanley, Bob "Bazooka" Burns, Country Washburne, Carl Grayson, Spike and Luther Roundtree on Burns' radio show, late 1942 or early 1943. (*Warren Dexter*)

said, 'I can make anybody laugh.' "

At the conclusion of the band's USO tour in the fall of 1944, they appeared on BBC Radio in *The Chamber Music Society of Lower Regent Street*. The program was well-received, but the Slickers were not entirely the Brits' cup of tea; they were forced to substitute a tuba note for the raspberry on "Der Fuehrer's Face."

Jones' special blend of music and chaos was more appreciated on the home front, where the band turned up on NBC's *Chase and Sanborn Program* as a 1945 summer replacement for Edgar Bergen and Charlie McCarthy. However, they played second fiddle to singer-actress Frances Langford, as well as the weekly guest star.

The show was broadcast from a different California service hospital each Sunday, catering to an audience of "fellows from your hometown and mine." Nearly all comedy programs followed the same pattern during World War II. But while the idea was patriotic, the shows were so heavily geared toward servicemen they almost always suffered as a result.

The enterprise was not without its rewards. "We traveled by bus when we did the shows," recalled Eddie Brandt. "We had such great fun. Once we spent a whole day riding on a bus with Groucho Marx—he brought his little four-string guitar and he sang songs all the way there."

Jones was heard regularly on the air—not so much as a comedian, but as a straightman for Langford. A typical exchange:

SPIKE: What would you like me and the Slickers to play next?
FRANCES: Why, Spike, how wonderful.
SPIKE: That we're going to play?
FRANCES: That I have a choice.
SPIKE: I take it you'd like something quiet.
FRANCES: Can you play something quiet?
SPIKE: Anything you suggest.
FRANCES: Then why don't you play pinochle?

There was little rapport between Jones and Langford, whom he had backed on a number of Decca records. "You didn't have the time to get to know people in those days. I was traveling so much, I didn't do that bit," recalled Langford, who would arrive the day of the show and do a quick rehearsal before the program. "The band played good music," she observed, "but after you saw them once or twice, that was it. The audience liked it, but they only saw it once."

By the time the series came to an end in late summer, Jones had reached a decision. He was tired of being someone else's straightman. He desired to star in his own radio program, and he wanted to depart from the variety format. He and his manager, Ralph Wonders, met with a young comedy writer named Charlie Isaacs that fall and discussed ideas for *The Spike Jones Show.*

The improbable result was a situation comedy which took place on the college campus of Subnormal Normal, and in an adjacent malt shop. Spike would play a perennial sophomore, the proprietor of the malt shop; Carl Grayson was cast as a professor and Red Ingle as a big dumb football player, with Ann Rutherford and Mabel Todd as coeds.

"Spike wanted a college premise. I guess he felt the City Slickers should be of the college age, and appeal to that level. I'm sure that's how it came about," recalled Isaacs. "Even though he was on solid ground with his music, Spike wanted to have a semi-storyline. But it was a very

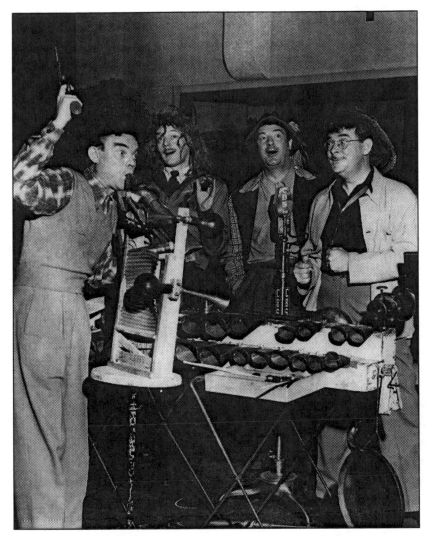

Spike rehearses with Carl Grayson, Dick Morgan and Red Ingle for a guest appearance at CBS, circa 1944. (*Larry Edmunds Bookshop*)

short script and he had a number of things he wanted to do musically.

"We cut exposition to the bone. You had to take what would be a well-developed scene...suddenly you're chopping like hell, because you're also trying to make room for music...and Spike wanted to talk funny, he wanted funny lines. It was like writing for Oscar Levant: he would keep yelling, 'Give me more lines.' I told Levant, 'You're doing a five-minute concerto.' He said, 'To hell with the concerto, I'll have more jokes.' "

Jones also allowed his co-stars to have their share of the laughs, as indicated by a scripted exchange between Jones and Todd:

MABEL: I always dreamed of meeting a man who was tall, dark and handsome.

SPIKE: But I'm not tall, dark and handsome.

MABEL: So if I can't get filet mignon, I take hamburger.

SPIKE: Mabel, isn't there anyone else on campus you like?

MABEL: Well, there's Red Bagle.

SPIKE: You mean the big fullback?

MABEL: Yeah. We broke up but I sorta like him…I like to run my hand over his head and feel the muscles.

The audition show was broadcast on NBC in November 1945. Despite the success of *Kay Kyser's College of Musical Knowledge*—the apparent inspiration—Jones' pilot failed to make the grade with prospective sponsors. Isaacs, who went on to write for almost every comedian in Hollywood, recalled it as "a jokey-joke kind of show," but not a fiasco. "I remember getting laughs. Ralph and Spike were very happy afterwards; everybody seemed to like it. We were all very elated, because Spike was happy."

Before long, Jones was back on the air. His Other Orchestra—early incarnations of which were heard on both *Furlough Fun* and *Chase and Sanborn*—broadcast over West Coast network Mutual-Don Lee from the Trocadero, throughout the spring of 1946. *Spike's at the Troc* featured Jimmy Cassidy and Helen Grayco on vocals, offering tunes like "September Song" and "E-Bop-O-Lee-Bop" until they wore thin. When the union insisted his broadcasts were "commercial" and the sidemen had to be paid accordingly, Jones could no longer afford to indulge himself.

Spike and his City Slickers resurfaced on radio 17 months later, in the fall of 1947, as the stars of a CBS variety show better suited to them than their ill-fated situation comedy. They shared the microphone with Columbia recording artist Dorothy Shay—the Florida-born "Park Avenue Hillbillie"—and the usual guest star, but the accent was on funny, and the focus was on them.

Spotlight Revue, sponsored by Coca-Cola and informally dubbed *The Coke Show*, was packaged not by the sponsor or the ad agency—as was then common—but by Jones' booking agency, the all-powerful Music Corporation of America. "MCA got Spike *The Coke Show*. That's why he left General Artists. They couldn't get him a radio show; they weren't

Tommy Dorsey matches wits with Spike on *Music America Loves Best,* NBC, 1945.

strong enough," stated Eddie Brandt. "MCA owned their own shows in those days. They would have him, the writers; they owned everybody on the show."

The contrivance was not uninspired. "Dorothy Shay was a perfect partner for Spike. You couldn't get a better combination," said Brandt. "Frances Langford was kind of aloof when we did *Chase and Sanborn*— like it was below her dignity. Shay was easier to get along with. We spent a lot of time with her and got to know her; she was more a part of the whole thing."

The program, which aired on Armed Forces Radio in an abbreviated version, was heard on Friday nights until January 1949. The series then switched to Sundays, becoming *The Spike Jones Show* in the process. The weekly event was unique by any name in that it traveled with the band, broadcasting from wherever *The Musical Depreciation Revue* was booked.

"They'd work the dates like a wheel," explained clarinetist Jack Golly. "They'd go into, say, Chicago, and then the first week they'd go out to Wisconsin, and the second week to Michigan—and then they'd come back into Chicago for the radio show. After they covered all those states, then they'd maybe move to Atlanta, or they'd move out to Baltimore, and do it from those locations."

Because the schedule was dictated by the lucrative road show, getting the series on the air week after week called for substantially more advance planning than most broadcasts required. "The writers would be part of the advance crew. They'd set up, in Boston or Atlanta or wherever we were going to originate the show. They'd meet with the guest star a day or two early. We'd start rehearsals for *The Coke Show* at 10 a.m. Sunday, and go right up to showtime; the show was done at 4 p.m. Eastern time. Then we'd come back at 8 or 8:30 and do the stage show," recalled Eddie Metcalfe.

"In the bigger cities, we'd do the radio show in a studio, where they had a seating capacity for an audience," said Golly. "You'd go to a smaller town—even Atlanta wasn't very big then—Spike would have to do the show from the auditorium, where we did the *Musical Depreciation Revue*."

The October 3, 1947 premiere offered humorist Victor Borge, who savaged "Clair de Lune" on the piano, Doodles Weaver and a certain broken-down race horse, a pair of numbers by the Big Band—a throwback to the Other Orchestra—and two by Dorothy Shay. It also introduced the public at large to a new comedian named Spike Jones.

Writer-producer Hal Fimberg's script gave him precious little to work with, but from the outset Jones saw the program as an unprecedented opportunity. As the show's emcee, he was entitled to deliver the punchlines on a weekly basis—with Shay as his straightwoman. If Oscar Levant could be funny, so could Jones:

SPIKE: Our clarinet player is making a fortune on something he invented. It's a clarinet shaped like a fish with a ladder on it.

DOROTHY: A clarinet shaped like a fish with a ladder on it?

SPIKE: Sure, for musicians who like to run up the scale.

DOROTHY: That's silly. You should put your money into something practical.

SPIKE: I have, Dorothy. Bubble gum. It's a growing business.

DOROTHY: Spike Jones Bubble Gum. That sounds good.

SPIKE: And my gum will have movie stars' pictures on it. Imagine, a guy blows a bubble and there's Lana Turner's face in front of his.

DOROTHY: What happens to Lana when the bubble bursts?

SPIKE: She can't tear herself away from his lips.

The jokes were better the second season, with Eddie Maxwell and Eddie Brandt (who generally worked as a team) and Jay Sommers at the typewriters. Jones' material was carefully tailored: "Incidentally, if you noticed that last Sunday there was an instrument missing from my band, it really wasn't my fault. During rehearsal Jack Benny sneaked in from next door and stole my washboard to do Ronald Colman's laundry."

By this time writers for other comedians were returning the name-dropping favor, knowing the reference was guaranteed to get a laugh. One night on *The Fred Allen Show*, after Senator Claghorn (Kenny Delmar) told Allen he was developing a giant magnet that would lift the Iron Curtain, Allen mused, "The senator had better be careful with that magnet. He'll pull Spike Jones off the air."

The writing sessions for Jones' radio program were "beyond description," according to Eddie Maxwell. "Luckily we all got along together well, and Spike seemed to instill the same sense of his humor in all of us, so it was a ball.

"We had to fit the material to the guest stars, but we'd always make them the funny guys. They'd sometimes sit in with us, but rarely would you find any of them who were equipped to improve anything," said Maxwell. "Spike would always offer ideas and gags. If the show was good he participated in the credit; if the show was lousy, we heard about it."

Jones rarely uttered a word that wasn't in the script. "I remember one time he ad-libbed," said George Rock. "It was one of the most un-funny things I ever heard. I think it was the only time he did, all the time I was with him. [Country singer] Eddy Arnold, who was known as the Tennessee Plowboy in those days, was on the show. Eddy said something

Will the real Peter Lorre please stand up and sing "My Old Flame"? Paul Frees,
Spike and the genuine article on *The Spotlight Revue*, 1948. (*Skip Craig*)

to him ad-lib so Spike called him 'Plowhead.' That's about as funny as it
got. You can see what his ad-lib abilities were."

The emergence of Spike as a funnyman was less a conceit than a
public relations move. He projected that image more so on radio than
any other media. It was not an easy step for someone as microphone-shy
as Jones, who had relied largely on Carl Grayson to announce the stage
shows up until his departure from the band the year before.

The bandleader had no shortage of comedians in his organization at
this point—notably Doodles Weaver, Freddy Morgan and Earl Bennett,
in the character of Sir Frederick Gas. But the program was simply too
good a vehicle for him, to leave matters entirely in their capable hands.

"He had to put himself before the public. There was no point in
him sitting back and letting someone else get all the kudos. He wanted
people to think he had all the talent, and I guess he obviously did," observed Rock.

"Spike was so uptight; he was always trying to be a Jack Benny. Spike
would try and get the writers to copy lines from Benny, and Fred Allen—
and of course when he would read 'em, nothing would happen," asserted

Jack Golly. "Benny could turn around and look at the audience and get a laugh. Spike always wanted to be able to do that, and he just couldn't do it.

"He always thought he could get so much out of a line. And he was probably the least talented of anybody. The guys that were funny were Freddy and Gas. Hell, they'd walk on the stage and the crowd would start to laugh, before they even said anything. Freddy was a genius when it came to dialect," said Golly.

"Jones had a bit—it was going to be Freddy, myself and him," recalled Earl Bennett. "I knew it wasn't working, and I think way down in his guts he knew it wasn't working. I was so green and naïve, I said, 'You know, Spike, this'll be a lot funnier if you just let Freddy and I do it.' And he said, 'Gas, I'm the star.' "

Despite Jones' efforts, Doodles Weaver was the show's top comic. As Professor Feetlebaum, he delighted audiences by screwing up the words of romantic ballads ("When April showers…she never closes the curtain") and interpolated all manner of gibberish, non sequiturs and throwaway jokes: "Speaking of birds, I was once arrested for feeding pigeons. Someone said, 'How can you be arrested for feeding pigeons?' I said, 'Well, I was feeding them to my brother.' "

Music was as essential to *The Coke Show* as comedy. The City Slickers would get the program rolling with an old standard like "Yes, Sir, That's My Baby" or "Way Down Yonder in New Orleans," played at breakneck speed. The openers were arranged by Jack Golly, who was featured with Dick Gardner on an assortment of woodwinds.

"The arrangements were all the same pattern. You'd open and then there'd be a funny chorus in the middle. For that funny chorus—anything I wanted, I could go out and buy," recalled Golly. "One day, I said, 'I'd sure like to have an E Flat clarinet.' And Spike said, 'Just go buy one.' He also bought us a bass sax. We'd get to the special chorus and Gardner and I would pick up these dumb horns and play the hell out of 'em."

The City Slickers demonstrated their versatility by making up the core of the show's big band. Eddie Pripps, musical director of the stage *Revue,* conducted the orchestra; he also traveled ahead of the unit, lining up talent to augment Jones' regular sidemen.

"We would add men wherever we were. In New Orleans, we added Al Hirt on second trumpet; he was just a local trumpet player. In New York, we used Billy Butterfield and Sammy Spear on trumpet, all the time we did the show there. We'd add two trumpets, two trombones, two

Jerry Colonna evidently forgot to read the fine print in his contract. Front, from left: Joe Colvin, Jones, Colonna, Earl Bennett and Joe Siracusa. Back: Roger Donley, Jack Golly, Doodles Weaver (kneeling), Dick Gardner, Dick Morgan, Freddy Morgan and Doc Birdbath (partly hidden). (*Ted Hering*)

saxophones; we had our own rhythm section," recalled George Rock.

"We had the big orchestra onstage, we'd play the opening theme; then during the announcement, we'd filter out the orchestra and come down to the Slicker setup," explained Joe Siracusa. "We'd go to our opening number, then we'd go back to the big band and play for Frank Sinatra, or whoever the guest was. It's hard to realize now, but we were playing with the biggest stars in the business."

The size of the budget in no way determined the magnitude of the guest list. "I think we paid $800 for Peter Lorre, $1,000 for Sinatra, $1,500 maybe for Gene Kelly. The whole show maybe had a $5,000 budget," said Eddie Brandt. "All those big stars, they loved doing *The Spike Jones Show*. They all wanted to get into a City Slicker number with Spike."

Some were happier to be there than others. "Don Ameche was warm, friendly, all the guys in the band loved him," recalled Earl Bennett. "You just wanted to hug the guy he was so great, how he could relate to people, even if you were nothing but sidemen. As compared to, say, Marlene Dietrich, who acted like they'd asked her to walk hip-deep in human excrement, by just being on stage with us."

Peter Lorre, whose film portrayals of villains and psychopaths obscured his gift for comedy, headlined one of the more memorable shows in the series. "We have a lot in common," the actor told Jones on the broadcast. "What you do to music, I do to people." Paul Frees reprised his imitation of Lorre singing "My Old Flame," after which Lorre tried to imitate Frees imitating him. After the show, he dryly told the impressionist: "You're too difficult to follow. I'm never going to work with you again."

"Lorre was in the dressing room one day, he was practicing Peter Lorre," said Eddie Brandt. "He didn't sound like Lorre anymore because everyone was so used to the mimics, how they exaggerated him. He sounded very feeble next to Paul." Earl Bennett concurred: "Frees amplified and expanded on Lorre's character and voice; it was a beautiful caricature. Frees was a consummate artist."

Bennett was modest in his assessment, however, according to Joe Siracusa. "Earl did 'My Old Flame' in *The Musical Depreciation Revue* for years. He made a disemboweled head of a woman, with the hair shooting out, and a white face, as a prop; he added another dimension to it on stage. He did it visually, and outdid Peter Lorre and Paul Frees."

While the emphasis in radio was necessarily on aural humor, the Slickers still put on a highly visual show. A great number of gags were pulled solely for the benefit of the studio audience. "If the situation called for pouring a glass of water on the stage, instead of a glass I'd take a five-gallon Sparkletts bottle and get water all over the place," said Siracusa, who served as sound effects man.

"There was a routine with Kirk Douglas on one show, where the guys were playing crooks. They rush into the room and he says, 'Okay, put the chair against the door, put the bed...put the couch...'—I literally did all that on the stage. I got as much furniture as I could and moved it. He says, 'We forgot the guy outside. Move the furniture.' So I took and moved the furniture again.

"Everything had a visual impact—the clothes we wore, the instruments we played, the way it was executed. We had to be very careful, doing radio, to make use of the visual gags in the proper spots," observed Siracusa. "If a guy walked in during a line, like Sir Frederick Gas

Frankie Little and Junior Martin join Spike and Doodles Weaver at a promotional event for Jones' Coke-sponsored radio show. (*Ted Hering*)

with his wild hair or George Rock with his kiddie outfit, or Dick Morgan with his 'thirsty camel' face, they'd disrupt the whole routine—so they had to time their entrances with the laughs. You can still hear surges of laughter on some of the shows, where somebody made an entrance during a line."

Eddie Brandt concurred. "A lot of our radio stuff, people must've wondered at home—what the hell was that big laugh? It would be a guy coming out in a wig or a girl's outfit. We did a lot of TV things on radio, but everybody did," noted Brandt. "There would be a five-minute laugh when Jack Benny warmed up his Maxwell; it was Mel Blanc doing all these crazy faces [for the studio audience] and nobody at home saw it."

As visual as the Slickers were, it was their aptitude for sound effects that captured the interest of Basil Rathbone when he appeared on Jones' program. The actor was treated to a special demonstration neither seen nor heard by the listening audience.

"Dick Morgan was a heavy eater; naturally, sometimes he'd have gas. He could release the gas at the most opportune or inopportune times," recalled Siracusa. "Rathbone was on the show, and he was so impressed with all of us and the funny noises we made. So George Rock said, 'That's nothing. Go ahead, show him, Dick.' And Dick raised his leg and released a torrent on cue."

Coca-Cola executives, who were not treated to Morgan's command performance, were displeased with the noise that *did* go out over the air. In the spring of 1949, the sponsor asked the band to "tone down" its raucous antics, which corporate officers apparently found inappropriate for their Sunday time slot. "Spike vehemently refused to compromise," mused Eddie Metcalfe, who recalled that Jones was soon replaced with Percy Faith and his Orchestra.

While the bandleader would no doubt like to have remained on the air, he was a bit too independent—and too forward-thinking—for a long-term relationship with the soft drink company. "It was awfully hard for him to make a decision to accept a sponsor for his show," said Siracusa, "because he ordinarily did not like to tie himself down to one product or one sponsor…something you could not release yourself from to go on to something else."

Jones made dozens of guest appearances, with and without the sound minds and bodies of his bandsmen, on local and network radio shows throughout the '40s and '50s. On *Music America Loves Best,* he played his somewhat less than sentimental version of "I'm Getting Sentimental Over You"—with Tommy Dorsey joining in on trombone. He backed Bing Crosby on "Love in Bloom" on Crosby's *Philco Radio Time* and turned up, sans Slickers, on *Ellery Queen* and *People Are Funny.*

The bandleader's most memorable guest shot came on *Truth or Consequences* late in 1948. Midway through the program, host Ralph Edwards told a Mrs. Andrews of Los Angeles, "For your consequence tonight we want you to sing 'Glow-Worm.' Behind the curtain we have a full orchestra to accompany you." He then introduced her to the conductor, a bearded gentleman by the name of Dr. Spikuro Jonesivini.

The contestant revealed a lush operatic voice as she began: "When the night falls si-lent-ly, the night falls si-lent-ly…"

Honk! Crash! Honkhonkhonk! Bang! Bang! Bang! Honkhonkhonk!

Mrs. Andrews continued gamely, in spite of the commotion. "Wait a minute!" screamed the host. "WAIT A MIIINUUUTE! WAAAIT A MIIINUUUUTE! WHAT'S GOING ON? WHAT IS GOING ON?!"

Edwards interrupted the rendition to reveal the conductor's true identity. "You were expecting maybe Toscanini?" quipped Jones. Following an encore of "The Glow-Worm," he reminded the host that Edwards was to guest on his show the following week. "I can't sing and I can't play an instrument," protested the host. "What can you do with me on your show?"

Jones chuckled. "Naive, isn't he?"

In 1951, the bandleader made another attempt at a weekly radio series. *Spike Jones' Symphony Hall* combined commentary on classical music by Jones, along with *The Coke Show*'s Roundtable Discussion segment, which had Dick Morgan, Earl Bennett and Freddy Morgan displaying their ignorance about the subject. For the audition record writer-director Jay Sommers borrowed some of his own jokes from the 1949 season, with good reason—he couldn't top them:

SPIKE: Doctor Morgan, what do you think of Tchaikovsky?
DICK: I think it's one of the finest breakfast foods on the market.

Jones' final attempt at radio was *Use Your Head* (1955), a quiz show which would have featured George Rock and other members of the band, with Spike as master of ceremonies. But by the early '50s radio found caught itself in the grip of radical upheaval and transition, as profit-minded advertisers began to abandon the medium for television; as a result, neither of Jones' last efforts made it beyond the audition or pilot stage.

Vantage Point: Joe Siracusa
Drums, 1946–1952

I've been a City Slicker all my life. I played a washboard when I was 12; I had a group called Doggie Joe and his Pups and I was doing comedy things with kazoos, frying pans and tin cans. So I think it was all predestined that I should end up with Spike Jones. Some guys wanted to be with Tommy Dorsey; I always wanted to be with Spike.

During the war I was in the army band, and they had a big contest. I was always clowning around on the stage; somebody said, "There's a novelty band classification, why don't you get a group together and do something?" Spike's records were becoming popular. I did "Sheik of Araby" and we did a takeoff on "Anvil Chorus," with the three of us doing sound effects. We won the contest.

After I got back to Cleveland, people kept saying, "You should be with Spike Jones." I composed a letter to Spike, and told him of my background; I said, "I'm willing to wager I can reproduce 75% of your sound effects, vocally, mechanically or musically." A month later, I got a handwritten card: "Dear Joe, we'll be in Cleveland in June [1946]. Looking forward to seeing and hearing you then. Sincerely, Spike Jones."

That was the first time I saw him perform, at the RKO Palace Theatre. I had only heard them on record. I went backstage; he was getting ready to go on. When he met people for the first time, he never got excited or showed any emotion. I said, "You had a great show out there." He said, "Yeah, nice to meet you. Appreciate your coming back." He shook hands and went onstage.

I said, "That's Spike Jones? Big deal." That night the secretary called and apologized: "Spike didn't remember who you were. He'd like to see you again." I went down and saw the show again, then went backstage. I was nervous. He put me at ease immediately; he said, "Relax. You're among friends."

I sang "Chloe" and "Sheik of Araby" and did some glugs for him. This was Red Ingle's last tour with the band. Spike was looking for somebody to understudy him. I couldn't join then; Spike had a commitment to his present drummer [Dick Peterson] and I was from a different local.

I moved to California and deposited my card in the union. He had nothing to lose; I was taking a gamble. One day Spike called and said, "We're going to rehearse at the Pasadena Civic Auditorium." I sat in with the band for the first time. There wasn't any music. I played the show for memory; I knew every number he had. Then he said, "We're playing a dance job at the Hotel Del Coronado" [San Diego]. They played a couple hours of dancing, then put on a show. I played a set and Spike said, "You've got the job." And that was my audition.

We were going on this tour, to try out *The Musical Depreciation Revue*. He took it out for 30 days, doing one-nighters. He said, "What kind of salary do you want?" I said, "You've been honest with me so far; whatever you say is fine." He said, "I'll give you $150 a week and this month will be your tryout. If you work out, I'll give you $200 and make it retroactive."

Now we go on this tour. I had never played a two-and-a-half hour show, and there was no music. If there's anything I can play, it's vaudeville. We played the first night, and before Spike dismissed the band he said, "Joe, you got the job, and you got the raise." That was my niche in life—I knew it, and he knew it.

To me, it was as natural as breathing to be in that band. My high school band director came to the show in Cleveland: "You're playing just like you did in school." I said, "Yeah, only now I'm getting paid." I didn't have to adjust my thinking at all.

I was able to express myself creatively with Spike. He would draw that creativity from you, just by the way he worked. I sat in on all the story sessions; I'm not a writer but I could think of gags and funny bits. I knew how to utilize his effects and work them into the arrangements. Spike used to kid me; he'd ask me what I thought of an idea and I'd say, "That's great." He'd say, "What am I asking you for? You're as crazy as I am."

I'd always carry my sketch pad with me. Spike would say, "If you ever get an idea, don't hesitate. Even if it's two o'clock in the morning, you come in and we'll talk about it." We worked on a City Slickerland before there was ever a Disneyland. When we were in Tucson or Phoenix we were looking at miniature train rides, with the idea of a park. I had my sketch pad; I was thinking of different rides. It became too big a project.

Once he said, "Hey, Joe, what about a one-man band? Think about it."

Joe Siracusa horns in on Helen Grayco's drum solo.

So I concocted this little array of instruments. I wore a football helmet with a gong. I'd shake my head and the gong would sound; I'd flop my ears and the castanets would play, then I'd blow the train whistle and the smoke would come out of my ears. I'd have the bulb under my arm for the water coming out of the ears. With the kazoo I'd play "Bye Bye Blues" and I'd keep going faster and faster—going crazy, so to speak—then two guys in white coats would come out and drag me off stage.

Then there was the two-headed drummer. I think it was something Spike had seen on *The Jack Benny Show* one time. The curtain would open and you'd see a drummer playing with two heads. Spike would say something like, "I was going to hire a man with three heads but I didn't think you would believe it."

Siracusa supplies glugs for "Hawaiian War Chant" in a turn at the mic, with Doc Birdbath, Dick Gardner and Spike joining in the fun. (*Ted Hering*)

The head was made out of papier mâché by Earl Bennett, who was an accomplished artist and sculptor. Unbeknownst to Spike, when we were in San Francisco I took the head down to the basement and drilled a hole through it. I inserted a rubber tube through the head, coming to the lips.

One night Spike introduced me on the stage, and I stood up with a cigarette. I took a drag on one head and the smoke came out of the other head. Then I reversed it; I took a drag on the second head, and smoke came out of the first head. Then I said, "And now, the *hard* way"—I took a drag on the cigarette and Roger Donley, the bass player, stood up and the smoke came out of his mouth.

They weren't just gags for the sake of the gag; they were well thought out. But as much as I liked to have fun, I always had an awareness—not to be overbearing, or disruptive—it was always in the spirit of the thing. I didn't do it to embarrass anyone, just to have fun.

The first gag I ever pulled, I didn't know Spike that well; I'd only been in the band a short time. George Rock played a number called "Minka." Spike would conduct a couple of chords and George would play a couple of cadenzas. Then Spike would run up and play the drums to George's trumpet solo.

One night, I took a chance. I knew Spike had a sense of humor, but I didn't know how far it would go. I sawed the drumsticks almost in half.

When Spike hit the drum, the sticks broke—but he was so fast, he picked up the other pair of sticks, and had the cowbell right in tempo. He flipped the sticks at me; he was muttering things under his breath but he was kidding about it. So that started it—I knew he could take a joke. From then on, it was every man for himself…

Spike kept abreast of everything topical. He was constantly listening to radio, he always had his finger on the pulse of what was happening, musically or news. If a record came out like "Riders in the Sky," before it was released to the public almost, we'd have an arrangement on it, and be doing it. Which is the way to be on top of those things.

The timing was so important in the show. Jack Teagarden, probably one of the greatest trombone players of all time, sat in with the band once. We had an arrangement of "Glow-Worm," where we played it very legitimately at first, where the gal sang. Then Dick Morgan came and sang with her, then we'd go into a fast verse—we'd double the time. And Jack Teagarden took a breath—took a breath—took a breath. He never caught up with us; he never played a note…

Spike could be very sarcastic; there were times when he could be vicious. But by the same token, he had a lot of self control. He was very careful about what he said on the stage—there was good reason for it. We were playing someplace; there was a girl about the sixth row, with binoculars, looking up at the stage. So Spike kiddingly said, "Hey, honey, what are you looking for? Blackheads?"

After the show there was a call for Spike at the hotel. He wasn't there so I took it. The caller says, "That was my daughter who had the binoculars at the show. She just got out of the hospital; she had an operation and doesn't see well. I thought it was very poor taste of Mr. Jones." Spike called and apologized, and also sent the young lady an RCA Victor record player and a set of records.

He would never do that knowingly. We were playing Chicago, and there was a sergeant sitting in the front row—asleep. Here was a perfect spot for a gag. Spike didn't say a word. Later, he said, "All I have to do is make some crack—this guy is probably some hero from Japan." He had to control himself not to say anything. He became very conscious and aware of people's feelings.

We were playing in Columbus, Ohio, and a woman came backstage with her son who was studying piano and happened to be blind. We heard him play; she was obviously looking to advance his studies. So I said, 'Yeah, we'll all pitch in…" Spike said, "Joe, you cannot cure all the ills of the world by yourself." He said, "It's already been taken care of, anonymously. I made a generous contribution, but no publicity. Can you imagine if it gets out? We'll get to Detroit, there'll be 14 kids there…

Spike set me up with a workshop. I had a complete workshop in my home, and a paint shop. When we did "Hawaiian War Chant" in the blackout, I painted all the instruments with fluorescent paint. The gentlemen wore white gloves; it looked like the instruments were floating in the air.

We would do a routine with a man with four arms playing the drums. Spike wore a black suit with chartreuse checks. My wife Eleanor designed a set of sleeves for me that matched his plaid; during the blackout, Spike would be playing a set of drums that were outlined in florescent paint. He would start playing first with one hand, then the second hand; in the meantime, I'd sneak behind him, covered with a black cloth, and suddenly a third hand would appear playing, and suddenly a fourth hand.

Just before I left the band, I created a harp that could pop popcorn. You could shoot arrows off the strings; it had a Coke dispenser, it shot ping pong balls and it squirted water. It also played a couple of notes.

Spike's band was originally a funny *sounding* group. They were funny maybe as far as costume, but they weren't a visual act—of course, that was before television, so a lot of groups weren't visual. When we got into the stage aspect of it, it was strange how so much of it came from within the group. It's not like we had a bunch of outside writers, and guys developing visual gags for him—a lot of it came from within. We all worked on the visual aspect of "Hawaiian War Chant," we all contributed.

The rapport of the band was excellent. But we were a close-knit group. The other acts were outsiders until they broke into our group. Some worked in nicely, but there were a couple of acts we didn't cotton to; they weren't part of our group. The City Slickers were like a family, even between tours. I lived with Roger Donley for six years; I spent more time with him during those years then I spent with my wife.

I had an offer from UPA Pictures to get into film editing, a very hard thing to do. I had to quit some time. I couldn't even face Spike; I had to call him on the phone. He made a lot of generous offers to come back. But Ralph Wonders was a businessman; he said, "Drummers are a dime a dozen. We can get somebody tomorrow." And that's when I left the band. If I had talked to Spike face to face, I could have never left.

Movie Madness
The Film Appearances, 1940–1954

Movies were the one medium where Spike Jones failed to make anything but the most fleeting of impressions, the one arena where he did not hold the reins. But it had its compensations. "I can't imagine him putting down anything that would make a buck," observed George Rock. "He was furthering his career and feathering his nest. Anything that would do it, he would do."

It is unlikely Spike ever visualized himself on a motion picture screen in his early years. In fact, he had little respect for the movies in his high school days—or, at any rate, didn't take them too seriously.

"A bunch of the guys from Poly High would go to shows together," remembered Hersh Ratliff, who recalled seeing *Wings* with Spike at the Biltmore Theatre in Los Angeles when the Academy Award-winning film came out in 1927. "We got kicked out of a couple of theatres because of raucous laughter. We always laughed in the sad places; there was weeping or crying on the screen and we'd all break out in laughter. The sad parts weren't dramatic, they were just silly."

A questionnaire filled out by Spike early in his career, at the behest of Metro-Goldwyn-Mayer's publicity department, provides an intriguing glimpse of the man on the subject of movies. Favorite actor? James Cagney. Favorite actress? Theda Bara. Favorite picture? *The Human Comedy.* What would you do if not in pictures? "Sleep." How often do you attend pictures? "No time now." What is your opinion of Hollywood? "Swell, just ignore it."

Jones' own work in motion pictures amounts to no more than a footnote in the annals of movie history. From their inauspicious debut in a series of shorts filmed at Hal Roach Studios, to their largely uninspired fade out at Universal Pictures a dozen years later, Spike and his Slickers

Lois James and Mitzi Uehlein provide the window dressing while Spike makes like his favorite actor, James Cagney, for the band's Soundie, *The Blacksmith Song,* 1942. (*Richard W. Bann*)

left little of an enduring nature on celluloid.

Spike began working in films during his early solo days, behind the scenes and occasionally in front of the camera. His efforts as a freelance studio musician were virtually anonymous, such as his presence on the soundtrack of Hope and Crosby's *Road to Morocco.* He was also the invisible man behind the drums in Victor Young's orchestra on a group of shorts in 1940—the very first Soundies session—providing a backdrop for the music videos of their day.

That same year, the young drummer was briefly seen playing a washboard in the Universal picture, *Give Us Wings.* The movie, which starred the Dead End Kids and Little Tough Guys, was not just a solo gig for Jones, however; the unidentified bandsmen who accompanied him were none other than the City Slickers, a year before they began using the name.

The Slickers made their real entry onto the Hollywood scene in a series of Soundies. Composer Sam Coslow and producer Herbert Moulton engineered the group's official film debut. As production head of Roosevelt-Coslow-Mills, Inc., one of several producers of jukebox movies in the early '40s, Coslow was in constant need of musical talent. Louis Armstrong, Duke Ellington, the Mills Brothers, Hoagy Carmichael and the Hoosier Hot Shots were among the entertainers he pressed into service.

"Spike was working down in a lousy neighborhood in Los Angeles," according to Moulton's partner, Duke Goldstone. "Herb and I took him out of Central Avenue, where he was working in some little club with his schnickelfritz band; we made a deal with him. The first break he had, really, was with us."

Early in 1942, the fledgling bandleader agreed to supply the music for Moulton's low-budget Soundies at union scale, with the Slickers acting as the uncredited house band; they backed a variety of performers, including Dorothy Dandridge (*Blackbird Fantasy*) and William Frawley (*The Yankee Doodler*). In exchange, he and his group were featured in four musical short subjects of their own.

The band's Soundies—*The Blacksmith's Song, The Sheik of Araby, Pass the Biscuits, Mirandy* and *Clink, Clink, Another Drink*—were non-theatrical 16mm shorts made to be shown on the Panoram, a box that swallowed dimes and projected the films on a square screen in juke joints, restaurants and cocktail bars. The machine itself, which employed a rear-projection system, can be seen in *Clink, Clink* displaying sing-along lyrics.

The songs were silly, production values were minimal and the band was not yet in its prime. But the Soundies, still in circulation today on video, furnish a fascinating look at Spike and the Slickers early in their career. *Clink, Clink*—the best of the four shorts—has the distinct plus of Mel Blanc in his first on-camera appearance. In *Pass the Biscuits* Spike can be seen flipping his drumstick in the air and catching it behind his back, a stunt that would become a trademark.

Moulton also added Jones to the talent lineup for "a Hollywood newsreel-type short" featuring columnist Hedda Hopper and other celebrities, but later regretted it. "We asked Spike to come and front the band. He was supposed to introduce people—and, boy, it was just a catastrophe," said Duke Goldstone. "At the very beginning, he wasn't very good as a stand-up front for a band. He was sort of a bashful guy."

When "Der Fuehrer's Face" exploded onto the scene in the fall of 1942, it was naturally translated to film. While the resultant Fox Movietone News short was a performance staged for the camera, it preserved for posterity a better record of the band in action than any of the Soundies, with Carl Grayson's comedic skills particularly well displayed. More importantly, the hit record resulted in two feature film appearances, visually introducing the band to general audiences for the first time.

Producer Mark Hellinger was the first to capitalize on the group's sudden notoriety, signing Jones and company for their feature debut in an all-star Warner Bros. musical which had just gone into production. Spike and his men received $5,000 for one week's work in *Thank Your Lucky Stars*. Unfortunately, the picture made little use of their talents, setting a precedent for the band's work in films.

The 1943 release starred Eddie Cantor in an on-target self-parody as an egotistical radio personality, and featured virtually every star on Warner's contract roster. The Slickers did an energetic rendition of "Hotcha Cornia," with Spike using everything in sight as a percussive instrument—everything, that is, except a goat that reportedly brayed in the key of C. They also provided straight accompaniment for a song performed by Dennis Morgan and Joan Leslie. Extant still photos of the band performing in tuxedos—one of which was published in *The Saturday Evening Post*—appear to be from a deleted sequence, although production records do not indicate such a scene was ever filmed.

Metro-Goldwyn-Mayer's *Meet the People*, which starred Lucille Ball and was loosely based on the radio program *It's Wheeling Steel*, promised the band a generous amount of screen time. Jones and the group were written into a number of sequences, including a comedy routine with Bert Lahr and a hillbilly number with singing comedienne Virginia O'Brien; they were guaranteed five week's work in the spring of 1943. In the end, however, they appeared in only two scenes, notably an elaborate production number called "Schickelgruber" which they rehearsed for 21 days.

The band was costumed in pantaloons and silk stockings for the scene, which featured drummer Beau Lee in an impressive take-off on Mussolini, partnered by a chimpanzee Lee remembered as "an irascible SOB." Recalled trumpeter Don Anderson: "We had to dance this silly dance. I never saw a script; we had a choreographer to teach us the number.

"We had to rehearse with this ape they made up to look like Hitler. At the end of this number, the ape climbs up on Mussolini's shoulders. We're all standing around, I'm in the back with this ape's ass right in my face. We started to do a take and the ape farted."

MGM's legal department never got wind of the chimp's offense. However, they forewarned producer E.Y. Harburg about fouling the air: "In connection with the line, 'But I get—[*shrug*] and you get—[*shrug*]

Beauregard Lee teams up with Jack the chimp for *Meet the People*, a 1944 release.
(*Scott Corbett*)

right in Der Fuehrer's Face,' there must be no 'razzberries' or other vulgar sounds, either in the vocal or musical score."

Jones might have had some reservations about the film, or at least the Slickers' contribution to it. "It's awaiting release right now," he told an interviewer at one point. "But I think they're going to keep it and release us." Despite a reported seven-year contract with MGM, *Meet the People* was the band's first and last film for the studio.

By the time the picture came out, the band had a third feature to their credit. In the spring of 1944, producer Fred Kohlmar hastily signed them to perform "Chloe" in Paramount's *Bring on the Girls*. Spike's wild burlesque of the song, as heard on Armed Forces Radio, had been a winner with the boys overseas; it cried out for visual interpretation. Kohlmar and his crew were more than equal to the task.

The Veronica Lake-Eddie Bracken vehicle was already in mid-production when the Slickers were brought in to film the unscheduled number. The movie's then-extravagant $1.5 million budget permitted not only such whimsical detours, but a lack of professionalism Jones himself would never have tolerated: Lake was late virtually every day; when the "peek-a-boo" blonde did show up, she didn't know her lines.

Kohlmar took full advantage of Technicolor, dressing the band in garish plaid and checkered suits—the forerunner of the crazy outfits they would soon adopt permanently—for their only color film appearance. Red Ingle, the chief perpetrator of mayhem on this occasion, changed costume repeatedly; in the course of his routine, he used an outhouse for a telephone booth, battled a midget fireman, mounted a camel and did a take-off on Ted Lewis.

Spike and the Slickers returned from their USO tour in the fall of 1944 to find themselves in great demand in Hollywood—or so it seemed. They were slated for but did not appear in *Duffy's Tavern,* Paramount's all-star film version of the popular radio program; they were also announced for projects at Disney (presumably *Make Mine Music*) and Columbia, but neither came to pass.

The labor unions were wreaking havoc with production schedules during this time by increasingly hostile means, including an eight-month walkout by studio painters. Although he and his sidemen had barely rested up from their overseas jaunt, Jones that winter decided the time was right to leave town once more. "I think one of the reasons we went on the road," said Hersh Ratliff, "was that Spike had some contracts coming up, but they were voided because of the film strike. We went on the road and he was supposed to do them after he came back."

The fall of 1945 found the City Slickers making two films almost simultaneously. *Breakfast in Hollywood,* a movie version of the morning radio show hosted by Tom Breneman, was an quickie independent production to which the band contributed two numbers. Del Porter sang a song dedicated to Hedda Hopper, while Red Ingle and Judie Manners reprised "Glow Worm." Beulah Bondi, in the nadir of her career, and other veteran character actors carried the plot.

The movie was a patchwork. "We saw nobody. We just worked on an isolated set at General Service Studios. All the Breneman stuff had been shot; he wasn't there. Everybody shot their own numbers and they just worked 'em in," observed Eddie Brandt. "We were all fitted into the picture."

Producer Daniel Dare allotted the band a generous amount of screen time in Paramount's *Ladies' Man*—the most they had received to date—but the Slickers were still relegated to comic relief, once more in support of Eddie Bracken. Spike had dialogue for the first time on screen, and sang a duet with George Rock on a Jule Styne-Sammy Cahn number;

Carl Grayson reprised "Cocktails for Two," and the band went to town on "Holiday for Strings" one more time.

Jones and his men were paid $5,000 a week for seven weeks, plus $2,500 apiece for their arrangements. "Those were the days of everybody stealing the money and running," Eddie Brandt remarked. "You could've done the whole thing in one day's work, in eight or ten hours. But that's how the studios did it; they spread it out over seven weeks."

"All we did was practice every day, and sit around and wait. The band played cards a lot. We used to go over and watch Bob Hope and Bing Crosby shoot pictures," said Brandt. "I was doing all kinds of out-side things for Spike; we conducted business on a lot of things we needed, buying props, booking ahead for tours."

Spike was assigned an idea man and a gag man on the film, along with a prop man who no doubt earned his salary—and was reportedly thrilled to see Jones vacate the premises. Rubber hands, odd-sized cock-tail glasses, imitation daisies and substandard ping pong balls were among the bandleader's requests. Another entry on the wardrobe sheet read like a personal calling card: "Bathing suit and two chicken heads, $125.00."

Dissatisfied with his film efforts to date, Jones and manager Ralph Wonders made attempts to get a project of their own going in 1946. "Ralph talked to me about trying to do a picture with the band; he had an idea he wanted to go with on a movie," recalled Charlie Isaacs, who had written their unsuccessful radio pilot the year before. "I said, 'Well, let me know.' Maybe he couldn't get a development deal; I didn't hear anything further about it." A commitment for three films at RKO Pic-tures was announced that spring, but none materialized.

Variety Girl, the Slickers' third effort for Paramount, and their second for Danny Dare, was filmed in the fall of 1946. This time they negotiated a raise, receiving $10,000 a week for two weeks, plus $500 a day for any en-gagements they were forced to cancel during their stint. The film, yet another all-star hodge podge, was headlined by Hope and Crosby; 15 writers were employed, not counting the gag men assigned to Jones and Hope.

Under the direction of veteran filmmaker George Marshall, Spike and company provided entertainment at a Hollywood party, with the guests—and themselves—ending up in the host's swimming pool. The band backed newcomer Mary Hatcher in the title role; among the Slick-ers participating in the fun were Mickey Katz, and Doodles Weaver in his first appearance with the band.

Hollywood trade paper *Variety* acclaimed the film "a smash comedy hit," but others were far less amused. "Perhaps Paramount was kidding, perhaps it said, let's see if we can put every celebrity on the lot together and still turn out a picture that will bring no credit to any of them," observed Seymour Peck of *PM*.

Though their three Paramount films got decidedly mixed reviews, Jones and his City Slickers came off well, particularly in *Bring on the Girls*. But unlike some of Hollywood's zanier comedians, they did only what they were told to do in movies. "Spike never said one word. As he did through his whole career, he relied on a known talent," stated George Rock. "Our stuff was all scripted and mapped out, bar by bar; it was never ad-libbed. It was done by skilled people. He never had some dummy do something when he could hire a talent to do it."

Indeed, Jones did not rely solely on the studios' judgment when it came to movies. His secret weapons were animation directors Fred "Tex" Avery and Frank Tashlin. "Spike would call them when he got a picture, and put them on salary," said Eddie Brandt. "Avery and Tashlin would just sit and draw gags. He paid them out of his own pocket. They did tons of gags, and he kept them all." What material didn't find its way into the scripts often ended up in Jones' stage revues and TV shows.

Although Rock contended that "Spike didn't balk at being directed" in movies, Brandt remarked, "I don't think they gave him any direction. He just did his number. The director would come in the late afternoon, make a few notes and leave. They marked the floor where the guys had to be for the camera."

Spike threatened to become "a full-fledged movie star" in 1950 when producer Harry Sherman signed him to appear in a picture called *Really, Mr. Greeley*. The bandleader was cast as "the reporter sent west by Horace Greeley when he gave with his famous 'Go West, young man.' Any resemblance to Greeley, the West or a newspaper reporter will be purely hilarious," according to a news item. The band's rendition of "Carmen" was planned as "one of the lowlights" of the film; "Wild Bill Hiccup" was to be another.

The following year it was reported that Tony Owen would produce the film and release it through RKO. A different synopsis was attached: the movie was now "a period piece about a barnstorming entertainer in the days of the early west, and Spike, of course, will play the barnstorming entertainer." Nothing ever came of the project.

Jones announced he was in preparation for another western about the same time, to be titled *Singing Goons*. He planned to make it in Technicolor and supply the Slickers with instruments to match their eyes, for example a blue sax for the blue-eyed saxophonist. "Only one of the boys presented a problem," he reported. "It was quite a job locating a blood-shot accordion." The project, however, was simply a gag—yet another jab at Vaughn Monroe, who had the starring role in Republic's *Singing Guns*.

When Jones' burlesque of "Ill Bacio" was released in 1951, within a few weeks of *Abbott and Costello Meet the Invisible Man*, someone made a suggestion to the bandleader: why not do a comic remake of *The Phantom of the Opera* with Bud and Lou? Spike approached the comedians with the idea, but nothing materialized.

In 1952 Joe Siracusa took Jones' recording of Frank Tashlin's "How the Circus Learned to Smile" to United Productions of America, the animation studio known for the Mister Magoo cartoons. "I had an idea for them to do a cartoon while we did the music and sound effects," recalled Siracusa. "Tashlin was a cartoonist to start with; he was still thinking in those terms. I thought it would make a great animated cartoon. It would have, but Spike and Steve Bosustow, the president of UPA, couldn't come to an agreement on it; there was a conflict of egos between them."

Jones finally returned to films after a seven-year absence when he was written into a picture planned for Abbott and Costello—but not *The Phantom of the Opera*. Universal-International's *Fireman, Save My Child* cast Spike and the Slickers in a role that did not exist in early drafts of the script, a role as a Keystone Cop-like fire station crew that was seemingly perfect for them—although the popular dixieland band, the Firehouse Five Plus Two, might have been a more logical choice.

When Lou Costello collapsed from exhaustion three days before the start of shooting in the fall of 1953, Jones emerged as the star of the film. Producer Howard Christie replaced Bud Abbott with studio contract player Hugh O'Brian and Costello with little-known nightclub comic Buddy Hackett. Director Charles Lamont backed out on the advice of his agent and the reins were taken over by Leslie Goodwins.

Had Costello's illness been the real reason for the team's departure, Universal might simply have postponed the film until he recovered. But his health was not the only factor. "They got into a big fight over who was going to have the television rights," asserted Earl Bennett. "By this time the word had gotten out, 'Get the TV rights'—so Costello and Abbott and Jones went around and around. Spike wouldn't give in and neither would they."

With the money-making comedy team out of the picture—which the studio had originally planned to make in 3-D before they departed—the budget plummeted. Where Abbott and Costello were contracted for $75,000 apiece, Hackett and O'Brian earned $11,000 and $4,250, respectively. Jones was paid $6,000 a week for five weeks, while his sidemen picked up a total of $4,050.

The role of Lt. McGinty of the San Francisco Fire Department required Jones to act funny rather than simply crack jokes, which he did reasonably well for an untrained comic. He also led the band in "The Poet and Peasant Overture" and several other numbers. Freddy Morgan and Earl Bennett pantomimed their way through a substantial amount of footage—so much so in one scene where Bennett's frizzy mop of hair caught fire that Hackett complained, "Who is the comedian in this picture?"

Several scenes featuring the band were trimmed or deleted. "The crap was left in there and the good stuff they cut out. It was a turkey," observed Bennett. "The only thing funny in that picture never made it on film.

"Nobody explained to [pianist] Paul Leu how you slide down a fireman's pole. I guess they figured we all knew. He was the first guy to make it to this pole—it was a full-length thing—and he went *whoosh*. He hit so hard he was numb; he just sat there, he couldn't move. So all the rest of the guys stacked up on top of him. If they'd had a camera on him—that would've been funny."

Newsweek's appraisal of the film as "an old-fashioned, Mack Sennett-type two-reel comedy stretched to the full length of six reels" was right on target. Director Les Goodwins, special effects man Nick Carmona and gag man Eddie Cline—another weapon on Jones' payroll—were all Sennett alumni, with Cline a one-time Keystone Kop.

Though the studio was obliged to hype its one-shot "new team" of O'Brian and Hackett, most of the publicity was centered around Spike and the Slickers. When the movie was released, Jones meticulous record keeping system came in handy; special attention was paid to those cities where the band had been most welcome on their tours. The exploitation packet included a list of Spike's records, and suggested that exhibitors arrange tie-in promotions with local disc jockeys.

Despite rumors that surfaced about Abbott and Costello's dissatis-

Jones and company heat up European movie screens in *Fireman, Save My Child.*

faction with the script, the slapstick comedy was no worse than many of those the team did appear in. Audiences couldn't complain they weren't warned at the outset, either; the film is prefaced with a note reading, "There may or may not be a plot to this story. If you can't find it, don't worry about it."

Jones himself was not happy with the end result, but he knew the studio's concerns were elsewhere. "No matter what you and I think," he told publicist Bill Doll, "Universal swears it's going to make a lot of money."

While there were promises of additional work, and no shortage of self-generated projects, the 1954 release was to be the band's last film appearance. That Jones was frustrated in his efforts to make any kind of impression in the medium is evident from his comments to MCA agent Harry Friedman.

"Although Universal ruined our arrangements completely in *Fireman, Save My Child* by bad editing and bad direction and photography, I know we could do some very funny things if we were handled properly in a motion picture," he told Friedman in a letter. "What I could do on a wide screen with a complete symphony orchestra shouldn't happen to Horace Heidt."

In 1960, Jones came up with a promising notion—a feature film based on the life of W.C. Fields. The idea might well have been inspired by longtime staffer Eddie Cline, who had directed Fields in four pictures and occasionally regaled Spike and his bandsmen with anecdotes about the great comedian.

After discussing the project with various independent producers and finding it a tough sell, Jones dispatched Cline to talk to director Frank Capra. The veteran filmmaker advised Spike "it would be ridiculous to think of a theatrical movie," especially with the restrictions Claude Fields had put on depicting his father's alcoholism.

Jones then pitched an abbreviated version of the idea as a TV special with Jack Oakie as Fields, and three of the comic's surviving contemporaries—Ed Wynn, Eddie Cantor and Buster Keaton—as themselves. Despite the trend toward sensationalism in films, he hoped such a program would "stimulate the movie industry into thinking what a great idea this would be for a picture." But, like so many of Jones' bright ideas, nothing ever came of it.

Keaton was enlisted as a gag writer on another unrealized project the following year. *Rides, Rapes and Rescues*, a tie-in with Spike's Liberty album of the same name, was planned as a satirical documentary that would utilize clips from silent movies. "Whether the theatre patron is a sophisticate or a slob," Jones promised, "after seeing this motion picture, he will say, 'This is the most fun I've ever had with my clothes on.'" Despite the levity, he was serious enough about the project to draw up a detailed budget and commission a script.

When Jones learned that Harold Lloyd was putting together a compilation of his work, he approached the silent film comedian and suggested a meeting would be mutually beneficial. "I think you will agree that a new dimension can be added to your project after hearing some of my musical ideas, both straight and satirical," he proposed. *Harold Lloyd's World of Comedy* went on to become the hit of the Cannes Film Festival without benefit of Spike's ideas, humorous or otherwise.

One last opportunity was dangled before Jones in 1961, only to be snatched away from him. Producer Joe Pasternak considered Spike and his cohorts for a sequence involving a "clown band act" in MGM's circus musical, *Billy Rose's Jumbo,* starring Doris Day and Jimmy Durante. Unfortunately, the scene was deleted during script revisions.

For all his attempts, Jones never translated his success to the big screen. "I don't think they ever captured Spike in movies," observed Eddie Brandt. "The films he did are too mechanical; they're not funny. *Fireman* was the only one—the picture wasn't a hit, but that's really Spike Jones. He didn't have that much acting talent, but they really captured him in that picture, the way Spike was in life," said Brandt.

Vantage Point: Earl Bennett
Comedian, 1947–1954

I studied to be an artist in Kansas City with a guy named Thomas Hart Benton. All I really wanted to do was be a painter. Then came the war. Where a lot of guys lost their lives, I just lost my opportunity to be an artist. The Kansas City Art Institute is where I learned to be an entertainer, to keep from starving to death. I found out if you were an entertaining kind of a guy, you'd get invited to parties and affairs where they'd set up buffet luncheons, and it was free food.

That's how I stayed out of combat—they decided I was worth more as an entertainer than I was an infantryman. When the stuff I offered at the USO clubs was a cut above the others who volunteered, they put me in regular entertainment units. When I got out of the army I was equipped with the material and experience to be a nightclub performer.

An agent got me a job at Bimbo's 365 Club in San Francisco. Bimbo's was one of Spike's favorite restaurants. He came in, Bimbo [Agostino Giuntoli] said he had a guy that would fit in Spike's show…I never dreamt I'd be in a show like that, and wasn't real sure I'd cut it, even when Spike decided he'd put me in the show.

When Spike saw me, he said, "You're going to be Sir Frederick Gas." I said, "Whatever you say, mister. If that's what it takes to get the contract signed, I'm Sir Frederick Gas." Spike thought that was a funny-sounding name; I have no idea where he got it. The character I did in nightclubs and in the army, I did with Spike. I didn't change the character, he just gave it a name.

I soon got the measure of Spike. He had an idea for a bit with a breakaway violin, and he wanted somebody to break it over his head. The stage manager, Les Calvin, took a standard old violin, filled it with balsa wood—it wasn't heavy, but it gave this thing strength—and cut it in two;

then he had a trigger thing, and he had made it with heavy coat hanger wire. It was not designed properly for a breakaway.

The only way you could make that thing come apart was to break it on Spike's head. I kept saying, "I don't want to do this." And he said, "Break the violin over my head." So finally at the right cue, I come up to him and I break this thing…it hurt him, and it terrified me. He stood there, and his eyes were kind of glazed for a minute, and he said, "Where you working next week?"

Being with the show was quite a bit of celebrity for a country boy to handle all at once, and I didn't handle it all that well. When we opened in San Francisco [in 1947], it was a big fanfare, a lot of money spent, and I'm sure Spike eagerly awaited the critic's reviews. The old Curran Theatre on Geary Street was as high as you could get in theatre—Paul Robeson [appeared there], Ethel Barrymore—so when I walked out on that stage with Spike, it was quite a moment for me. It was as good a performance as I ever gave.

The next morning, we all went and got a paper. *The Chronicle* said, "Spike Jones opened at the Curran last night…and there was a very funny man in the show named Sir Frederick Gas." So I'm just ecstatic—it never occurred to me the show didn't get a good review. I was too wrapped up in myself. Spike was having breakfast in the same restaurant I was, and he came by my table and said, "Did you see the review in *The Chronicle*?" I said, "Yeah, wasn't that great?" I was so naive.

Spike said, "Aw, shit!" He turned on his heel and stalked out of the restaurant. I didn't think there was such a thing of being too funny. It's a very crippling thing, to know you can be just so funny, but don't be any funnier than that. In other words, if you really want to make it, don't be funnier than the star…

Spike could be very acerbic. I had to go to a war surplus store in Chicago in the dead of winter and get a ski trooper's parka because I would be wringing wet with sweat backstage. The old timers, they would underdress so they had their street clothes underneath their costumes; they were ready to walk right out the stage door the minute the curtain dropped. It would take me forever to get my hair dried and combed down, get my clothes changed—when I come out, everybody's gone. And I was always by myself. But when I got the parka, I could go right out in the deadly cold wind.

One day they had a big storm, and they piled the snow along the sides of the streets; it was about four feet high. That's where you had to stand and try and get a taxi. And I wasn't having any luck; I was all by myself again. Every headlight that came by, I'd wave at it. Here comes a big car and it pulls up, and it's Spike. I thought, "Thank God." Spike rolled down his window and said, "Whatsa matter, Gas?" I said, "I can't get a taxi to stop." He looked at me for a minute and he said, "Don't worry, the first dog sled that comes by will pick you up," and he drove off and left me there. That's very typical of Spike's humor…but I love the line. It was worth it.

There was a part of Spike that was pretty super. He really wanted to be a pal. He found a restaurant that did such food you couldn't believe— we were in Canada, where at that time a good restaurant wasn't that easy to find. He told everybody to be there at a certain time, and the whole restaurant was turned over to the band; it was one of the best meals. The whole thing was on Spike, and it was a really nice evening.

You get bored doing one-nighters. At the end of a tour…the jokes are almost a tradition. The only joke we got Spike in on one time was actually on Doodles Weaver. We were in New England, and we outnumbered the audience. The people in New England didn't care for us. The folks Down East just walk to a different beat; we were a little bit bodacious.

We were doing a matinee, and there must have been 30 people in the audience. So Spike was going around saying, "Cut this number, cut that number…" I began to notice all these props and things that weren't going to be used.

Weaver had a thing in his act; they would go to a blackout and put a green spot on him. And he'd throw this real wild scraggly black wig over his head and come out in this spot, and the band would play some weird kind of ethereal music. And he'd say, "The Five O'Clock Shaaadow…" And he'd stand there for a minute and say, "I haven't got a finish," and they'd bring the house lights up.

So I thought, we'll give him a finish. The only lights on stage were this green spot. I talked Doc Birdbath into coming out on stage in his long underwear, with a flit gun full of powder. I actually talked Spike into putting on a headless man costume, and he put that on. Les Calvin came out without his teeth; it didn't look like Les. And Frankie Little went across the stage wearing [Junior Martin's] Frankenstein head. We gave something to practically everybody who didn't have to be on the band car.

Dolores Marlin takes a break from acrobatics to straighten out Earl Bennett.

And when Weaver turned around to see what this wild reaction from the audience was, here's the whole stage full of these cavorting creatures he couldn't recognize—what with the green light, and Doc squirting a cloud of talcum powder in the air, the whole thing was very strange. And Weaver admitted later he really thought, just for a few seconds, "I've lost it, I've gone over the edge." But Weaver made a fantastic recovery. He got the tub we dumped the cowbells out of, sat down in it, got Spike's baseball bat, and was rowing himself along singing, "Some enchanted evening..."

That was a touch of surrealism the people in New England expected from Spike. That piece of business got the biggest hand in the whole show. They applauded like crazy; they figured that was part of the show. We had a helluva time getting Spike to put on the headless costume, 'cause he figured we were going to send him out by himself; he thought the joke was going to be on him.

I had Frankie Little squirt Spike with a seltzer gun one time from a balcony, in Texas, when we were doing a show to an empty house. Everybody'd go to the ballgame during the state fair; they wouldn't come to the show. We played to empty houses, so we did the show for our own benefit. Frankie and I would get into a fight up in the balcony, and Spike sprayed us with seltzer. The next day, I got a bottle for Frankie and said, "You squirt him back." We had a big laugh…

I just loved Frankie. He was an absolutely delightful little man. And George Rock and I would get into competitions about who got Frank to ride with them. Just being with Frank was a kick in the head. Rock used to just look at him and break down in tears, 'cause he just got such a kick out of this funny little bitty guy with his little bitty hat…and this little world he'd arranged for himself backstage; he'd drive nails where he could hang hats and things and get at 'em. And this just delighted George.

In Boston, they had a star dressing room on stage level. It was like a hotel room. But it was too small for Spike, with all of his wardrobe changes. He got a kick out of Frank too, because Frank was self-sufficient—he'd always build this little nest for himself.

Spike said, "Frankie, how'd you like to have this dressing room all to yourself?" And Frank was in Seventh Heaven. So he said, "Hey, you guys, c'mere"—to Rock and I—"Come over here and look at my dressing room." We said, "Oh, boy, Frank, that's terrific." He said, "Would you guys like to dress with me?" We said, "Yes!" Anything to be involved with Frank, we'd rush in there. It wasn't any time at all before we were saying, "What can we do to Frank?"

One time I got a big ball of string, and I strung string all around the room like a big cobweb. Then we sat down and shut the lights off, and waited for Frank to come in. And he comes in and gets all entangled in the string, and he's howling. Rock had this high pitched laugh—he'd get so tickled—and Frank was so mad, he'd say, "Shut up, you damned hippopobamus," and George couldn't quit laughing. Frank, all he had to hit him with were some feathers, and this got George tickled. George very nearly died; he damn near laughed himself to death 'cause Frank was hitting him with feathers.

The funny thing about those two, there was almost a love affair.

George would do things like grab Frank and pick him up and put him on his lap at the poker game. And Frank would say, "Aw, c'mon, dammit, c'mon, George," and George would hang onto him. And Frankie loved it. But he had to protest vehemently. And George would say, "Well, give me a kiss and I'll turn you loose." Finally, he'd kiss him on the cheek, and George would put him down.

Frankie was the center of attention. And that's what he loved. In fact, if you didn't give him a bad time, he felt unloved and insecure…

We did a "family show." But we were asked to do late late shows at the Flamingo Hotel in Las Vegas, the third show on a Saturday night at three in the morning. Strictly adults—and a gambling audience is kind of hard to reach anyway. So Spike had seen this bath mat made out of female breasts—it was foam rubber, painted pink with red nipples. And he said, "Gas, I want you to do a bit with this." What he came up with was for me to sit down and take my shoes off, open this suitcase and take this bath mat out, then get up and walk on these rubber tits.

The bit didn't last too long. I hated it. There wasn't anything about it that was funny I could see. To keep from feeling totally empty about it, I started humming an old children's Sunday school song, "Jesus Loves Me, This I Know." Rock got it right away, and he was dying with laughter.

Finally Spike said to Rock, "What's Gas humming when he's out there?" When they told him, he had a fit. He come and grabbed me, he said, "Don't you know I have a reputation…" If he's got a family show, what's he doing with a bath mat like this? I don't think I did anything except make it at least palatable. But when Spike found out what I was doing, he just came down on me. This was his attempt to do an adult kind of thing—and yet it terrified him so, and he was so insecure with it…

Spike had great doubt, great fear of failing on TV. He was so hyper, so worried about his first appearance on TV being successful, the guy had an asthma attack. He was in the wings waiting, very close to air time; he was having a helluva time breathing. I went to Helen and I said, "Spike's not well." I said, "Why don't you get the hell out of this business, take the money and go someplace and buy a little cabin by a stream…he's going to die from this." And she looked at me like I was out of my cotton-picking mind. Spike was gasping for breath all through that show.

I was sort of the band's artist in residence. The Art Institute of Chicago was having one of the first big shows of Van Gogh paintings. It was the talk of the town. So Jones comes to me and says, "Gas, I'd like for you to take me over to the Art Institute." So we went, and I explained as best I could, not being a consummate expert on Van Gogh...

We get to the cornfield, with the crows, which was Van Gogh's last painting; Van Gogh shot himself, as everyone knows, shortly after he finished the painting. And Spike says, "What's the meaning of it?" And I said, "The best thing I can tell you, Spike, is you're pretty much in the same boat. You stay up all hours; you're burning the candle at both ends, you're doing the TV shows, you're doing the stage shows, you're doing one-nighters, you're doing records, you're doing movies..." I said, "You're burning yourself up just like Van Gogh. It's the same kind of fatal genius." He didn't want to hear this; he turned on his heel and walked away. And I realized what I said...hadn't been diplomatic.

Frankie Little, the troupe's morale booster. (*Gloria Gardner*)

After the show, people would come up to us and say, "You guys seem to be having so much fun on stage." There was a love affair going on between the show and the audience that was dampened, frankly, by a manager who was just a little too greedy. Ralph Wonders sapped the life out of the show with all his shenanigans. He would short-count the poor guys who sold programs.

He was dead set against Spike giving any bonuses, even war bonds at Christmas; it started off with $50 bonds, then went down to $25, then just disappeared. Then Spike was told he should seek his own social level. Spike said, "I can't go out to dinner with you guys anymore"—the word had come down to him it wasn't smart to be seen with the sidemen. This is the sort of thing that took the heart out of it. Wonders pushed it to where it wasn't fun anymore.

I was fed up anyway with one-nighters. We had Thanksgiving dinner in Bishop's Cafeteria in Davenport, Iowa, four years in a row. Going down this line and trying to talk the woman out of the end cut on the roast for your Thanksgiving dinner—it just wasn't going anywhere. And the empty seats were beginning to show up. It was the dead of winter in Schenectady, New York [1954], and I had come down with the flu. Spike wasn't very sympathetic with something like that; his attitude was, no excuse was good enough.

They came around and said, "We're going to play a club, and the guy can't cut the nut"—in other words, he couldn't pay Spike's price. I knew George Rock, Billy Barty and others weren't asked to take the cut in salary. And it burned me up that I was one of the people—I wasn't the only one—who was asked. I was so miserable, doing shows with the flu and being away from my wife, who was pregnant then. When it came time to take the cut, I said, "No, I'm not going to do it." Spike was furious.

That night Roger Donley cut my hair, right after the show. He gave me a real close cut. I went to Spike's dressing room—the breach had been established, everybody knew I was leaving—the only thing he could think to do was slam his dressing room door real hard. *Wham!* To show me how angry he was with me. It wasn't a happy finish.

Down the Tube
The Television Shows, 1950–1962

For all Jones' savvy in masterminding his career and merchandising his mad commodity, he was always a little out of sync with television. They could never figure out quite how to make the best use of each other's capabilities, the medium that killed radio and the man who murdered music. But from the outset, Spike was excited and challenged by the possibilities it offered, and he was anxious to give the new-fangled invention a try—at a time when many of his contemporaries were afraid and uncertain.

"There was a big battle between the East Coast and the West Coast. New York had a grip on TV and they wanted to keep it all on the East Coast; they didn't want Hollywood to get involved in it," explained Earl Bennett. "And Spike knew Hollywood was going to get involved; he was one of the people trying to break through that, and show that you could do TV on film."

Jones might have shared Bob Hope's concerns as well: "All I know about television is that I want to get into it as soon as possible—before Milton Berle uses up all my jokes."

No coaxial cables existed to transmit television from East Coast to West—which received broadcasts by kinescope, a week late—when Jones decided to enter the infant medium. His decision to get into TV coincided with the arrival of his son in May 1949. Appearing on San Francisco radio, he announced the birth of Spike Jr.—"his burp sounds just like a cello," said the proud father—and reported he was going to try out new material during *Musical Depreciation Revue* matinees, for a television show starting in January.

A series of 39 half-hour shows were planned, but only two, at a cost to Arena Stars of $34,000, were ever filmed. "Wild Bill Hiccup" and "The Foreign Legion," written largely by Eddie Maxwell and directed by

Eddie Cline, were filmed during the summer of 1950 with a 16mm Multicam system developed by Jerry Fairbanks. The shows circulated around Hollywood for two years, with no takers.

The pilots did nothing to disprove the statement that TV stood for "Tired Vaudeville"—as one Hollywood funster quipped. Spike's monologs relied on jokes that were tired even then: "We always try to give every song a finished performance, and our performances have finished many a song. Yet composers are continually after us to play their material, and when we do—they're still after us."

"Wild Bill" was based on a number the band had recorded for Victor; it made a weak selection for record-buyers and, elongated to 26 minutes, an even less enthralling television show. But Jones was deliberate in his choice of material.

"I've just got to make good on television, because of my son, Spike Jr. He's only a baby," Jones *père* told his intended audience, 'but he loves to sit and watch television, especially those shoot-'em-up westerns. I was gone so long on the last tour he thought Hopalong Cassidy was his father."

Eddie Cline's Sennett-trained touch was well in evidence. Even prehistoric gags—like a bullet-riddled villain (burlesque comic Billy Reed) taking a drink, and spurting water from the bullet holes—came off funny. But the dialog was stilted and the timing uneven. Spike (as Wild Bill, and the Captain of the Legion) displayed plenty of ham yet was awkward and ill at ease. There was no pretense of sophistication; at one point, he turned to the camera and asked, "Isn't this silly?"

But the humor was no more primitive than the medium. "I think the shows were well done, for what they were, for the time we did them," said Joe Siracusa. "A lot went into them—jugglers, dancers, singers, giants, midgets, all in one show. Remembering lines, singing songs, acting...it was quite a feat. It was unusual for a band to be so versatile, and do all those things; it was quite a coup for a group of musicians."

When NBC finally signed Jones to make his network television debut on *The Colgate Comedy Hour* in February 1951, they took no chances—Edward Sobol, who had piloted Milton Berle's *Texaco Star Theater* during its first season, was brought in to produce the show. Spike also played it safe. With a $40,000 contract in his pocket, he stayed away from the burlesque skits and did what he did best—musical depreciation.

The script attributed to Jay Sommers was largely a conglomeration

Jones and Freddy Morgan stage "Chinese Mule Train" for the cameras. Bright lights and heavy equipment were a requisite of early television. (*Ted Hering*)

of old gags and routines from Jones' stage production, but the material was still funny, as sold-out crowds attested. Better yet, nothing quite like it had ever been seen on TV.

Getting the program on the air was no easy task. "Back here at Studebaker Theater [Chicago] where 18 directors and Eddie Cline are making a ragout of tasteless hash out of our TV show," Doodles Weaver noted in his diary during rehearsal. By the time the results were broadcast—live— two days later, things fell into place. "A Jesus by the name of [director] Kingman Moore has appeared to overrule Cline, Sobol & [Ralph] Wonders," observed Weaver. "So, instead of a jumbled chaos of insanity speeding outward, the emanations leaving the Studebaker Theater were quite acceptable."

The show got off to a fast start with a full-scale rendition of the old Slicker stand-by, "In a Persian Market." Earl Bennett crooned "My Heart Cries For You," with water squirting from his glasses at appropriate moments—a gag borrowed from the Korn Kobblers. A young man sang "Laura" while Spike chased a woman with a sword.

Jones traded quips with singer Gail Robbins about his physique ("It's all there, sewn right into the jacket," he assured her) and introduced his string section—a trio of yo-yos. The Slickers accompanied her on "Be

My Love," smashing their instruments at the conclusion, along with the cameraman's breakaway camera.

Mike Wallace, the band's sometime radio announcer, appeared to do a shampoo commercial. Jones conducted "The Poet and Peasant Overture" with a toilet plunger. Freddy Morgan made faces and plump LaVerne Pearson sang "Glow Worm." Roger Donley plucked a skunk from his tuba and Dick Morgan shorted out an amplifier with his steel guitar.

For his part, Weaver demonstrated his Pootwaddle Portable Sink and followed with a partly-improvised Ajax commercial, during which he poured soap all over himself—the only new bit in the program, and one of the funniest. In fact, it was too funny for Spike, who got upset with the comic for ad-libbing. "I doubt Weaver did anything like that during rehearsal," said Earl Bennett. "That was the high point in the whole show. The Ajax people were delighted with it."

Critical reaction was mixed. "That was no atomic bomb flash on your television screen last night," observed Larry Wolters of *The Chicago Tribune*. "Whatever it was, it was the most riotous entertainment we've seen since Olsen and Johnson were in their prime. Spike Jones was a natural to follow Martin and Lewis, who appeared last week. But who can keep up with this Jones? Wonder if even Spike can?"

Art Cullison of *The Akron Beacon Journal*, offended by some of the physical comedy, was less complimentary. "A new low in television humor was hit in Spike Jones' debut, leaving a bad taste in the mouth of anyone sitting in a family group watching the show," he asserted.

"Jones brought out of the audience a big, bouncy lady stooge [LaVerne Pearson] who looked like she had just finished a turn on the burlesque circuit. She did one of those muscle control acts, moving about several portions of her anatomy. That was bad enough," frowned Cullison. "Then at the end of the show, a midget [Frankie Little] walked onto the stage...his appearance alongside the girl from Minsky's was sickening."

Jones, who chewed gum throughout the hour program, appeared far more comfortable and relaxed on camera than he had in the pilots. In actuality, however, he was anything but. "There was a scene where he was going to hypnotize me to do a levitation bit, and I'm supposed to not be affected by his attempts," recalled Bennett. "I'm eating a banana, and he knocks the banana out of my hand. Spike was so uptight, he hit my hand so damn hard he almost broke my thumb."

The carefully-planned show—"we rehearsed the hell out of it," said

Spike rehearses half-dressed for his network TV debut on *The Colgate Comedy Hour,* 1951. (*Ted Hering*)

Bennett—was seriously marred by only one thing: the cameramen couldn't keep up with Jones. "He was so fast they missed everything," noted Eddie Brandt. "By the time they cut to the tuba pouring the water he was on something else. TV was great for Spike, but it was too new then, too tough. It couldn't catch him in the beginning."

As the bandleader told a magazine writer: "The transition from other mediums to television has presented some special problems. The full scope of our slam, bang and beep is limited by mechanical restrictions."

"It was so primitive…to think that was big-time television," mused Bennett. "There was a bit where Spike had a Tarzan outfit; a skin with the tail on it. The guest star [Gail Robbins] was supposed to step on the tail, and I was supposed to provide the squeal with my reed. I confiscated a mike, laid it down, laid on my stomach, looked underneath the curtain and watched their feet—and when I saw her foot step on the tail, I made the noise in the mike. That's how primitive it all was; it was almost like a high school play."

Industry reaction to the program was not positive, judging from an extant inter-office memo. Told that a Jones TV show was available for fall, a rep for McCann-Erickson ad agency "let out a scream and said no. It appears MCA showed them the hour kinescope show he did for Colgate and from what she said it was pretty bad. She said MCA had been showing this all over town as far as she knew, and the reaction was the same as hers."

Though Jones' television debut was a qualified success, his follow-up appearance that September—a *Colgate Comedy Hour* emanating live from Rockefeller Center in New York City—was an unqualified disaster. NBC producer Ernie Glucksman had gone beyond the call of duty, flying out to various towns on the *Musical Depreciation Revue* itinerary to meet with Spike, to discuss and plan the show. Glucksman was a TV veteran who had worked on *Your Show of Shows* and produced Dean Martin and Jerry Lewis' *Colgate* segments—but no amount of experience or planning could have prepared them for what happened.

The theme was variety—everything from a baseball skit to a parody of a British movie to the "Foreign Legion" sketch. A revolving stage made such diversity possible; while the "Legion" segment was in progress, the baseball set would be readied on the back side, away from the camera. All went well, until the revolving stage got stuck. The theatre's chief electrician, Frank Eisner, ran to the switchboard to correct the problem; he dropped dead of a heart attack, collapsing over the switches.

"The rest of the show was complete chaos," Jones recalled of the live broadcast. "To top the whole thing off, in New York City there is a law that you can't move the corpse until the coroner has examined the body. So, here in the middle of an English drama or a baseball sketch, or Helen singing a song...were cops, priests, coroners and everyone else that would be concerned with a man dying, walking in front of the cameras and through all the scenery."

The studio audience of 3,200 people apparently had no clue what was amiss, nor did viewers at home. Meanwhile, pandemonium reigned backstage: "They had to try to take that set down manually and rebuild it," explained juggler Bill King. "I had a bit in the first segment where I was a tough New Yorker, and I was eating peas out of a can with a knife. They put the camera back on me and I ate damn near a can of peas, while they were trying to get the set torn down.

"That thing got pretty wild; all these stagehands were cussing back there, 'Spike Jones killed our electrician.' We didn't have anything to do with it, but they always want to blame somebody for something," said King. Remembered Bernie Jones: "In *Variety* it said, 'Master electrician drops dead'—and on the other side, 'Spike Jones show is slow-moving,' panning the hell out of it. Spike was furious over that."

Veteran director Eddie Cline (left) assists as Billy Barty and Earl Bennett rehearse the Liberace sketch, 1954. (*Skip Craig*)

The bandleader survived the debacle, reteaming with Ernie Glucksman in 1952 for two segments of NBC's *All-Star Revue*. The shows, broadcast from Hollywood's historic El Capitan Theatre, featured old standards like "The Poet and Peasant Overture" and such guests as Billy Eckstein and Liberace. Both programs won glowing reviews. *Variety* described the first broadcast as "a fast-moving parade of pandemonium," calling it "TV's fastest show and one of its funniest."

The loudest laugh, provoked by a sketch about an all-girl band, was not scripted—nor did it come from the audience. "When Spike laughed, it would turn into a scream sometimes. You could hear him a mile away," said Bernie Jones. "We were all dressed like women: long dresses, lipstick, eyelashes. Spike and Hugh Herbert were talking; Hugh reached inside his blouse—on camera—and pulled out the ball that formed his breast. He took it out and bounced it and put it back in. Spike let out that scream and fell on the floor laughing."

No one laughed at Jones' next effort, despite the fact that it featured Buster Keaton and was directed by his frequent associate from the silent era, Eddie Cline. "It was some kind of a pilot thing. Spike was putting up the money; the Slickers were all in it," recalled Earl Bennett.

"Keaton would say to Eddie before a take, 'I've got an idea for a piece of business...' Eddie'd say 'No, no...we'll do it like it's written.' If Eddie could have been flexible and let Keaton do what the old man knew was funny—it probably would have been something. But Cline was too insecure. I think that was the end of the project. The thing wasn't even worth putting together."

Jones finally won his own television series three years after his debut. As usual, he hired the best talent he could get. Ed Sobol, who had produced Spike's first *Colgate Comedy Hour* appearance, returned to handle the same chores; Bud Yorkin, who began his career as stage manager on *Colgate,* signed on as director of *The Spike Jones Show*. Yorkin and Jones became and remained close friends.

The 1954 series—broadcast Saturdays on NBC, from January to May—reflected the changing face of the band. Personnel at this stage included George Rock (trumpet), Bill DePew, Bernie Jones and Bill Hamilton (sax), Ray Heath (trombone), Roger Donley (bass), Freddy Morgan and Jad Paul (banjo), Dick Shanahan (drums) and Paul Leu (piano). Helen Grayco, "the contrast to our musical snake pit," sang at least one song on every show, and took part in the sketches.

Earl Bennett (in his last season with Spike), vaudeville headliner Peter James and midget actor-comedian Billy Barty provided the laughs. An odd assortment of guest stars contributed to the levity, including Margaret Truman, Harpo Marx, jazz pianist Art Tatum and children's TV favorites "Buffalo Bob" Smith and Howdy Doody.

The comedy had some punch to it, according to Bill King, because Jones and company were finally in the hands of a director who knew what to do with them. "Bud Yorkin was great. On *The Colgate Comedy Hour*, some director would come in and say, 'Do it this way'—and damn it, it wouldn't work that way, it had to be done the tried and true way, the way we did it," stated King.

"A lot of these guys hurt Spike because they'd want to do it their way...I'm not saying their way was wrong, but it wouldn't work for us. That ruined a lot of the TV shows because they had no idea of Spike's sense of comedy."

If he was no longer able to direct, Eddie Cline's sensibilities were still in tune with his employer's. "He was very good on knowing how to time bits, and things like that," said King. "We might be doing a bit and it wouldn't work right, and Eddie could look at it a little bit and explain to you how it worked and everything." Eddie Maxwell concurred: "Cline

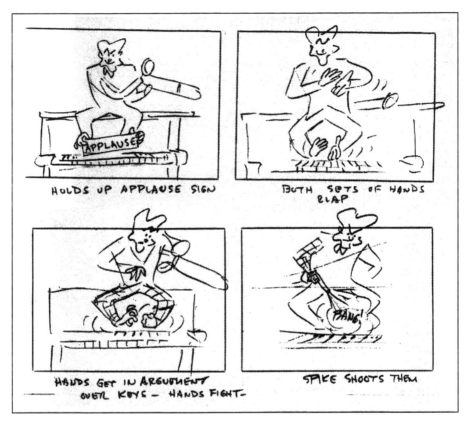

HOLDS UP APPLAUSE SIGN

BOTH SETS OF HANDS CLAP

HANDS GET IN ARGUMENT OVER KEYS — HANDS FIGHT

SPIKE SHOOTS THEM

Tex Avery sketched these gags for Jones' 1954 TV series. (*Mark Evanier*)

helped us a lot, because he brought a lot of his slapstick education to the show. He earned his keep."

The bandleader welcomed the input of everyone in the organization. "He was very open-minded," said Bernie Jones. "He'd say, 'What do you think about the show? Any suggestions?' I said, 'Spike, if you don't mind my saying so, I think you should smile more. You use that deadpan face as a comedy thing, but it makes you look so bored and uninterested.'

"I said, 'I think if you used a few zany faces now and then, it would be more personable for kids.' Next thing on the show, he's making all kinds of faces. Then he got to watching the band. He'd say, 'You goddamn guys stand there like a bunch of clods. Gotta get some action in this. Smile, do some things.' "

Spike—who once told a friend he was hesitant to go into television because "Jimmy Durante went on TV and shot 18 years of material in about three shows"—was in constant need of ideas. Freddy Morgan, Sol

Meyer (co-writer with Morgan on the band's "Bottoms Up" album), Eddie Brandt and Joe Siracusa (who had by then left the band) contributed to the supply, along with Maxwell and Cline. Even Harpo Marx reportedly took part in the writing sessions when he appeared on the show.

Animator Tex Avery and cartoonist Virgil Partch (best known for "Big George!") were also put to work, dreaming up gags at the drawing board. Avery, who directed some of the wildest and most surreal cartoons ever made and is generally credited with the creation of Bugs Bunny, had always wanted to be a live-action gag writer. Jones gave him the only such opportunity he would have in the course of his long career.

"Everybody would throw ideas. There wasn't anybody who was assigned to be the big brain," observed Eddie Maxwell. "Spike never let you forget he was the head, but he didn't whip us. He functioned more as an editor, because although he had a good sense of comedy, he never said anything funny. But he had a good reaction to comedy; he would either like something immediately or just be cold to it."

Billy Barty took center stage in one of the most outrageous pieces of funny business the bandleader and his staff ever concocted. "He knew I did impersonations," recalled Barty. "One day he said, 'Did you ever do Liberace? He's the latest thing.' I had never even seen Liberace, but I had heard his voice."

Barty turned up on the season's fifth show in tuxedo, tennis shoes and silver toupee, seated at a miniature piano. Mimicking Liberace's effeminate speech and manner flawlessly, he sang "I'm in the Mood for Love," with Earl Bennett (as brother George) backing him on the tree branch violin. "I fall down, go boom," Barty exclaimed, when he slid off the piano bench. The topper was a candelabra that spewed shaving cream all over them.

"We were going to do 'September Song' and for some reason NBC couldn't clear it. We were doing the show, and that morning Spike called an emergency meeting; they called up Jimmy McHugh and cleared 'I'm in the Mood For Love.' We threw that in fast," said Barty, who recorded the number with the band for RCA Victor and reprised it regularly in Jones' stage and TV shows. Liberace himself was "the greatest audience," reported the comedian. "He loved it."

The sketch was perhaps the band's high water mark in television, although the City Slickers' potential was never tapped by the little screen. "I don't think we had the opportunity to do what we could have done on television," said Joe Siracusa. "TV was really our medium; it's just that we never got our feet wet."

The spontaneity of live broadcasting was like a shot of adrenalin for the band. "It was like an opening night every night, rather than something you got accustomed to doing," enthused Helen Grayco. "All the boys loved being in television. And Spike was thrilled. I think he enjoyed that more than any part of the performing end of his career."

Jones' first series ranged from inspired buffoonery to beleaguered slapstick, as in the tiresome "Foreign Legion" sketch—but even that hackneyed routine could be saved by Barty's energetic Jimmy Durante impression. The program, however, was not the audience-pleaser his stage revues had been. "Even the most dyed-in-the-wool follower of Jones' musical mayhem must have found this a pretty dull offering," noted *Variety*.

"Enjoyment of Spike Jones is a curious and contagious disease," observed Don Freeman of *The San Diego Union*. "It strikes unexpectedly against the victim's more rational judgment. The hard-shell intellectual, most of all, puts up the fiercest resistance on the ground that Jones is insufferably lowbrow."

The lowest common denominator was clearly what the bandleader had in mind in 1955 when he dreamed up *Seven O'Clock Spiketacular*—a daily early morning comedy-variety show that would feature everything from amateur songwriters to puppets giving weather reports, to wrestling films with humorous commentary.

Billy Barty, he proposed, could do a daily feature in a rabbit costume, conducting a toy band in a pantomime of pop records. Dialect comedienne Minerva Pious could appear regularly as a gossip columnist, reminiscent of the Mrs. Nussbaum character she played on Fred Allen's radio show. Jones could stage a jitterbugging contest, tour a cartoon factory, visit movie stars on location or have Liberace give kids a piano lesson.

"I don't think we should confine ourselves to any format that would please a minority of viewers or listeners, but should always keep in mind the entire family as potentially our audience," he noted in a lengthy program outline. The show failed to sell.

During the three years that would go by between series, Jones guest-starred on other shows. Ernie Kovacs—a big fan of Spike's who did wonderfully zany things with music himself—late in 1956 invited Jones to be on *The Tonight Show*, of which he was then part-time host. Unfortunately, the pro-

Spike and Freddy Morgan slice up "Mack the Knife" for home viewers.
Audiences never tired of Freddy's antics—or his faces.

ducers of *The Perry Como Show* had just signed the bandleader for a guest shot, and forbade him to appear on anyone else's program prior to theirs.

The 1957 edition of *The Spike Jones Show*—which CBS aired live on Tuesdays, from April to August—marked a radical departure in style. Music and comedy were still the name of the game, but Helen Grayco was more prominently featured, and the band was in essence no longer the City Slickers. Jones dressed his men in pastel-colored tuxedos and called them The Band That Plays for Fun. But the fun was distinctly subordinated.

"Spike called and asked me to come to the house," remembered Joe

Siracusa. He said, 'We're having a creative meeting and I'd like to have your comments.' I was still thinking like a Slicker—funny suits, gunshots—he said, "No, no, this is a whole new approach. It's all changed. If Lawrence Welk can do it, so can I.' I said, 'I have nothing to contribute then. I don't think that way.' "

Danny Arnold, who later went on to create *Barney Miller,* was one of the writers in tune with the new thinking. The guest list—which included the Mills Brothers, Nelson Eddy, Carol Channing, Gordon MacRae and the King Sisters—also reflected the change in tempo.

Eddie Brandt, who co-wrote the series, felt the director made the series work where other attempts had failed. "TV was hard for Spike until he got Dik Darley, who really sat down and planned everything. Darley wasn't creative, but he was a great mechanical director. He methodically worked out everything by the second and by the bar," said Brandt. "I had to stick with him and count the bars—'at 16 bars you cut to this.' He wasn't a music man, and yet he was the best one for Spike."

Jones concurred: "I was very fortunate to have a wonderful producer-director. Dik Darley was just sensational and he knew what we wanted. Every four bars or every eight bars we change cameras, change shots, change angles. That compared to an ordinary sketch that Jackie Gleason or Red Skelton would do—it couldn't be compared—so it was very difficult for the director."

The bandsmen varied from week to week. Among the regulars were George Rock and Cappy Lewis (trumpet), Brian Farnon, Gil Bernal and Clyde Amsler (sax), Phil Gray (trombone), Eddie Robertson and Larry Breen (bass), Dickie Phillips (guitar), Freddy Morgan and Jad Paul (banjo), Hal Hidey and Arnold Ross (piano) and Carl Fortina (accordion). Comedians Peter James and Paul "Mousie" Garner augmented with prop instruments and scripted silliness.

Critical reaction was generally favorable. "It was, for Mr. Jones and his confederates, a program marked by decorum," said *The New York Times* of the premiere. "There were some novelty numbers but they were balanced by conventionally popular offerings without benefit of cowbells, shrieks or alarms." Jones, they noted, spent most of the evening in "a dark business suit that would pass muster at a librarian's convention."

Singer-saxophonist Gil Bernal, who described the show as "a combination of *Lawrence Welk* and *Laugh-In,* stated, "Spike was always thinking what it was going to be like the next time around. He thought it was time to move on. He wanted to present just a band making music, having fun; he always tried to move along with the times."

"Spike could just as easily have gone the Lawrence Welk route," ventured George Rock, "and would have been a much bigger success in TV—but certain things he demanded really detracted from the show, and took it from being what it could have been."

Jones was clearly jealous of Welk. They had both been perceived as purveyors of corn in the early '40s, when the former drummer was depreciating popular music, and the farm boy-accordionist was touring middle America with a dance band. Now Welk had suddenly parlayed his comparatively modest achievements into a television phenomenon. But Welk would do whatever it took to please an audience; Jones was too restless to emulate the "champagne music" maker's bland formula for widespread acceptance.

"A show like Welk's was generally the idea, but Spike still insisted on some things…that kind of ruined the commercial value. Spike was literally paying for those shows. The people who were sponsoring the show [Liggett & Myers] wouldn't pay for some of the those things—he had to pay for them out of his own pocket. In my opinion he would have been much better off had he gone with more musical numbers, and maybe featuring the Slickers more," said Rock.

When trombone virtuoso Tommy Pederson and former Slicker pianist Frank Leithner reprised "The Flight of the Bumble Bee" on one broadcast, they decided to find out how far the money would go. "We did something like four run-throughs and two dress rehearsals, then we put the show on live" said Pederson. "Then we had to do the same thing for the West Coast.

"Spike's manager—naturally, he tried to stick up for the boss—he said, 'Look, I'm going to pay you the same as the rest of the boys.' I said, 'The hell you are. That's not enough.' I told Frank to get up and walk out with me, and we both left. The day of the program, his manager calls up again, and says, 'Okay, you win.' And we each got $500 for the show," recalled Pederson.

"Spike didn't pay anything extra if he didn't have to," said banjoist Jad Paul, who appeared on several of Jones' TV series. "I did a commercial one time; I didn't get paid for it. Even though I wasn't a comedian, I still did a lot of scenes and bits. All of us musicians were doing AFTRA [American Federation of Television and Radio Artists] things—acting bits, singing bits, and all that stuff—and we weren't getting paid AFTRA money,

Spike clowns with George Rock, Len Carrie, Gil Bernal and Joyce Jameson on *Club Oasis*, 1958. (*Ted Hering*)

we were just getting musicians' scale. We didn't even belong to AFTRA."

Jones was back on NBC in 1958 on alternating Saturday nights, as summer host of *Club Oasis*. Format and personnel were much the same. Doodles Weaver and Feetlebaum were back in harness after a long absence, along with actress Joyce Jameson—who played everything from Vampira to Little Orphan Annie—and funsters Len Carrie and Ken Capps. Spike added Hymie Gunkler on sax and Jimmy Bryant on guitar; Phil Stephens took over on bass and Dick Shanahan returned on drums. Dik Darley again directed, co-producing the series with Tom Waldman.

"Maybe it's age, maybe it's tired blood or maybe it's just a new understanding of the TV medium, the capacity of TV screens and the mood of TV living rooms, but Spike and his 'band that plays for fun' seem to have toned down considerably," observed Janet Kern in *The Chicago Ameri-*

can. "They still play for fun—but the fun isn't nearly so raucous and ear-splitting as it used to be. They still play for laughs—but their satire isn't nearly so cruel or sloppy as it used to be."

Certainly the humor was more sophisticated. "It was a thinking person's comedy," suggested trombonist Phil Gray. "You had to think a little bit—not get hit over the head. You maybe thought about it a second. Then the joke would come to you. Some of it was slapstick, some of it was subtle. I remember singing 'Gigi,' singing it seriously; at the end of the number, on my last phrase, the camera pans in to a picture I'm holding—a gal with crossed eyes and no teeth."

While the bandleader disappointed old fans with such material, he won new ones. His difficulties in the early years of television were largely "because of his deadpan personality. He wasn't called Mr. Warmth," noted Billy Barty, who felt the more receptive welcome had little to do with Jones' mastery of the medium. "Let's put it another way—maybe people accepted him for what he was. Spike never changed that much. The show didn't change much in those four years either."

Jones was even less personable off camera than on. "When I think of the guy, I think of how abstract he was. He had a perverse sense of how to relate to people," reflected Jad Paul. "We were playing a nightclub up in Montreal, and he would turn around with his back to the audience and conduct—and he looked at me and just gave me a dirty look, which he was very good at. And I looked at him, and I mouthed, 'You sonuvabitch.' Because I was bugged. I thought, 'Why is he giving me dirty looks?'

"I was sitting next to Freddy Morgan, and he went and did some kind of a bit, and Spike came over and sat in Freddy's seat and said, 'You know, Jad, the funniest thing happened to me today…' He kind of made friends with me, just after I literally called him a son of a bitch," mused Paul. "He kind of admired someone who stood up to him—he called me for every TV series he had after that."

The bandleader could be coarse and unpleasant with guest stars who stepped out of line or technicians who didn't do their job. Fans and others he had only fleeting contact with also were subjected to his roughhewn manner. "Spike had a tremendous power to retaliate verbally with people," said Bernie Jones. "If he opened fire on you, you knew it."

Gil Bernal recalled: "We were rehearsing on a soundstage one day. There was a studio tour; people were walking through. This guy walked in and said, 'Oh, hi, how you doin', Spike? I watch your show all the time.' He said, 'Good thing you changed that routine you were doing at the end of the show. Made you look kind of faggy.' Real tact. Without even looking up, Spike said, 'Yeah, well blow it out your ass.'"

Jones' razor-sharp tongue and often scathing remarks obscured a much less public side of him. "He was sensitive as the dickens but he didn't want you to know it—and of course everybody did know it," observed harpist Charlotte Tinsley.

"He could be very emotional," concurred Linda Jones. "I didn't see him cry often but certain things would bring up an emotional reaction," she said, recalling an incident after the cancellation of *Club Oasis*. "On the last show he invited everyone from NBC to lunch at a restaurant, and he was thanking the sound man, and this one and that one...he got to the end and just broke down crying. He was very moved by things."

While Jones' daughter also saw her share of his acerbic side, she was uncertain of its source. "I think it was just part of his nature. I don't know if he realized it hurt people, at the time," she reflected. "I don't know where a sarcastic attitude comes from. Maybe from the upbringing he had. Maybe because he'd been hurt. Who knows? But he could say things definitely that would have smarted."

Many people unquestionably deserved the tongue lashing they got. At other times, Jones' sarcasm was seemingly unprovoked. When a Los Angeles lawyer wrote a satirical song and sent it to him on speculation, the bandleader wrote back, "All I can say is that if you aren't a better attorney than you are a songwriter, I pity your clients."

The attorney got the last word. "I regret that you have converted your sense of humor to hostility," he replied. "You used to be funny." He addressed the letter to Jones care of CBS: "If not there, please forward to Forest Lawn."

Though Spike was dead to the fledging composer—and not in the peak of health as far as the record industry was concerned—he continued to find new life on television. *Swinging Spiketaculars,* a nine-episode series broadcast on CBS during the summer of 1960, featured Helen and The Band That Plays for Fun. The regular cast included Joyce Jameson, impressionist Lenny Weinrib and comedian Bill Dana, doing his then-popular Jose Jimenez routines—with Jones as straightman. The bandleader also gave a weekly tongue-in-cheek commentary on subjects ranging from ballet to songwriting.

The show, produced and co-written by Dana, represented a turn in yet another direction. "I was an infantry soldier in World War II, so I really had a great affection for what Spike did," stated Dana. "I told his agent, Frank Cooper, 'I'm sure I could do that, but that's not my strong suit.' He said, 'No, we want to go 180• from that, and we'd like to get the smart, hip…'—today it would be *Saturday Night Live*; then it was *The Steve Allen Show* we were emulating."

Bill Dana, co-writer Don Hinkley and director Robert Sheerer were acquainted with Steve Allen not as at-home viewers but as in-studio associates. They were not only modeling Spike's show after the renaissance man's innovative comedy-variety program, but "apparently trying to fashion Jones in their old boss' image," observed *Variety*. "Much of Jones' zaniness has been put under control and he comes across as a likable restrained funnyman."

The well-received *Spiketaculars*, sponsored by General Foods, were done on a weekly budget of $19,500. "Spike might have taken $5,000 off of that. I know my salary was $750. That was for performing, being executive producer, head writer and…I remember doing something unpleasant with a broom," quipped Dana.

"Spike was the final arbiter, but he really let me take complete charge. That was the quid pro quo, for doing this thing sort of as a labor of love. It was summer stock; it felt like, 'Hey, gang, let's put a roof on this place and do a show.'

"It was very exciting in terms of the experimentation. We did an awful lot with very little. I had a big argument with CBS—we tried to get a disclaimer that this was 'live on tape.' They wouldn't let us do that, for some reason, but we had no money to edit. So we did the show exactly as it was going to be on the air, on tape in front of a live audience."

Spike and Helen resurfaced on CBS in 1961 as a summer replacement for Danny Thomas. General Foods again signed on as sponsor; only Don Hinkley returned to the creative staff. He was joined by writers Sheldon Keller and Mel Tolkin—a veteran of *Your Show of Shows*, who wrote the pilot for the new venture—and Ernie Kovacs' one-time producer, Perry Cross. Dana made a guest appearance as Jose Jimenez on the premiere, which featured a burlesque on the advantages of a summer camp for boys.

The off-season to which Jones was regularly assigned had as many perks as the boy's camp. "A summer series gives me a chance to get away from my kids while they're out of school," he explained in *The Los Angeles Mirror*, as he ventured once more into the No Man's Land of television

Terry-Thomas (on hood of car), Edie Adams, Debbie Dawson, Betty Kovacs (behind stepmother Edie), Mannie Klein (trumpet) and Freddy Morgan (banjo) join Spike in his next-to-last TV appearance on Adams' variety show in 1964.

programming. "Can you possibly compare the comforts of rehearsing six days a week in a beautiful air-conditioned studio to being home with a 10- and 12-year-old suddenly let out of stir?

"Very seriously, the tremendous advantage in a summer series is the fact that the networks, advertising agencies and sponsors don't seem to go into shock if your show is not in the Top Ten during this period. They are very lenient in allowing us to try new ideas...This year, our policy is, 'If you don't like our show, wait a minute.' "

TV was almost always a joking matter. "If we could talk the Westerns and Private Eyes into using real bullets for about three weeks, it might be possible for us to have a steady series again," he told critic Janet Kern.

While Jones rarely made a straightforward statement for public consumption, he offered a simple rationale for his short-lived efforts on the tube in later years. "By the time you go on in the summer, the Fall has all been bought," he said in a radio interview. "It's almost impossible to get on in the winter, if you're trying to prove yourself in the summer."

Spike never stopped trying to prove himself, if only to himself. Among the projects he tried but failed to market in the early '60s were a series of specials based on his record albums; a mini-series called *The Fabulous Phonograph*; a situation comedy featuring himself and Helen as a show business couple; and a collection of fractured fables called *Scary Tales* (e.g., *Little Red Riding Hood Meets the Werewolf.*) Not all his ideas were "lowbrow." He also wanted to remake *The High and the Mighty*, with Brendan Behan and David Susskind—jokingly, at least.

When NBC asked Jones to host *The Jack Paar Show* for a week in the spring of 1962, he decided as much as he needed the television exposure, it was neither worth the effort nor the risk involved. "I do not feel that it is entertainment that they are looking for on this program so much as a most controversial character, on and off camera, as Jack Paar obviously was," he explained to publicist Bill Doll.

"I'm sure the viewers tuned in Paar to see an emotionally unbalanced person saying and doing things that no one else could dare get away with. In other words, if I did anything controversial enough to cause a person to continue to tune in, I would probably be blasted for the fact that it was in bad taste, bawled out by network executives and a few other things."

Two of Jones' closest behind-the-scenes associates disagreed on whether he was a man ahead of or behind the times. "Today, Spike would have been a smash," contended producer Bud Yorkin. "He was very inventive; he had a tremendous mind. I've always felt he would have made a great network president. I never went to his house that he didn't have another idea—not for him, but for television. He was light years ahead of himself; he had ideas for game shows that went on the air 10 years later."

Eddie Brandt held a vastly different opinion. "Spike had a lot of specials he was trying to sell. But he was already over the hill as far as the entertainment business goes, and he was pretty sick," said Jones' longtime staff writer. "I don't think he would have sold these things if he was well; he couldn't sell anything anymore. I think his day was over with the *Club Oasis* show. When he came back with the 1960 show, that clinched it. It was not the City Slickers."

In retrospect, it was 1955 and not 1960 that apparently marked the turning point in Jones' understanding of the medium—and how to manipulate it—as well as his radical change in direction. He clearly aspired to be someone other than the leader of the City Slickers from that point on, and his proposal for the daytime *Seven O'Clock Spiketacular* suggests that person was not so much Lawrence Welk, as Ed Sullivan:

"I think the approach to use regarding me is to get them to think about Spike Jones not so much as a bandleader, but, a showman and salesman with a warm, friendly personality, 19 million ideas, and, entertaining gimmicks with family appeal…in addition to the talent that surrounds me."

The program outline, which was never meant to seen by the public, also reveals a man who would do anything to draw an audience or attract a sponsor. "On our recent [1954] television series, we considered the colored people as a tremendous percentage of the buying public. If it means the City Slickers and I should play an actual basketball game against the Globetrotters with Billy Barty biting Goose Goslin on the leg while I am flying on a wire as Superman trying to put the ball in the basket, we should go this route. When Neilsen calls you on the phone, they don't ask what color you are!

"I would like to do all of the commercials personally on this type of show. I do think that in daytime television it is more effective for the artist and personality to do his own commercials. I think there is a warmth and sincerity that will move merchandise better and faster than a cold, filmed pitch! If I made children ask their parents to change to L&M cigarettes…I'm sure as hell that I would be able to get rid of a box of Kellogg's corn flakes with the ideas I have in mind."

On the Road Again
The Revue & Other Insanities, 1950–1961

Des Moines. St. Louis. Springfield. Grand Rapids. Oshkosh. Winnipeg. Nashville. Little Rock. Shreveport. Birmingham. El Paso. Tucson. Wichita. Cheyenne. *For the Love of Mike, Don't Miss Spike!*

Come hell or high water, the fans were ever faithful. In Portland they stood in the pounding rain; in Boston they trudged through the snow. In Mason City, Iowa, they turned out 3,000 strong, in the midst of a raging flood.

In Fargo, North Dakota, the band was greeted at the depot by a young man in a gaudy handsewn Slicker suit made of awning material. He wore a battered derby and carried a metallic blue trombone. But 18-year-old George "Skip" Craig was no ordinary fan; when Doodles Weaver admired his red-and-white football jersey backstage, Craig literally gave the comedian the shirt off his back and went home half-dressed 200 miles.

When the band settled into Minneapolis' Lyceum Theatre for a two-week run in March 1950, he was religious in his attendance. "I'd buy a cheap seat and when the lights went out I'd sneak down in front," said Craig. "It was the sound that got me. It really gave me a thrill when the band got rolling.

"I started going to every show, and the local human interest columnist did a column on me. In the article, I said, 'If only I could sit in just once with the City Slickers, I'd be the happiest guy in the world.' That night I was sitting in my usual seat. Spike sent his valet out at intermission and called me backstage, and said, 'You're in the show Sunday.' I flipped. Spike put me in both shows, afternoon and evening; they gave me one of Weaver's old suits and a prop horn. They sat me up in back and they gave me little bits to do."

Craig, whom Spike designated "Number One City Slicker Fan," knew he didn't have the talent to become a bona fide Slicker—but told Jones to keep him in mind if he ever needed somebody to go for coffee, shine the men's high-button shoes or chase after the pigeons. That fall he took a chance and ventured to Hollywood. Before long his "ridiculous dream" came true; he was hired on as wardrobe boy, and whenever they played his home area he was allowed to sit with the band. He even got to march in the Santa Claus Lane parade with them.

Nineteen fifty was a transitional year for Jones and his *Musical Depreciation Revue.* Television was beginning to muscle its way into the national consciousness and radio was eroding in popularity. If his fans wanted to stay home and watch Uncle Miltie instead of driving into town to see his show, the bandleader couldn't stop them.

But there was still an audience for the stage revue. When Spike advertised a children's show at the Flamingo Hotel in Las Vegas late that year, the 2,000 tickets reportedly sold out within two hours. Those who had seen the live show knew that neither Spike nor Milton Berle could do anything on television as entertaining as what Jones and company did on stage.

"The TV shows could never live up to the *Revue.* You couldn't do that show every week and make it funny," said Eddie Brandt. "Nothing was ever going to top the *Revue.* It took all those years to get it to where it was a solid two hours of laughs. We were in Canada once in a place with 18,000 people. I was in the back room with Ralph Wonders, counting the gate. The laughs would take three minutes, to go from the front of the audience to the back."

But not everyone found the show to their liking. There was no middle ground when it came to the band, as Robert E. Thompson noted pointedly in the *Fort Wayne Journal-Gazette:* "Them Slickers weren't 'xactly taken to the bosom of all the popeelation, but them as did like 'em thought them Slickers was jes about the dang-blastedest, routin'-tootin'est gang what ever set toe an' heel in Indiana. In fact, them Slickers was sorta like Scotch whisky and buzzard pie…Either you loves 'em dearly or you jes don't want no truck o' any kind with 'em. Ain't no inbetween."

The road show changed little over the years, despite attempts to the contrary. Introducing a new number into the line-up was always a problem. "We worked on 'Some Enchanted Evening' for about four months, and finally put it in the show," recalled Eddie Metcalfe. "But in order to put it in we had to take something out. So we took out 'Laura.'

"When we were ready to close the curtain, the people were screaming for 'Laura.' You couldn't take anything out because people had become accustomed to seeing it. We thought they'd like to see something new. We were shocked to find they didn't want that; they wanted to see the old numbers again."

"Hawaiian War Chant," an elaborate production done in blacklight, evolved into "The Man With the Golden Arm." In the original number, Jones grew a second set of hands while playing the drums. He later embroidered the routine so he was flanked by three sets of drums on either side, all in different colors.

"The guys on stage right had the golden arm on the right side, the guys on stage left had the golden arm on the left side—the arms were phosphorescent," explained Phil Gray. "We wore black cloaks; all the audience could see would be the derby, the golden arm, a set of gloves, the drumsticks, and the drums."

There were times when simple was best. "When Dick Morgan and I did 'Riders in the Sky' as a duet, everybody loved it," said Earl Bennett. "It was a very funny [stage] routine; it got terrific laughs. When we got to Las Vegas, Spike wanted to add showgirls…he was going to make a big production. He wanted us to stop and do a tap dance; neither of us were dancers. We did it one time at the Flamingo Hotel, and it died a terrible death."

In a playful jest at his audience, Jones got a tremendous amount of mileage out of "The Poet and Peasant Overture." Year after year, he introduced it as "a number we're doing for the first time tonight"—even two and three times in the same town. But by the time Freddy Morgan mugged his way through the "premiere performance" on NBC's *Colgate Comedy Hour* in 1951, the number was already an old reliable.

The routine was not original with Spike. He lifted it unhesitantly from the repertoire of Frank and Milt Britton, who, like Olsen and Johnson, were a prime source of material for him. The main difference in the reworked number was that Freddy played one too many notes on a banjo instead of a trombone. But Morgan took "Poet and Peasant" further than Jones intended.

Originally it was just a quick bit during the opening fanfare—the band paused, Freddy did an extra twang, Spike grimaced and the number continued. When the audience howled at the comic's moronic faces, the routine grew and grew until it was nearly 15 minutes in length, produc-

Spike brings out the wacky in Waikiki, with a little help from Eddie Kop, Joyce Tanai and Elsa Edsman. Honolulu, 1951. (*Scott Corbett*)

ing some of the loudest and longest laughs of the night. "We thought it was a perfect vehicle for Freddy," said Joe Siracusa. "He was a natural."

If Morgan did not quite rival Doodles Weaver in the audience's affections by this time, he proved an able farceur. He was also a big winner in the all-night poker sessions on the train.

The Slickers played for high stakes: "One night Dick Morgan got up to go to the bathroom," recalled Bill King, "and we were still playing poker, about 3 or 4 in the morning. We said, 'C'mon, Dick, sit down.' He got in the game and lost about $30. I can still hear him: 'It cost me $30 just to take a piss!' "

Weaver, who relieved himself of cash as freely as the proverbial drunken sailor, would not have cared about loosing the money. He was even less adept at handling his growing popularity; he did things in public other people would not dare to do, and got away with them because he was well known. At times, he was so drunk he didn't know what he was doing.

Jones and Weaver eventually locked horns in a clash of personalities that almost erupted into violence. "I wasn't party to the falling out, as to being able to say I understood what was going on. I know Doodles was getting kind of unfunny. When he was drinking, his sense of humor was blunted, or his timing," ventured Earl Bennett. "But one time up in Doodles' dressing room in the old Studebaker Theatre in Chicago—awfully close to show time—I blundered into the room, to ask Doodles about God knows what, and these two guys [Spike and Doodles] were damn near at fisticuffs; they were very red in the face, both of them.

"I thought for a bit I was going to be witness to some kind of a physical encounter with these two guys," said Bennett. "I knew then that things were terribly wrong—you kind of knew Doodles was through. They didn't care that I was there; they were so mad, they didn't give a damn. I was so shocked to see anybody [Doodles] speak like that back to the star. Nobody said anything, took issue with Spike—what he said went and that was it; if you disagreed, you just shut up and walked away. I'd never seen Spike mad enough like he was willing to double up his fist and hit back. But they were very angry men."

Within days of his dismissal from the band in 1951, the comedian's brother, NBC executive Sylvester "Pat" Weaver, signed him for a television series. Some of his associates thought he had engineered his own exit. "Doodles started goofing off with Spike on purpose, so Spike would fire him, 'cause he had that show," asserted Bill King.

Ultimately, it was the comedian's fondness for the bottle that led to his termination, after a drunken party in Peoria, Illinois. It took Weaver over two decades to face the truth. "The constant parties and disinterest I had in [the] show make Spike, Ralph [Wonders] and MCA decide to axe me, and I don't blame them a bit…what a fool I was," he acknowledged in his diary. "But I was hooked on having fun and parties, not a human bean [sic] at all."

Other members of the company came and went without much notice, but Doodles—whose new comedy-variety series and $1,000-a-week NBC contract lasted only 13 weeks—was conspicuous by his absence. Spike doctored publicity photos of the show's ensemble, painting a beard and glasses on the comedian, so he could continue to use them after he sent Weaver packing.

While he remained with the band until the conclusion of their Hawaiian tour in May 1951—alongside his temporary replacement, Guy Raymond—the diary reveals Doodles was given notice in March. Weaver's departure was marked by yet another party when the troupe returned from Honolulu: "Big homecoming celebration," he jotted. "Everyone got loaded."

Peter James, a burlesque comic who specialized in legmania and physical gags, was soon brought in to fill the gap. His elaborate magic act, "The Great Screwdini" (worked into "That Old Black Magic"), took the place of "William Tell" at the end of the first half. Nobody could replace Weaver, just as no one had ever quite replaced Red Ingle—but Jones made no half-hearted attempt to please the audience.

"Spike really splurged on this number. He paid over $5,000 for props; he didn't care what it cost," said Peter James. "I'd come out and louse up all the magic. I had everyone in the band as my assistant. At the beginning, I'd say, 'Everybody pick a card.' Then I'd say, 'Hold up your card please.' At the end, we'd walk off the stage and everybody would still have their hands up. That was 'The Great Screwdini.' "

Freddy Morgan and Earl Bennett became the show's principal comedians on Doodles' departure. From then on, Jones always had at least two head-liners; if one became hard to handle, he featured the other one. Mack Pearson, a vaudevillian of the black-tie-and-bare-feet school of humor, acted as James' stooge; he further clowned during off-hours for Spike's own amusement.

Virtually every member of the company was pressed into service, in the name of getting laughs. Tap dancer Ruth Foster and juggler Bill King appeared in the comedy sketches, as did the Wayne-Marlin Trio, a spectacular acrobatic act that traveled with Jones for several years. "I was hired as a dancer, but with Spike you did everything," said Foster. "When you auditioned for him, and you were a dancer, he saw way beyond that."

Stagehand Art Remmert and master carpenter Lester Calvin often did funny bits in the show. Calvin, a one-time burlesque comic, would take his teeth out and sing, "They try to tell me I'm too young..." The venerable Eddie Cline was also called upon to do the occasional bit, or perform *Hellzapoppin*-style, as a plant in the audience.

Even the singers were comediennes. "I didn't have to worry about keeping a straight face," reflected Eileen Gallagher, "because I was supposed to be the lady who won the *Queen for a Day* contest. I would come out dressed as an ordinary lady; I would be giggling all the time. I would pretend I was nervous and didn't know what to do, and all I could do was laugh," she said, recalling the routine she and her predecessors did.

"Spike would say to me, 'Is there anything else we could do for you, Mrs. Gallagher, that would make your reign as Queen for a Day more enjoyable?' And I would say, 'Oh, yes, I've always loved to sing, and I would just love to sing with your band.' Spike would say, 'We don't have any music, Mrs. Gallagher...' And I'd say, 'Oh, but I just happen to have some music here.' And I would pull the music for 'Glow-Worm' out of my big purse, and give it to him.

"Then he would allow me to sing; I'd go to the microphone and say, 'Can I have an arpeggio please?' He'd say, 'Mrs. Gallagher, if you can find one here, you can have it.' I'd start off with the obbligato, I'd do that three or four times, and then I'd get to a real high note and I'd hold it—then Dick Morgan would say, 'Turn the page, you blockhead.'"

LaVerne "Effie" Pearson, who replaced Gallagher, probably garnered more laughs than all her predecessors with the "impromptu" interview routine, which was loaded with double entendres. When Pearson began to giggle helplessly, her stomach quivering and her big rhinestone belt buckle bouncing up and down, audiences went into hysterics. Eventually she expressed a desire to sing: "If I could go back home and say I sang with Spike Jones, that would be the thrilling end of everything." She did, and it was.

Toward the end of her song Pearson would do a big bump and grind, followed by a tumultuous explosion. The Slickers would fall off the stage, the backdrop would crash to the floor, the instrument stands would collapse; finally, George Rock would reappear with a flattened trumpet.

As Pearson did the bump, a stagehand would fire a double-barreled shotgun, packed with wadding, into a 55-gallon oil drum. One St. Patrick's Day, the Irish stagehand got blind drunk—and very nearly put an end to the show. "He saw two barrels, and shot the wrong one," remembered saxophonist Bernie Jones. "He blasted a big round hole in the curtain, a foot and a half across. The shot just missed Dick Gardner's head."

The stagehand was fired immediately, as was anyone else who didn't carry their share of the load. "As long as Spike thought you were trying, and giving it your best shot all the time, he was very good to you," asserted Jones. "But he had no patience with people he thought were flaking off."

The Bird of Paradise employed by Peter James in his magic act could also be a problem. The bird, which was supposed to lay a golden egg, did absolutely nothing—like the Great Screwdini—but was a necessary prop. In Las Vegas, they rented a goose to play the part; in Boston, however, they had to settle for a wild turkey.

"This bird was scared to death," said Bernie Jones. "All of a sudden it started flapping. I was trying to hang onto it; it got loose and I had hands full of feathers. It got out into the audience and the stagehand had to go down and get ahold of it and put it back in the cage. We finally got a duck named Toby and carried her with us."

Dick Morgan was far more difficult to replace. His sudden departure from the band in 1953—via a fatal heart attack at the age of 48— deeply saddened his associates, who looked up to him. "Dick was a joy. He was an inspiration," said Joe Siracusa. "He was like a big brother to us. We came to him with our problems."

"He was a much-loved man," concurred Earl Bennett, who recalled a cherished moment one night in New Jersey when Morgan took his fellow Slickers by surprise. "The audience was nasty. Someone threw a lemon from a balcony, and hit Dick's guitar and broke it. Then they gave him a bad time when he was out there performing.

"He was doing 'Glow-Worm' or something and they were yelling at him; someone made a smart-ass remark. He turned to the audience— which was very unlike Dick—and he yelled in the microphone, 'Ah, go shit in your hat.' We were a little shocked because it was not Dick Morgan's style. He just didn't do this sort of thing—but they'd pushed him too far. We were very proud of him," said Bennett.

The circumstances of Morgan's death were tragic. "We'd be on these long tours, and his wife sued him for divorce," said Bill King. "That broke Dick's heart; they had a child 8 or 10 years old. He hadn't drank for years. He went to drinking; he wanted to try and get straightened up and they put him on Antabuse—a drug to get you off drinking—and he died. The heart attack was brought on by taking him off whiskey and putting him on that drug; it was fairly new."

Earl Bennett's "very unpleasant" departure in 1954 was more predictable, given his sometimes contrary relationship with Jones. When the comedian—who was billed as Sir Frederick Gas throughout his stint— was asked to take a cut in pay for a club engagement, he flatly refused. He was let go without an afterthought and blackballed from the entertainment business: "Ralph Wonders told all the agents I was trouble," stated Bennett. "After being on TV and on records and playing all the cities in the United States, I come back to Hollywood and all the agents had the word; they said, 'We never heard of you.' "

Bennett went on to became a film editor at UPA, as had Siracusa, who quit two years earlier when he tired of life on the road. The next Sir

The Slickers join a St. Louis parade, circa 1952. From top left: Bernie Jones, Dick Morgan, Peter James, Mack Pearson (partly hidden), Freddy Morgan, Spike and Bill King. The young lady next to Spike was part of a roller skating act in the revue. (*Earl Bennett*)

Frederick, slapstick comic Paul "Mousie" Garner, was already waiting in the wings when his predecessor departed. Garner adapted "Chloe" and "You Always Hurt the One You Love" to his own style. He got his laughs with broad physical humor, copying his teacher, Ted Healy—the Three Stooges' mentor—who had literally banged the lessons into him. But with Bennett gone, Freddy Morgan emerged as the top funster.

Billy Barty was Morgan's chief competitor for the audience's affections the remainder of the decade. The 3-foot-11, 86-pound midget, who was working in nightclubs when he joined Jones circa 1953, quickly proved his talent was far out of proportion to his size. He played the drums, sang, danced, and did impressions—not only Liberace, but Louis Armstrong, James Cagney and even Elvis Presley.

The diminutive entertainer, who started in movies at the age of three—at a dollar a day—was hired at $200 a week. "Spike and I hit it off right at the beginning. He knew I wasn't a yes man; he knew I was my own boss. And he accepted me for just being me," ventured Barty. "Spike wanted me to sell programs. He said, 'That's how Frankie Little made his money.' I said, 'That's good for Frankie. I'll make my money entertaining.' I think that's what sold me to Spike; I was honest and frank right in the beginning.

"We got along really well. Eight years I was with him, I never had a contract. Spike offered me a steady contract; I don't know why I didn't take it. I figured I could do just as well without one," said Barty. "I always got along fine with him. If I wanted a raise, I got it."

Barty eventually made as much as Freddy Morgan—$600-650 a week—more than twice as much as most of the Slickers. That salaries stayed at the level they did is evidence of Jones' attempts to treat his sidemen well, despite the myriad of headaches that began to plague his operation.

The remarkable longevity of the revue had been due to many factors, but Jones was primarily responsible for his own success. "Spike was the best promoter," asserted Eddie Brandt. "He set it up for people in the future. He would be working the Flamingo Hotel in Las Vegas, and he'd have all the promoters from the country come out there—at his expense—for three or four days. They'd sit around the pool during the day and line up the whole tour.

"He invited everybody out there—the guy who had the whole Chicago area, the guy who had the Detroit area, the guy who had New York. They'd say, 'Give me 11 dates around Chicago; I want these nights.' They would rent the auditorium together, and the guarantee would be set."

The revue—retitled *Musical Insanities* in 1953—remained popular, but by the mid-'50s the financial picture was beginning to change, thanks in part to television. "What finally killed it was Dean Martin and Jerry Lewis. They came along demanding $10,000-a-night guarantees—with no promotion," said Brandt. "They'd hit a town where they wouldn't make it and the promoter would lose a fortune. They just came and did the show; Spike worked on the whole thing, promoted it in advance. He sent a promotional man, sent flyers, sent the records, bought spots on everything; he was a helluva promoter. He could have put anything out, he promoted it so hard."

Jones refused to acknowledge the downward trend. "When the house was full and people were laughing and getting their money's worth, Spike would say, 'Aren't these people great—the salt of the earth,'" observed Earl Bennett. "When the empty seats began to show up and the responses were not the kind he wanted to hear, he'd come back offstage and say, 'Buncha hicks, buncha farmers...' Like it was their fault. Very sad."

The bandleader wouldn't admit he was outmatched by the little box in people's living rooms, even to himself. On January 19, 1953, he scheduled the usual evening performance opposite a national event—the birth of "Little Ricky" on Lucille Ball's sitcom. He should given the band the evening off. "It was murder for me," he later admitted. "The *I Love Lucy* fans were glued to their TV sets by the millions."

Despite Jones' unabashed optimism, he couldn't overlook the bottom line: expenses were rising uncontrollably, while the house guarantees remained the same. In some cases, the percentages were even smaller than what they had been in the past—in spite of Ralph Wonders' attempts to strike a better bargain.

The 46th Street Theatre in New York offered Spike a guarantee of $15,000 a week plus 25% of the profits—"a sensational deal," as far as MCA's booking agents were concerned. But Jones and Wonders decided they couldn't possibly make any money on it. When the Broadway Theatre asked for a rental fee of $8,000, Spike and his business advisors calculated they would have to gross $35,000 a week just to break even; the preopening advertising costs alone would run $15,000.

Jones replaced his private train with a caravan of buses and trucks when the Pullman cars became economically unfeasible, but the show's overhead was still exorbitant. While he whittled the company down to a more manageable payroll, he still carried a troupe of 15 to 20 people.

Although the revue remained their primary enterprise during the '50s, Spike and his managers had their hands in everything from concert tours to dry cleaners. At one point they contacted Moss Hart about the possibility of staging Broadway shows in Las Vegas; they toyed with the idea of producing *Pajama Tops*—an English translation of a French stage farce—for over a year before dropping the project. "What can I say? We were looking for ways to make a buck," conceded Dick Webster.

Though neither Jones nor his managers would admit it to anyone outside Arena Stars or MCA, they actually lost money on a number of engagements. They often took a gamble when filling holes in their itinerary, accepting minuscule guarantees and even no guarantees. As long as they had a fighting chance to come out on top, they would consider a booking.

Spike was willing to accept almost any reasonable offer to go overseas, but the cost of taking his ensemble was almost prohibitive. And the natives—particularly the English—were not all that friendly. When the

London Palladium offered him $25,000 a week for an eight-week run in 1948, the British musicians' union squelched the deal; they insisted one of their members be employed in America in exchange for every sideman Spike brought with him. Jones sent them a batch of recordings "to prove we weren't musicians," but the answer was still no.

The irrepressible bandleader tried to save face by claiming *he* turned down the offer, saying he'd rather turn his cowbells loose on Peoria, Illinois, for half as much. "There are plenty of sad little towns right here in the U.S.," he told the media. "Why not cheer up the home folks first?" But Jones was ever anxious to take his show to Britain; he made many failed attempts over the years.

An offer for Spike to take the revue abroad materialized late in 1953, but proved unfeasible. A tour of Western Europe was proposed, with the possibility of a full month in Sweden alone, and a guarantee of $15,000 a week. But they would only be allowed to take 50% of the money home from the Continent in U.S. dollars, and there were no guarantees things would go smoothly once they were on foreign soil.

Europe's loss was Australia's gain when Spike took a troupe of 21 Down Under. While his drawing power was beginning to wane at home, he was greeted by huge crowds on the 1955 tour. Thousands of fans welcomed them at the airport in Melbourne; 77,000 people squeezed into a boxing arena to see the band during their stay in Sydney.

Jones decided to play it safe and tailor the show to the audience. In addition to the old standards—which included the *world* premiere of "The Poet and Peasant Overture"—the band gave "Waltzing Matilda" the typical City Slicker treatment. He also employed a cricket bat as a baton. "The National Anthem was the only tune which came out straight," noted the *Sydney Daily Telegraph*.

Apart from a few well-timed local jokes, however, the Aussies saw much the same show Jones staged at home. The opening number started with a bang: Mousie Garner sounded a sour note on the bagpipes and got his kilt shot off. Then the proceedings were interrupted by a loud knock, as usual; when the bassist turned his fiddle around, out climbed an irate Billy Barty.

At times the crowds played havoc with the program. "In Adelaide, the show was to go on at 7:30," recalled George Rock. "Billy had to be in the fiddle before the curtain went up, naturally. He was inside ready to go and they decided to hold the show a half hour, because there was a big

Billy Barty, pound for pound the biggest talent in Jones' troupe.

line of cars trying to get into the parking lot. But nobody knew he was in there; we were all backstage.

"When he did come out, he was *furious*. He was purple, and he was dripping sweat. Instead of doing his bit, he came out shaking his fist at us: 'You dirty...' And everybody in the band was a bastard because we hadn't let him out of the bass fiddle."

Barty remembered the incident differently. "They delayed the show, but the bass was already on stage—it was visible to the audience. I couldn't get out because I'd ruin the gag," he contended. "They didn't forget about me; they had to leave me in there, or I'd ruin it."

Jones was guaranteed $163,000 for the tour, including transportation costs; he grossed $313,780 for 43 performances. Despite the success of the trip Down Under, though, he never returned. "Spike could've stayed there a year," said Bill King. "He said he could've made a million dollars, but [you couldn't bring the money out, due to regulations]. His opinion was, who wants a million dollars in Australia?" Subsequent offers to appear in Formosa and Japan did not work out, nor did a proposed tour of South Africa.

The company toured Canada on several occasions, but the results were sometimes unsettling. "We were playing Quebec one time," said Barty. "Except for the pratfalls, everything died. Dialog—died. My impressions—died. It was a French-speaking audience. Anything where somebody would get hit, somebody would fall down, hilarious. Acrobats, fine; half-man gag, fine. 'Two Front Teeth'—blecch."

Barty, who once faked a drowning in a Las Vegas swimming pool to promote the revue, fondly recalled Jones' unabashed sense of humor. "He loved jokes—as long as it didn't interfere with your work," said the comedian. "Your work came first. He knew what he wanted, and he got what he wanted; as long as you delivered there was no problem.

"Sometimes we went to the movies together. Spike would always buy me children's tickets: 'One adult, one child.' There were a lot of gags he'd do. With his deadpan face, he could tell you what you thought was the truth and be putting you on; you wouldn't even know it."

The bandleader milked every conceivable situation for a gag. "He always had sensational ideas, whether it was going to Australia and bringing back a kangaroo, or whatever the hell it was," said producer Bud Yorkin. "He wanted me to drive down Sunset Boulevard with him; I said, 'Not me.' But he did. He put the top down on his car and propped that sonuvabitch up in the back seat with a harness or whatever, and drove down Sunset—just he and the kangaroo." Affirmed Peter James: "Spike always wanted to do something to get a laugh."

Freddy Morgan's mind worked much the same way. "I was straightman to Freddy in 'The Poet and Peasant Overture' when we did it in live shows in 1957 and '58," said trombonist Phil Gray. "He'd tell a funny joke or say, 'Look at that gal…' He'd smoke a cigar before he came onstage, eat garlic for dinner, the whole bit—trying to break me up."

Trombonist Abe Nole, one of Gray's predecessors, recalled, "Spike hired me because when Freddy licked my nose with his tongue [during

Spike and Helen get the royal welcome on their 1955 visit to Australia. (*Ted Hering*)

my audition] I didn't laugh. I just sat there waiting for my next cue."

Although he made no attempt to restrain Morgan, Jones toned down his humor as he continued to travel with annual editions of *Musical Insanities,* which he eventually dubbed *Spiketaculars.* In place of the garish plaids he once favored, his sidemen wore pastel-colored tuxedos. "They were a little bit on the zooty side—tuxes with full lapels, matching bowties, shirts, shoes—in light blue, pink, purple," noted Gil Bernal. "It was a departure from what had been, which was really outlandish—but it was still loud; you wouldn't walk out in the street wearing something like that."

In 1958 Jones hired June Wilkinson to walk out on stage wearing something far more attention-getting. It wasn't hard—the teenaged *Playboy* model, who reportedly measured 43-22-37, turned plenty of heads. "Spike called me The Bosom. He put me in dresses that were so low cut, I practically had to glue myself in," recalled Wilkinson. "Once I went out and bought a high-neck black dress. He saw me in it backstage and said, 'Get that dress off—you don't sing *that* good.'

"He was still doing crazy stuff then. That's what he hired me for—gags. I remember one gag for publicity photographs. Spike had me stand at the state line, in Nevada, with my breasts hanging in California. Just for publicity."

Jones might have been living out a teenage fantasy when he hired the British-born actress-model. According to Carl Vidano, he once told the members of the Five Tacks, "My greatest ambition in life, music-wise, is to make enough money so that I can rent a half-acre of breasts and just wallow in them."

But not everyone was so inclined. "When we did the show at Harrah's Club in Lake Tahoe, Spike was lecturing about Latin instruments, and using double entendres," said Phil Gray. "He had a bit worked out. June had a low cut gown on; she was going to saunter on stage maybe in back of him as he was talking about the maracas, and bend over. He had this whole script rigged up. We did a run-through for Bill Harrah, and Harrah wouldn't allow it in the show."

Despite such titillating routines, Jones was no longer wallowing in box office receipts. While the aforementioned failure of Martin and Lewis to promote their stage appearances—and the phenomenal popularity of television—sounded the death knell of the roadshow business that was the cornerstone of Jones' empire, they were only partly responsible for its demise.

Ultimately, the unions shut the door on one-nighters with their notorious "feather-bedding" practices. They demanded that Spike—and others who toured—hire a set number of stagehands, despite the fact he carried his own. They also insisted he pay for musicians in the pit.

Bookings for the revue were hindered by other factors as well. "One of the main problems with not playing more places was that Spike always tried to package Helen with the deal," observed one of his associates. "A lot of buyers just weren't interested in buying a female vocalist. It put an extra cost on a package they didn't go for either."

Jones could not have continued making the tours much longer had

June Wilkinson spices up the menu.

the myriad of problems not brought an end to them. The five-pack-a-day smoking habit he had grown accustomed to as a young freelance musician was beginning to take its toll; after two decades of abuse, his lungs were starved for air.

"Whenever we'd get into altitudes like Reno and Tahoe he had an oxygen tank in the wings," recalled Phil Gray. "He'd take a few whiffs of oxygen after the opening number so he could catch his breath. When someone else was performing he'd walk offstage; he was having trouble breathing in those altitudes."

By the late '50s Spike could no longer hide his shortness of breath from those around him, nor was the sad irony of his puffing for air during cigarette commercials lost on TV audiences. The problem developed

Len Carrie, Billy Barty, Helen and an unidentified showgirl join Spike for a
toned-down stint in Las Vegas, circa 1959. (*Ted Hering*)

gradually; the oxygen tank first rented on an as-needed basis eventually
became a permanent backstage fixture. By the time emphysema was diagnosed in 1960—at the age of 48—he was chronically ill.

It was a less informed era. "When he was diagnosed, it was the first
time any of us had ever heard the word emphysema," stated Linda Jones.
"We didn't know what it was. He said, 'What have I got?' We did not know
the word. And of course, he did not want to give up the smoking…"

With the tour business gone, and his health ebbing, Jones' stage
appearances grew much less frequent. One by one, his trusted cohorts
departed for greener pastures. Freddy Morgan, whom Spike often called

in the middle of the night to work on an idea, was tired of getting up at 3 a.m. on Jones' sudden whim. "Spike had control of his life 24 hours a day," reflected Morgan's widow.

George Rock, Billy Barty and Bill King sought work elsewhere when engagements began to dry up. "The show just quit," said King. "It wasn't that I quit him or he quit me; the business quit us."

"Spike had run out of work," stated Rock, who went on the Las Vegas-Reno-Lake Tahoe circuit with a sextet. "I wouldn't have left otherwise. But it got to a point where Arena Stars didn't have enough money to pay me. Spike would call and ask me to come over, and he'd give me a personal check; $200 a week for staying home and doing nothing. We weren't doing anything, and there was no organization as such any more."

The trumpet player's departure sounded a sad note on a merry old horn, marking the last exit at the end of the long and prosperous road traveled by the City Slickers. "He absolutely was the thing that held the whole outfit together," said Jad Paul. "If it hadn't been for George Rock, I don't think Spike would have been as big as he was."

As though Jones didn't have enough troubles, his old pal Donnell "Spade" Cooley—whose own career as a bandleader was falling apart—also contributed to them. When the self-proclaimed King of Western Swing murdered his estranged spouse (singer Ella Mae Evans) in July 1961—and was convicted and sent to prison—the former King of Corn unwittingly took part of the rap. A segment of the public, it seems, misread "Spade and Ella" for "Spike and Helen" during the sensationalized trial.

Even after being blamed for Cooley's ignominious deed, Jones was harder to stop than the proverbial runaway train. "I tried to get him to retire for a year before he retired," said Dick Webster. "We were at Harrah's Club in Lake Tahoe, late in 1961; he was getting pretty sick. I said, 'Spike, this is ridiculous.' He finally gave in and said, 'Go back and make arrangements to close down the office'—which I did. That was pretty much the end."

But Jones wasn't dead yet. Refusing to idle away his remaining years, he busied himself with a endless slate of projects, and continued to make appearances in Reno and Las Vegas—without Arena Stars, without a personal manager, and without his most valuable associates. As long his name could sell seats, he gamely carried on.

In the Groove
The Post-Victor Recordings, 1955–1965

By the late 1940s Spike Jones' influence in musical circles had spread far and wide. There were bands doing his material, like Freddie Masters' group. There was a polka bandsman named Walt Solek calling himself "the Polish Spike Jones." Among others turning out occasional Jones sound-alike discs were Eddie Brandt and his Hollywood Hicks (headed by Jones' longtime staff writer), the Korn Kobblers ("Sylvia") and Red Fox and his Musical Hounds. Mickey Katz replicated the Slicker sound on "There's a Hole in the Iron Curtain." Arthur Fiedler and the Boston Pops got into the act with "The Glow Worm Turns."

Even the Firehouse Five Plus Two was accused of trespassing when they spiced traditional jazz with comic sound effects. "When people first started listening to us, they said we were imitating Spike Jones. They soon found out we were pretty serious," noted bandleader Ward Kimball. "Our approaches were different. He wanted you to know it was funny; we were serious, but we sounded like we were having a good time."

Jones had been without peer in the field of musical humor for more than a decade when things began to sour at RCA in the early '50s. But he was well aware of stiff competition rising in the ranks. The most serious contender to the throne was the Musical Hounds' one-time guitarist, Stan Freberg, who had scored high marks with parodies like "John and Marsha" and "St. George and the Dragonet."

The young comedian cultivated a taste for satire at an early age. "I loved Spike Jones, and I grew up listening to his wonderful records. My dream was maybe to perform with him," recalled Freberg. "Later on, I became friends with Spike, after I began making records. He was a little bit hostile to me...I was careful never to use a gunshot, because Spike used a gunshot like a musical instrument."

Jones would never admit the newcomer's work had a vitality and a freshness his lacked at this stage, but the bandleader—whose own lampoon of *Dragnet* was feeble compared to Freberg's—was himself among the up-and-coming satirist's fans.

"Freberg was his idol," asserted Bernie Jones. "One time Stan happened to walk in the studio when Spike was recording. Spike said, 'Get out of here, you genius.' He was kidding but he said, 'Get the hell out of here. I don't want you stealing anything.'

"Spike read *Billboard* magazine and all the trade papers; he was always on top of everything, what was moving and what wasn't," observed Jones. "He wanted to stay current, and he was trying to match anything that came along."

But the bandleader was not always as prescient as he appeared. Instead of fighting fruitlessly with the brass at RCA Victor in the final years of his tenure with them, he should perhaps have paid heed to the old adage, "If you can't beat 'em…"—and joined the competition at Capitol Records. Although the label was home to Nat King Cole and Frank Sinatra, musical humor was clearly appreciated; Stan Freberg, Mickey Katz, Red Ingle, Jerry Lewis, Mel Blanc, Jerry Colonna and Yogi Yorgesson (the "Scandihoovian" comedy characterization of Harry Stewart) were all in Capitol's stable.

When Katz told an associate he moved from Victor to Capitol because of "artistic freedom," he apparently wasn't joking. "Capitol has always come up winners. They had the guts to try novelty things in different combinations," observed country and western artist Cliffie Stone, who produced many of the label's novelty releases. "I've always thought RCA was somewhat like the government. At Capitol, I could walk in right into [co-founder] Johnny Mercer's office and sit down and talk to him—we could release a record in two days. We didn't have to go through merchandising or promotion."

Jones had fallen victim not only to RCA's cautious and conservative ways, but to occupational hazard. "The problem with novelty is, you have to top yourself every time," said Stone. "I think you can follow yourself as a singer, but when you're doing novelty records, you have to do a better one each time."

In the spring of 1955—while Spike's relationship with RCA continued to disintegrate—the Slickers recorded a pair of dixieland-flavored numbers, "Double Eagle Rag" and "Pick-It-You-Peasant." The tunes were issued by Decca Records as a single credited to the Banjo Maniacs.

During the same session, the band did a corny rendition of "Cherry Pink and Apple Blossom White"—a send-up of Perez Prado's current RCA hit. They also recorded a mambo about nuclear testing in Nevada titled "No Boom Boom in Yucca Flats," written and sung by Billy Barty. The results were released to unsuspecting record buyers on the Starlite label, with the culprits credited as Davey Crackpot and the Mexican Jumping Beans. The gunshots, belches and sneezes on "Cherry Pink," however, clearly identified the perpetrator.

When Jones at last aligned himself with another record company, it was one associated more with jazz than comedy. Early in 1956 he began recording on the Verve label for jazz impresario Norman Granz, who gave him a freedom he had not enjoyed in years. His first release for Verve, while hardly his best effort, proved far superior to most of the selections he recorded in his last years with RCA.

"Spike Spoofs the Pops," an extended-play 45, offered four silly songs for the price of two: "Love and Marriage," "The Trouble With Pasquale," "Sixteen Tacos"—sans apologies to Tennessee Ernie Ford or composer Merle Travis—and "Memories Are Made of This." The latter, a send-up of Dean Martin's current hit, featured Gil Bernal and the Canine Nine.

With one-man zoo Doc Birdbath retired from the fold, Spike literally went to the dogs. "I got a tape recorder and went to the pound," recalled Bernie Jones. "The dogs seemed to hit certain notes. I couldn't get a D-note so I barked that one myself."

Between July and September of 1956 the bandleader recorded two albums of his own, and supervised a third featuring Freddy Morgan. "Spike Jones Presents a Xmas Spectacular," a collection of holiday songs, hymns and carols, was followed by "Dinner Music for People Who Aren't Very Hungry," Spike's second 12" LP and in many ways his best.

The Christmas album—which featured monotonous vocals by the Jud Conlon Singers with interference by the City Slickers, toned down for the occasion—was enough to give almost any Spike Jones fan seasonal indigestion. Only George Rock provided any fun, singing "I'm the Angel in the Christmas Play" in his high-pitched child's voice. But even Rock had lost his holiday spirit by this time. "Something goes well and then you beat it to death," he lamented.

"Dinner Music," however, was the most inventive thing Jones had done in years. Ironically, the project had been conceived for RCA. Touted as a Hi-Fi demonstration, the album reprised a number of his old hits, including new, albeit inferior, versions of "Pal-Yat-Chee" and "The Jones Laughing Record" (retitled "The Sneezin' Bee"). The selections were all newly recorded, except for "Cocktails for Two" and "Chloe," which were dubbed from old Standard transcriptions and re-equalized for Hi-Fi.

As with some of his most memorable work, it was not so much what Jones did but how he did it. The album poked hilarious fun at audio technology, and produced some truly innovative effects: "garbage disposal...garbage disposal grinding up violin...garbage disposal grinding up violinist..."

But the times they were a'changin', and rock 'n' roll was beginning to rear its ugly head. "Every time I got ready to release this album—I had made it as raucous and cacophonous as possible—Elvis Presley would put out another 'Hound Dog' or something," Jones observed. "I'd go back to the studio and overdub some more dropping garbage cans. It was rather anti-climatic when it finally came out. 'Hi-Fi' was a cliché word by that time, so the album didn't do as great as it should have."

Presley was an irresistible target. On one TV program, Spike presented a pair of pants playing a guitar and announced, "For the first time on television, the bottom half of Elvis." Gil Bernal, who performed swivel-hipped rock 'n' roll parodies on Jones' TV and stage shows, reflected: "I was doing not a direct take-off on Presley, but we would get into things that were satires of that kind of music. Except a lot of people thought we were doing it on the square."

Asked by one disc jockey if he were bitter about the overwhelming popularity of rock 'n' roll, Jones replied, "No...I just resent it because I don't think it's music, and it's certainly hurt the record business from the artistic standpoint." He was unrelenting in his criticism of most of the hits: "When medical research is making such wonderful progress toward discovering cures for diseases we never believed possible, why can't we cure things like 'Wake Up Little Susie'?"

British humorist Gerard Hoffnung, who was lauded by *Time* magazine as "a sort of highbrow Spike Jones," avoided the bandleader's creative headaches by making fun of classical music. His 1956 "evening of symphonic caricature" at London's Royal Festival Hall and the resulting album—based on a book of zany cartoons Hoffnung had drawn—opened with an overture that employed three vacuum cleaners, an electric floor polisher and a rifle. His stellar rendition of "Lochinvar" was annihilated by kettle drums, pots and pans, broken glass, gongs, sirens and cuckoo clocks.

Still trying to get a head: The maestro drums up a little publicity for
"Spike Jones in Stereo" with the help of Lynne Cartier, alias Vampira.

Jones might have followed the lead of his British counterpart, whose
droll horseplay won Hoffnung an international reputation before his untimely death a few years later—but he was never one to follow. Instead of
returning to the classical field, Spike choose a new direction.

The restlessness which resulted in the Other Orchestra fiasco in
1946—and subsequently in "Bottoms Up" and other departures—began
to reemerge at Verve. In 1957 it manifested itself in "Hi-Fi Polka Party."
Ever the perfectionist, Jones went to great pains to achieve an authentic
sound, even hiring the conductor responsible for the then-current hit
record of "Beer Barrel Polka." Country Washburne (alias Johnny Freedom) returned to play tuba, with Rock joining in on trumpet and Bernie
Jones (alias Ole Svenson) fronting the band.

Spike paid tribute to a number of well known polka personalities by naming the selections after them ("The Frank Yankovic Waltz"), but once again chose not to put his own name on the album. Only after its release did he acknowledge The Polka Dots was really The Band That Plays for Fun.

The album might have sold twice as fast had it carried the original title and cover art. "Spike had a nude gal sitting on an accordion. This was the planned cover," recalled Eddie Brandt. "He wanted to call it 'Squeeze Box'—that's what an accordion is. You couldn't do that then; today you could. He was great at things like that."

By this time Spike was treating his personnel with somewhat more consideration than he had in the early years. He helped Bernie Jones put together a band of his own to capitalize on the success of the album, and produced a single to spotlight singer Gil Bernal. Jones also supervised a recording session for Billy Barty, but the tunes—written by Barty himself—were never released.

The record projects which consumed his dwindling energy in the middle and late 1950s say less about Spike Jones than the world around him—a world that, perhaps without his fully realizing it, was beginning to close in on him.

The guys who had served Uncle Sam in World War II, and did for his career what Jones did for their morale, were getting married and raising families. Their offspring were spinning hula hoops instead of Spike's records. The younger generation's idea of a platter party was to "Shake, Rattle and Roll" with Big Joe Turner and "Rock Around the Clock" with Bill Haley and his Comets, not sit and snicker with the City Slickers.

When they wanted a laugh, they dropped The Coasters' "Yakety Yak" or "Along Came Jones" on the turntable—Top 40 hits in the tongue-in-cheeky tradition of rhythm and blues pioneer Louis Jordan, a prime influence on Haley.

Debasing popular music was a stock in trade that had never let Spike down. But rock 'n' roll was so coarse and crude and foreign to his ear, his creativity was stifled. "How can I wreck something that has already been ruined in its original version?" he said in defense of his inability to satirize the music of the day. "In its regular contemporary form it's about as funny as you can get."

The bandleader wasn't trying to be funny when he spoke his mind to TV critic Hal Humphrey: "What can a washboard and banjo accompanying an exploding trombone possibly do to exaggerate a recorded version of 'Shimmy Shimmy Ko-Ko Pop,' which was sung and popularized by a quartet that blended like four seagulls with their feet caught in a garbage disposal? Even a belch, or the raspberry we used on 'Der Fuehrer's Face,' would be a musical improvement."

Music wasn't the only thing changing. The industry itself was evolving in ways that put a chokehold on the imagination. "Every one takes themselves so much more serious now than ever before. The clearances you have to go through now are unbelievable," Jones vented to one interviewer. "On record it's worse than anything; we can satirize things on television, you just never would get permission to do on record. It's there for posterity when it's there on a record."

While Stan Freberg had no problem picking up where Jones left off, and ribbing a trend he likewise detested—witness his savage lampoon of the Platters' hit, "The Great Pretender"—within a few years he too found himself stranded by the tastes of the record-buying public.

Having ditched the Slickers in favor of The Band That Plays for Fun, Jones concentrated on TV and one-nighters and took a hiatus from the record business. He approached Bill Haley himself about teaming up for a tour—a sure sign of what was happening to his audience—but MCA dragged their feet and nothing came of the plan, despite an agreement with Haley's manager.

In 1959, after nearly two years of inactivity in the studios, he signed a deal with Jim Conkling to do an album for the then-new Warner Bros. Records. The result, "Spike Jones in Stereo" (originally titled "Spike's Stereo Spooktacular") was as complex as its creator, as intricate as anything the maestro ever conceived. Its execution was largely the work of old hands, including writers Eddie Brandt and Eddie Maxwell.

Paul Frees, the man of 1,000 voices who had made "My Old Flame" so memorable, was hired to breathe life into the material. Among his vocal guises were Dracula, Frankenstein, Alfred Hitchcock and (who else?) Peter Lorre.

Loulie Jean Norman, a frequent vocalist on Spike's Victor sessions, lent her voice to Frees' "ghoulfriend," Vampira, on "I Only Have Eyes for You" and "My Heart Sings." Thurl Ravenscroft, whose talents had enriched "Bottoms Up," "Dinner Music" and other recordings, graced "Teenage Brain Surgeon" with his glorious basso profundo.

Carl Brandt (no relation to Eddie), one of the arrangers on "The Railroad Hour" with Carmen Dragon, did the arrangements for the LP. He did his job so well he was employed in the same capacity on all of Jones' future albums. But it was not an easy task.

"The 'Spooktacular' was a complicated album," stated Brandt. "Spike had a million voice tracks. We finally broke it down and ended up scoring it like a movie, because it had to be done in bits and pieces. Nothing was ever done in haste; it took a lot of thinking. I made conductor sheets—which side the stereo was supposed to come from, and all the effects—it was like a regular score."

Among the album's highlights was a stereophonic belch that traveled from one speaker to the other, and back again. "Spooktacular Finale," with its raucous, noisy jug band sound, was as close as the LP got to the old Slicker spirit—which was closer than everything that was to follow.

Just prior to the "Stereo" album, Jones recorded "The Late Late Late Movies," a zany parody of television programming. The session, which cost him $1,200, was financed out of his own pocket; before he could even consummate his deal with Warner Bros., however, he signed a contract with Alvin Bennett of Liberty Records and sold them the master tapes.

The resulting album was "Omnibust," which poked fun at everything on TV from kiddie shows ("Captain Bangaroo") to Lawrence Welk ("Ah-1, Ah-2, Ah-Sunset Strip"). The material itself was uneven and heavy-handed.

"It would have been nicer if we could have had an audience reaction on our albums," mused Eddie Brandt. "Even the guys who did it in front of audiences would sweeten it; the things that didn't get real good laughs, they'd go in and add them. Mort Sahl would add laughs to his nightclub shows at Radio Recorders, where we were editing our stuff."

Jones needed all the laughs he could get; the competition was gaining on him, and in many instances outdoing him. A California raisin farmer and a Harvard math professor were among those making advances into his market. And if Ross Bagdasarian's Chipmunks and Tom Lehrer's devilishly clever patter songs were not enough to contend with, TV game show producer Allan Sherman was looming on the scene with his first album ("My Son, the Folk Singer"), destined to become a huge success.

But if the movers and shakers were ready to write him off, Spike paid no heed. Given his involvement on the Board of Governors of the National Academy of Recording Arts & Sciences, he was evidently held in high esteem within the industry at this time, regardless of his dwindling popularity.

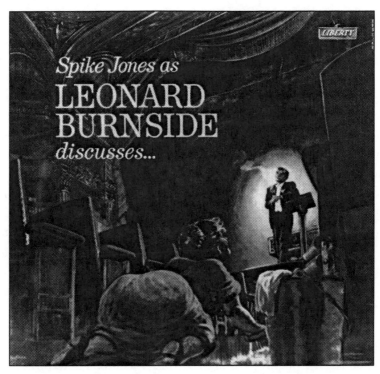

The hottest unreleased comedy album of 1960. (*Ted Hering*)

Working at a feverish pace, he began cranking albums out back to back, working on several projects at once. While he had deals cooking all over town, he was to remain with Liberty for the balance of his career. The label was aptly named: they gave him carte blanche to do whatever he pleased. They also paid for his studio time, which Warner Bros. would not.

No less than three album projects got the green light in 1960. When RCA issued "60 Years of Music America Loves Best," Jones couldn't resist a parody. Before long he was taping "60 Years of Music America Hates Best," harpooning all types of tunes. "Pimples and Braces"—a send-up of the Champs' chart-topper, "Tequila"—"Mairzy Doats" and a reprise of "I Kiss Your Hand, Madame ('Cause I Can't Stand Your Breath)" were among the selections.

Equally amusing were the titles devised solely for the liner notes, or the amusement of the media: "Your Folks Can Put Me in Jail for Loving You, but They'll Never Stop My Face from Breaking Out."

"Leonard Burnside Discusses," a series of mock lectures satirizing conductor Leonard Bernstein, from the pen of Bill Dana and Don Hinkley, was Jones' next effort. It was a telling indication of the competition: Mike Nichols and Elaine May, Bob Newhart, Jonathan Winters, Shelley Berman and Dana himself were *talking* their way up the charts.

"Whether one's musical taste is [Van] Cliburn or the Chipmunks…whether he laughs at Mort Sahl or the Three Stooges, he will enjoy these lectures on musical depreciation," Jones told the press, hyping his product as "the hottest talking comedy album of the year." But the LP, which featured studio adaptations of sketches from his 1960 summer TV show—with canned laughs—was never issued.

Undaunted, Spike poured his energies into another project. "Rides, Rapes and Rescues," a tribute to an era that vanished before he was graduated from high school, musically recreated every genre of silent movies under Jones' constant and careful supervision. Carl Brandt, who shared writing credits with Jones, was conductor as well as arranger on the LP.

The album featured a talented instrumental duo identified only as Hangnails Hennessey and Wingy Brubeck. Spike got carried away in some of his publicity, claiming he himself played drums on the album. John Cyr, who had first worked with Spike on the "Charleston" album a decade earlier, was in fact the drummer; Bobby Van Eps accompanied him on piano.

While the song titles were somewhat zany, the music itself was genuine. "It's the real thing. They updated the harmony a little, but the essence is absolutely authentic. When we were boys, they had piano players in the movie houses, and Bobby had good ears," said his brother, George Van Eps. "My mother was a fine pianist, and Bobby would go in and listen to her back a picture; he knew all the different clichés they played for chase scenes, and so forth."

Exploiting "Rides" for all it was worth, Jones pitched one of the cuts to TV comic Soupy Sales as soundtrack for a pantomime. He promoted the album as atmosphere to coffee houses and nightclubs that showed silent movies, and even to the teenage market as "a new sound" for dance parties. He got additional mileage by sending bosom buddy June Wilkinson to radio stations, offering disc jockeys a free Hangnails Hennessey manicure—with a three-foot carpenter saw.

Although Spike seemed to go into hibernation in 1961 as far as the public was concerned, nothing could have been further from the truth. In actual fact he had his hands in so many pies no one could keep track of him. However, it was to be nearly three years before he brought another album project to fruition.

An aural biography of Ernest Hemingway was one of many LP ideas he tried to get off the ground in the interim. Another was "Play Along With Spike," one of a series with the surreptitious Hennessey and Brubeck combo.

Jones also poured gallons of time and energy into his wife's faltering career during this period. To anyone who would listen, he proposed an album with Helen singing theme songs from popular foreign films, a hodgepodge of Hawaiian songs and similar packages—in short, anything that might be commercial.

The Hawaiian album was a pet project he pitched repeatedly. With some exotic arrangements, and a title like "Adventures in Paradise"—to take advantage of the hit TV show of the same name—Jones was sure it would sell; he had proved more than once he could merchandise almost anything with the right gimmick. Helen had recorded for various labels in the '50s, including a few RCA subsidiaries, but no one was quite as enamored of her voice as Spike.

"Persuasive Concussion" was a satire on then-current percussion albums that Jones promised would sound "like Mighty Joe Young attending an Arthur Murray dance party in a boiler factory." He clinked and clanged his way through Raymond Scott's deliciously weird "Powerhouse" and, in a throwback to the "Dinner Music" LP, inventive new versions of his old stand-bys; he even talked Red Ingle into doing "Chloe" one more time. But it was not like old times.

"Spike called him to do this record," stated Don Ingle, "and Dad said, 'How much?' He gave him a figure and Dad said, 'Not enough.' First time in his life he ever got smart. Dad floated a figure, and Spike sort of hesitated for a minute and finally said, 'Well, okay.' And Dad said, 'Fine, I'll send you a contract.' And he did...the only time he finally got what Spike promised."

The album was half-finished when Liberty interrupted with an idea for something entirely different. "Everybody was ready to write Spike off," contended Don Blocker, then head of A&R at Liberty. "He wasn't a has-been but we couldn't find a market with the comedy albums; we couldn't sell the old Spike Jones. Then I suggested he do an album of dixieland stuff."

"Washington Square"—recorded in the fall of 1963—was a departure from almost everything Jones had done previously. The LP featured his so-called New Band, which combined folk music with traditional dixieland jazz. It was Liberty's idea, he explained at the time, "to try to get an additional image for us; not a new image but an additional image."

The album was "just a temporary musical disarmament until rock 'n' roll blows over," Jones asserted, though he was forced to admit: "It's been eight years blowing over, and it's blowing better now than ever."

However casual the concept sounded, it was a deliberate and calculated move. "It was more of a marketing scheme than anything else," admitted Blocker. "But it worked. 'Washington Square' sold 75,000 copies. That doesn't sound like much now, but it was big in those days."

The title tune—a sparkling rendition of the Village Stompers' then-current hit—was accompanied by an odd choice of material. "If I Had a Hammer," "Red Sails in the Sunset," "Whistler's Muddah" (a retread of "Dance of the Hours," minus Doodles Weaver's commentary) and other standards were done in high style.

Above all, the performances were solid; up-and-coming talents like Tommy Tedesco (dominating the album on banjo) and old-timers Johnny Cyr and Nick Fatool (alternating on drums) gave the LP a touch of class. The album was followed in quick succession by "Spike Jones New Band," "My Man" (which added Other Orchestra alumnus Eddie Kusby on trombone) and "The New Band of Spike Jones Plays Hank Williams Hits."

The New Band contained not one former City Slicker among its members. Spike at times claimed otherwise for the benefit of the press— a reverse of the tactics he had employed on "Hi-Fi Polka Party," apparently hoping to cash in on whatever value such pretense might have.

Moreover, although he picked the tunes and the personnel, Jones' New Band was his in name only. In addition to doing the arrangements, Carl Brandt served as the bandleader—a fact both he and Spike were careful to obscure from the record-buying public.

Asserting dixieland and country and western were a less strenuous way for an aging musical satirist to make a living, Jones told one interviewer, "It makes it a lot easier—I can sit home and phone my part in from now on, compared to getting a mental hernia trying to think of 'Chloes' and everything."

The ironic joke was close to the truth, yet Spike was much involved in making the albums. While Dave Pell was the accredited producer, Jones himself performed that function. "Spike knew what he wanted and I basically knew what Spike wanted, so there really wasn't too much for anybody else to say," noted Brandt. "I'm not denigrating anyone else, but it's just one of those things where we got in and did what we had to do and got out. Anybody else was there strictly as a company representative."

Though the hard core fans—those who had never left him—felt Spike

Helen, Spike and disc jockey-friend Larry Finley (right) relax at a party, at KRHM,
Los Angeles, 1960. (*Ray Avery*)

more or less deserted them with some of his offerings in later years, he was
still a satirist at heart. "The New Band albums were done basically tongue-
in-cheek," asserted Brandt. "They weren't drop-your-pants style like 'Cocktails for Two,' but there were some pretty corny licks on those things. They
were not meant to be 'uptown'—they were a little bit down-the-nose."

The albums were also more than a little bit eye-on-the-dollar. "I don't
know how much Spike liked country and western," said Brandt, in regard to
the LP of Hank Williams tunes. "I think he'd like it if the album sold; if it
didn't sell, he probably wouldn't like it. Spike was a practical guy. He didn't
have any delusions of grandeur about being artistic or anything like that.

"In the final analysis, it's what happens at the bottom line. You're not in
this business to diddle around and make records just for the sake of making
records; you're in it to make a buck if you can. He was very pragmatic—get
the job done the best way you can, as economically as you can. This is what a
lot of people in the record business today seem to forget all about."

While the New Band was as contemporary as Spike ever got, he kept
up to date. While he failed to comprehend the popularity of most '60s

groups and their work, he had a pragmatist's admiration for the Beatles: "They know they're in it for the loot, and they've got a tremendous gimmick going," he remarked to talk show host Bill Ballance. "They have a tremendous sense of humor in their press conferences…"

Asked if he thought the Beatles would be just a fad when they burst on the U.S. scene early in 1964, Spike shrugged, "I wouldn't make any predictions. I don't know what could ruin them…dandruff?"

The state of the art in those days did not encourage him. "I see absolutely no future in the music business…you'd have to be one of a very select few to get anyplace," he told disc jockey Norman Pringle. "As far as records are concerned—if you attain the height of some of your current rock 'n' roll artists of today, if you don't get the second record to follow up the first, you're back to stealing hubcaps again."

While he largely left the pop and rock parodies to others, Jones' renewed comic sensibilities are evident in "Nyet!"—an hilarious satire on life in the Khruschev-era Soviet Union—and the two album projects he was working on when he died. "Persuasive Concussion," which Jones labored at on and off—might well have salvaged his reputation, had he lived to complete it. It is apparent from the extant acetates in his files and the selections posthumously released that Spike hadn't lost his touch for musical depreciation. The Slickerish instrumentals and requisite sound effects he had long disdained were in full bloom, modernized perhaps but more than a little reminiscent of the glory days at RCA Victor.

"Ghoul Days," which he planned with Eddie Brandt as a follow-up to the "Spooktacular," was less promising—but would probably have been welcomed by the admirers Spike hadn't alienated with the New Band albums.

"We had three songs. We were doing it over the phone; I was working in Alaska. I didn't know he was as sick as he was," mused Brandt. "Spike said, 'We're going to do this album if it's the last thing we do.' It was the last thing we did, but we didn't finish it."

Their morbid imaginations ran rampant with possibilities: "Moonlight and Rodents. Holiday for Strychnine. Tennessee Vaults. Butcher Arms Around Me. Homicide and Jethro. Artie Shroud. Rodgers and Heart Attack. Embalm Monroe…"

But Jones ran out of oxygen long before he ran out of ideas. Though he was blessed with imagination enough for two lifetimes, he had barely enough air for one—and a brief one at that.

Down Beat
Spike's Last Years, 1962–1965

Spike Jones was never the picture of robust health, even in his prime. His thin, undernourished frame and hollow chest were generally disguised by expert tailoring—but his sallow complexion was all too obvious.

"I never did like his color. Even in the Paramount Theatre days, he didn't look real healthy. His color wasn't good at all, even way back then," said clarinetist Willie Martinez.

While he fathered a fourth child in 1958—daughter Gina Maria—by the late '50s it had become increasingly obvious to Jones' friends and associates he was not a well man. But he continued to push himself at a relentless pace, determined to make the most of every moment. The internationally renowned bandleader was no less driven at the end of his career than the teenaged entrepreneur who drummed all over town for a dollar a dance.

What kept him going full speed? "Maybe he figured if he stopped, he'd die," speculated Linda Jones. "Maybe it was based on the convictions of some people who didn't realize how bad his physical condition was—a lot of people felt it was like talent going to waste, that he shouldn't be just sitting in the backyard writing, or on the phone planning things, but he really should be working. Maybe he felt the pressure from that."

Jones, who aged rapidly in his last years, rarely acknowledged time was running out, or even that he was short of breath. "He told me he knew he had emphysema a few years before he died," remembered long-time friend and associate Harry Geller. "But it was always gags, always a laugh, nothing very serious. He knew he was ill; he knew smoking was at the base of most of what ailed him, and yet he carried on. I never saw anybody before or since that smoked as incessantly as he did."

Despite the ever-present oxygen tank, he was unable to kick the habit. "I used to take him out to UCLA Medical Center for therapy," said his former manager, Dick Webster. "I'd take Spike down once a week; he'd come out, get in the car and light up a cigarette."

Realizing his projects and ideas and turning them into tangible products during those final years grew into a strenuous undertaking. Even a simple maneuver like descending the stairs of a studio, after a recording session, was a difficult task.

The illness was hard not only on Jones, but on those around him. "One of the saddest memories I have," reflected Bill Dana, "was when we did the 'More Jose Jimenez' album that used some of the bits I had done on Spike's TV show. Taping at a speed of 15 inches per second, we had to edit out his heavy breathing.

"You didn't notice it on television, but when you sat in a room with these huge speakers, you could hear this emphysema that finally did him in," recalled Dana. "I really loved the man, and we were close to tears; we looked on the floor of the editing room and there was a very eloquent picture of a man who was in terrible trouble with his lungs."

Public appearances became not only fewer but far less prestigious. By the early '60s, the big Strip hotels in Las Vegas were no longer calling on him. The Riviera, the Flamingo and the Tropicana—where Jones was breaking attendance records as late as 1959—stopped booking his act; he was relegated to playing the Showboat, which hired many country and western attractions and lesser names.

The act—a modified, scaled down version of the stage revues—featured new arrangements and a crew of 12. While the show was a far cry from the heyday of the City Slickers, it was a small miracle to those involved—and a backstage drama of major proportions.

"Spike was still the leader. We carried him through pretty good," said comedian Peter James, who served as Jones' constant companion and manager during those last years. "I was with him all the time. He depended on me; if he wanted anything done, he'd call me. I'd be there with the oxygen all the time, and the wheelchair.

"I used to take him from the dressing room to the stage in the wheelchair. I'd wheel Spike into the wings; he'd get out of the wheelchair and go on," he revealed. "Then we started using a clip-on mic, so he didn't have to leave the cowbell set. He did the whole show sitting down."

In May 1964 Spike and Helen went on tour with *The Show of the Year,* a revue that packaged them with Homer and Jethro and the TV stars of *The Beverly Hillbillies.* The show marked yet another comedown in his career.

Spike's popularity was in decline, Jayne Mansfield's in ascent, at the time of this autograph session (with Mickey Hargitay and Helen Grayco) in Las Vegas.

"When we came into a town, the carpet was laid out—for the Beverly Hillbillies—and Spike was in the background," recalled James. "Until I stepped in. I said, 'Wait a minute. Spike is the star. You're not going to step on him. He's the star of the show, and he should be treated that way.' I fought and fought. I used to call ahead, so when we got into town we would be the big deal instead of them."

By the time Jones played Disneyland that August, he was almost too sick to continue the charade—but never quite. "Even on stage he had one of these little inhalators, like you'd use for an asthmatic," said Joe Siracusa. "He'd breathe in and make the announcements and go offstage. He wasn't really partaking in the show."

In a change of pace that delighted fans too young to recall *The Musical Depreciation Revue* in its prime, the repertoire for the theme park engagement reverted to vintage Slicker material. Former associates like Siracusa, however, were present only in the audience.

In a desperate attempt to get away from the heavy Los Angeles smog, Jones moved with his family to 490 Martin Lane in Trousdale Estates. High in the hills above Sunset Boulevard, he was able to breathe a little bit easier. But his last-ditch effort was far too late to make much difference.

In January 1965, Spike opened at the Roaring '20s in San Diego, California. On January 29, toward the end of the engagement, he suffered an asthma attack and was rushed to the hospital by air ambulance. He had scarcely recovered when he was back in action the following month, at the Showboat in Las Vegas.

"He would work two shows, and I would come in and do the last show," recalled Spike Jr. One memorable evening, "I had taken his place for the third show. He was sitting on the steps watching, and I remember making him laugh, and it's probably the biggest high of my life."

The gig, however, was not a cause for celebration. "My wife and I went backstage to see him," said George Rock. "I cried. I couldn't face him; I've never seen a man look so ill and still be alive. He wanted to see our son—he was godfather to the boy. We promised we'd come back and bring him, but I couldn't go back. That's the only time I ever lied to him, but I just couldn't go back, I couldn't face him again. For days it just haunted me."

"People were walking out at the Showboat," recalled comedian Mousie Garner. "He looked like death. They couldn't say the show was bad; they just couldn't look at him."

Freddy Morgan was working in Reno when Jones called and asked him, for old times' sake, to appear with him that March at Harrah's Club, Lake Tahoe. Morgan told Jones not to go, advising him he wouldn't be able to breathe in the high altitude. His was not the only plea that fell on deaf ears.

"I went to see Spike at the Showboat to see what kind of staging he would need, because he was playing in our lounge," recalled Bob Vincent, then Harrah's entertainment director. "He was laying on a cot with an oxygen mask over his face, when I went backstage. He was having trouble breathing. I told him, 'At 8,000 feet, Tahoe's not good for you in your condition.' He gasped, 'Everything's going to be all right, don't worry about it. I'll be okay; just be sure you've got an oxygen mask for me.' "

The bandleader's eldest daughter was also concerned. "I was at the house the night before they were going to go, and he was not well at all," affirmed Linda Jones. "I thought, 'How is he going to get on an airplane tomorrow?' It would have been impossible to picture this man being well enough the next day—to go anywhere. I went home, and the next day I

The Jones family puts on a happy face—despite Spike's illness—for a 1960 TV interview. From left, Spike Jr., Dad, Linda, Helen, baby Gina and Leslie.

get a call from my dad—sounding fine, like a miracle: 'I know you were worried about me last night, but I'm going.' "

Jones was no less demanding of himself than he was of others. "I fought with Spike, but he wouldn't give up," said Peter James. "I said, 'Let's not go to Lake Tahoe.' He said, 'We have to go. I've got these people on my hands.' I said, 'The hell with the people, think about yourself. They can make money without you.' He said, 'No, the show must go on.' He loved the business. He loved to perfect things. And when they went over...ohhh. That's what he used to love."

On March 23, Jones collapsed at Harrah's. He was put aboard an emergency plane and flown back to Los Angeles, where he was admitted to Santa Monica Hospital. His 15-year-old son—who had seen the stage show perhaps 100 times—took a leave of absence from school to play the remainder of the engagement.

Jones remained on the critical list for nine days, and spent an additional week in the hospital before being released. "We were all so glad when my dad would get out of the hospital, we didn't realize he might die—he was okay. If he got well and got home from the hospital, everything was all right…I refused to believe anything was going to happen to him," said Linda, who was little more aware than her younger half-siblings of just how critical Jones' condition was.

But the bandleader—with a little help from close friends like Danny Thomas and Loretta Young—had come to terms with his hastening illness. "Spike knew he was dying. He just had to go on; he figured he would make it," said James. "But that's what did it, up there in Tahoe, that altitude."

James moved into the Trousdale mansion to take care of Jones during his last days. Toward the end, he was literally carrying his boss around. "Spike had lost so much weight, he was like a baby," mused James' ex-wife, actress Ruth Foster.

Jones couldn't bear to sit still and let nature take its course. "He liked to get out, to get some fresh air," said James. "He wouldn't let loose. He was always going; he wouldn't want to lay in bed, he wanted to get out."

"Each day Peter would take him for a drive, and they'd drive around Beverly Hills," said Foster. "Spike would say, 'Let's hurry back, let's get back.' Each day it got shorter and shorter, and finally he wouldn't leave the house because he was so scared without the oxygen. I believe the family had to call in a psychiatrist, because they felt he was hooked on the oxygen, that it became a mental thing. Even when he could be without it, he was scared to be away from it."

Despite heavy medication, Spike remained sharp and alert in his last days. "He was weak, but quite lucid when I last saw him," said Bud Yorkin, who spent the evening with Jones on April 29. "I was trying to talk him into going out to dinner. Helen wanted to see if we could get him pepped up. He agreed that we'd all go out to dinner, but it never happened."

The next morning, Jones complained of a headache. He felt well enough to go for a car ride that afternoon, but later in the day, a nurse noticed an irregularity in Spike's pulse. His personal physician, Dr. Joseph Schwartz, was summoned to the house.

Jones died in his sleep on Saturday, May 1, 1965, at 3:15 a.m. He was found by his nurse. "They had given him quite a few shots—one for his respiratory condition, one for his allergies, one for vitamins—and they were a little concerned about all the shots they gave him," revealed Foster. "They gave him one to relax him and tranquilize him, and I guess he was so tranquilized he just slept on; he usually had to have the oxygen all the time."

Dr. Schwartz determined the immediate cause of death as an excess

Jones never lost his appreciation for fine art. (*Ted Hering*)

of carbon dioxide in the lungs and respiratory insufficiency. "Emphysema" was close enough for the media, although one Los Angeles newspaper attributed Jones' demise to a heart ailment.

On May 4, a requiem Mass was held at St. Victor's Church in West Hollywood. Jones—"painted up so he looked like a wax dummy," said one friend—played to a full house. An overflow crowd of roughly 400 gathered to pay their last respects, including a host of show business personalities; few of his associates showed, apart from current personnel. Entombment followed in the mausoleum at Holy Cross Cemetery in nearby Culver City.

"Spike Jones wanted people to be happy. He wanted them to smile and to lift up their hearts in a time of war and the rumors of war," stated the Rt. Rev. Msgr. John Devlin. The 53-year-old bandleader—who outlived his mother by only three and a half years—was eulogized as "a genius in the clothes of a musical satirist. His was a gloriously fantastic imagination, and he used it to make people forget for a moment the nervous tension of our era."

The pastor spoke of Jones' courage and nobility of character, his recent conversion to Catholicism and his first communion. Msgr. Devlin quoted Spike as saying the latter "was one of the great experiences of his life, and [he] said his newfound faith had given him strength to bear the ill health which plagued him for the last year of his life."

Jones' oversized funnybone also helped to sustain him. "He always had the humor, in spite of not being well," stressed Linda Jones. "A few years prior, when my dad first got ill, he had to go to Denver to make a speech, and I went with him. And when we got off the plane in Denver, where the altitude is severe, I had to call the fire department for him. He was standing there with the oxygen mask on and the fireman said to him, 'Tell me, Mr. Jones, are you on your way into Denver or on your way out?' And he took the mask off, and with that look, he said to him, 'I'll let you know in a minute.'

"He handled his illness with as much humor as he possibly could," stated Linda. "He was very valiant, very brave; he wasn't the kind to whimper or complain. A lot of people milk it for all they can get—it just wasn't his way. I felt he was very humble in life, and very valiant in facing death."

Clearly, Jones understood the concept of mind over matter. The ideas never stopped flowing, even on his deathbed. The last project to reach fruition was an Italian restaurant. Spike Jones' Oodles of Noodles opened on La Cienega Boulevard in Beverly Hills not long after his passing. The establishment opened with a big splash, but was short-lived.

Jones' estate was estimated at over $300,000. His first wife, Patricia, filed suit, claiming she was awarded $750 a month for life—hers, not his—at the time of their divorce; she asked for a lump sum to cover her life expectancy. Three years later, a court awarded her over $114,000. By then, however, claims against the estate had whittled it down to less than $40,000—with claims of $53,000 outstanding. The former chorus girl died in 1977.

Helen Grayco briefly resumed her singing career after Jones' death, with little success. In 1968, she married New York restaurateur William Rosen in a brief Las Vegas ceremony; for a number of years they ran a popular West Los Angeles café called Gatsby's, where she occasionally performed. Now retired, and recently widowed for the second time, she keeps current in music.

In the late '60s and early '70s Spike Jones Jr. attempted to follow in

Spike Jones Jr. (third from left) tried to carry on with the Barstow Filharmonic.
(*Scott Corbett*)

his dad's footsteps, a decision which "upset the hell out of my mother."
He recorded a few sound-alike discs, including an amusing parody of
"Raindrops Keep Fallin' On My Head," and hit the road with a rock 'n'
roll-oriented version of the City Slickers.

"A lot of things that I wanted to find out from my father, I never
really had the opportunity to find out, because he was sick," stated Jones
fils. "Once I started performing I had thousands of questions to ask him.
'How do you do this?' 'What do you do in this particular area?' There
were a whole bunch of questions that never really got answered."

The bandleader's son soon found that cowbells and electric guitars did not mix. As he once observed: "The problem was that people who came to see me expected to see the old Spike Jones, and I was doing a hipper thing." More to the point, he was heir apparent to an act too tough to follow.

Spike Jr. has since turned to a myriad of enterprises, establishing a reputation as a producer of special events and live television broadcasts. His projects have included *The 52nd Presidential Inaugural Concert Celebration at the Lincoln Memorial,* ABC's millennium New Year's Eve TV special and the Primetime Creative Arts Emmy Awards; he has produced and directed programs for HBO, Showtime, A&E, Nickelodeon and the History Channel. He currently lives in Los Angeles, where he is president of SJ2 Entertainment. His 21-year-old son, Taylor, is a personal trainer and an actor who has appeared in films and plays.

Linda Jones served as assistant to top literary agent Irving "Swifty" Lazar for 18 years. The Beverly Hills resident is completing a book on the life of Billy Barty titled *Long Story, Short,* a project she began with the former City Slicker and beloved character actor before his death late in 2000. Her daughter, Alexandra Hughes, is a costume designer for films and television.

Leslie Ann Jones, who has racked up over 25 years as a recording engineer and record producer, is Director of Music Recording and Scoring for Skywalker Sound, George Lucas' audio post-production complex in Marin County, California. She resides in Oakland where she serves on the city's Cultural Arts Commission, as well as the advisory boards for the nearby Ex'pression Center for New Media and UCLA Extension's Recording Arts program. Leslie is a past Chairwoman of the National Academy of Recording Arts & Sciences' Board of Trustees, and still serves on several national committees, having clearly inherited her father's multi-tasking abilities.

Spike's youngest daughter, Gina Jones, produces television and radio commercials, marketing health and beauty products. She lives in Los Angeles with her husband Terry Sullivan, and their preschool-aged son Nicholas, who appears to take after his grandfather. "He's a real ham," she reported. "He discovered the camera the day he was born."

The bandleader's multimedia omnipresence is a legacy especially treasured by Gina, who was two months shy of her seventh birthday when her father passed away. "Because we have the records, the TV shows, the films—I know his voice, I know how he looked, I know how he moved," she affirmed. "I don't remember anything personal, but I'm luckier than most people who have lost a parent that young."

Life After Death
The Second Coming of Spike Jones

On Sunday, February 26, 1995, Spike Jones made music history once more, nearly 30 years after his death. With his loved ones in attendance at Universal CityWalk, the bandleader was honored with a posthumous Grammy for "Cocktails for Two," as his half-century-old RCA recording was inducted into the Hall of Fame. It was long overdue, but the recognition that had eluded Spike during his lifetime was finally his.

Time has been kind to Jones in the four decades since he passed from the scene. In recent years there has been a tremendous resurgence of interest in the bandleader who once billed himself as The Wizard of the Washboard. His memory has been kept alive by LPs, CDs, videos, cable TV broadcasts, radio specials, books, documentaries, websites, a fan club, a postage stamp and a variety of tributes both live and recorded.

As Joseph Laredo observed in his liner notes for a 2002 compilation of radio transcriptions, "Even the most daunting challenges of this fledgling millennium seem somehow less intimidating when you can march bravely into the future to the beat of the birdaphone."

Spike's sphere of influence has grown wider over the years. He has been cited as an inspiration to artists as diverse as rock composer Frank Zappa, comic George Carlin, painter Ed Ruscha, satirist "Weird Al" Yankovic, singer-songwriter Jimmy Buffett and British comedy troupe Monty Python.

The foremost musical humorist of the late 20th century, Peter Schickele, considers himself a student of both Jones and Hoffnung. The perpetrator of P.D.Q. Bach has recalled a misspent youth acting out Spike's records with his brother and friends, forming a comedy band called Jerky Jems and his Balmy Brothers while in his early teens. Prolific jazz keyboardist Chick Corea has stated that he found Jones "a breath of fresh air" in contrast to his serious musical education, which included a stint at Julliard.

Jones' renaissance has been attributed partly to radio personality Dr. Demento, otherwise known as Barry Hansen. The Doctor, who began playing zany novelty records from his collection on a Los Angeles underground rock station in 1971, has gleefully introduced Spike to new generations. In addition to Demento's syndicated program, Jones' work has been faithfully included in the good doctor's "Greatest Novelty Hits of All Time" audio and video releases, and other compilation albums.

"Spike was a major inspiration for me, all the way from the early exposure when I was a child, to when I started doing the show. He's the King of Dementia," asserted his dedicated disciple. "I owe my career in many ways to Spike Jones and his music."

Why has Jones' work withstood the test of time so well? "It's good-hearted fun, expertly rendered. The musicianship is still absolutely tip-top," said Demento. "Spike developed the idea of silly music to a virtuosity that had been unknown. Nobody before that really came close to him, with the amount of effects he used, and the dexterity with which he used them—especially in his golden age, from 1944 to about 1951.

"Spike was the first one with his use of sound effects...and glugs and all sorts of things like that, to really completely upset the normal foundations, the normal parameters of what popular music performance was supposed to be..."

The continuing interest in Jones' work did not surprise Joe Siracusa. "Spike always made it a policy not to date himself, whenever possible," observed the former City Slicker. "He was very sharp in that respect. That's why his records are still funny, because they're not dated. The kids think Spike Jones is something new."

The bandleader's son concurred. "It's surprising how many 9-year-olds and 12-year-olds are familiar with what my father did," Spike Jones Jr. told an interviewer. "A lot of it has to do with Weird Al [Yankovic] and Dr. Demento, and the nature of the music and the comedy itself. It is timeless from the standpoint that you really don't have to know or understand the music he was satirizing at the time to make the guns work for you or the ducks falling, and all of the other stuff that went with the band."

Chief among the "other stuff" that has won over the younger generation are the vocal interpretations of George Rock and Doodles Weaver, as fresh and appealing as they were decades ago. "My Two Front Teeth" and "The William Tell Overture" are evergreen.

Former bandsmen and family members gather for a 1988 documentary. Clockwise from top left: Bernie Jones, Joe Siracusa, Eddie Brandt, Spike Jones Jr., his son Taylor, Billy Barty, Leslie Ann Jones and Linda Jones. (*Scott Corbett*)

The technology employed by Jones also helps contemporary audiences appreciate his work. "I always marvel at what he was able to do live in a single track recording studio, based on what is done today in multiple tracks," said Spike Jr. "His stereo console and home equipment was always state of the art, and very much up to date."

Dozens of compilation albums have been released on record, cassette tape and compact disc since Jones' death, thanks to a loyal cult of fans. A ready market for virtually anything created by the bandleader has resulted in the reissue of not only his most popular records, but also much obscure material—including Standard Radio transcriptions, V-Discs, radio broadcasts, movie and TV soundtracks, and selections RCA Victor (now BMG Music) chose not to release during his lifetime.

RCA's "The Best of Spike Jones" (originally titled "Thank You, Music Lovers!") has been continuously available since it was first issued in 1960. The album—which reprised a dozen of his most memorable tunes—reportedly sold in excess of 100,000 copies in the first decade of release. The original LP is still prized for the cover art by *Mad* illustrator Jack Davis, depicting Jones being attacked by an angry crowd.

Foreign compilations have been much sought-after by U.S. collectors, notably the 1973-74 German RCA set of three double-albums—"Spike Jones Murders Them All," "…Murders Again" and "…Can't Stop Murdering." The latter, which includes such long-suppressed numbers as "Rum Tee Diddle Dee Yump," "Fiddle Faddle," "Alto, Baritone and Bass" and "Rickeyshaw," is still in demand, despite subsequent CD reissues of the material.

One of the more entertaining compilations of the pre-compact disc era was "The King of Corn"—a long out-of-print LP comprised of tunes like "Sound Effects Man" and "People Will Say We're in Love" from *Furlough Fun* and *Bob Burns* shows. "The Uncollected Spike Jones," released by the aptly-named Hindsight Records, vindicated Jones' 1946 experiment with his Other Orchestra; it proved the bandleader could have done what Tommy Dorsey did with equal finesse, had he chosen to follow that path.

Harlequin Records of East Sussex, England, has been responsible for more compilations of Jonesiana over the years than any other label, initially on LP and tape and more recently on CD. Their releases, obvious labors of love produced by lifelong fan John Wood, have drawn from Standard transcriptions, V-Discs, radio airchecks, film soundtracks, RCA rejects and alternate takes, to the delight of European and American collectors alike. In 1998 they issued Spike's complete Bluebird recordings, including "Beautiful Eggs." Such recent efforts as "Fonk" have brought still more rarities out of mothballs.

Good Music Records' "Spike Jones: The Man Who Murdered Music" dusted off several forgotten items from the maestro's archives, including "I Wuv a Wabbit," which subsequently became a much-requested listener favorite on a children's radio program in the Philadelphia area, WXPN's "Kids Corner." The arguable high note of the CD, an instrumental version of "Carmen" from the unfinished "Persuasive Concussion" album, was presented with much fanfare as a world premiere on "The Dr. Demento Show."

The 1994 compilation was but one of three notable releases that year. Demento himself co-produced a near-definitive double CD for Rhino Records, "Musical Depreciation Revue: The Spike Jones Anthology." All the familiar "best of" selections were included, along with a sizable number of first-time reissues. Catalyst/BMG Classics' compact disc compilation, "Spiked! The Music of Spike Jones," included two previously unissued Liberty recordings—"Powerhouse" and "Frantic Freeway"—as well as the complete "Nutcracker Suite."

The near-simultaneous release of the Rhino and Catalyst albums resulted in an abundance of press. "How innocent it all sounds now. And how precious, in a musical age that has no room for a modern Spike Jones," observed Richard Corliss in *Time* magazine. "The new Spike CDs are a welcome reminder of a time when pop music was so demure and so universal in its appeal that a daredevil insider could give it the razz."

Better yet, as collector Mike Kieffer pithily observed: "These CDs allowed us commoners finally to hear most of Spike's great studio recordings without the interference of the great RCA Echo-and-Stereo Machine used extensively on '60s and '70s reissues."

Spike Jones Jr. has done much to revive his father's work for new generations to enjoy. Not content to simply license the reissues and compilations of others, he has taken an active role in perpetuating the Jones legacy. "The Craziest Show on Earth"—a boxed set of LPs comprised of largely unfamiliar tracks from the radio and television shows—was followed by "Spike Jones Presents World War II" on cassette and the reissues of the first two Verve albums, "Dinner Music" and the "Xmas Spectacular." Spike Jr. has packaged and repackaged the television shows, most visibly in the multi-volume "Best of Spike Jones" for Paramount Home Video.

Rare TV and movie footage was also incorporated into *The Spike Jones Story*, a documentary produced by Storyville Films of Copenhagen. The Danish-financed film aired on European television and was seen on public broadcasting stations in the U.S.

The bandleader's old 78 rpm records and albums are still treasured despite the avalanche of compilations—several of the originals, inexplicably, have never been reissued—and pristine specimens often command high prices at auctions and record collectors' conventions. The online auction site, eBay, has been a boon to collectors, lowering the price of rarities and making items easier to find.

"By the Beautiful Sea," pulled off the market by RCA due to its supposedly dirty lyrics, is among the scarcest of Jones' records today. But the rarest discs of all are the special wartime issue of "SNAFU" and the souvenir pressing of "All Hail COINegie Tech!" A single copy of the former is known to exist; there are only two of the latter, which was handed out at a jukebox convention.

Joe Siracusa's spare-time effort to revive the Slickers and pay tribute to his former boss—which resulted in the LP, "The New Society Band Shoves It In Your Ear!"—demonstrated it was possible to capture the essence of the band without mimicking it. There have however been many attempts to recreate the Slicker sound in recent decades.

The Clams, a New York-based band that "existed for one weekend"— just long enough to record a 45 rpm single—came closer than most with "Close to You." As banjoist-vocalist Pete Levin recalled, "It took four of us to overdub the percussion track (glass, birdcalls, gunshots, etc.), simulating what Spike did by himself. The record got heavy top-40 play for a couple of weeks then disappeared because you couldn't buy it anywhere."

Unlike the one-shot Clams, the Rubber Band enjoyed a measure of high-profile success, appearing on *The Tonight Show*. The group, led by Los Angeles artist Llyn Foulkes, recorded an equally laudable attempt on 45, emulating Jones with "Bye Bye Blackbird." The Cornball Express also made an admirable effort with "Almost Degraded."

Ray Stevens, a prolific purveyor of novelty singles since the early '60s, paid homage to Spike on CD with a dead-on sound-alike parody of Kris Kristofferson's "Help Me Make It Through the Night." The Belgian group, Telex, performed a song called "Spike Jones" on their "Looney Tunes" album, using digital samples from Jones' rendition of "I'm Getting Sentimental Over You."

Bob Kerr and his Whoopee Band, a British group that has toured for over three decades, performs raucous renditions of Jones' hits in their stage act. "We are very much doing Spike's stuff," acknowledged Kerr. "Our show is a complete comedy-with-music show and our best features and most-applauded numbers are when we do 'Cocktails,' 'Chloe,' 'You Always Hurt' and the rest of those wonderful numbers immortalized by Spike. We play all over Europe and the story is the same—they all loved Spike," reported the bandleader, who included three of the numbers in his album, "Molotov Cocktails for Two."

In 1987, the New York Jazz Repertory Ensemble, led by banjoist Eddy Davis, staged *The Best of Spike Jones* at Michael's Pub in New York. Armed with starter pistols, cowbells, bird calls, taxi horns, a toy skunk and a Chrysler brake drum salvaged from a junkyard, the group reprised "Cocktails for Two," "Holiday for Strings" and other hits from the maestro's canon.

"Ever since I was a little kid I've heard the records and always wanted to be a part of a band like this," said Davis, a longtime member of Woody Allen's jazz group. "Probably almost every musician I've known in my life has wanted to be part of a band like this, and it never happened."

Davis' seven-piece ensemble appeared at the Boston Globe Jazz and

The New York Jazz Repertory Ensemble pays tribute to Jones, 1987. Clockwise from bottom right: bandleader Eddy Davis, J.J. Silva, David Grego, Cynthia Sayer, Simon Wettenhall, Joe Muranyi and Todd Robbins.

Heritage Festival, the Sacramento Jazz Jubilee and the Showboat Hotel in Atlantic City. Despite the group's success in recreating Jones' instrumentals, they had difficulty with vocal interpretations—especially the glugging chorus on "Hawaiian War Chant." "It was practically enough to give you epilepsy," said pianist-washboardist-sound effects man Todd Robbins.

Production designer C. Robert Holloway ran into similar problems when he devised and staged *An Evening with Spike Jones and his City Slickers* in New Orleans in 1992. Although he managed to adapt "Carmen" to the stage—"we took it off the record note-by-note"—he conceded, "The one number that seems to bedevil us, and doesn't seem to quite work, is 'The William Tell Overture,' but…I thought it was very important that we do it for this incarnation, so the purists wouldn't beat me up."

The first half of the show was a full-scale recreation of *The Musical Depreciation Revue,* which employed tuned cowbells reportedly used by Jones. But because Holloway "didn't want to do a museum piece," he came up with a second act in which "God sends Spike back for one more night, to tackle the music that's come along since his death"—

Mick Jagger, Diana Ross, Michael Jackson, Madonna and others, appropriately "Spike-ified."

Eos Orchestra, an adventurous New York-based ensemble that prides itself on "the rediscovery of important neglected works and composers," offered an evening of *"Out There" Music* featuring four of Jones' unfinished numbers in 1999. "They did them with an 80-piece orchestra, sound effects and everything," marveled Spike Jr. "And it was just outrageous."

Carl Mack, the xylophonist and "new vaudevillian" who portrayed Jones in the New Orleans revue, reprised his role in 2003 when the Kentucky Symphony Orchestra presented *Who Spiked the Symphony?* The show, performed old-time-radio style for a live audience, assaulted Cincinnati with renditions of "Shh! Harry's Odd (Scherezade)" and "Carmen" (from "Persuasive Concussion"), along with "The William Tell Overture" and other familiar items.

Ultimately, no one has succeeded in taking the bandleader's place. "Nobody is Spike Jones," stated his longtime publicist, Buddy Basch. "Somebody said to Guy Lombardo, 'What happens to New Year's Eve when you die?' And he said, 'I'll take it with me.' He wasn't kidding. Same thing with Spike Jones—there was only one."

It is not only that Jones was *sui generis;* his uniqueness is also a matter of timing. He was very much the product of an era, a time that has passed as surely as the man himself.

"He occupies a unique place in Americana—there was no one else quite like him. A lot of people tried the same thing, and many were successful to some degree, but he was the one who became a household word," stressed Gil Bernal. "I wonder what would he have done with today's musical scene, would he have been able to satirize it? I imagine he would have had a ball."

Those who knew him disagree on whether Jones himself would have succeeded today. "I personally think he was way ahead of his time, as far as the comedy and the quickness of it," noted Phil Gray. "He had so much comedy packed into a short time. When I saw *The Benny Hill Show*, I said, 'I wish Spike were alive to see this,' because he would have gone ape over it. A lot of the stuff Hill did was Spike Jones; he copied a lot of the schtick."

"Had he lived I think probably Spike would've been the biggest thing in the music business," observed friend Harriet Geller. "He was some kind of cockamamie genius; he had an enormous gift for wonderful ideas."

Countered Eddie Brandt: "I think his day was over. He never would

Spike up the band: Carl Mack tunes up for a 2003 concert with the
Kentucky Symphony Orchestra.

have had anything again. But he was one of a kind; there was nobody like him. 'Spike Jones' is a magic name today, wherever you go in the world."

From reruns of TV's Korean War era sitcom, *M*A*S*H*, to comparisons with contemporary musicians, the name—which remains synonymous with musical humor—still surfaces with frequency today. "It's unusual to have your father's name mentioned in the newspaper, or to see him on television so long after he has died," reflected Linda Jones. "It's as though he's not dead—like he is still somehow with us."

The name is often confused these days with that of journalist-turned-filmmaker Spike Jonze, best known perhaps for *Being John Malkovich*. The director's pseudonymous salute to the bandleader (his real name is Adam Spiegel) is not appreciated by the Jones family.

Others have confused the bandleader's name with African American filmmaker Spike Lee. Prospective patrons of Robert Holloway's New Orleans revue inquired, "Is this going to have Malcolm X in it?" The faux pas was also made at a Manhattan city council hearing by New York State Assembly Speaker Mel Miller, who declared, "As Spike Jones says, you have to do the right thing."

Clearly, the right thing to many is to pay homage and perpetuate the legacy. To this day fans recall the sensation caused by world champion iceskater Scott Hamilton, when he used "You Always Hurt the One You Love" as the basis for a routine he performed at the 1984 Winter Olympics in Sarajevo.

The Spike Jones International Fan Club is defunct, but former members still talk about the group's one and only gathering. The club's 1989 convention, held in the Los Angeles area, was attended by Jones' four children and many of the surviving members of his band.

While the club still serves as an information clearinghouse and maintains archives, there is no central repository for Jonesiana. The warehouses where the bandleader stored his prized possessions were emptied when he died, and their contents scattered to the winds. Many of Jones' crazy props and costumes were sold at auction, with some of the instruments going to Drum City; his personal scrapbooks were unceremoniously unloaded in a St. Vincent de Paul thrift store, and salvaged by a fan who chanced upon them. Some of the loot simply went to the incinerator.

Although the bandleader's recordings are not heard on the radio as frequently as they once were, he still has his allies in the broadcasting world. Skip Marrow of KBRD AM in Olympia, Washington, is one of the more ardent ones. "I will play as many as eight to ten Spike Jones records in a day, maybe 30 in a week. KBRD plays the music that Skip likes and nothing else. It's my passion and I'll do it no matter what," he asserted.

"The senior vice president of a billion-dollar company said to me, 'As I drive by the station I reach for my checkbook to give you a donation, and then Spike Jones comes on the air, and I put it back in my pocket.' " Reported one listener: "In answer there is more Spike than ever on the station."

Jones has been honored by not one but three stars on Hollywood's celebrated Walk of Fame: one for records (1500 Vine Street), one for radio (6290 Sunset Boulevard) and one for TV (6826 Hollywood Boulevard). Few entertainment personalities share the distinction. In 1991 the bandleader was pictured on a commemorative stamp issued by the island of Grenada, one of four marking the 50th anniversary of the USO.

But perhaps the most significant memorial to Spike Jones today is the place he occupies in the hearts and minds of his former associates. The seasons they spent on the road with him were, for many of the City Slickers, the best years of their lives.

"It was a very happy period in my life," observed Joe Siracusa. "I can't think of any other band I could've worked in and been that happy. Or that I could have contributed [to] as much.

"Some of the guys griped, but I can honestly say I can't remember one time where I really suffered or where I wasn't enjoying myself. Through all the years, Spike was very generous to me, financially and with his praise," said Siracusa. "In later years, I wrote and thanked him for every night I played. I said, 'There hasn't been a night I played that stage I didn't have as much fun as the audience.' And I meant it."

"Working with Spike was a great experience," said Eddie Metcalfe. "It was a good time to travel because there was a great deal more appreciation for that type of show, and we traveled in some pretty good style; today the bands fly everywhere. It's an era that has slipped by us, and that's one band that has not been replaced."

Appendix A: Oodles of Doodles
Weaver, Man & Legend

Doodles Weaver lived in the towering shadows of his father, his brother and his own formidable legend. He could never compete with any of them. He gave up trying when he died by his own hand in 1983, putting an end to his tortured existence. But the legend lives on.

The best known member of Spike Jones' organization was the nut his boss only pretended to be. Where Jones was happy to retreat to his relatively normal private life under a cloak of craziness, Weaver basked in the notoriety won by wacky exploits both real and wildly exaggerated, until the legend became larger than life and began to torment him.

The line between fact and fiction was blurred in both their lives. Where reality ended and fantasy began, in Weaver's case, is almost impossible to determine. While he was a student at Los Angeles High School, he purportedly announced he was going to commit suicide at noon one day, then threw a football tackling dummy off a rooftop, dressed in his clothing. When his well-to-do parents went to Europe, he reportedly hung a sign in front of the family mansion that read DOODLES' NIGHTCLUB, and proceeded to turn it into one.

There was no end to the stories attending his years at Stanford University, beginning with his arrival on campus, when he supposedly had a chauffeur roll out a red carpet for him at the door to the freshman dorm. While at Stanford, legend has it he paid his tuition in pennies...hung an *autographed* picture of Jesus in his room...sped down Market Street in San Francisco, dressed as Christ...mounted a beer tank behind the driver's seat of his car, with a long tube he could drink from...drove a rented car backwards on city streets to reduce the mileage...took apart a Model A Ford and hauled it to the top of a tower where he reassembled it, piece by piece.

"He spent a good part of those years after leaving Stanford trying to erase the legends of his time. He never succeeded. As fast as he stamped them out, others took their place," wrote a newspaper columnist. "New ones surfaced years after he left Stanford."

According to legend, Doodles once donned a bra and wig, leaned out a fraternity window and screamed, "Help me! I'm being attacked!"...took a dormitory fire hose and laced it through the balustrade of a staircase, then turned it on full blast...flooded a frat house and mixed the water with Jello...bought a horse from a glue factory, herded it to the second floor of the dorm and shot it...turned up in the arms of a newly-completed statue, when it was ceremoniously unveiled...stole five cupid figurines from a nearby cemetery and used them to mark freshly dug graves on a frat house lawn...and, in a final act of defiance when he earned his B.A. in Humanities and Sciences, roller-skated up to the university president to collect his diploma.

"During the 35 years since my graduation," the comedian observed early in 1973, "I've heard more invidious, insidious, invalid, inane, insane and incredulous stories about myself on the campus than I care to recall. I was no angel, but I was no practical joker, horse-shooter, roller-skater [or] car-wrecker either."

Weaver spent the early successful years of his career building up and encouraging the legend. His fellow City Slickers had little doubt the tales of Professor Feetlebaum's past had at least some basis in fact; the offstage antics they witnessed firsthand did nothing to convince them otherwise. "That was part of his glory," said his close friend and rival comedian, Earl Bennett. "He didn't want to be like anybody else, he wanted to be an original."

But by the early '50s, with his career slipping into decline, Doodles began denying the stories that followed him everywhere. "Contrary to popular belief, my undergraduate existence was not a series of idiotic pranks, wildman gyrations, and uninhibited calisthenics of a gleeful, thoughtless buffoon whose main motive seemed to be the invention of sordid practical jokes," Weaver contended, "but that of a near-normal energetic young man who used the Stanford stage as a good foundation for a career that has been highly rewarding."

During a comeback in the early '60s, while busy with a flurry of movie roles, he announced he was writing a book called *The Legend of Doodles Weaver.* He said he would recount all the stories—"half truths, quarter truths and no truth at all"—and compare them with the facts.

The accounts of his college foibles and follies had begun to hamper his career, he complained. Producers and directors did not take him seriously any more. "All anyone wants to talk about is what I did at Stanford," he lamented.

While the comedian no longer encouraged such stories, he actually did little to discourage them. "We used to go to Catalina," said his son, Win, "and we couldn't walk more than 10 feet without hearing somebody go, 'Doodles!' [and relate some real or imagined Stanford prank]. He'd just kind of laugh; he laughed with everybody and they all carried on, and he just let it go. He never really stopped anybody, except maybe the press. He might not have liked it, but he didn't seem to take offense.

"As soon as he became physically ill, about 1972 or '73, for some reason he had a change of heart toward the stories. I don't know why. Perhaps he just didn't feel good. He actually started to become bitter. It became almost an obsession as soon as he got ill.

"Towards the end, he'd stop the guy cold in his tracks and say, 'That didn't happen, it's not true.' Whether my father did half the things or not, we don't really know," said Win Weaver, "and he probably didn't remember himself."

The fake suicide was a tale that followed Doodles from Los Angeles High to Stanford to USC, where he took classes in the early '50s; it was one he could never live down. "My father told me that whole story," recalled Win. "He used to have these stuffed animals his nanny had made for him, and one was Felix the Cat; one day he took the thing to school and threw it off a building. That's really all he did, was throw this cat over the roof, as a gag, as high school kids would do. It was about four feet tall; it was large enough where somebody would look and see the shape of a body. He probably got a reaction from a few of his friends—and it has become something tremendous."

The story about Weaver turning his parents' house into a nightclub, said his son, "was 100% true. I guess he didn't make the boat to Europe. His brother and two sisters went with the family, and he stayed home and called every one of his friends over to that place. He got the keys to the liquor cabinet…and they had a wild party for two or three days, or a week, and drank all his dad's Scotch. You hear about it today; he did it then, when it was completely unheard of."

Doodles denied he painted the estate black, as legend has it, or turned the place into a shambles. He admitted to holding dancing contests and imitation gambling, serving soft drinks out of whiskey bottles, turning the front lawn into a miniature golf course and staging automobile races on the circular driveway. "My aunt (his sister) told me when she came home, she noticed all of her diving cups were gone," said Win. "They'd have contests, and my father would give them one of her diving trophies. She never did really forgive him for that."

The story about dismantling and reassembling a Model A Ford was false, Weaver's son noted, but derived from a similar incident in which a friend of his built a midget race car, piece by piece, and then accidentally smashed it up. The beer tank behind the driver's seat was fact—but was similarly perpetrated by someone else.

"A friend of his did it and he got nailed for it," said Win. "Harry Gentry was another party animal. He had a Stutz Bearcat, with two stainless steel gas tanks in the back. He drained one out and put booze in it, during Prohibition or soon after; he had the hose, and he used to drive around. He'd pick you up and say, 'Here, have a sip.' "

But unlike Weaver, who mixed drinking and driving with seeming impunity—and wrecked dozens of cars in his lifetime—Gentry's luck ran out. "He was a race car driver. He was at the track; there was a problem with the car. The steering came undone and he was killed instantly. That was tragic for my father—Harry was his closest friend. He never did get over that death. I used to watch him cry, thinking about it. Gentry's ghost was always with him; he always believed the ghost was by his side."

The signed picture of Jesus was another tale that followed Weaver throughout his life, as surely as the ghost of his departed friend. It supposedly adorned the wall of his room at Stanford—where it got him kicked out of school—and later went with him when he toured with Spike Jones. Everyone in the band heard about it, but apparently no one ever saw it. "I don't think it was on the train," said Earl Bennett. "Jones wouldn't have allowed him to have it."

"According to my father, he did not have the painting of Jesus in his room signed, 'To Doodles, Love, J.C.' He vehemently denied that," said Win. "The decency issue bothered him." Weaver himself told a Stanford newspaper reporter: "What sort of revolutionary pervert would desecrate a picture of Jesus?"

But his son conceded: "I wouldn't put it past him to have a picture, maybe something small he might've written on, because he was always doing goofy things. He might've just had a wallet-size portrait and showed it to friends, and that was all it took—one drunken party where they all sat around and laughed about it."

The other story Doodles adamantly denied—to no avail—was the one about the horse in the bedroom, and the many variations on it. "Supposedly, it was anywhere from having it just living in his room, to sleeping with it, to shooting it," recalled Win. "My father was terribly offended by the sex thing—he was very conservative when it came to sex—but the shooting thing was when he really hit the ceiling. He became very, very angry.

"He may have had a toy horse or something. There might've been a small horse; he might have tried to walk it up the stairs when he was drunk. He would do something like that," said his son. "Next thing there's a story that Doodles has a horse in his bed."

Weaver was shocked when he saw the 1978 movie, *National Lampoon's Animal House,* in which John Belushi and his college pals shoot a horse in a frat house. "They basically took a lot of the things he had done [or supposedly did]...My father thought they carried it a bit too far," said Win, "but I could tell his ego was satisfied: 'Even though it didn't happen, the great thing was, they remembered me.' "

The most famous Stanford story, about Weaver turning up in the arms of the statue, smoking a cigar and barking like a seal, was one prank the campus cut-up proudly admitted. "I think he did do that. He didn't seem to shun from that like he did the horse story or the Jesus portrait. I don't recall him ever really denying it," said Win. "I must interject, that would be something he would probably admit to doing because it wasn't profane—even if he didn't do it, he might've gone along with that one. He was under a tremendous amount of pressure to come up with these stories, and confirm them and elaborate on them."

The deviltry Weaver engineered during his five-year stint with the City Slickers was no less outlandish, and no less memorable, than the stuff and nonsense of the Stanford legends. Even when he was sober. "He'd do the damnedest things," said saxophonist Bernie Jones. "One time we had to get on the train early in the morning. He'd already gotten on ahead and he was sitting in the dining room with a napkin over his head, covering his face, wearing dark glasses and a hat. He was supposed to be the invisible man or something; he was sitting there like he was ordering breakfast, knowing we were coming in. He was always pulling

Doodles in the early days of his movie career, table-hopping at the Brown Derby—
one of the comedian's tamer off-screen antics.

stuff like that—with him, the show was always on."

"Doodles did a lot of wild things," concurred Earl Bennett. "He had a sense of humor that was so far out, so separate, all his own thing—it was almost so unique that sometimes it didn't fit with the Spike Jones show.

"It's hard to illustrate. Weaver had his own language he brought from Stanford. 'Birankins' was a woman's breasts. Your 'rear duty instrument' was your behind. I forget what a 'glibwicket' was. He could talk dirty and nobody knew."

"Doodles would give me a 'pootwaddle'—one time it was a bunch of tin cans that had fallen off a wedding vehicle, that had all been mashed flat. It was like a modern piece of sculpture," said Bennett. "He gave it to me and said, 'Here's your pootwaddle for this week.' So I'd give him a pootwaddle. One time it was a wind machine I stole from the backstage of an old theatre in Missouri.

"These pootwaddles, we didn't have any place to put 'em, so we had 'em between the Pullman cars, that narrow passage you go through. Finally we had quite a pile of 'em, and they were highly treasured things. I wish I had some of them today," said Bennett. "Ralph Wonders, the manager, got on the train drunk one night and fell over these things. So he just opened the door of the Pullman car and stood there, 60 miles an hour, throwing these things off. The next morning all our pootwaddles were gone. It was the kind of thing…you were able to keep your sanity by being a little bit insane. It was just sheer joy."

Weaver's behavior almost made him an outcast within the Jones troupe. "Nobody in the band would go along with Weaver on these wild, far out things. He had a kind of genius that was not all that pleasing to a lot of people; they didn't understand, they were too conservative," said Bennett. "I was one of the few people who could get into that with him, this kind of surreal world he could branch off into; [clarinetist] Jack Golly also dug these things Doodles did, and they would get into it."

Professor Feetlebaum was always a little out of touch with reality. As Golly remembered: "One day Doodles said, 'It's such a drag to get your laundry done; I have to leave it at a hotel, then they have to send it or I have to get back.' My wife, who traveled with the band, said, 'All we do is go to a laundromat.' Doodles says, 'That's a good idea.' The next day he shows up—his suitcase was a pillow case, and he always carried comic books—and we went to the laundromat. And Sir Frederick Gas [Bennett] was with us.

"We put our stuff in the washing machines. Right away Doodles and Gas started doing this German submarine bit. Gas did all kinds of dialects—he'd open the door of the washing machine, and Doodles would make believe he was putting in a torpedo. They'd close the door and then they'd put their fingers in their ears; before you knew it, there were all kinds of people outside laughing at them," said Golly. "Anything they could figure out like that, anyplace—no matter what, they'd do it and get away with it. Being with them used to embarrass me, then I found out they didn't give a damn."

One thing Weaver did care passionately about, throughout his life, was sports—be it professional, amateur, collegiate or makeshift. "They'd park the Pullman cars sometimes out in railroad yards, and out in this yard, there was a place the guys who worked there could take a shower. So Weaver got permission for he and I to go take a shower," recalled Bennett. "We wrapped our towels around us like Roman togas. They had two carts, a heavy iron cart and a bigger one made out of wood—and we had a chariot race. We went around and around this abandoned railroad yard, pulling the carts.

"We were the charioteers, the horses, the whole bit. Old Dood was very competitive; he took the race seriously. He picked the iron cart 'cause it was the smallest, but actually it was the heaviest. I lapped him several times before the race was over. He didn't take his beating too graciously. He wanted to win that chariot race."

It wasn't all fun and games. "Sometimes, if we were sharing a room, Weaver would come back drunk," remembered Bennett. "He came in one night and woke me up at some godawful hour and said, 'The monster is loose...' I rolled out of bed and I was so furious, I said, 'You sonuvabitch, I'm going to subdue you!' He got in bed and started to cry."

Doodles was deeper than most of the City Slickers would have imagined. Beneath the joker's mask was a man who felt, privately, that he was superior to them. "The butter-brained adolescents of the Spike Jones troupe make it exceedingly difficult to maintain a high standard of thought and to keep continual a perpetual search toward great truths and fundamental beliefs," Weaver observed in his diary.

His mind worked in mysterious ways. "He was tremendously involved with science fiction. A.E. Van Vogt was his favorite author," said Bennett. "When I'd say, 'You can't do that, Weaver,' or 'We'll never get there in time'—he'd say, 'Just Van Vogt it, Gas. Van Vogt it.' In other words, tune into a different wavelength and go for it, and it'll work out. He would investigate and do things I would never have gotten involved in, and that was Van Vogting it.

"One morning we were coming into Champaign, Illinois. Only we hadn't been hooked up to the train yet. Weaver came and woke me up in the Pullman and said, 'Gas, get up, get dressed.' I learned whenever he called—it was like Sherlock Holmes shaking Dr. Watson, 'The game is afoot...'—I'd just get dressed and go, without question.

"Doodles said, 'There's not going to be a diner on this train'—no coffee, nothing. He also found out they had an inter-urban line, that ran into Champaign from this little town we were in. After we got off and ate breakfast we got on the inter-urban. We got into Champaign so much sooner than the band, we went to a lake, rented a boat and went fishing."

The comedian's primary recreation, however, was people. Not the dignitaries they sometimes rubbed elbows with, not people in showbiz, not fans—just plain folks, the plainer the better. "Weaver would find these bums and old drunks, or just lost souls—he called them 'roosterfish.' He would spot these characters—he'd bring 'em backstage and introduce 'em as his relatives," said Bennett.

"Doodles was always bringing somebody backstage for the performances," concurred Jack Golly. "He'd pick anybody up—in a bar, or someplace. Spike used to get really upset about it. Finally he wouldn't let him do it anymore."

"Weaver would look for these guys," said Bennett. "And he would take 'em out to dinner, to big hotel rooms, all kinds of places. He had an audience, that's what it was. He wasn't alive unless there was somebody watching these things. And he needed a stooge—so I was the straightman.

"We had one guy who said he was talented, and would we audition him—Weaver just looked at me and winked, and said, 'You bet.' This guy would go behind a curtain, and then come out—and he hadn't done anything, nothing was different. Then he'd do his impression of whoever, whatever—and we'd say, 'Oh, that's terrific.' And there was no impression—this was a roosterfish. The more we encouraged him, the more he would do it," said Bennett.

"There was a guy who lived in the back of a truck, just the shell. Weaver says, 'What do you do for a living?' The guy says, 'I'm a chicken plucker.' And he was. Weaver says, 'How do you do that?' The guy says, 'I haven't got a chicken, but I'll show you with my hat.' Nobody had ever taken any interest in this poor guy his whole life, until Weaver came along and said, 'Gas, you gotta come and meet the chicken plucker.' And of course, he'd take him to dinner and the whole thing."

Weaver was, in fact, making fun of the people he befriended. "Right to their face," said Bennett. "But they were lovin' it. 'Cause they were street people and they were getting all this attention—comin' backstage and shaking hands with (to them) celebrities. He'd laugh right in front of these people; they wouldn't be offended, this is the damnedest thing. He'd go up to a cop on the Canadian side of the border and pinch his cheek and go, 'You rascal you...' Anyone else would've killed him. But he was so tickled Doodles came up and did that to him."

The comedian was every bit as tickled as the objects of his ridicule, and every bit as needy of the attention. Although he was the scion of a wealthy Los Angeles industrialist—who made his fortune in the roofing business during the boom years of the '20s—he was equally needy as a boy.

"My father was the youngest of four children," said Win Weaver. "His mother raised the eldest three. When Doodles was born, they had some money and hired a nanny to take care of them. He got detached from his parents; the nanny did most of the actual upbringing. She was gentle and kind but didn't ever set him in one direction or another. She let him grow like a weed."

Sylvester L. Weaver Sr., who became president of the Los Angeles Chamber of Commerce, had little time for his younger son. "My grandfather was busy working, so my father had to have fun by himself; he'd goof around and make weird noises. His father never sat him down and made him be responsible, never made him do anything. Literally spoiled him. That was his biggest downfall, next to the booze. Doodles wasn't at fault for his life, as much as it was probably his parents' fault," said Win.

"My father never had to work. When he went to Stanford, he didn't take it seriously. That's why he didn't study like he should have; he goofed around and partied. He knew that no matter what happened, he was going to eat. He was kicked out of Stanford two or three times—probably because they caught him drunk, and he was slightly unruly."

While Doodles made a spectacle of himself, his older brother Pat climbed the corporate ladder at Young & Rubicam; he soon moved from the prestigious advertising agency to American Tobacco Company and later NBC, where he created *The Today Show* and *The Tonight Show* and went on to become president of the network.

"I think Doodles had to live in kind of a never-never-land," ventured Earl Bennett. "My guess is that he felt rejected by his folks, and Pat was such a success…he could not compete with his brother in the real world, on that level, so he just went off and became a whole different kind of an animal.

"Doodles didn't have a chance with Pat. So the only thing he could do was be a wild and crazy man, which Pat Weaver didn't know how to do—and get attention in that direction. Doodles was a very neurotic and tortured man, I think. He'd resort to all this stuff to escape from it."

"My father definitely was intimidated by Pat, and rightly so," concurred Win. "He just knew he couldn't live that life. He said, 'You couldn't coop me up in a high-rise office building with phony executives…' He admired and respected his brother, but…there was almost an attitude of,

'You might be great, Pat, and you might have it together—but I had all the fun.' "

As Doodles reflected in his diary: "About the time Pat became head man of the world's largest & most influential broadcasting enterprise, I voted myself King of Muscle Beach…Pat must have read Pop's books on success while I was playing football, making model airplanes, dating L.A. Hi cuties & taking my wondrous trips to Avalon [Catalina]."

Weaver could wax philosophical, but he played the fool every waking hour and played it to the hilt. "My father lived life in the fast lane; he was an extremist in having fun," said Win. "Anything that could be done to make the situation funnier, he would do. Let's face it, he liked getting high. The alcohol just made it that much easier to be silly and goofy."

The drinking and the clowning also made it that much easier to escape the dark realities of his life. "My father had a lot of guilt," said Win. "He was terrified of getting killed in World War II. He was 28 or 29 and he was afraid he'd get drafted; he got married and proceeded to have a child. He kind of used them as an excuse to get out of the war. Unfortunately, the marriage was a drunken mess.

"He couldn't take care of the kid; he wasn't responsible, he didn't know how. He was still a kid himself. My father never did grow up. The daughter was raised by someone else, and I think he had a tremendous amount of guilt his entire life regarding that whole thing. I think half the time he got drunk, it was because of that and maybe a couple of other things he had done."

Despite his personal problems—including four broken marriages—Weaver enjoyed a measure of success before and after his stint with Spike Jones, in nightclubs, films and television. But he never realized his full potential or scaled the heights of contemporaries like Danny Kaye, to whom he was often compared by critics. "Doodles was a genius at comedy. He could've been one of America's great funnymen," said Earl Bennett. "But as the years went by and the alcohol took its toll, he just began to lose the edge of his genius."

On top of everything else, he could not deal with his advancing age and the inevitable hardening of the arteries exacerbated by years of high living. Weaver competed regularly in senior athletic contests and won a flock of medals, despite a heart condition. He gamely continued making personal appearances, including one of Dr. Demento's live shows. But he became increasingly despondent over his health.

304 Spike Jones Off The Record

"The sad joke is, we all have to quit. I don't want to quit, but I don't feel good," he stated in his last known interview. "All my life I've been funny and clever but I can't do it any more. I can't make people laugh because I feel lousy. I've tried everything; I've been to the doctors, I've tried all the different magic pills…I had the heart bypass, it didn't make any difference." When he could no longer bear the pain, he shot himself in the chest with a .22 caliber pistol.

Reflected Win Weaver: "Before he died, he admitted to me, 'I had a great life, but I made one tremendous mistake—alcohol.' He said, 'Alcohol was the single biggest thing that destroyed me.' He'd be on top of it, then he'd go get drunk and just blow it. The drinking was his downfall, and the pills followed. The doctors gave him these Miltowns [tranquilizers]. He got hooked on those, and that just wiped him out. That was the end of it.

"What really killed him, more than him killing himself, was that all his friends were party animals, and they all were dying like flies. I believe he only had two or three left by the time he died; he watched them all die. Imagine everybody you know, that you associated with, is dead—and you're the only one left. It's very lonely. He wanted to call somebody up and say, 'Hey, remember the time…' and he couldn't—they were all dead. You can only take that for so long."

Appendix B: Who's Who
The Spike Jones Disorganization

It would be well nigh impossible to list everyone who worked with Spike Jones over the course of his career, let alone provide biographical sketches of them. With apologies to those excluded for lack of space, the following Who's Who represents primarily those who recorded with Jones during the RCA Victor period (1941-55) or toured with The Musical Depreciation Revue *at its peak (1946-53). No attempt has been made to include those who left the band after only a few weeks or months, or the later stage and TV personnel; others were uncooperative, or wholly obscure. Only the main entries have been indexed.*

ANDERSON, DON (Donald H. Anderson), *trumpet*
Born Apr. 26, 1912, Thief River Falls, Minn. Anderson, who began his career in Seattle at 17, recorded with Seger Ellis and His Choirs of Brass, Ray Noble, Freddie Slack and Ben Pollack early in his career; he also worked with Vincent Lopez prior to joining Spike on trumpet (1941-43). He worked concurrently with Gordon Jenkins, David Rose and others, and later played with Joe Venuti and Victor Young. His radio credits include *Fibber McGee and Molly, The Great Gildersleeve, The Eddie Cantor Show, The Al Jolson Show, Amos 'n' Andy, The Bob Hope Show, The Chase and Sanborn Hour, The Abbott and Costello Show, The Frank Sinatra Show* and *The Dinah Shore Show.* After five years on staff at 20th Century-Fox (under Alfred Newman) Anderson moved back to Seattle, and started his own dixieland group. Died Sept. 17, 1986, Port Townsend, Wash., age 74, after a long illness.

BALLARD, KAYE (Catherine Gloria Balota), *vocals*
Born Nov. 20, 1928, Cleveland. Ballard was an usherette at RKO's Palace Theatre in Cleveland when Jones hired her to sing and do impressions in his stage shows, where she was initially billed as Kay Ballad. After leaving the band in 1946, she toured with Vaughn Monroe and Stan Kenton. Ballard went on to a national tour with Phil Silvers in *Top Banana* and the Broadway musical *The Golden Apple*, eventually finding TV fame with *The Mothers-in-Law* (1967-69).

She has been seen in movies (*The Ritz, Baby Geniuses*), off Broadway (the New York Shakespeare Festival revival of *The Pirates of Penzance*) and on (*Nunsense*). She has toured extensively in warhorses like *Gypsy* and *Annie Get Your Gun*, as well as *The Full Monty* and a pair of one-woman shows.

BARTY, BILLY (William John Bertanzetti), *comedian*
Born Oct. 24, 1924, Millsboro, Pa. Barty, who appeared in over 200 films by his own estimate, made his movie debut at the age of three in the Vitaphone two-reeler, *Wedded Blisters*. He played Mickey Rooney's kid brother in a number of "Mickey McGuire" comedies and turned up in some of Mack Sennett's early sound shorts; he also appeared in *Alice in Wonderland, Footlight Parade* (notably in the "Honeymoon Hotel" sequence), *Gold Diggers of 1933, A Midsummer Night's Dream* (as Mustard Seed), *Roman Scandals, The Bride of Frankenstein, Nothing Sacred* and other films of that era. He played the drums and did impressions in a vaudeville act with his sisters (1934-42), traveling throughout the U.S. and Canada. Barty then attended Los Angeles City College, where he majored in journalism and participated in intramural sports, and lettered in basketball at California State University, Los Angeles. He was working in nightclubs when he joined Spike circa 1953; his impression of Liberace became an audience favorite soon after its debut on Jones' TV series. After hosting a children's show on Los Angeles television (1963-67) Billy won acclaim for television and movie roles, notably his dramatic performance in *Day of the Locust*. TV appearances included *Alfred Hitchcock Presents, Peter Gunn, Circus Boy, Get Smart, Little House on the Prairie, Phyllis, The Golden Girls* and *Frasier;* he was seen in such films as *W.C. Fields and Me, Foul Play, True Confessions, Legends, Willow, Tough Guys,* "Weird Al" Yankovic's *UHF,* Mel Brooks' *Life Stinks,* and *Radioland Murders,* in which he sang "That Old Black Magic" with a Jones-like band. He also toured with Donald O'Connor, with whom he played the London Palladium. In 1957 the 3-foot 9-inch Barty founded The Little People of America, while working with Spike in Reno; he later established the Billy Barty Foundation to further aid and support persons of small stature and increase public awareness of dwarfism. Died Dec. 23, 2000, Glendale, Calif., age 76, of heart failure.

BENNETT, EARL *see* GAS, SIR FREDRIC

BERNAL, GIL (Gilbert Bernal), *saxophone, vocals*
Born Feb. 4, 1931, Los Angeles. Bernal was 19 when he had the good fortune to join Lionel Hampton on sax, at the close of the big band era. He later formed his own combo, recording for RCA, Columbia and other labels. He joined Spike in 1955 (replacing Bernie Jones) and became a featured performer in the band's stage and TV shows; he also recorded the vocal for "Memories Are

The cast of *The Musical Depreciation Revue* at the Civic Opera House, Chicago, 1949. Back row, from left: Dr. Horatio Q. Birdbath, Dick Morgan, Paul Leu, Joe Siracusa, Junior Martin, Merle Howard, Doodles Weaver, Bob Perry. Front row: Spike, Paul Judson, Joe Colvin, George Rock, Earl Bennett, Bill King, Gladis and Gloria Gardner, Betty Jo Huston, Frankie Little, Ina Souez, Helen Grayco, Betsy Mills, Paulette Paul, Dick Gardner, Freddie Morgan and cartoonist Milt Gross, who designed the curtain. (*Dr. Horatio Q. Birdbath*)

Made of This," backed by a canine chorus. As a solo artist with Quincy Jones (a fellow Hampton alumnus), he has been heard on the soundtrack of such films as *In Cold Blood* and *In the Heat of the Night,* as well as *Forrest Gump* and *Buena Vista Social Club.* Bernal appeared for many years at Del Conte's restaurant in Torrance, Calif., and still performs at various jazz clubs in the Los Angeles area.

BIRDBATH, DR. HORATIO Q. (A. Purves Pullen), *vocal effects*

Born Feb. 2, 1909, Philadelphia. Birdbath grew up on a farm where he learned to mimic birds and barnyard animals. After a stint on the Chatauqua circuit "Whistlin' Pullen" spent a decade with Ben Bernie (1931-41). with whom he appeared in films (*Shoot the Works, Stolen Harmony*) and recorded "Let's All Sing Like the Birdies Sing." Between engagements, he was the mouthpiece of Cheetah in Johnny Weissmuller's MGM *Tarzan* films; he lent his talents to Disney features, as well as Mickey Mouse, Betty Boop and Popeye cartoons. He was also heard on such radio programs as *The Jack Benny Show, The Jimmy Durante Show, The Hardy Family* and *National Barn Dance* (alias Trailer Tim). Doc joined Spike in 1945, supplying vocal effects for many of the classic Victor recordings ("Laura," "Love in Bloom," "Ill Barkio," etc.) and assisting in public relations. He left the band to manage a toy shop; he went on to provide the voice of Bonzo in *Bedtime for Bonzo* and Pierre the Parrot in the Enchanted Tiki Room at Disneyland and Disney World. Doc, who imitated over 300 birds and 700 animals, spent his later years entertaining children and appearing on San Francisco radio programs. Died Oct. 18, 1992, Woodland, Calif., age 83, of heart failure in his sleep.

BOTKIN, PERRY L., *banjo*
Born July 22, 1907, Springfield, Oh. Botkin, who recorded with Hale Byers at the age of 19, played guitar with Paul Whiteman early in his career. He worked with Benny Goodman, Glenn Miller and the Dorsey Brothers, and recorded with the Wabash Dance Orchestra, Roger Wolfe Kahn, Skinnay Ennis, Red Nichols, Jack Teagarden, Victor Young, the Foursome, Ella Logan, the Boswell Sisters, Jerry Colonna and Frankie Laine. Radio kept him busy as well, working with Al Jolson, Eddie Cantor, Bob Hope, Bing Crosby and John Scott Trotter (*Kraft Music Hall*). As contractor for Young and others, Botkin frequently employed Spike for studio work. The City Slickers' original banjo player (1940-42), he left the band shortly before its rise to fame. Botkin occupied his schedule with radio, TV (*The Beverly Hillbillies*) and movies (*Birth of the Blues, Murder by Contract*) for the remainder of his career. His son, Perry, Jr., co-wrote the popular "Nadia's Theme." Died Oct. 15, 1973, Van Nuys, Calif., age 66, in his sleep.

BRANDT, CARL (Carl Edwin Brandt), *arranger*
Born Aug. 15, 1914. A native of California, Brandt began his career as a child in vaudeville. He worked with Dick Jurgens for many years, first on violin, then on sax, clarinet and vocals. After World War II he rejoined Jurgens as an arranger, then moved to Los Angeles where he worked in radio (*The Railroad Hour*) and recording studios on a freelance basis. He made a series of albums under the name Raoul Meynard at Warner Bros. Records, where he also did arrangements for "Spike Jones in Stereo." He and Jones reteamed for Spike's 1960 TV show, "Rides, Rapes and Rescues" (for which Brandt wrote several original tunes) and the four "New Band" Liberty albums—on which he functioned as bandleader (uncredited) and arranger. He later worked in movies (*The Incredible Mr. Limpet*) and television (*Eight is Enough*). Died Apr. 25, 1991, Los Angeles, age 76.

BRANDT, EDDIE (Edward August Brandt), *writer*
Born Aug. 5, 1922, Chicago. Brandt, who served a stint in the Navy during World War II, was assistant manager of Grauman's Egyptian Theatre when Spike hired him as a bandboy in 1944, replacing Marty Pecora; he moved into Jones' house where he was "on call 24 hours a day." Brandt began doing comedy bits with the band and soon became a prolific writer of songs and material for

Jones' radio and TV shows, movies and records—beginning with the idea to do a takeoff on "My Old Flame." He did an uncredited rewrite on "Two Front Teeth," and wrote or collaborated on "Happy New Year," "People Are Funnier Than Anybody," "Ill Barkio," "None but the Lonely Heart," "Carmen" (with Jay Sommers), "Wild Bill Hiccup," much of the material on the "Spike Jones in Stereo" and "Omnibust" LPs and several unfinished TV projects. At Jones' death, Brandt was working on the unrealized album, "Ghoul Days." In the late '40s and early '50s he fronted his own Slicker sound-alike band, the Hollywood Hicks. He contributed parody songs to Joan Davis' radio show, and created material for Eddie Cantor, Teresa Brewer, Vaughn Monroe and Spade Cooley; he also wrote for Bob Clampett's animated TV series, *Beany and Cecil*, and Hanna-Barbera studios. He subsequently opened Eddie Brandt's Saturday Matinee, a flourishing video and movie memorabilia store in North Hollywood.

BRUNN, LOTTIE, *juggler*
Born 1925, Aschaffenburg, Germany. Brunn began her career at age 14 in her hometown near Frankfurt, partnered with her brother Francis. They entertained European audiences during World War II, coming to the U.S. with Ringling Brothers in 1948. She began touring as a solo act in the '50s, performing in Jones' *Revue* and also working with Tommy Dorsey, Milton Berle and the Harlem Globetrotters. Brunn headlined at Radio City Music Hall, traveled the nightclub circuit and appeared on *The Ed Sullivan Show* before retiring in the '80s due to arthritis; she taught juggling at Ringling's Clown College and elsewhere.

CARLING, FOS (Foster G. Carling), *writer*
Born Mar. 14, 1898, St. Paul, Minn. Carling wrote songs for many films, including Disney's *Song of the South, The Plainsman, Lady of the Tropics, The Renegade Trail* and *Hit Parade of 1947*. Among the songs he penned for Jones, or had recorded by the Slickers, were "Clink Clink, Another Drink" and "City Slicker Polka" (both with Phil Ohman), "The Blacksmith Song" and "The Yankee Doodler" (both with Phil Boutelje) and "SNAFU." He also scripted the band's Soundies, and wrote special lyrics for Spike's "Nutcracker Suite" with Country Washburne, his frequent collaborator—with whom he later teamed on Red Ingle's "Tim-Tayshun" and "Cigareets, Whiskey and Wild, Wild Women." Died Jan. 30, 1976, Los Angeles, age 77.

CARLYLE, AILEEN (Aileen Bauer), *vocals*
Born Mar. 5, 1906, San Francisco. Carlyle (sometimes billed as Carlisle) attended college in Paris; she made her stage and film debuts in 1926, in *Passions* and *Sweet Adeline* respectively. She subsequently appeared on the New York stage in *No Strings,* and was seen in such movies as *The Virginian, Her Majesty Love,*

Blessed Event, The Country Doctor, Rose-Marie, Conquest, Holiday, The Women, Mrs. Miniver and *Notorious.* After her tenure with Spike—replacing the band's original "Glow Worm" singer, Judie Manners—Carlyle appeared in *Father of the Bride, Harvey, Three for the Show* and other films. She also became a songwriter and a member of ASCAP. Died May 3, 1984, Los Angeles, age 78.

CLINE, EDDIE (Edward Francis Cline), *director, adviser*
Born Nov. 7, 1892, Kenosha, Wisc. Cline began his career in the theatre; he made his film debut in 1913 as a Keystone Cop and subsequently became assistant director to Mack Sennett. He shared writing and directing credit with Buster Keaton on 17 of Keaton's silent shorts (including such gems as *Cops* and *The Playhouse*) and co-directed with him the feature-length *The Three Ages.* Over the course of his career he directed innumerable Ben Turpin, Slim Summerville and Andy Clyde two-reelers, four Wheeler and Woolsey features, three with Olsen and Johnson (including *Crazy House*) and four with W.C. Fields (*Million Dollar Legs, My Little Chickadee, The Bank Dick* and *Never Give a Sucker an Even Break*). He directed two never-broadcast 1950 television pilots for Jones and contributed countless gags and routines to the band's stage revues and TV shows, remaining on the payroll for over a decade. Died May 22, 1961, Los Angeles, age 68.

COLVIN, JOE (Joseph Frederick Colvin), *trombone*
Born Feb. 5, 1920, Drumright, Okla. Colvin played with Jan Savitt and Rudy Vallee, and toured with Tommy Dorsey and Frank Sinatra on USO camp show circuits during World War II. He also taught music before joining the Slickers on trombone (1947-52). While in the band he met and married Gladis "Pat" Gardner of the Slickerettes; he subsequently held a staff position at Paramount Pictures, and played for the Los Angeles Rams' football team band. After a brief fling as a restaurateur with his Danish Kitchen, he grew orchids, and then started a successful nursery business in Malibu, Calif. Died Aug. 23, 1987, Los Angeles, age 67, of throat cancer.

CRONE, HERM (Herman Francis Crone), *piano*
Born Feb. 6, 1906, Shamokin, Pa. Crone worked with Jack and Charlie Teagarden, Frankie Trumbauer and Red Nichols during the big band era; he also played with a number of small bands in the Chicago area. A one-time member of Freddie Fisher's and Mike Riley's novelty bands, he was Roy Bargy's pianist-arranger (*The Jimmy Durante Show*) when he joined Spike in 1943. When time permitted, he wrote arrangements for the Merry Macs. After a stint with fellow Slicker Red Ingle, he quit the music business and went into real estate. Died 1984, Cleveland, age 78.

DAUGHERTY, CHICK (Harry Joseph Daugherty), *trombone*
Born May 14, 1915, Missouri. Daugherty, who grew up in Los Angeles, was active in music circles during the early '30s before serving in the Armed Forces. He worked with Glen Gray and his Casa Loma Orchestra and Orrin Tucker prior to joining the Slickers on trombone in 1944; he left Spike after two years of playing movie theaters and Victor sessions, and soloing with Jones' Other Orchestra. Daugherty later toured with Russ Morgan and played with Red Ingle's Natural Seven, before quitting the music business to drive a taxi for Yellow Cab Co. Died Mar. 29, 1966, Inglewood, Calif., age 50, of a cerebral hemorrhage.

DePEW, BILL (William H. DePew), *saxophone*
Born Oct. 14, 1914, Wilkinsburg, Pa. DePew started with Benny Goodman on sax and clarinet in his teens, recording extensively and appearing in several films with him; he later made Goodman's all-star list and worked with Jimmy Dorsey. In the late '30s he played with Bob Crosby and Lyle "Spud" Murphy and also had his own band. He did radio work with Ben Pollack (*The Joe Penner Show*), Opie Cates (*Lum 'n' Abner, The Judy Canova Show*), Bud Dant (*The Dennis Day Show*), Gordon Jenkins (*The Dick Haymes Show*) and others (*Lux Radio Theatre, Mayor of the Town*) before joining Spike on sax for several years beginning in 1950. He later returned to Pittsburgh where he played with Ralph DeStefano. Died Nov. 29, 1971, Monroeville, Pa., age 57, of a heart attack.

DONLEY, ROGER B., *tuba*
Born Oct. 13, 1922, Quincy, Ill. The son of a piano teacher, Donley started on piano and accordion at age five; he later switched to trumpet and finally bass. In 1942 he enlisted in the Army Air Force and served in the Air Force Band, which took him to China, Burma and India, where he performed with the Calcutta Symphony. After eight years on tuba and bass with Spike (1947-55), he joined Joe Siracusa in the editing department at UPA; he later worked for Jay Ward (*Fractured Flickers, George of the Jungle*) and Bill Melendez (*The Charlie Brown and Snoopy Show*), and freelanced at other animation studios. Died Aug. 16, 1995, Thousand Oaks, Calif., age 72, of a heart attack.

FOSTER, RUTH, *dancer*
A native of Cincinnati, Foster began her dancing career as a youngster. After appearing in Chicago area night clubs and the New York stage, the former Miss Cincinnati performed overseas with Bob Hope, Milton Berle, and her husband, Peter James; she and James also entertained troops in Korea. She played the Earl Carroll Theatre in Los Angeles before accepting a job in Jones' *Revue* for 40 weeks; it lasted eight years. Following her 1951-59 stint as dancer-comedienne in Spike's stage and TV shows, she turned to acting with regular roles on *Ben Casey, Little House on the Prairie* (as the postmistress) and *Highway to Heaven*.

FREES, PAUL (Solomon Hersh Frees), *vocal impressions*
Born June 22, 1920, Chicago. Frees toured in vaudeville in his youth, under the name Buddy Green. Within a year of his 1946 move to Hollywood Jones hired him to do impressions for "Pop Corn Sack," then the Peter Lorre imitation on "My Old Flame." He returned for "Too Young," "Deep Purple," "Little Child," "Spike Jones in Stereo" and "Omnibust." One of the busiest voices in the entertainment business, Frees served as the narrator for radio's *Suspense* and *Escape*, and TV's *The Dudley Do-Right Show* and *George of the Jungle*. He was also heard as Boris Badenov on *Rocky and His Friends*,Ludwig Von Drake and the Pillsbury Dough Boy. Frees' film credits included *A Place in the Sun*, *The Thing*, *The War of the Worlds*, *Suddenly*, and *Gay Purr-ee*. He provided many voices for Disneyland, notably the ghost host of The Haunted Mansion. Died Nov. 1, 1986, Tiburon, Calif., age 66, of an overdose of pain medication, an apparent suicide.

GALLAGHER, EILEEN (Eileen Turner), *vocals*
Born Sept. 15, 1930, New York City. Gallagher, who had her own program on WBRY in Waterbury, Conn., migrated to Colorado after finishing high school and won a statewide singing contest. The soprano was all of 17— and planning a career in opera—when she auditioned for Spike, and replaced Ina Souez in 1949. In addition to the *Revue* and Jones' CBS radio show, she recorded "Carmen" with the band; she left the group to get married, a "big mistake" she later regretted. Gallagher subsequently worked with Jimmy Durante and sang in nightclubs in Chicago, Los Angeles and San Francisco.

GARDNER, DICK (Richard Booth Gardner), *saxophone, clarinet*
Born Jun. 18, 1918, Mintvale, Utah. Gardner had just graduated from the University of Iowa and was working in a radio orchestra (KSL, Salt Lake City) when the U.S. entered World War II; he immediately enlisted in the Flying Cadets. He was playing with a small combo in a Hollywood nightclub when Joe Wolverton introduced him to Spike. He played baritone sax, clarinet and violin during his tenure with the Slickers (1946-51). Gardner was called back into the Air Force during the Korean War, during which he was stationed in Tokyo; he retired from the military with 26 years active duty. He worked with local combos in Sacramento before moving to Minneapolis, where he played sax with Jules Herman before joining the Kenwood Chamber Orchestra on violin, with whom he remained active until the end. Died Sept. 6, 1994, Richfield, Minn., age 76, of a stroke.

GARDNER TWINS, THE, *dancers*
Born Nov. 2, 1929, Lansing, Michigan. Gladis and Gloria Gardner, Siamese twins who were separated at birth, made their show business debut as children, singing on local radio stations. They soon moved to Los Angeles, attending Hollywood High School and appearing in such films as *Heart of the Rio Grande* with

Gene Autry, *The Late George Apley* and *The Bachelor and the Bobby Soxer*. In 1947 they replaced the singing Nilsson Twins in Spike's troupe; as the Slickerettes, they danced in the *Revue* and appeared in the band's earliest TV shows. The Twins left after three years with the band when Gladis married Slicker Joe Colvin. They were replaced by Evelyn and Betty. Gladis died Feb. 11, 1981, Los Angeles, age 51, of cancer. Her sister continued to run the family's nursery business until she retired a decade later; Gloria died Nov. 28, 2000, Tehachapi, Calif., age 71, of cancer.

GARNER, MOUSIE (Paul A. Garner), *comedian*
   Born July 31, 1909, Washington, D.C. Garner, who got his start as a piano player, toured in vaudeville with an act called Jack Pepper with Mustard and Ketchup (he was Mustard). He auditioned for Ted Healy when the Three Stooges temporarily left their mentor for greener pastures in 1931, and was hired as a replacement; he and his partners played Broadway in *Crazy Quilt* and then went into vaudeville as The Gentlemaniacs (an act later revived with fellow Slickers Billy Barty and Peter James). During World War II Garner toured with the USO in Olsen and Johnson's *Sons o' Fun*. He was working nightclubs when he joined Spike's *Musical Insanities* in 1954, replacing Earl Bennett; he remained with the band for six years. After a recurring role on TV's *Surfside 6* and numerous appearances on *The Red Skelton Show*, he appeared in such films as *Last of the Red Hot Lovers, Stoogemania* and *Radioland Murders*. In 1992 he was seen in the Las Vegas revue, *Hanky Panky*. Died August 8, 2004, Glendale, California, age 95 of natural causes.

GAS, SIR FREDERICK (Earl Fred Bennett), *comedian, vocals*
   Born Nov. 5, 1919, Kansas City, Kansas. Bennett was graduated from the Kansas City Art Institute, where he studied with muralist Thomas Hart Benton. He began performing in USO shows during a stint in the Army Air Corps. After the war, he was seen in Los Angeles nightclubs—Jay C. Flippen's short-lived Chez Cobar, Billy Gray's Bandbox—and briefly with Marie Wilson in Ken Murray's *Blackouts*. He also appeared "as a screen test" in the Universal film, *The Egg and I*. A 1947 engagement at Bimbo's 365 Club in San Francisco led to the job with Spike, who christened him Sir Frederick Gas. He was spotlighted in the *Revue* and contributed the vocals on such Victor records as "Riders in the Sky" (with Dick Morgan), "Carmen" (with Eileen Gallagher) and "Tennessee Waltz" (with Sara Berner); he was prominently featured in the bands' radio and TV shows, and the film, *Fireman, Save My Child*. After leaving the band in 1954, Bennett joined the editing staff at UPA and occasionally did voices for cartoons (including an old prospector in *Magoo Beats the Heat*) and commercials. He then moved to Hanna-Barbera for several years, where he specialized in sound effects and worked on *Scooby-Doo*, and such films as *Charlotte's Web*. In the late '80s he was coaxed back onstage to reprise "Chloe" with Joe Siracusa's band. He happily

devoted his retirement to painting before his eyesight failed; in 1993 his work was exhibited at the Albrecht-Kemper Museum of Art in St. Joseph, Mo., in the collective show "Under the Influence: The Students of Thomas Hart Benton." He also appeared in Ken Burns' documentary on the artist.

GOLLY, JACK (John Edward Gollobith), *saxophone, clarinet*

Born Oct. 17, 1922, Hanover, Ill. Golly began his career shortly after graduating from high school; during his four-year stint in the Army he conducted a 24-piece orchestra. He was playing with Marion and Jimmy McPartland at Chicago's Brass Rail when Spike hired him "because I looked funny enough." During his gig on alto sax and clarinet with the City Slickers (1948-49), he arranged the fast-paced opening numbers for Jones' CBS radio show. Golly left to form his own orchestra, which was featured regularly on WGN radio and TV in Chicago, for six years. He was then signed by the Mutual Radio Network as Musical Director of the show "Florida Calling;" based in Tampa, he led a popular dance band for over four decades before retiring.

GRAY, PHIL, *trombone, vocals*

Born Aug. 8, 1925, Utica, N.Y. Gray toured with Frankie Masters and Henry Busse, with whom he also recorded, before joining Spade Cooley for seven years in 1950. When Cooley's TV Hooper ratings began to slide, Jones suggested he try an all-girl western band—and picked up "the boy singer who plays trombone." During his stint with Spike (1957-59), Gray also went on the road and recorded with Ray Anthony; he left Jones to join George Rock's sextet. He then enjoyed a long engagement on TV's *Polka Parade*. His film credits include *Sound Off, The Glenn Miller Story, Mame, Funny Lady, New York, New York* and *For the Boys*. He was featured in later years with the Harry James ghost band (lead by Art Depew) and the Ben Grisafi Big Band. Died Jan. 8, 2004, Los Angeles, Calif., age 78, of lung cancer.

GRAYCO, HELEN (Helen Constance Greco), *vocals*

Born Sep. 20, 1924, Tacoma, Wash. Jones' second wife, one of 12 children of Italian-born parents, began her singing career on a Seattle radio station as a child. She attended a professional children's school in Hollywood and won a contract with Universal Pictures, which was soon cancelled; she was later heard on Los Angeles radio stations KHJ and KFWB. She also toured briefly with Stan Kenton's band, and made radio transcriptions with Red Nichols. She was appearing with Hal McIntyre in 1945 when Spike hired her to perform on an occasional basis; she soon became the band's "torch singer," offering ballads and pop songs in the stage and TV shows. She married Jones in 1948 and gave him three children, Spike Jr., Leslie and Gina. Grayco made few recordings with Spike ("Rhapsody from Hunger(y)" and "None But the Lonely Heart" for RCA,

"E-Bop-O-Lee-Bop" and "I've Got the World on a String" for Standard transcriptions) but on her own recorded for such labels as Mercury, London, Verve and RCA subsidiaries "X" and Vik; her albums include "The Lady in Red" and "After Midnight." She also appeared in the film *Cha-Cha-Cha Boom*, and performed in Las Vegas with Joe E. Lewis and Dick Shawn. Following Jones' death she remarried, and operated Gatsby's restaurant in Los Angeles for several years.

GRAYSON, CARL (Carl Frederick Graub), *violin, vocals, vocal effects*
    Born Jul. 23, 1908, Canton, Oh. The son of a Swiss German immigrant, Grayson made his professional debut at 19 as a violinist and vocal soloist in RKO stage presentations. Early in his career he was heard as a staff artist on WLW, Cincinatti, then the most powerful radio station in the country; he toured with Harry Sosnik and other orchestras, and played the Kit Kat Club in London with Johnny Hamp. In 1936, he was appearing at the Chez Paree in Chicago as a soloist with Henry Busse—with whom he recorded "Two Seats in the Balcony"—when he caught the ear of Columbia Pictures' president Harry Cohn and was signed to a movie contract. As "Donald" Grayson he sang in such films as *Dodge City Trail, It Can't Last Forever, Outlaws of the Prairie, Call of the Rockies, Cattle Raiders* and *The Old Wyoming Trail;* he also worked with the Sons of the Pioneers and reportedly became a bandleader of some standing. He joined the City Slickers on violin when the group was in its embryo stage, fronting the band for its 1940-42 engagement at the Jonathan Club. Prized by Spike for his innate comedic abilities and unique vocal effects (especially the *glug*), he was heard on two of the Slickers' biggest records: "Der Fuehrer's Face" and "Cocktails for Two." Fired for his alcohol problem in 1946, Grayson returned as a guest three years later—to record glugs for "Morpheus" and "Carmen." He also worked briefly with Eddie Brandt and his Hollywood Hicks. Died Apr. 16, 1958, Glendale, Calif., age 49, of cancer and liver disease, after a long illness.

GRIFFITH, JEFF (James Jeffrey Griffith), *saxophone, vocals*
    Born Feb. 13, 1916, Los Angeles. Following his short stint in the band circa 1947, Griffith became a prolific character actor, largely in western movies and television shows. Usually billed as James, his film credits include *The Law vs. Billy the Kid* (as Pat Garrett), *Masterson of Kansas* (as Doc Holliday) and *The First Texan* (as Davy Crockett); he made numerous appearances in such TV series as *The Lone Ranger, Dragnet, Wagon Train, Perry Mason* and *Gunsmoke*, and enjoyed a lengthy run in an L.A. stage production of *The Drunkard*. Died Sept. 17, 1993, Avila Beach, Calif., age 77, of cancer.

HALL, CANDY (Russell R. Hall), *bass*
    Born Apr. 30, 1912, Santa Monica, Calif. Hall won early renown when he was hired by Gene Austin to take over for Leo Dunham (who had replaced

Candy Candido) in the team of Candy and Coco, opposite Otto Heimal. He appeared in films with Austin and also did a stint with the singer in Ken Murray's *Blackouts*; he simultaneously worked with Mike Riley's novelty band. Hall, who knew Jones in his high school days, joined the Slickers for a year on bass in 1945, replacing Country Washburne. He later recorded with Red Ingle, managed an amusement park in California and served as entertainment director for Harrah's Club, Lake Tahoe, before retiring. Died Mar. 25, 2001, Reno, Nev., age 88.

HEATH, RAY, *trombone*

Born Oct. 9, 1924, Toldeo, Ohio, Heath joined his first band at age 16. He perfomed with Dick Stabile, Vaughn Monroe, Artie Shaw and Harry James before joining Spike on trombone for three years (1954-1957), replacing Abe Nole. He later worked with Russ Morgan, Spade Cooley, Bob Crosby and Henry Mancini. His TV credits include *The Colgate Comedy Hour* with Martin and Lewis, *The Adventures of Ozzie & Harriet* and *Polka Parade*. Died Jan. 12, 1991, Davy, W. Virginia, age 66.

HOEFLE, CARL *piano, writer*

Born May 22, 1898, Philadelphia. Hoefle toured in vaudeville (with an act called Tom, Dick and Harry) and worked as a song plugger for Leo Feist before moving to Los Angeles, where he became contractor for Roy Rogers' and Gene Autry's radio shows. Hired as the Slickers' part-time pianist in 1942, he also served as the band's contractor. Hoefle and Del Porter became partners in the music publishing business with Tune Towne Tunes, and collaborated on roughly a dozen songs recorded by Spike (including "Pass the Biscuits, Mirandy," "Serenade to a Jerk," "Blowing Bubble Gum" and "Ya Wanna Buy a Bunny?"). Died Dec. 21, 1967, Los Angeles, age 69.

HUDSON, BRUCE (Bruce Robert Hudson), *trumpet*

Born Apr. 14, 1908, Copperas Cove, Tex. Following an eight-year stint with Ben Bernie (1930-38), Hudson spent 30 years with Gordon Jenkins' orchestra; he also did radio work with John Scott Trotter (*Kraft Music Hall*), Jeff Alexander (*Amos 'n' Andy*) and Meredith Willson (*Maxwell House Coffee Time*). He played trumpet on the City Slickers' initial Victor and Standard Radio sessions in 1941. Died Aug. 14, 1989, age 81.

HUSTON, BETTY JO, *dancer*

Born 1925, Bakersfield, Calif. Huston worked in vaudeville and nightclubs, and appeared in the films *Nob Hill* and *Wonder Man*, before being featured as an acrobatic dancer in Spike's stage shows circa 1945-1949. Her marriage to trumpeter George Rock, during her stint with the band, produced two children. Huston later opened a health spa in Las Vegas.

INGLE, RED (Ernest Jansen Ingle), *saxophone, comedian, vocals, vocal effects*
Born Nov. 7, 1906, Toledo, Oh. Ingle, who started on the violin at the age of 5 and was occasionally "tutored" by family friend Fritz Kreisler, switched his allegiance to the sax at 13. He was just 15 when he played his first professional job with Al Amato in 1922. Early in his career he toured with various groups fronted by Jean Goldkette, including the 1927 Greystone Orchestra, alongside Bix Beiderbecke and Frankie Trumbauer. After leading the band at the Merry Gardens Ballroom in Chicago and playing a stint with Maurice Sherman, he joined Ted Weems on tenor sax for a decade (1931-41), vocalizing on novelties and ballads. With Weems he was heard on "The Man From the South," "Jelly Bean," "Sittin' Up Waitin' For You," " 'Tain't So" and other records, *The Jack Benny Show* (as Cringoline, the vault watchman), *Fibber McGee and Molly*, and NBC's *Beat the Band*. During World War II, he trained pilots and served as Director of Visual Education for the Civil Aeronautics Administration. On his return to Los Angeles in 1943, Ingle enlisted in the City Slickers where his contributions were many – most visibly the vocals on "Chloe" (hilariously rendered in the film, *Bring on the Girls*) and "The Glow Worm." He created gags and vocal effects (hiccups, howls, oinks, etc.) for "You Always Hurt the One You Love" and many other records; he was also the band's resident caricaturist. After leaving Spike, he played character parts on *The Fitch Bandwagon* and other network radio shows, and freelanced in movies, underscoring Gale Storm features at Monogram Pictures. He also co-starred, to rave reviews, in the Los Angeles and San Francisco Civic Light Opera productions of *Rosalinda* (Max Reinhardt's adaptation of *Die Fledermaus*). When his tongue-in-cheek recording of "Tim-Tayshun" (with Cinderella G. Stump, alias Jo Stafford) became an overnight hit, he put together his own novelty band to capitalize on the unexpected success; over 3 million copies were pressed. Ingle's Natural Seven featured Country Washburne and several other former City Slickers; among their Capitol recordings were "Cigareets, Whiskey and Wild, Wild Women," "Them Durn Fool Things " (with June Foray), "Moe Zart's Turkey Trot" and "To Reach His Zone." They also filmed several numbers for Snader Telescriptions, a forerunner of music videos, and appeared on TV's *Pantomime Quiz*. After disbanding in 1952, Ingle briefly rejoined Ted Weems and played with Eddy Howard; he also opened a saddlery. In 1963 he reprised "Chloe" for Spike's unfinished "Persuasive Concussion" album. Died Sept. 7, 1965, Santa Barbara, Calif., age 58, of an internal hemorrhage.

JACKSON, KING (Kingsley R. Jackson), *trombone*
Born Jan. 17, 1906, Austin, Tex. The Slickers' original trombonist (1940-42) played on the band's Cinematone, Victor and Standard sessions of the period, as well as the Soundies, and doubled as arranger on *The Sheik of Araby*. Jackson worked with Marshall Van Pool and recorded with Seger Ellis, Wingy

Manone and John Scott Trotter, was also heard on such radio shows as *Kraft Music Hall, The Eddie Cantor Show, Burns and Allen, The Don Ameche Show* and *The Baby Snooks Show* (with Carmen Dragon). During World War II he played in the Coast Guard band; after his discharge from the Armed Forces, he joined fellow *Kraft* alumnus Red Nichols. Jackson's distinctive trombone was heard on Jones' 1948 radio shows (as part of the big band) and the "Charleston" album; he also recorded with Mickey Katz before quitting the music business to operate a catering truck. Died Jan. 24, 1984, Riverside, Calif., age 78.

JAMES, PETER (Peter James Accardy), *comedian*
Born 1908, New York City. James, a one-time professional boxer, was a teenaged chorus boy when Ted Healy decided he had the makings of a comic. He eventually made a name for himself as Bobby Pinkus in vaudeville and burlesque, and toured Europe and the U.S. as a headline act, playing such showplaces as New York's Paramount Theatre and the London Palladium. He also worked with Tommy Dorsey during the Sinatra period, and Spade Cooley. With his wife, dancer Ruth Foster, he joined Spike's *Revue* as a featured comic in 1951 (replacing Doodles Weaver). In the '60s he acted as Jones' manager and remained with him until the bandleader's death; he then revived his own nightclub revue, *Fun For Your Money.* Died Sept. 16, 1986, Los Angeles, age 78.

JONES, BERNIE (Bernard Edgar Jones), *saxophone, vocals*
Born Dec. 23, 1911, Portland, Ore. Jones (no relation to Spike) worked with Jimmie Grier and served on staff at CBS before touring with Ozzie Nelson's band, with which he appeared on the *Red Skelton* and *The Adventures of Ozzie and Harriet* radio shows. He joined the Slickers on sax in 1950 and was often featured on vocals as Ole Svenson, a carry over from the Nelson band. He also co-wrote songs for the "Bottoms Up" and "Hi-Fi Polka Party" albums during the six years he appeared in Spike's stage and TV shows. Bernie then traveled with Horace Heidt (appearing on his variety series, *Swift Show Wagon*) and formed his own comedy outfit, Ole Svenson's Smorgasbord Band. A long stint on TV's *Polka Parade* (with a number of former Jones associates) was followed by on-camera appearances in several films, including *Homer and Eddie, Sunset* and *Dick Tracy*, and cable TV's *The Man Show*. Still active in the Los Angeles area, Jones has taken up painting in recent years.

JUDSON, PAUL (Irving Franklin Judson), *vocals*
Born 1916, Seattle. Judson, who attended the storied Pasadena Playhouse, appeared on Jones' 1947-48 radio shows and simultaneously toured with the *Revue*. He also contributed straight vocals to such RCA recordings as "I Kiss Your Hand, Madame" and "My Old Flame," and sang at Spike and Helen's wedding. Judson performed in nightclubs and TV commercials after leaving the band, and later became a teaching golf pro. Died Feb. 9, 2001, Pinehurst, N.C., age 84.

KATZ, MICKEY (Meyer Myron Katz), *clarinet, vocals, vocal effects*

Born June 15, 1909, Cleveland. Katz, who began competing in amateur nights at 12, toured with Phil Spitalny when he was 17. He later worked with Maurice Spitalny at Cleveland's Loew's State and RKO Palace Theatres, and led a comedy band, Mickey Katz and his Krazy Kittens. During the war he accompanied Betty Hutton on a USO tour. He then played clarinet with the City Slickers for two years (1946-47), during which he recorded "Jones Polka," wrote specialty material and helped conduct the show; he quit to start another novelty band of his own. Katz and his Kosher Jammers (who included Mannie Klein on trumpet and Si Zentner on trombone) recorded briefly for Victor and extensively for Capitol, producing some 99 singles and a dozen albums—among them such popular English-Yiddish parodies as "Tico Tico," "Borscht Riders in the Sky," "Duvid Crockett," "The Barber of Shlemiel," "Kiss of Meyer," Herring Boats Are Coming," "Yiddish Mule Train," "There's a Hole in the Iron Curtain" (an inspired duet with Mel Blanc, very much in the Jones style) and an LP of klezmer instrumentals (reissued on CD as *Simcha Time*). In 1948 he starred in the hit variety show, *Borscht Capades*, which introduced a 15-year-old entertainer destined for stardom—his son, Joel Grey, who would win a Tony and an Oscar for *Cabaret*. Katz did a stint as a disc jockey (KABC, Los Angeles), toured England, Australia and South Africa, played the Florida condominium circuit and treated Southern California audiences annually to *Chanukah in Santa Monica*. He also headlined the Broadway revue, *Hello, Solly*, and appeared in the film *Thoroughly Modern Millie*. He did not live to see granddaughter Jennifer Grey's success in the hit movie *Dirty Dancing*. Died April 30, 1985, Los Angeles, age 75, of kidney failure.

KING, BILL (William Martin King), *juggler*

Born Dec. 18, 1919, Muncie, Ind. King started his juggling career as an amateur at age 12, turning professional in 1937. While stationed in Texas during World War II, he appeared in the service musical, *Three Dots and a Dash*; he later toured North Africa, Italy, England and France with the USO. He performed in vaudeville and nightclubs before joining the City Slickers in 1946 as a featured act in the *Revue*—in which he juggled "13 pieces of live fire," including a headpiece with four torches, during "My Old Flame." He also appeared on the band's TV shows. After leaving Jones in 1959, he returned to playing club dates in the Midwest and opened a theatrical agency in Ohio called Variety Attractions. King appeared at the New Mexico State Fair and the Showboat in Las Vegas in later years. Died April 17, 1996, Phoenix, age 76.

KLINE, WALLY (Merle Weldon Kline), *trumpet*

Born Nov. 10, 1912, Lincoln, Neb. Kline, who grew up in Los Angeles, worked with various local bands early in his career; as a member of Everett Hoagland's band, he accompanied Tony Martin on a personal appearance tour.

He also traveled with Will Osborne and played the Million Dollar Theatre in Los Angeles before joining the Slickers on trumpet (1943-44). After a stint on the staff of NBC, he joined Kay Kyser; he later freelanced and worked as a business agent for the American Federation of Musicians. Died Nov. 16, 1984, Orangevale, Calif., age 72, of a heart attack.

LaVERE, CHARLIE (Charles Lavere Johnson), *piano*
Born July 18, 1910, Salina, Ks. LaVere worked with Spike in the Johnny Cascales band, and played alongside him on many freelance recording sessions, before playing piano for the Slickers on a part-time basis in 1942-43 (on *Furlough Fun,* etc.). During his long career he recorded with Jack Teagarden, Ben Pollack, Bing Crosby and his own group, LaVere's Chicago Loopers; he also worked with Wingy Manone, Henry Busse, Paul Whiteman, Frank Trumbauer, John Scott Trotter, Country Washburne and many others. Died Apr. 28, 1983, Ramona, Calif., age 72.

LEE, BEAU (Beauregard Wilmarth Lee), *drummer, manager*
Born Oct. 5, 1898, Chicago. Lee, a descendant of Robert E. Lee, was graduated from Hollywood High School. He got his start in a drums-and-piano act with Howard Smith, which toured the vaudeville circuit and played Australia; he also performed Down Under with Harvey Ball and his Virginians early in his career. In the '30s, he played drums and sang with Everett Hoagland, at the Rendezvous Ballroom in Balboa, Calif., alongside Stan Kenton. He later played with Nick Cochran's band and toured with Hoagland before joining the Slickers on drums in 1943. Lee, who appeared with the band in the film *Meet the People* (as Mussolini), served as Spike's business manager for most of time in the band. He retired in 1946 due to a serious illness, unable to work again. Died Jan. 22, 1962, Los Angeles, age 63, of a heart attack.

LEITHNER, FRANK (Frank Russell Leithner), *piano*
Born Nov. 7, 1905, Inwood, N.Y. Leithner recorded with his own orchestra in 1929, before becoming Frances Langford's pianist; he was also one of Rudy Vallee's original Connecticut Yankees. He left Vallee in 1933 to join George Olsen, for whom he did his famous sneeze long before he joined Spike. He was steadily employed on radio (*The Jack Benny Show, Burns and Allen, The Eddie Cantor Show, The Red Skelton Show, The Great Gildersleeve, Duffy's Tavern* and many others) when he became the Slickers' second piano player (1942-44); he also did a number of the band's arrangements. He kept busy with radio and TV work afterwards (including *The Adventures of Ozzie and Harriet,* with boyhood friend Ozzie Nelson, and *The Curt Massey Show*), but returned to contribute sneezes to "Morpheus," "Dinner Music" and other Jones records, as well as the 1957 CBS TV series. He also recorded with Frank Sinatra, Ray Noble, Cookie

Fairchild, Carmen Dragon and Red Ingle ("Moe Zart's Turkey Trot"). Died Mar. 22, 1964, Los Angeles, age 58, of a heart attack while driving.

LEU, PAUL, *piano, arranger*

Born Apr. 2, 1913, Delta, Oh. Leu started his career as a classical pianist. He played with a number of dance bands, including Henry Busse, Red Nichols and Russ Morgan; he also recorded with Bing Crosby and Kenny Baker, before joining Spike in 1947 for roughly eight years. Leu was credited with many of the Slickers' arrangements; he also wrote special material for Doodles Weaver and the Gardner Twins, and composed the unrecorded "City Slicker Boogie." Died Jul. 8, 1990, Las Vegas, age 77.

LITTLE, FRANKIE (Pasquale Scalici), *comedian*

Born Sept. 2, 1900, Milwaukee. A one-time batboy for Babe Ruth, Little was a dwarf who entered show business at 16, in a bicycle act that played the Keith-Orpheum vaudeville circuit and often shared the bill with Burns and Allen. He reportedly appeared in the film classic, *The Wizard of Oz*, and was seen in Soundies with Harry Lefcourt's Red Jackets. He was working in nightclubs, after many years as a clown with the Sline Circus, when he joined Jones in 1946; in addition to doing comedy bits in the stage and TV shows, he sold programs in the lobby. He returned to the circus (alias Pudgy the Clown) after six seasons on the road with Spike, and later operated a newstand in Wisconsin. Died Dec. 31, 1989, Milwaukee, age 89.

MARTIN, JUNIOR (Joseph Lockard Martin, Jr.), *actor*

Born 1916, West Bridgewater, Pa. Martin, who stood 7 feet, 7 inches, was raised in Colorado; he was working as a doorman at Grauman's Chinese Theatre when he made his film debut. He was an imposing presence—often billed as Lock Martin—in such pictures as *Lost in a Harem* and *Lost in Alaska* (both with Abbott and Costello), *Sherlock Holmes and the Spider Woman*, *Beyond the Blue Horizon*, *Anchors Aweigh*, *Blaze of Noon*, *Invaders From Mars* and most memorably *The Day the Earth Stood Still*, as Gort, the giant robot. A natural for sight gags in Spike's *Revue* and first TV pilots, he also came in handy for promotional stunts until he left the band in 1950. He later appeared on television with Art Linkletter, Alan Young, Groucho Marx and Frank Sinatra. Died Jan. 19, 1959, Los Angeles, age 42, of cancer.

MARTINEZ, WILLIE (William Sosa Martinez), *saxophone, clarinet*

Born Sept. 25, 1912, Mexico. Martinez, who began performing in his teens, was playing tenor sax and clarinet in a burlesque show in 1934 when he first met Spike. They then worked together in Fuzz Menge's band at the Club Ballyhoo, and Rube Wolf's orchestra at the Paramount Theatre. Martinez went on to record

Standard transcriptions with Frank Trumbauer; years later, he played baritone sax and clarinet with the City Slickers for two seasons on the road (1953-54). Died Jan. 1, 1992, Norwalk, Calif., age 79, of cancer.

MAXWELL, EDDIE (Edward Maxwell Cherkose), *writer*

Born May 25, 1912, Detroit. Maxwell migrated to Hollywood in 1936, where he got his start writing for the Yacht Club Boys (*Pigskin Parade,* uncredited). Billed as Chekose, he wrote material for the Ritz Brothers at 20th Century-Fox (*On the Avenue*), while Republic Pictures kept him busy as a tunesmith for Roy Rogers (*Under Western Stars*), Gene Autry (*Melody Ranch*), Smiley Burnette and The Three Mesquiteers. His other films include *New Faces of 1937, Village Barn Dance* and *Charlie McCarthy, Detective.* During World War II he reported to Ft. Roach (aka Hal Roach Studios), where he contributed gags for training films. He wrote for such radio shows as *The Eddie Cantor Show, The Abbott and Costello Show* and *The Mel Blanc Show* before joining Spike, circa 1948. Maxwell contributed to Jones' stage revue, radio series and TV shows, in addition to the records—which included "Pal Yat Chee," "Morpheus," "Ugga Ugga Boo Ugga Boo Boo Ugga," "Mommy, Won't You Buy a Baby Brother," "Charlestono-Mio", the unjustly rejected "Alto, Baritone and Bass," "Fiddle Faddle," special lyrics for "Yes, We Have No Bananas" and "Rudolph, the Red-Nosed Reindeer," and later "Teenage Brain Surgeon." He also wrote for Homer and Jethro, Danny Thomas, Rudy Vallee, Tony Martin, Josephine Baker, Bob Hope, Nelson Eddy, Monte Hale, Freddie Martin and nightclub comic Billy Gray; his TV credits include *I Love Lucy* (songs only), *The Jimmy Durante Show, The Donald O'Connor Show* and the animated *Beany and Cecil.* Maxwell's "Breathless" was a hit record for the Merry Macs; his "Pico and Sepulveda" became the theme song for radio personality Dr. Demento. Died Nov. 21, 1999, Los Angeles, age 87.

MEISSNER, ZEP (Joseph James Meissner), *clarinet*

Born Aug. 14, 1915, Glendive, Mont. Meissner worked with Charlie Barnet, Bob Crosby and Pee Wee Hunt before joining Spike on clarinet (1944-46); he handled arranging chores when the Slickers played for dancing and recommended Helen Grayco to his boss. He continued playing with his own groups after leaving Spike, and worked as an arranger for Lawrence Welk at the Aragon Ballroom. He later opened a music store in Los Angeles. Died Dec. 7, 1998, North Hollywood, Calif., age 83, of heart disease following a stroke.

METCALFE, EDDIE (Edwin C. Metcalfe), *saxophone*

Born Jul. 20, 1918, Pittsburgh. Metcalfe began his career as as a juvenile actor, appearing in O'Neill's *Strange Interlude* with Gladys George before he "got the music bug." After a stint as staff vocalist on Pittsburgh's KDKA—during which he had his own show—he was featured on sax and vocals with Dick Barrie,

Leighton Noble (1941-46) and Tommy Tucker. Metcalfe spent two seasons with the Slickers (1948-50); he quit the group to join the sales department of KTTV, Los Angeles, occasionally playing sax for the L.A. Rams band. In 1989 he retired from his longtime position as general manager of the ABC-TV affiliate in Fort Wayne, Ind., to become a management consultant; now fully retired to the golf course in Tucson, he remains on the Board of Trustees of a college in Ft. Wayne.

MEYER, SOL, *writer*
    Born Dec. 28, 1913, Jersey City, N.J. Meyer served with the Glenn Miller Army Air Force Band during World War II. He wrote or co-wrote a sizable amount of material for Jones, including "The Blue Danube," "I Dream of Brownie With the Light Blue Jeans," "Christmas Cradle Song," the "Bottoms Up" and "Hi-Fi Polka Party" albums (with Freddy Morgan and Bernie Jones), "Spike Jones in Stereo" (with Eddie Brandt, Eddie Maxwell and others), and the TV shows. Meyer also wrote for radio (*The Eddie Cantor Show*) and films. Died Aug. 12, 1964, New York City, age 50.

MORGAN, DICK (Richard Isaac Morgan), *banjo, guitar, vocals*
    Born Jan. 25, 1905, Boulder, Colo. Morgan worked with Glenn Miller in his college days; in the late '20s he recorded with Ben Pollack, Jimmy McHugh's Bostonians, Benny Goodman's Boys and extensively with Irving Mills—alias Mills' Musical Clowns, Mills' Merry Makers, the Kentucky Grasshoppers, etc.—with whom he recorded "Icky Blues." He was a featured comedian with Horace Heidt and later sang with Alvino Rey ("The Skunk Song") before joining Spike on banjo and guitar (1944-53). Morgan, who was nicknamed "Icky Face," was equally known for his clowning and his abilities as a dialectician; he contributed vocals on such numbers as "Riders in the Sky" (as the drunken cowpoke, I.W. Harper) "MacNamara's Band," "By the Beautiful Sea" (as the carnival barker) and "It Never Rains in Sunny California." He was prominently featured on *Spotlight Revue* and seen in the band's early TV shows. Died May 17, 1953, North Hollywood, Calif., age 48, of a heart attack.

MORGAN, FREDDY (Phillip Fred Morganstern) *banjo, vocals, comedian, writer*
    Born Nov. 7, 1910, New York City. Morgan, who was raised in Cleveland, started out on the ukelele. At 14 he formed the banjo duo of Morgan and Stone (with school chum Leo Livingston) and went into vaudeville. Their first real professional engagement was in 1927 at New York's Paramount Theater, where they were under contract for 51 weeks; they later played the famed Palace Theater with Joe Cook's *Fine and Dandy* (1931) and traveled Europe. During World War II, Morgan started the European Theatre Artists Group (the forerunner of the American USO) with Bebe Daniels and Ben Lyons; afterwards he took a USO show to Tokyo. He joined Spike on banjo in 1947, bringing along his skills

as a mimic and dialectician. Best remembered for "Chinese Mule Train" and the "Poet and Peasant" routine, Freddy collaborated on a number of songs and much other material for the group (including the "Bottoms Up" LP). He was featured in *Fireman, Save My Child* and the band's radio and TV series. The prolific composer ("Hey, Mr. Banjo") recorded with fellow Slickers Jad Paul (for Kapp, as the Sunnysiders) and Mousie Garner (for RCA, as The Alley Singers); for Verve he made the solo album "Mr. Banjo" under Spike's supervision. After leaving Jones in 1959, he toured Europe, Asia and Australia (1960-63) and played Reno with his own group, Freddy Morgan and the Idiots; he did two albums for Liberty, "Bunch-a-Banjos" and its followup, "Bunch-a-Banjos on Broadway." He was also heard on TV's animated *Beany and Cecil.* Died Dec. 21, 1970, Alameda, Calif., age 60, of a heart attack, in the midst of his stage act at a naval base.

NILSSON TWINS, THE, *vocals*

Born circa 1925, Wichita, Kansas. Elsa and Eileen Nilsson, the band's original Slickerettes, sang with Ted Weems and appeared in the film *Hiya, Sailor,* before joining Spike in 1943. They sang on his radio broadcasts and Standard transcriptions, and accompanied the band on its USO tour of England and France; they were later replaced by the dancing Gardner Twins. The Nilsson sisters also appeared in a number of Soundies, and recorded a pair of LPs for Del-Fi in 1959.

NOLE, ABE (Albert A. Nole), *trombone*

Born Nov. 26, 1921, Altoona, Pa. Nole went on the road with Red Norvo after graduating high school, then joined Ina Ray Hutton. He enlisted in the Navy, earning a B.A. in music after the war. He then worked with Buddy Baker, who got him an audition with Jones; he played trombone on tour and record with the Slickers for over a year (1953-54). He later performed with Wayne Newton. Died Apr. 19, 1985, Las Vegas, age 63.

NORMAN, LOULIE JEAN, *vocals*

A much–in–demand studio vocalist, Norman's soprano graced many of Spike's RCA recordings, including "Pop Corn Sack," "Carmen," "Too Young" and "I Saw Mommy Kissing Santa Claus;" she was subsequently featured as Vampira on "Spike Jones in Stereo" and also heard on "Omnibust." She lent her voice to a number of movie musicals, including *Easter Parade, The Harvey Girls, Hit the Deck* and *Porgy and Bess* (dubbing Diahann Carroll), and vocalized the wordless theme for the *Star Trek* TV series. Norman, the wife of conductor Gordon Jenkins, also recorded with Ray Conniff, Henry Mancini, Frank Sinatra, Elvis Presley, Sam Cooke and Joe Williams.

PAUL, JAD, *banjo*

Born 1926, Los Angeles. Paul began his career in vaudeville in the late 1930s, appearing in "kid acts." He performed as a single while still in his teens; he later did an act with his wife before joining Spike on banjo for his 1954-58 TV shows and recordings, taking over for Dick Morgan's short-term replacement, Hayden Causey. After leaving Jones, he played the Nevada hotel circuit with his own band, and appeared on the syndicated TV show, *Polka Parade*. With Freddy Morgan—with whom he had done an act in the early '40s—Paul recorded for Decca (as the Banjomaniacs) and extensively for Kapp (as the Sunnysiders); he also recorded for Liberty under his own name. He can be heard on the soundtrack of such films as *Doctor Zhivago* and *Paint Your Wagon*. Paul additionally performed in piano bars in the Los Angeles area before retiring.

PEARSON, LaVERNE, *vocals*

A native of Chicago, "Effie" Pearson had trained for a career in grand opera before she read in Louella Parsons' syndicated column that Jones was looking for a fat lady who could sing. The blonde soprano admitted to weighing 240 pounds and won the role, replacing Eileen Gallagher circa 1950. Pearson sang "Glow Worm" in the *Revue* and Spike's early TV shows, including his *Colgate Comedy Hour* debut, and accompanied the band on their Australian tour. She also performed with Jimmy Durante in his nightclub act. Died Oct. 2, 1981.

PHARES, BETTY, *dancer*

Born 1924, Ukiah, Calif. As one third of the acrobatic dance trio Lindsay, Laverne and Betty, Phares toured with Ted Lewis, entertained the troops during World War II and appeared in a number of films, including *Gents Without Cents* with the Three Stooges and *Song of Nevada* with Roy Rogers. Replacing the Gardner Twins as Slickerettes in 1949, Betty was partnered first with Evelyn Lunning in Jones' *Revue*, and subsequently with Lucille Winters and Diane Robinson. She retired from show business when she got married in 1952.

PORTER, DEL (Delmar Smith Porter) *clarinet, vocals, writer, arranger*

Born Apr. 13, 1902, Newberg, Ore. At the outset of his career Porter played violin with Stuffy McDaniels and his Bungalow Five, with whom he traveled the country in the early '20s. He played with Glen Oswald's Serenaders at the Cinderella Roof in Los Angeles, then toured the Northwest with Dwight Johnson's Strollers and Cole McElroy and his Spanish Ballroom Orchestra for several years. In 1928 Del became a member of the newly-reorganized vocal quartet, the Foursome, with Raymond Johnson, Marshall Smith and Dwight Snyder. The group was playing one-night stands in Los Angeles when Mack Sennett hired them to sing background in short comedies; they also appeared in *The Wild Party* with Clara Bow and *Stolen Heaven*. Their dismal New York debut in *Ripples* was soon followed by the hit George and Ira Gershwin musical, *Girl Crazy* (1930)—in which they stopped the show with the song, "Bidin' My Time." Afterwards they sang with Roger Wolfe Kahn (alias the Kahn-a-Sirs) and traveled with the Smith Ballew-Glenn Miller band, then went back to Broadway in Cole Porter's *Anything Goes*. The Foursome returned to Hollywood for *Born to Dance*, remaining to make semi-regular appearances on *Kraft Music Hall*. During this time they recorded with Bing Crosby, Dick Powell, Red Nichols, Ray Noble, Shirley Ross and Pinky Tomlin; Spike drummed in the backup group on the quartet's own Decca recordings, including some with Crosby. Porter continued working with the Foursome (which broke up late in 1941) while he began the Feather Merchants. As Jones' partner, he exerted substantial influence on the embryonic City Slickers from their earliest days, as lead vocalist, clarinetist, arranger ("Hotcha Cornia," "Der Fuehrer's Face"), and composer ("Siam," "Pass the Biscuits, Mirandy" and others with Carl Hoefle). Porter continued to write for Jones after leaving the Slickers in 1945, and returned to do vocals for the "Charleston" and "Bottoms Up" albums; "My Pretty Girl" (written by Porter and Ray Johnson) was recorded by Jones, Lawrence Welk and Cliffie Stone. In addition to his music publishing business, Tune Towne Tunes, Del later wrote jingles for Paper Mate pens. He also recorded with his Sweet Potato Tooters (for Capitol transcriptions), as well as Mickey Katz ("Tiger Rag"), Bob Hope ("Home Cookin' ") and Spade Cooley ("Chew Tobacco Rag," alias Andy Climax). He continued to dabble in songwriting in his later years. Died Oct. 4, 1977, Los Angeles, age 75, of a respiratory ailment after a long illness.

RATLIFF, HERSH (Herschell Edison Ratliff), *tuba*

Born 1909, Oswego, Kan. Ratliff was a member of Spike Jones and His Five Tacks during their school days together at Long Beach Poly High; he and Jones later played together in Everett Hoagland's band. Following a six-year stint as soloist with the Long Beach Municipal Band, he joined the Slickers on tuba (1944-45), but his health forced him to quit. Ratliff later earned a teaching credential and taught music and history at the high school level in Central California, while playing one-night stands with his own dance band. He performed for eight years with the San Jose Symphony before retiring. Died Jul. 26, 1995, age 86.

RAVENSCROFT, THURL, *vocals*

Born 1914, Norfolk, Neb. Ravenscroft provided the striking basso profundo voice of the Mellomen quartet heard on many of Jones' records, including the "Bottoms Up" album; he sang sans quartet on "Wyatt Earp Makes Me Burp" and "Teenage Brain Surgeon." Beginning his career as a studio singer in 1933, he was a member of the Paul Taylor Chorus before he and three others quit to form the Sportsmen Quartet, featured on *The Jack Benny Show*. With the Mellomen, he was later heard in such Disney films as *101 Dalmations* and *Lady and the Tramp*; he provided voices for The Haunted Mansion and other Disneyland attractions. Ravenscroft also sang back-up for

Frank Sinatra, Stan Freberg and Rosemary Clooney ("This Old House"), but is best known as the voice of Tony the Tiger.

ROBINSON, ROBBIE (Robert F. Robinson), *trombone*

Born Feb. 10, 1923, Sedalia, Mo. Robinson worked with Jan Savitt and served in the Air Force before playing trombone with the Slickers (1946-47). He later worked with Billy May, Matty Malneck, Harry James and Red Nichols; he was a member of Disneyland's house orchestra, playing dixieland and big band, for 25 years (1961-1985). Still active in the Los Angeles area, Robinson plays regularly with the Alumni Band and the Crazy Rhythm Hot Society Orchestra.

ROCK, GEORGE (George David Rock), *trumpet, vocals, vocal effects*

Born Oct. 11, 1919, Farmer City, Ill. Rock, who began singing at age four, attended Wesleyan College on a football scholarship before switching to music studies; he turned professional at 20 when Bob Pope offered him a job on trumpet. He worked with Howard Fordham in a St. Joseph, Mo., gambling club, then toured with Don Strickland and played with George Jessel in vaudeville before joining Freddie Fisher's popular Schnickelfritz Band in Dec. 1940. With Fisher he played Gene Austin's Hollywood nightclub, the Blue Heaven, recorded for Decca and made a number of radio and movie appearances (including *The Farmer's Daughter, The Sultan's Daughter, Jamboree* and *Seven Days Ashore*). He worked briefly with Charlie Barnet and Mike Riley, joining the Slickers immediately after their 1944 USO tour. Rock quickly became the star of the troupe, supplementing his virtuoso trumpet solos ("Minka") with comic vocals ("Ya Wanna Buy a Bunny?"); his high-pitched child's voice sold over two million copies of "All I Want for Christmas (My Two Front Teeth)." He was also responsible for numerous uncredited vocal effects, including the Woody Woodpecker-like laughs and raucous belches so often heard on the Victor records. One of his proudest moments was performing "Blowing Bubble Gum" for President Truman. Rock left Jones early in 1960 to play the Las Vegas-Reno-Lake Tahoe circuit with his own sextet. After taking three years off to run his own gun shop, he worked with Ed Chilleen and Turk Murphy, then returned to Lake Tahoe with a quartet. George later sang with Phil Gray's band, and recorded an album and made appearances with fellow Slicker alum Joe Siracusa's New Society Band; in his last years, he played and sang with Merle Koch's jazz band in Virginia City, Nev. Rock returned to his hometown near the end, serving as grand marshal of the town's sesquicentennial parade. Died April 12, 1988, Champaign, Ill., age 68, of a heart attack after a long bout with diabetes.

ROUNDTREE, LUTHER (Luke Ervan Rountree), *banjo*

Born Aug. 4, 1905, Mount Pleasant, Tex. "Red" Roundtree, who turned professional at 19, started by playing guitar with various bands in the South, including Gene "Blue" Steele (1929-32). He had his own "hillbilly show" on Memphis radio station WMC for eight years before he moved to Los Angeles and joined the Slickers on banjo. During his 1942-43 stint with the band he was featured as Cousin Luther on *The Bob Burns Show*. He later recorded with Red Ingle ("Tim-Tayshun"), Bing Crosby, Tennessee Ernie Ford, Tex Ritter and Stan Freberg, and was paired with Dick Roberts as the Banjo Kings. Roundtree did freelance work at film studios (*Syncopation*) and served on staff at NBC; he also played in Country Washburne's band on *The Curt Massey Show* and subbed with the Firehouse Five Plus Two. Died Apr. 30, 1990, Van Nuys, Calif., age 84, of a stroke.

ROYSE, GIGGIE (Gilbert A. Royse), *drummer*
    Born August 21, 1905. Royse performed with the Johnny Noble Orchestra in Honolulu before Spike hired him to replace Beau Lee on drums in 1945. He toured with the Slickers for a year, during which he appeared on *The Chase and Sanborn Program* and in the films *Ladies' Man* and *Breakfast in Hollywood*. His recordings with the band included "The Nutcracker Suite" and a rejected version of "Hawaiian War Chant," for which he provided the vocal. Royse also had his own orchestra at one point. Died December 1980, Las Vegas, age 75.

SIRACUSA, JOE (Joseph James Siracusa), *drummer*
    Born Feb. 3, 1922, Cleveland. Siracusa, a third generation musician, worked with the Cleveland Philharmonic prior to a stint in the army—during which he played timpani in the El Paso Symphony and accompanied Danny Kaye on a tour of the Philippines. He was playing in the Cleveland Municipal Band when an audition with Spike led to six years on drums with the Slickers (1946-52); he also constructed many of the zany instruments and props. He left to become head film editor at UPA (home of Mister Magoo cartoons), where his staff included Jones alumni Earl Bennett, Roger Donley and wardrobe boy Skip Craig. Siracusa later moved to Format Films, Warner Bros. and DePatie-Freleng, then served as music editor at Marvel Productions for many years. He also worked with Henry Mancini, Ernest Gold, Jay Ward, Ross Bagdasarian and Chuck Jones during his long career in animation, which was capped with the prestigious Annie Award in 1991. The New Society Band (aka the Funharmonic Orchestra) was Siracusa's part-time attempt to revive the Spike Jones style; he featured several former City Slickers with the group on the album "The New Society Band Shoves It in Your Ear" and in concerts. He remains active despite retirement, entertaining senior citizens.

SLICKERETTES, THE *see* NILSSON TWINS, THE; GARDNER TWINS, THE; PHARES, BETTY.

SOMMERS, JAY, *writer*

Born Jan. 3, 1917, New York. Sommers, who began his career circa 1940 as a writer for Milton Berle's radio show, was best known as the creator of TV's *Green Acres* and its radio predecessor, *Granby's Green Acres*. He wrote for Jones' radio and TV shows for several years, and was responsible for the operatic spoof, "Carmen" (with Eddie Brandt). He also wrote for such radio series as *The Eddie Cantor Show, Lum and Abner, The Red Skelton Show, The Durante- Moore Show* and *The Victor Borge Show*. Sommers' TV credits include *The Buster Keaton Show* (writer-producer), *My Friend Irma, The Adventures of Ozzie and Harriet, Petticoat Junction* (writer-producer), *Alice* and *Hello, Larry*. He wrote the screenplay for the film *All Hands on Deck*. Died Sep. 25, 1985, Los Angeles, age 68, of congestive heart failure.

SOUEZ, INA (Ina Fayar Rains), *vocals*

Born June 3, 1903, Windsor, Colo. Souez made her European operatic debut at 18 as Mimi in *La Boheme*, and established herself as Mozartian *prima donna assoluta* during her 1934-39 reign at Britain's prestigious Glyndebourne Festival. During the same period, she performed Verdi Requiems throughout Scandanavia. When her London apartment was destroyed in a bombing raid, she returned to the U.S. and joined the Women's Auxiliary Corps. Following an engagement with the New York City Opera, she replaced Aileen Carlyle as Spike's "Glow Worm" singer in 1947; after her stint with Slickers, the former diva devoted herself to a teaching career. She recorded arias on the New Sound label circa 1960. Died Dec. 7, 1992, Los Angeles, age 89, of a heart attack.

SPICER, WILLIE, *sound effects*

Perhaps the most versatile of all the City Slickers, Spicer manipulated the Collidophone ("Little Bo Peep Has Lost Her Jeep"), the Sneezaphone ("Hotcha Cornia"), the Hiccuphone ("The Sheik of Araby"), the Birdaphone ("Der Fuehrer's Face"), the Trainaphone and the Anvilaphone. Willie was, however, a figment of Jones' imagination, a name invented for record labels.

STANLEY, JOHN J., *trombone*

Born Jun. 11, 1916, Indiana. Stanley played with Everett Hoagland's jazz band (with future Slickers Beau Lee and Wally Kline), and Seger Ellis and his Choirs of Brass (with King Jackson, Stan Wrightsman and Don Anderson), before replacing Jackson as Slicker trombonist (1942-44). He had also done studio work in Hollywood prior to his stint with the band. Stanley left Jones to become a staff musician at Warner Bros. and Universal Studios, returning briefly to the fold in 1947. He later appeared as a sideman in the film, *The Glenn Miller Story* (1954), and recorded with Dean Martin, but ultimately quit the music business to go into the construction field. Died Jul. 3, 1984, age 68.

STERN, HANK (Henry P. Stern), *tuba*

Born May 8, 1896, New York City. Stern, the Slickers' original tuba player (1941-42), recorded extensively with Ben Selvin, Victor Young, the Dorsey Brothers and the University Orchestra. He also recorded with the California Ramblers, Joe Venuti and his New Yorkers, the Wabash Dance Orchestra, Sam Lanin, Merle Johnson and his Ceco Couriers, McKinney's Cotton Pickers, the Ipana Troubadours, Cookie Fairchild, Judy Garland, Bing Crosby and Paul Whiteman (Capitol's "History of Jazz" series) during the course of his career. Died Dec. 25, 1968, Los Angeles, age 72.

TINSLEY, CHARLOTTE (Charlotte Laughton), *harp*

Born June 12, 1910, Goodwell, Okla. Tinsley assisted her parents in teaching harp in music school and played in the family orchestra at an early age. She was heard on local radio stations and in Tulsa nightclubs, and played with the Oklahoma Symphony before moving to Hollywood. Tinsley joined Spike on the harp in 1944 (as soloist on "Holiday for Strings"); she performed with the band on radio and records, and was a member of Jones' Other Orchestra. She worked extensively with Dimitri Tiomkin in motion pictures and was also heard on radio (Art Linkletter's *House Party*, *The Chesterfield Show*, *Fibber McGee and Molly*). She later became a teacher. Died Jan. 22, 1998, Riverside, Calif., age 87.

VAN ALLEN, DANNY, *drummer*

Born June 3, 1914, Douglas, Ariz. Van Allen, a Poly High pal of Spike's who went into vaudeville with a dancing act when he was 16, joined Del Porter and the Feather Merchants on drums in 1939; as a part-time drummer for the City Slickers, he subbed for Beau Lee on the *Bob Burns* radio show. As a member of Carmen Miranda's back-up group, the Banda de Luna (1940-47), he appeared in several films. He later operated a restaurant in Northern California, while playing one-night stands. Died Jan. 20, 1997, Lafayette, Calif., age 82.

WASHBURNE, COUNTRY (Joseph Howard Washburne), *tuba, arranger*

Born Dec. 28, 1904, Houston. Washburne won local fame playing bass horn in John "Peck" Kelley's Galveston band, in the '20s. Before joining Spike, he was best known for his 1931-42 stint with Ted Weems, who featured him on the band's Victor, Decca and Columbia recordings; he also recorded with Jimmy McPartland's Squirrels, Wingy Manone, Eddie Skrivanek, Nappy Lamare and LaVere's Chicago Loopers during his career. Country played tuba and string bass for the City Slickers on an irregular basis for four years (1942-46), and wrote special material for Spike (notably for "The Nutcracker Suite"). He later recorded with Red Ingle's Natural Seven for Capitol, and was featured with Marvin Ash and Pete Daily on the same label. Radio listeners heard him on such shows as *Fibber McGee and Molly*, *The Great Gildersleeve*, *Beat the Band* and *The Roy Rogers Show* (with his own band); beginning in 1950, Washburne led the band on Curt Massey's

CBS radio and NBC TV shows for more than a decade, hiring a number of former Slickers as sidemen. In his later years he operated a music studio. A gifted composer, Country wrote or collaborated on such songs as "Oh, Mo'nah" (featured by Weems), "One Dozen Roses" (a hit for the Mills Brothers), "Them Durn Fool Things" (featured by Ingle) and "Lawrence Welk Polka" (for Jones' "Hi Fi Polka Party" album). Less known was his genius as an arranger, which shone brightest in the Slickers' renditions of "Cocktails for Two" and "Chloe," and Ingle's parody of "Tim-Tayshun." Died Jan. 21, 1974, Newport Beach, Calif., age 69, of a heart attack.

WAYNE-MARLIN TRIO, THE, *acrobats*

(George Wayne Long) Born Nov. 12, 1908, Kansas; (Glenn Marlin Sundby) Born Nov. 4, 1921, Minneapolis; (Dolores Sundby) Born Aug. 11, 1924, Minneapolis. George and Glenn teamed in 1939 as Wayne and Marlin. After working at Radio City Music Hall, they were seen in Mike Todd's *Star and Garter* with Gypsy Rose Lee and appeared at the Stage Door Canteen; they then toured the world with the USO. Glenn brought his sister Dolores into the act in 1945. The trio was working at the Desert Inn in Las Vegas when their daring acrobatics became a part of Jones' *Revue* and TV shows; they spent five years with the bandleader (1951-1955), departing after the Australian tour. The trio then broke up with Dolores getting married. George, tired of traveling, became a Jesuit Brother; Glenn went into real estate, then published a magazine for gymnasts. George died March 1979, Carson City, Nev., age 70. Glenn lives in Oceanside, Calif., where he founded the International Gymnasts Hall of Fame in 1987 with Dolores' assistance, and currently publishes a quarterly called *Acro*.

WEAVER, DOODLES (Winstead Sheffield Glendenning Dixon Weaver), *comedian, vocals*

Born May 11, 1913, Los Angeles. Weaver made his debut singing "St. James' Infirmary" on a local radio station while still in high school. In 1937 he was graduated from Stanford University, where he appeared in the *Gaieties*—and excelled at basketball, football and tomfoolery—to become a popular nightclub comic. He headlined at the Ambassador Hotel's Cocoanut Grove in Los Angeles, and was featured on Rudy Vallee's radio program; he first assaulted the Broadway stage in *Meet the People* (1940). During the war he enlisted in special services, performing in military hospitals; he also worked with Horace Heidt before returning to Broadway in *Marinka*. He joined the City Slickers in 1946, performing his classic horse race routine (which Jones backed with "The William Tell Overture") and other material on the band's records, road tours and radio shows (alias Professor Feetlebaum) for five years. He flopped with a television series, then went back with Heidt. Doodles appeared in over 100 films and TV movies following his feature debut in *My American Wife*. Among his films were two Our Gang shorts, *Hockey*

Homicide and other Disney cartoons, *Topper, Swiss Miss* with Laurel and Hardy, *Another Thin Man, A Yank at Oxford, Reveille with Beverly, The Story of Dr. Wassel* (his favorite), *Variety Girl* with Spike, *Gentlemen Prefer Blondes, Inherit the Wind,* Hitchcock's *The Birds,* and several with Jerry Lewis, including *The Ladies' Man* and *The Errand Boy;* later pictures included *Cisco Pike, Macon County Line* and Woody Allen's *Everything You Always Wanted to Know About Sex* (from which his scenes were deleted). Weaver made his TV debut on the premiere broadcast of NBC's *Hour Glass* variety series in 1946; he brightened Jones' first *Colgate Comedy Hour* and the later *Club Oasis* series with his presence. He had four TV shows of his own—including the syndicated *A Day with Doodles*—and was seen in recurring roles on *The Lawman, Batman* and *Starsky and Hutch.* He recorded the album "Feetlebaum Returns" in 1974 and in his later years was a frequent medal-winner in the Senior Olympics. Died Jan. 13, 1983, Burbank, Calif., age 69, of self-inflicted gunshot wounds.

WEBSTER, DICK (Richard Eugene Webster), *manager*

Born Oct. 8, 1909, Silverton, W.V. Webster began his career "in short pants" as a violinist; he appeared in vaudeville with Slim Martin and provided mood music for actors in silent films. He subsequently sang with the Yale Collegians and played with Jimmie Grier's orchestra; his violin was also heard on Eddie Cantor's radio program. He was a talent booker with General Artists when Ralph Wonders enlisted him to help run Jones' organization. As personal manager, talent scout and eventually president of Arena Stars, Webster worked for Jones 14 years (1948-1961), longer than most of the City Slickers. He later managed Johnny Carson and singer Jimmy Dean. Died Dec. 5, 1993, Thousand Oaks, Calif., age 85, after a long illness.

WOLVERTON, JOE (Ralph Edwin Wolverton), *banjo*

Born July 8, 1906, Carbon, Ind. Wolverton entered vaudeville in 1926, touring with an act called Banjo Land, and subsequently teamed as a duo with his first wife. He then played briefly with Gene Austin, and toured the Midwest with Rube Tronson's Cowboys. In 1932 "Sunny Joe" Wolverton and his hillbilly band, the Scalawags (with 17-year old Les Paul), performed on KMOX, St. Louis. He and Paul, whom he claimed he "taught everything," later reteamed as the Ozark Apple Knockers on WBBM, Chicago. He appeared on a number of Hollywood radio programs (*Burns and Allen, The Judy Canova Show, The Dinah Shore Show*) and had his own novelty group—the Local Yokels—on NBC's *Our Half Hour;* he then played with Spike on guitar and banjo, replacing Red Roundtree (1943-44). Wolverton briefly rejoined the Slickers after a stint in the army. In the '50s he arranged for other bands and worked with Polly Ship's all-girl orchestra in Las Vegas and

Japan; he later returned to the Orient, touring military bases with a single act, before retiring to Arizona. Died Aug. 27, 1994, Cottonwood, Ariz., age 88.

WONDERS, RALPH J., *manager*

Born Jan. 8, 1896, Gettysburg, Pa. Wonders spent six decades in management; as head of CBS' Artists Bureau, he brought the then-unknown Mills Brothers to the attention of his boss William Paley and set their career in high gear. He subsequently became West Coast Vice President of General Artists Corporation, where he handled Jones. Wonders left GAC in 1946 to become Spike's business manager and president of Arena Stars; he also served as best man at Spike's wedding to Helen. After his dismissal from the band, he worked for impresario James Doolittle and managed Los Angeles' Greek Theater. Died Nov. 3, 1977, Santa Monica, Calif., age 81, of a bacterial infection.

WRIGHTSMAN, STANLEY, *piano*

Born June 15, 1910, Gotebo, Okla. Wrightsman, who joined his father's band at 14, left his Missouri home at 16 to work with a quintet; he then played in territory bands before taking a staff job at WKY Radio in Oklahoma City. He traveled with Hogan Hancock, Marshall Van Pool and Henry Halstead early in his career, before joining Ben Pollack in Chicago (1935-36). He freelanced in Los Angeles studios and recorded with Seger Ellis, Wingy Manone, Santo Pecora and Artie Shaw prior to becoming the City Slickers' original pianist (1940-42). During his career he recorded with Bob Crosby, Rudy Vallee and his Connecticut Yankees, Barney Bigard, Nappy Lamare, Pete Fountain, The Banjo Kings, Eddie Miller, George Van Eps, Rosemary Clooney, Wild Bill Davison and Bob Scobey; he also worked with Jack Teagarden, Matty Matlock and Wayne Newton. He can be heard on Jump Records' "Jazz Party at Pasadena" and GNP's "Dixieland Jubilee," plus the soundtracks of such films as *Picnic*, *The Five Pennies* and *Pete Kelly's Blues*. Died Dec. 18, 1975, Palm Springs, Calif., age 65.

WYLIE, FRANK (Franklyn Wylie), *trumpet*

Born Apr. 23, 1918, Los Angeles. The band's original trumpet player (1940-41), Wylie participated in the early Cinematone and "home recording" sessions; he left the band just prior to the first Victor sessions. He was credited by Del Porter with having invented the familiar Slicker "tag" used to end their renditions. A busy studio musician, Wylie played with Horace Heidt after leaving Jones, and later became the first trumpeter at Disneyland's *Golden Horseshoe Revue*. Died Sept. 3, 1970, Costa Mesa, Calif., age 52.

Appendix C: For the Record
by Ted Hering and Skip Craig

The following career index was distilled from information collected primarily by two of Spike Jones'
most dedicated fans, over a period of several decades. Further acknowledgements will be found in
Notes and Sources.

Discography

PRE-CITY SLICKERS (JONES AS SIDEMAN)
This list is representative of Spike Jones' work as a sideman but incomplete. Spike also backed Lily
Pons and other artists on various labels. The number of sessions post-dating the City Slickers' Victor
debut indicates the part-time nature of the band in its early years.

Recorded	Orchestra	Label	Artist
8/9/36	Victor Young	Decca	Gene Austin
1/18/37	Cy Feuer	Vocalion	Phil Harris
1/24/37	Feuer	Brunswick	Alice Faye
9/20, 11/15?/37	Perry Botkin	Decca	The Foursome [2 sessions]
11/9/37	Rhythm Wreckers	Vocalion	Jerry Colonna
1/20-12/19/38	John S. Trotter	Decca/Brunswick	Bing Crosby [6 s]
1/28, 4/25/38	Feuer/Sosnik	Decca	Pinky Tomlin [2 s]
4/6-4/25/38	Harry Sosnik	Decca	Frances Langford [3 s]
4/16/38	Sosnik	Decca	Dick Powell
4/16/38	Sosnik	Decca	Connee Boswell
4/22/38	Sosnik	Decca	Kenny Baker
4/22/38	Sosnik	Decca	Bobby Breen
4/22/38	Trotter	Brunswick	Betty Jane Rhodes
4/25, 8/21/38	Sosnik	Decca/Brunswick	Judy Garland [2 s]
7/1/38	Young	Decca/Brunswick	Crosby & Johnny Mercer
7/17, 9/13/38	Botkin	Brunswick	Ella Logan [2 s]
8/12, 8/21/38	Sosnik	Decca	Dick Powell & Foursome [2 s]
8/15/38	Sosnik	Decca	Pinky Tomlin & Foursome
10/12/38	Lou Bring	Victor	Jean Sablon
10/14, 10/18/38	Botkin	Brunswick	Hoagy Carmichael & E. Logan [2 s]
11/19-12/18/38	Young	Decca	Frances Langford [4 s]
3/15-12/15/39	Trotter	Decca	Crosby & Foursome [3 s]
5/24, 11/16/39	Cascales	Cinematone	John Cascales [2 s; unconfirmed]
5/27-10/28/39	David Rose	Columbia	Martha Raye [unconfirmed]
7/29/39	Young	Decca	Garland
7/5/39	Young	Decca	Shirley Ross & Foursome

1/5, 10/8/40	Feuer/Botkin	Columbia	Mary Healy [2 s]
1/19/40	Lou Bring	Victor	Dorothy Lamour
2/25-12/20/40	Trotter	Decca	Crosby [3 s]
2/29/40	Jerry Joyce	Columbia	Eddie Cantor
3/7/40	Bring	Victor	Gracie Fields
3/15/40	Sam Freed	Columbia	Eddie Anderson
4/2/40	Botkin	Columbia	Ella Logan [unconfirmed]
6/5/40	Botkin	Columbia	Marie Green & The Merry Men
9/21/40	Bring	Victor	Kenny Baker
9/22/40	Botkin	Columbia	Fred Astaire
10/17/40	Botkin	Columbia	Six Hits and a Miss
12/9/40	Trotter	Decca	Crosby & The King's Men
12/18/40	David Rose	Decca	Garland
12/24/40	Young	Decca	Tony Martin
1/4/41	Botkin	Columbia	Marie Green
1/30/41	Botkin	Columbia	Jerry Colonna
2/1/41	Young	Decca	Tony Martin
2/20/41	Bring	Victor	Dinah Shore
1/7/41	Lou Kosloff	Decca	Andrews Sisters
3/27/41	Bring	Decca	Joan Merrill
4/28/41	Frank Tours	Victor	John Charles Thomas
5/13/41	Bring	Victor	Allan Jones
5/18/41	Botkin	Columbia	Ella Logan
5/23-7/9/41	Trotter	Decca	Crosby [4 s]
5/27-7/8/41	Young	Decca	Connee Boswell [3 s]
6/25-7/9/41	none/Young	Decca	The King's Men [4 s]
6/27/41	Slack	Decca	Freddie Slack & His Eight Beats
7/5, 9/12/41	Young/Kosloff	Decca	Merry Macs [2 s]
7/8, 7/14/41	Young	Decca	Crosby [2 s]
7/16-8/24/41	Young	Decca	Irene Dunne [3 s]
7/29/41	Trotter	Decca	John Scott Trotter Orchestra
8/4, 8/11/41	Johnny Bond	Okeh	Dick Reinhart & Vera Woods [2 s]
8/12, 8/29/41	Young	Decca	Carol Bruce [2 s]
8/27/41	Bring	Victor	Tito Guizar
9/9/41	Young	Decca	Frances Langford
12/15-17/41	Bring	Victor	Lena Horne [unconfirmed]
1/16/42	Frank Tours	Victor	John Charles Thomas
1/24-6/12/42	Trotter	Decca	Crosby [7 s]
1/26, 1/27/42	Young	Decca	Crosby [2 s]
1/26/42	Vic Schoen	Decca	Andrews Sisters
1/28/42	Young	Decca	Betty Jane Rhodes
2/1, 7/19/42	Young	Decca	Tony Martin [2 s]
2/2/42	Young	Decca	Gracie Fields
2/6/42	Young	Decca	Frances Langford
2/20/42	Daffan	Okeh	Ted Daffan's Texans
3/6/42	Lou Bring	Victor	Rudy Vallee
3/27, 5/11/42	Carmichael	Decca	Hoagy Carmichael [2 s]
5/28-6/27/42	Botkin	Decca	Arthur Schutt & Marlene Fingerle [3 s]
6/26, 27/42	Trotter	Decca	Fred Astaire [2 s]
7/27, 28/42	Bring	Victor	Gail Laughton [2 s]
7/30/42	Paul Weston	Victor	Dinah Shore

CINEMATONE CORPORATION

Record	Title	Recorded
Johnny Cascales, Musical Director (Jones' participation assumed):		
demo	Sugar Blues (*Cinema-Fritzers*)	5/29/39
demo	Runnin' Wild (*Penny-Funnies*)	5/29/39
demo; VS-1002	Hot Lips (*Cinema-Fritzers*)	5/29/39
demo	Sweet Adeline (*Penny-Funnies*)	5/29/39
VS-1006	Now Laugh (*Penny-Funnies*)	5/29/39
	Anything Goes	8/15/40
	Fine and Dandy	8/15/40
	I Can't Love You Anymore	8/15/40
	I'll Never Smile Again	8/15/40
	Imagination	8/15/40
	Johnson Rag	8/15/40
	Make Believe Island	8/15/40
	Nearness of You	8/15/40
	When the Swallows Come Back to Capistrano	8/15/40

AUDITION RECORDS

A single audition record labeled Spike Jones Quartet, dated 4/14/39, is extant on acetate.

Among the numerous audition records Jones made during the embryonic years of the City Slickers are extant acetates of the following, recorded at NBC or Cinematone, 1940-1941: Barstool Cowboy From Old Barstow; Beautiful Eggs; Behind Those Swinging Doors; Caravan; The Covered Wagon Rolled Right Along; Don't Talk to Me About Men; Fine and Dandy; Fix Up the Spare Room, Mother; Hot Lips; I Wonder Who's Kissing Her Now?; I'll Lend You Anything; The Nearness of You; Red Wing; She Wouldn't Do What I Asked Her To; Sweet Adeline; Medley No. 1: You're Driving Me Crazy/Am I Blue?/I Wonder Who's Kissing Her Now?/Chant of the Jungle/ Dream House; Medley No. 2: I'll Never Smile Again/Make-Believe Island/Imagination.

VICTOR - BLUEBIRD 78S

Records are listed in the order of release, within each category. No attempt has been made to list foreign issues; reissues have also been generally excluded.

A note on the Victor singles: The release dates indicated are those of the 78s. The first Jones record to be released on 45 rpm was The Nutcracker Suite *(Apr. 1949 reissue); simultaneous issue of 45s began with* Morpheus *(Dec. 1949). 45s are indicated by a single asterisk (*). Jones' singles were reissued in the Popular Series, as well as the Collector's Series, the Gold Standard series and the Little Nipper series; they were also repackaged for EPs.*

Record	Rel.	Title	Matrix	Recorded
B-11282	10/41	Behind Those Swinging Doors	PBS-061519	8/8/41
		Red Wing	PBS-061517	8/8/41
B-11364	11/41	Barstool Cowboy From Old Barstow	PBS-061518	8/8/41
		The Covered Wagon Rolled Right Along	PBS-061520	8/8/41
B-11466	3/42	Clink, Clink, Another Drink	PBS-072021	1/12/42
		Pack Up Troubles in Your Old Kit Bag	PBS-072023	1/12/42
B-11530	5/42	Little Bo Peep Has Lost Her Jeep	PBS-072237	4/7/42
		Pass the Biscuits, Mirandy	PBS-072239	4/7/42

B-11560	8/42	Come, Josephine, in My Flying Machine	PBS-072238	4/7/42
		Siam	PBS-072236	4/7/42
B-11586	9/42	Der Fuehrer's Face	PBS-072524	7/28/42
		I Wanna Go Back to West Virginia	PBS-072528	7/28/42
30-0812	4/43	Oh! By Jingo	PBS-072526	7/28/42
		The Sheik of Araby	PBS-072527	7/28/42
30-0818	10/43	Hotcha Cornia	PBS-072524	7/28/42
		The Wild, Wild Women	PBS-072020	1/12/42

VICTOR 78s & 45s - POPULAR SERIES

20-1628	12/44	Cocktails for Two	D4-AB-1056	11/29/44
		Leave the Dishes in the Sink, Ma	D4-AB-1058	11/29/44
20-1654	3/45	Chloe	D5-VB-1011	1/13/45
		A Serenade to a Jerk	D5-VB-1010	1/13/45
20-1733	10/45	Holiday for Strings	D4-AB-1057	11/29/44
		Drip, Drip, Drip (Sloppy Lagoon)	D5-VB-1012	1/13/45
P-143	11/45	**The Nutcracker Suite**	WP-143*	
20-1739/47-2795*		The Little Girl's Dream	D5-VB-1134	9/27/45
		Land of the Sugar Plum Fairy	D5-VB-1135	9/28/45
20-1740/47-2796*		The Fairy Ball	D5-VB-1136	9/28/45
		The Mysterious Room	D5-VB-1137	9/28/45
20-1741/47-2797*		Back to the Fairy Ball	D5-VB-1138	9/29/45
		End of the Little Girl's Dream	D5-VB-1139	9/29/45
20-1762	11/45	The Blue Danube	D5-VB-1129	9/10/45
		You Always Hurt the One You Love	D5-VB-1128	9/10/45
20-1836	3/46	Old MacDonald Had a Farm	D6-VB-2027	2/11/46
47-0180*		Mother Goose Medley	D6-VB-2025	2/11/46
20-1893	6/46	The Glow-Worm	D6-VB-2026	2/11/46
		Hawaiian War Chant	D5-VB-1131	2/11/46
20-1894	6/46	I Dream Of Brownie with the Light	D6-VB-2024	2/11/46
		Blue Jeans/Jones Polka	D6-VB-2063	5/6/46
20-1895	6/46	That Old Black Magic	D5-VB-1127	9/10/45
		Liebestraum	D5-VB-1130	9/10/45
20-1983	10/46	Minka	D6-VB-2065	5/6/46
		Lassus' Trombone	D6-VB-2066	5/6/46
20-2023	11/46	The Jones Laughing Record	D6-VB-2163	9/28/46
		My Pretty Girl	D6-VB-2175	10/7/46
20-2118	1/47	Laura	D6-VB-2064	5/6/46
		When Yuba Plays the Rumba on the Tuba	D6-VB-2067	5/6/46
20-2245	5/47	Love in Bloom	D7-VB-455	2/10/47
		Blowing Bubble Gum (Bubble Gum Song)	D7-VB-456	2/10/47
20-2375	7/47	Our Hour	D7-VB-1304	7/15/47
		Pop Corn Sack	D7-VB-1303	7/15/47
20-2592	12/47	My Old Flame	D7-VB-1367	10/7/47
		People Are Funnier Than Anybody	D7-VB-1140	11/5/47
20-2820	3/48	Down in Jungle Town	D7-VB-1113	10/30/47
		Ugga Ugga Boo Ugga Boo Boo Ugga	D7-VB-457	2/11/47
20-2861	4/48	William Tell Overture	D7-VB-1368	10/7/47
		By the Beautiful Sea	D7-VB-1162	11/13/47

20-2861	4/48	William Tell Overture (*reissue*)	D7-VB-1368	10/7/47
		The Man on the Flying Trapeze	D7-VB-357	3/24/47
20-2949	8/48	I Kiss Your Hand, Madame	D7-VB-2341	12/4/47
		I'm Getting Sentimental Over You	D7-VB-1163	11/13/47
20-3177	11/48	All I Want for Christmas (My Two	D7-VB-2342	12/4/47
47-2963*		Front Teeth)/Happy New Year	D7-VB-2409	12/23/47
20-3338	1/49	The Clink, Clink Polka (*reissue of B-11466*)	PBS-072021	1/12/42
		MacNamara's Band	D9-VB-501	1/6/49
20-3359	2/49	Ya Wanna Buy a Bunny?	D9-VB-503	1/6/49
47-2894*		Knock, Knock (Who's There?)	D9-VB-502	1/6/49
20-3516	7/49	Dance of the Hours	D9-VB-644	5/24/49
47-2992*		None But the Lonely Heart	D7-VB-2381	12/30/47
20-3620	12/49	Morpheus	D9-VB-685	7/31/49
47-3126*		Wild Bill Hiccup	D9-VB-643	5/24/49
P-277	2/50	**Spike Jones Plays the Charleston**	WP-277*	
		(*Reissued as 10" album, LPM-18*)		
20-3675/47-3198*		The Charleston	D9-VB-2611	12/17/49
		Charlestono-Mio	D9-VB-2615	12/18/49
20-3676/47-3199*		Black Bottom	D9-VB-2616	12/18/49
		Doin' the New Raccoon	D9-VB-2612	12/17/49
20-3677/47-3200*		I Wonder Where My Baby Is Tonight	D9-VB-2613	12/17/49
		Varsity Drag	D9-VB-2614	12/17/49
20-3741	3/50	Chinese Mule Train	E0-VB-3404	3/10/50
47-3741*		Riders in the Sky (*2 masters*)	D9-VB-645	5/24/49
20-3827	6/50	I Know a Secret	E0-VB-3508	1/4/50
47-3827*		Charlestono-Mio (*reissue*)	D9-VB-2615	12/18/49
20-3912	9/50	Yes! We Have No Bananas	E0-VB-3757	8/9/50
47-3912*		Yaaka Hula Hickey Dula	E0-VB-3756	8/9/50
20-3934	10/50	Mommy, Won't You Buy a Baby Brother	E0-VB-3507	1/4/50
47-3934*		Rudolph the Red Nosed Reindeer	E0-VB-3743	8/9/50
20-3939	10/50	Molasses, Molasses	E0-VB-5562	9/25/50
47-3939*		Baby Buggie Boogie	E0-VB-3754	8/9/50
20-4011	1/51	Tennessee Waltz	E0-VB-5051	12/8/50
47-4011*		I Haven't Been Home for Three Whole Nights	E0-VB-5052	12/8/50
20-4055	2/51	Peter Cottontail	E1-VB-500	1/3/51
47-4055*		Rhapsody from Hunger(y)	D9-VB-686	7/31/49
20-4125	4/51	My Daddy Is A General To Me	E1-VB-529	1/19/51
47-4125*		Ill Barkio	D7-VB-2408	12/23/47
20-4209	7/51	Too Young	E1-VB-663	7/9/51
47-4209*		So 'Elp Me	E0-VB-3758	8/9/50
20-4546	2/52	Deep Purple	E2-VB-5240	1/25/52
47-4546*		It Never Rains in Sunny California	E2-VB-5241	1/25/52
20-4568	3/52	Down South	E2-VB-5250	2/4/52
47-4568*		I've Turned a Gadabout	E2-VB-5255	2/4/52
20-4669	4/52	There's a Blue Sky Way Out Yonder	E2-VB-5253	2/4/52
47-4669*		Stop Your Gamblin'	E2-VB-5254	2/4/52
P-3054	5/52	**Bottoms Up** (*reissued as 10" album, LPM 3054*)		
20-4728		Bottoms Up	E2-VB-5273	2/26/52
		Cheerio	E2-VB-5270	2/12/52
20-4729		Sante	E2-VB-5269	2/12/52
		Salute	E2-VB-5271	2/17/52

20-4730		Drink to the Bonnie Lassies	E2-VB-5272	2/17/52
		Slante	E2-VB-5268	2/12/52
20-4731		A Din Skal, A Min Skal	E2-VB-5239	1/25/52
		Gesundheit Polka	E2-VB-5230	1/25/52
20-4875	8/52	Hot Lips	E2-VB-5358	7/1/52
47-4875*		Hotter Than A Pistol	E2-VB-5356	7/1/52
20-5015	10/52	Socko, The Smallest Snowball	E2-VB-6985	9/19/52
47-5015*		Barnyard Christmas	E2-VB-6984	9/19/52
20-5067	11/52	I Saw Mommy Kissing Santa Claus	E2-VB-6991	11/6/52
47-5067*		Winter	E2-VB-6990	11/6/52
20-5107	1/53	I Went to Your Wedding	E2-VB-6980	9/16/52
47-5107*		I'll Never Work There Any More	E2-VB-5279	2/26/52
20-5239	3/53	Lulu Had a Baby	E3-VB-0561	2/11/53
47-5239*		The Boys in the Back Room	E2-VB-7000	11/6/52
20-5320	5/53	Three Little Fishies	E3-VB-0570	2/11/53
47-5320*		A Din Skal, A Min Skal (reissue)	E2-VB-5239	1/25/52
20-5413	8/53	God Bless Us All	E3-VB-0154	7/22/53
47-5413*		I Just Love My Mommy	E3-VB-0155	7/22/53
20-5472	10/53	Dragnet	E3-VB-0191	9/9/53
47-5472*		Pal-Yat-Chee	E0-VB-3403	3/10/50
20-5497	10/53	Where Did My Snowman Go?	E3-VB-2004	9/25/53
47-5497*		Santa Brought Me Choo Choo Trains	E3-VB-2005	9/25/53
20-5742	5/54	I'm In the Mood for Love	E4-VB-3145	4/4/54
47-5742*		Secret Love	E4-VB-3144	4/4/54
20-5920	11/54	Japanese Skokiaan	E4-VB-5784	10/17/54
47-5920*		I Want Eddie Fisher for Christmas	E4-VB-4560	10/22/54
		(Harry Geller, leader)		
20-6064	3/55	Hi Mister!	F2-PB-0444	2/15/55
47-6064*		This Song Is for the Birds	F2-PB-0445	2/15/55

VICTOR 78s & 45s - LITTLE NIPPER SERIES

Y-377	7/49	**How the Circus Learned to Smile**		
Y-387/WY-387*		(record with picture book)		
45-5224/47-0192*		Part 1	D7-VB-2366	12/11/47
		Part 4	D7-VB-2369	12/15/47
45-5225/47-0193*		Part 2	D7-VB-2367	12/15/47
		Part 3	D7-VB-2368	12/15/47
Y-472	10/53	A Toot and a Whistle and a Plunk and	E3-VB-2002	9/25/53
WY-472*		a Boom/Captain of the Space Ship	E3-VB-0117	6/22/53

VICTOR EPs — POPULAR SERIES

EPA-440	1/53	**Carmen Murdered!**		7/31/49

(Never issued in 78 or 45 rpm; issued as 10" LP,
"Spike Jones Murders Carmen and Kids the Classics,"   LPM-3128)
Overture: Bizet Gets the Business/The Bubble Gum
Girls Stick Together/Carmen (A Square in Seville
Don Schmozay and Soldiers/March (April, May, June
and July)/Carmen Kills a Cadenza/The Giggle Song
Typewriter Solo for Twelve Fingers/Toreador Song (It's
the Bull)/Finale (Also End)

STARLITE 78S & 45S
Alias Davey Crackpot and the Mexican Jumping Beans

1371	6/55	Cherry Pink & Apple Blossom White	ST-1371-1	5/19/55
ST-45-1371*		No Boom Boom in Yucca Flats	ST-1371-2	5/19/55

DECCA 78S & 45S
Cindy Walker and the City Slickers:

5992		Waltz Me Around Again Willie	DLA 2731	9/5/41
		Don't Talk to Me About Men	DLA 2733	9/5/41
6022		I Want Somebody	DLA 2732	9/5/41
		He Knew All of the Answers	DLA 2730	9/5/41

Alias The Banjo Maniacs

29623	8/55	Pick-It-You-Peasant	W88214T2A 5/19/55
9-29623*		Double Eagle Rag	W88215T2A 5/19/55

VERVE 78S & 45S

V-2003	2/56	**Spike Spoofs the Pops #1**		
V-2003x45*		Little Child/*Love and Marriage***	20,058/60**	1/24/56
		The Trouble With Pasquale		1/24/56
		Memories Are Made of This	20,059	1/24/56
		16 Tacos	1/24/56	

** *(Track replaced on alternate issue — other tracks identical)*

V-2026		Wouldn't It Be Fun to Be Santa Claus' Son	20,283	7/25/56
V-2026x45*		My Birthday Comes on Christmas	20,273	7/25/56
V-10037		I'm Popeye the Sailor Man	20,683	2/11/57
V-10037x45*		My Heart Went Boom Boom	20,682	2/11/57

Alias The Polka Dots (Supervised by Jones)

V-10054		The Happy Trumpets Polka	20,912	2/11/57
V-10054x45*		The Lawrence Welk Polka	20,915	2/11/57

Gil Bernal (Supervised by Jones)

V-10087x45*		Tab, Rory and Rock, Rock	21,328	8/31/57
		Take Me Back	21,329	8/31/57

VERVE LPS

MGV-2021	10/56	**Spike Jones Presents a Xmas Spectacular**	7/25/56

(reissued as "*Let's Sing a Song of Christmas,*"
"*It's a Spike Jones Christmas*")
Jingle Bells Medley/Two Front Teeth/The Night
Before Christmas Song/Rudolph the Red-Nosed
Reindeer/Silent Night/Sleigh Ride/My
Birthday Comes on Christmas/Snow Medley
Nuttin' For Christmas/Deck the Halls Medley
White Christmas Medley/Angel in the Christmas
Play/Christmas Cradle Song/Frosty the Snowman
Hark Medley/Christmas Alphabet Medley/Santa
Claus' Son/Christmas Island/Victor Young Medley
Here Comes Santa Claus/What Are You Doin' New Eve?

MGV-4005	**Dinner Music for People Who Aren't Very Hungry**		9/15/56

Space Ship Landing/Assorted Glugs, Pbrts,
and Skks/Ramona/Mischa's Souvenir/Black and
Blue Danube Waltz/Stark's Theme/The Old Sow
Song/Pal-Yat-Chee/How High the Fidelity
Cocktails for Two/Wyatt Earp Makes Me Burp
Woofer's Lament/Memories Are Made of This?
The Sneezin' Bee/Little Child/Brahm's Alibi/Chloe

MGV-2065	**Mr. Banjo** — *Freddy Morgan (Supervised By Jones)*	8/23/56

Alias The Polka Dots (Supervised by Jones)

MGV-2066	**Hi-Fi Polka Party**	2/9/57

Lawrence Welk Polka/Pennsylvania Polka
Bottoms Up Polka/Happy Trumpets Polka
Pretty Girl Polka/Six Fat Dutchmen Polka
Ron Terry Polka/Whoopee John Polka/Frank
Yankovic Waltz/New Beer Barrel Polka
Funny Punny Polka/Strip Polka

WARNER BROS. 45

5116*	10/59	I Was a Teenage Brain Surgeon	B10,663	6/3/59
		Monster Movie Ball	B10,666	6/3/59

WARNER BROS. LP

B-1332	10/59	**Spike Jones in Hi-Fi**	5/22/59
WS-1332		Spike Jones in Stereo	

I Only Have Eyes for You/Poisen to Poisen
Teenage Brain Surgeon/(All of a Sudden)
My Heart Sings/Everything Happens to Me
Monster Movie Ball/Tammy/My Old Flame
This is Your Death/Two Heads Are Better
Than One/Spooktacular Finale

KAPP 45

(Jud Conlon, leader; supervised by Jones)

K-314 X*	12/59	I Want the South to Win the War for Christmas	K-4204	11/17/59

KAPP LP

Bill Dana (Jones as straightman; from CBS-TV soundtracks)

KL-1215	**More Jose Jimenez**	8/1/60

The Submarine Officer
The Judo Expert/The Piano Tuner
The Piano Tuner (Again)/The Artist
The Jose Jimenez Jammock Salesman
Warmup from Spike Jones Show

LIBERTY 45s

F-55191*	The Late Late Late Movies, Part 1	45-LB-954	1/20/59

		The Late Late Late Movies, Part 2	45-LB-955	1/20/59
F-55253*	2/60	Ah-1, Ah-2, Ah-Sunset Strip, Part 1	LB-1080	c. 12/59
		Ah-1, Ah-2, Ah-Sunset Strip, Part 2	LB-1081	c. 12/59

"Hangnails Hennessey and Wingy Brubeck"

F-55317*	11/60	Silents Please!	LB-1211	11/11/60
		Keystone Kapers	LB-1210	11/10/60

The New Band of Spike Jones (Supervised by Jones)

55649*	10/63	Green Green	LB-1767	9/18/63
		Ballad of Jed Clampett	LB-1768	9/16/63
55684*	3/64	Dominique	LB-1834	1/28/64
		Sweet and Lovely	LB-1835	1/28/64
55718*		I'm in the Mood for Love	LB-1907	5/14/64
		Paradise	LB-1908	5/14/64
55768*	3/65	Jambalaya	LB-2007	c. 8/64
		Hey, Good Lookin'	LB-2008	c. 8/64

(The New Band without Jones' supervision)

55788*	4/65	Let's Kiss Kiss Kiss	LB-2046	3/26/65
		Star Jenka	LB-2047	3/26/65

LIBERTY LPs

LRP-3140	4/60	**Omnibust**	1/20/59
LST-7140		Ah-1 Ah-2, Ah Sunset Strip/Loretta's	
		Soaperetta/Captain Bangaroo/The Late	
		Late Movies, Part 1/The Wonderful World	
		of Hari Kari/I Search for Golden Adventure	
		in My Seven Leaky Boots/A Mudder's Day	
		Sport Spectacular/The Late Late Late Movies,	
		Part 2	
LRP-3154	8/60	**60 Years of Music America Hates Best**	7/8/60
LST-7154		I Kiss Your Hand, Madame/Knock, Knock,	
		Who's There?/River, Stay 'Way From My Door	
		Pimples and Braces/Hut Sut Song/Strip Polka	
		Mairzy Doats/The 20s Roar/Melody of Love	
		Three Little Fishies/Kooky, Kooky, Lend Me Your Comb	

John Cyr and Bobby Van Eps — Alias Hangnails Hennessey and Wingy Brubeck
(Supervised by Spike Jones)

LRP-3185	1/61	**Rides, Rapes and Rescues**	10/27/60
LST-7185		Keystone Kapers/Silents Please/Lips That	
		Touch Liquor Shall Never Touch Mine	
		A Mustache, a Derby, a Cane and a Cop	
		Theda Barracuda Meets Rudolph Vaselino	
		The Great Train Robbery/Madame Fifi's Can-Can	
		The Beautiful Bathing Beauties/The Winning	
		of the West/Curses! If Jack Dalton Were Only	
		Here/The Cotton Pickin' Peasant Overture	
		The Star and Stripes Flicker Finale	

Various artists (Narration and stereo demonstration by Jones)

LST-101		**This is Stereo**	9/61
		Feetlebaum Bombs in Louisville *(from "Omnibust,"*	
		(originally "A Mudder's Day Sport Spectacular")	

The New Band of Spike Jones (Carl Brandt, leader; supervised by Jones)

LRP-3338	12/63	**Washington Square**	9/16/63
LST-7338		Alley Cat/Ballad of Jed Clampett/Frankie and	
		Johnnie/Maria Elena/Green Green/Washington	
		Square/September Song/Blowin' in the Wind	
		Puff (the Magic Dragon)/Red Sails in the Sunset	
		Whistler's Muddah/If I Had a Hammer	

LRP-3349	4/64	**Spike Jones' New Band**	12/30/63
LST-7349		Dominique/Kansas City/Whispering/Java	
		Deep Purple/Charade/There! I've Said It Again	
		Stoplight/Mañana/For You/Hey Mr. Banjo	
		Sweet and Lovely	

LRP-3370	6/64	**My Man**	5/8/64
LST-7370		Sophisticated Lady/Temptation/Paradise	
		Stairway to the Stars/I'm in the Mood for Love	
		Lefty Louie/Ballin' the Jack/Harlem Nocturne	
		The Glow-Worm/Shangri-La/The Stripper	

LRP-3401	4/65	**The New Band of Spike Jones Plays**	8/64
LST-7401		**Hank Williams Hits**	
		Jambalaya/I Saw the Light/Move It On Over	
		Weary/Blues from Waitin'/There'll Be No Teardrops	
		Tonight/Your Cheatin' Heart/Hey, Good Lookin'	
		Cold Cold Heart/I'm So Lonesome I Could Cry	
		Kaw-Liga/I Can't Help It/You Win Again	

Special Purpose Pressings

Transcription

78 rpm souvenir for National Assn. of Broadcasters
Alias The Country Dodgers (Labeled "A Standirt Production")

072248	10"	Your Morning Feature (Virgin Mary Sturgeon)	4/20/42

Radio Recorders

Pressings for radio broadcast

RR9345	12"	Chloe (*Command Performance*, with Bob Hope)*	12/25/43
RR8692		Black Magic (*Treasury Song Parade*)	6/28/43

* *An alternate without Hope, from same source, was issued as RR12334; flip side B-149.*

RR10520	10"	Cocktails for Two (*Command Performance*)	4/1/44
RR10518		The Glow-Worm (*Command Performance*)	1/15/44
RR10521	10"	SNAFU (*Command Performance*)	1/15/44
RR10519		City Slicker Polka (*Command Performance*)	4/1/44

Pre-release pressing

None	12"	Riders in the Sky (*The Spike Jones Show*)	5/21/49

Allied/International Artists

| 2158 | 10" | Holiday for Strings (*Bob Burns Show*) | | 4/27/44 |

RCA Victor

78 rpm souvenir for Coin Operators Assn. convention

| | 1947 | All Hail COINegie Tech! # | D7-CB-416 | 1/6/47 |
| | | My Pretty Girl | D6-VB-2175 | 10/7/46 |

 # An alternate take is extant on acetate.

45 rpm EP gift premium with RCA phonographs

SPD 6	1955	**Platter Party** (*Side 14 of 10-record set*)		
599-9049		Come, Josephine, in My Flying Machine	PBS-072238	4/7/42
		Fiddle Faddle	E0-VB-3402	3/10/50

Rainbo Record Company

Cardboard 78 "thank you" promo for radio stations

| None | 8" | Happy New Year! from the Spike Jones Show | | 12/17/48 |
| | | (*The Spotlight Revue; contains excerpts of "Jingle Bells"*) | | |

RADIO STATION PROMOS - RCA VICTOR

In addition to the standard white-label 78, 45 and LP "disc jockey samples" made available to radio stations by the various labels, RCA issued these unique promotional records:

DJ-613	10"	Trailers for Use with Spike Jones' "All I Want For Christmas" (*7 tracks*)		
20-3156	10"	Dance of the Hours	D9-VB-644	5/24/49
		Spike Jones Describes the Musical (?) Instruments used in "Dance of the Hours"	D9-CB-1346	
20-3934	10"	Mommy, Won't You Buy a Baby Brother?	E0-VB-3507	1/4/50
		Audio Disc for Use In Programming	E0-QB-13282	
	12"	Andre Koroshovsky and his Foster Parent — Spike Jones (*for use with E0-VB-3507*)	E0-CC-1299	c. 1/50
	12"	Spike Jones Asks Georgie Rock, "Did You Really See Mommy Kissing Santa Claus?"	E2-KB-6686	c. 11/52
		Georgie Rock Reminds You — Days 'Til Christmas	E2-KB-6687	c. 11/52

V-DISCS

VP-32	36	Der Fuehrer's Face (*Bluebird*)	D3-MC-123	7/28/42
VP-352	113	You Can't Say No to a Soldier		11/43
		That Old Black Magic	D3-MC-442	11/43
VP-353	113;115•	Chloe	D3-MC-443	11/43
VP-380	125	Hotcha Cornia		11/43
		Down in Jungle Town	D3-MC-451	11/43
VP-420	125	As Time Goes By		11/43
		Barstool Cowboy (*Bluebird*)	D3-MC-486	8/8/41
VP-939	348;128•	The Great Big Saw (*Standard*)		6/12/44
		Cocktails for Two (*Standard*)	D4-TC-441	6/12/44

VP-1511	551	You Always Hurt the One You Love	8/45
		Siam	D5-TC-1322 8/45
VP-1513	540	The Blue Danube	8/45
		Toot Toot Tootsie, Goo'Bye	D5-TC-1324 8/45
VP-1536	570	Minka	8/45
		MacNamara's Band	D5-TC-1336 8/45
VP-1748	640	Fairy Ball (*Victor*)	9/28/45
		Mysterious Room (*Victor*)	D5-TC-1595 9/28/45
JDB-183	709	Hawiian War Chant (*Victor*)	2/11/46
		Jones Polka (*Victor*)	D6-TC-6027 5/6/46

• *Navy Department numbers*

STANDARD RADIO TRANSCRIPTIONS

Cindy Walker and the City Slickers:

R-127
8/15/41
Salt River Valley, Bear Cat Mountain Gal, Don't Talk To Me About Men, Hillbilly Bill, Don't Count Your Chickens, I Want Somebody, Ridin' for the Rancho, Round Me Up and Call Me Dogie, Love Has Been the Ruin of Many a Maid, Barstool Cowboy from Old Barstow

R-131
12/17/41
Travelin' In My Shoes, He Knew All of the Answers, You've Got My Heart Doing a Tap Dance, The Old Wrangler, It's All Your Fault, Song of the Cowboy, I Don't Trust the Men, Homesick, Now or Never, It Never Can Be

R-136
5/11/42
You're From Texas, The Farmer's Daughter, How Many Apples Does It Take to Make a Pie?, Sweet Something, The Rose of the Border

R-143
5/11/42
Gonna Stomp Those City Slickers Down, 'Til the Longest Day I Live, That Big Palooka Who Plays the Bazooka, Bye Lo Baby Bunting, Into the Sunrise

Spike Jones and his City Slickers:

R-129
11/24/41
Hi! Neighbor, Behind Those Swinging Doors; Clink, Clink, Another Drink; Barstool Cowboy, Moo Woo Woo, Fort Worth Jail; Pass the Biscuits, Mirandy; Last Horizon, Don't Talk to Me About Women, Big Bad Bill

R-132
2/27/42
Little Bo Peep Has Lost Her Jeep, Trailer Annie, Siam, Hotcha Cornya, Hey Mable, Boogie Woogie Cowboy, Dodging a Gal from Dodge City, A Serenade to a Jerk, Ridin' Home With You, Now Laugh

R-136
4/20/42
That's What Makes the World Go 'Round, Don't Give the Chair to Buster, 48 Reasons Why, De Camptown Races with Gestures, The Blacksmith Song

R-138
7/31/42
Sheik of Araby, Oh! By Jingo, Red Wing, Der Fuehrer's Face, I'm Going to Write Home

R-138
4/20/42
Three Little Words, When Buddha Smiles; You're A Sap, Mister Jap; Pack Up Your Troubles, Never Hit Your Grandma With a Shovel

R-141 7/31/42	I'm Goin' Back To West Virginia, Water Lou (Sloppy Lagoon), St-St-Stella, I Know a Story, Hi Ho My Lady
R-141 7/17/42	John Scotter Trot, Cheatin' On the Sandman, The Girl I Left Behind Me, Sailor With the Navy Blue Eyes, Camptown Races No. 2
R-143 7/17/42	Come, Josephine, in My Flying Machine; Love For Sale, Moanin' Low, Horsie Keep Your Tail Up, Yankee Doodler
R-150 c.6/44	Down in Jungle Town, Whittle Out a Whistle, By the Beautiful Sea, At Last I'm First With You, Liebestraum, City Slicker Polka, Red Grow the Roses, Jamboree Jones, Down By the O-Hi-O, Casey Jones
R-151 6/12/44	Cocktails for Two, Mary Lou, Paddlin' Madelin Home, He Broke My Heart In Three Places, They Go Wild, Simply Wild, Over Me, Sailin' On The Robert E. Lee, The Great Big Saw Came Nearer and Nearer, It Had To Be You, His Rocking Horse Ran Away, Oh How She Lied to Me
R-167 c.8/45	Toot, Toot, Tootsie, Goodbye, You Always Hurt the One You Love, The Glow-Worm, Chloe, The Blue Danube, That Old Black Magic, Holiday for Strings; No, No, Nora; Row, Row, Row

* All 1942 dates are in question.

Spike Jones and his Other Orchestra:

Z-213 4/26/46	Spike Speaks (Spike Jones' Theme), Rhumba Rhapsody, E-Bob-O-Lee-Bop, Minka, Laura (*with the City Slickers*), Lovely, Warsaw Concerto, September Song, Hardly Ever Amber
Z-214 4/29/46	I Only Have Eyes for You, When Yuba Plays the Rumba on the Tuba, Spike Rocks the Troc, I've Got the World on a String, Pico Pick Up, Chameleon, Perfidia, Young Man With a French Horn, I'll Never Be the Same

VICTOR REJECTS & UNREALIZED PLANS

One-of-a-kind acetates of the following same-session alternate takes are extant:
Red Wing, Behind Those Swinging Doors; Come, Josephine, in My Flying Machine (1942); Der Fuehrer's Face; The Jones Laughing Record, All Hail COINegie Tech!, Ugga Ugga Boo Ugga Boo Boo Ugga, Pop Corn Sack, Our Hour, Riders in the Sky, Dance of the Hours, Chinese Mule Train; Yes, We Have No Bananas; Hot Lips, Varsity Drag, I Wonder Where My Baby Is Tonight?, Rudolph the Red Nosed Reindeer, Hi Mister!

##	Beautiful Eggs (*2 takes*) (*Written by Alfred Bryan and Herman Paley;* *vocal by Del Porter*)	PBS-072022	1/12/42
##	Hawaiian War Chant (*Vocal by Giggie Royse; narration by Carl Grayson.* *Alternate version of 20-1893, recorded 2/11/46.*)	D5-VB-1131	9/10/45
	Goldilocks and the Three Bears (*Intended as a four-part sequel to "The Nutcracker Suite;"* *vocal by George Rock, as Baby Bear. Unfinished; only audition* *with piano accompaniment extant.*)		1945

**	I Wuv a Wabbit		2/11/47
	(*Written by Mickey Katz; vocal by Arthur Q. Bryan,* *as Elmer Fudd. Unslated.*)		
**	My Cornet	D7-VB-356	3/24/47
	(*Written by Del Porter and George Rock; vocal by Rock.*)		
	MacNamara's Band		11/5/47
	(*Alternate version of 20-3338. Unslated.*)		
***	Rum Tee Diddle Dee Yump	D7-VB-2380	12/30/47
	(*Written by Freddy Morgan and Earl Bennett;* *vocal by Bennett, alias Sir Frederick Gas.*)		
#	Rum Tee Diddle Dee Yump (*2 takes*)	D9-VB-500	1/6/49
	(*Vocal by Sir Frederick Gas and his Sadivarius*)		
	A Goose to the Ballet Russe	D9-VB-686	7/31/49
	(*Vocal by Freddy Morgan and Helen Grayco. Test pressing;* *alternate of 20-4055, retitled "Rhapsody from Hunger(y)."*)		
	Mommy, Won't You Buy a Baby Brother	E0-VB-3506	1/4/50
	(*Written by Eddie Maxwell; vocal by George Rock. Alternate* *version of 20-3934 with "Happy Birthday" introduction.*)		
#**	Fiddle Faddle (*2 takes*)	E0-VB-3402	3/10/50
	(*Written by Leroy Anderson, parody by Eddie Maxwell;* *vocal by Homer and Jethro. Issued as special pressing:* *"Platter Party" SPD 6.*)		
•***	Come, Josephine, in My Flying Machine	E0-VB-3755	8/9/50
	(*Vocal by the Boys in the Back Room and King Jackson;* *updated version of B15560.*)		
#**	Alto, Baritone and Bass (*2 endings*)	E1-VB-662	7/9/51
	(*Written by Eddie Maxwell; vocal by Maxwell.*)		
¥***	What Is a Disc Jockey?	E1-VB-700	7/24/51
	(*Written by Ross Mullholland and Sheldon Allman;* *narration by Mulholland, as Larry Monroe.*		
	Bottoms Up	E2-VB-5273	2/17/52
	(*Vocal by Del Porter and The Mello Men; alternate* *version of 20-4728.*)		
20-4839 47-4839*	(All of a Sudden) My Heart Sings	E2-VB-5290	6/14/52
	(*Narration by Freddy Morgan, alias "The Contented Mental."* *Originally coupled with "I'll Never Work There Anymore;"* *pressed but not released. Issued on Armed Forces Radio* *transcription disc P-2566.*)		
	Under the Double Eagle	E2-VB-5357	7/1/52
	(*Written by Franz Josef Wagner; performed by* *Spike Jones and his Country Cousins*)		
	Keystone Kapers	E2-VB-5359	7/1/52
	(*Credited to Lindley Jones; performed by* *Spike Jones and his Country Cousins*)		
**	Winter	E2-VB-6990	11/4/52
	(*Vocal by the Mello Men; alternate take of 20-5067.*)		
	I Saw Mommy Kissing Santa Claus	E2-VB-6991	11/4/52
	(*Vocal by George Rock and the Mitchell Boy Choir,* *alternate version of 20-5067.*)		
	I Saw Mommy Screwing Santa Claus		11/6/52
	(*Special lyrics by Freddy Morgan; vocal by Rock. Unslated.*)		

		Oh Happy Day	E3-VB-0560	2/11/53

Oh Happy Day   E3-VB-0560   2/11/53
(Written by Don H. Koplow and Nancy B. Reed; vocal by Dick Morgan and Sir Frederick Gas)

20-5392*   #   Are My Ears on Straight?   E3-VB-0116   6/22/53
47-5392   *   *(Written by Mel Leven; vocal by Marian Richmond. Originally coupled with "Captain of the Space Ship"; pressed but not released. Issued on Armed Forces Radio transcription disc CH-78.)*

Gerald McBoing Boing   E3-VB-2003   9/25/53
(Written by Gail Kubik and Dr. Seuss; vocal by the Mello Men)

20-5602   ••   My Heart Went Boom Boom   E3-VB-2043   12/21/53
(Written by Freddy Morgan; vocal by Betsy Gay and Marjorie Rayburn as the Sorghum Sisters.)

47-5602*   #   Rickeyshaw   E3-VB-2044   12/21/53
(Written by Larry Coleman, Joe Darion, Norman Gimbal, Bernie Jones and Bill Whlpley; vocal by the Sorghum Sisters, Coupled with "Boom Boom"; pressed but not released. Acetate distributed to disc jockies on limited basis.)

LPM-3216   **Music for Leasebreakers — "A Study in Low Fidelity"**   c. 1953
(Alternately titled "Spike Jones' Dinner Music." Planned as 10" LP; recorded but not released. A shorter version of the album recorded for Verve in 1956.)

Issued on the 1974 German RCA LP "Can't Stop Murdering" (PJM 2-8021).
Issued on the 1998 Harlequin CD "The Bluebirds" (HQ CD 100).
**   *Issued on the 1994 Good Music CD "The Man Who Murdered Music" (DMC1-1210).*
***   *Issued on the 2002 Harlequin CD "Fonk" (HQ CD 178).*
•   *Reportedly issued on Scandinavian RCA 78.*
••   *Issued on the 1997 Eagle Records CD "The Masters" (EAB CD 040).*
¥   *Issued on the 1955 Australian RCA 78 (EA-4178).*

Planned But Not Recorded

Boogie Woogie Cowboy   1942
(Written by Dean, Stratham, Blair and Snow; intended for Bluebird)
SNAFU   1942
(Written by Foster Carling; intended for Bluebird.)
City Slicker Polka   1942
(Written by Foster Carling and Phil Ohman; intended for Bluebird.)
I Surrender, Dear   1946
(Written by Gordon Clifford; parody by Doodles Weaver)
Really, Mr. Greeley   c. 1950
(Written for Spike, Earl Bennett, Freddy Morgan and George Rock; to coincide with unrealized film of same name.)
Dragnuts (to You)   c. 9/53
(Alternate version of E3-VB-0191. Two drafts extant in script form.)
Hail to Subnormal Normal c. 1953
(Spike Jones and his Colleejuns, with Wally Cox as Mr. Peepers.)
Christmas Story   1955
(Written by Roy Robert Gillespie; intended for Little Nipper series with Jones as narrator.)

Copies of many other songs which may have been planned for recording—by Eddie Maxwell, Freddy Morgan, Sol Meyer, Paul Frees and others—were found in Jones' files.

V-Disc Rejects

VP-420	125	Shoo Shoo Baby	11/43
		(Written by Phil Moore; vocal by the Nilsson Twins; replaced with Barstool Cowboy*)*	
VP-1228		Beautiful Eggs *(Unissued Bluebird master)*	D5TC 252 1/12/42
		Holiday for Strings *(Victor master)*	11/29/44
VP-1580		Holiday for Strings *(Victor master)*	D5TC 1405 11/29/44
JDB 97		Mother Goose	D6TC 5280 c. 1946
		Old MacDonald Had a Farm	

Verve Rejects

Rock and Roll Waltz	1/24/56
(Vocal by George Rock; presumably intended for "Spike Spoofs the Pops.")	
The Story of Christmas Medley	8/2/56
The Spirit of Christmas	8/4/56
(Deleted from "Xmas Spectacular")	
Billy Barty selections (Supervised by Jones)	10/21/57
Satellite Baby/Little Things Mean a Lot	
Elevator Shoes/Why Oh Why/Sayo Nara GI	
Freddie Morgan selections (Supervised by Jones)	12/13/57
Smiles/Banjo Party/Save Your Sorrow for Tomorrow/Tiptoe Through the Tulips	

Warner Bros. Rejects

Who's Sick? *(9 takes)*	5/22/59
Who's Sick?	6/3/59
(Deleted from "Spike Jones in Stereo")	
William Tell Overture *(Vocal by Doodles Weaver)*	10/59

Planned But Not Recorded

I Was the Son of a Teenage Brain Surgeon	1959
March of the Martians (Take Me to Your Bleeder)	1959
I'm in Love with the Invisible Man from the Forbidden Planet	1959
(Intended for "Spike Jones in Stereo.")	

Liberty Rejects & Unrealized Projects

Keystone Kapers	10/27/60
Stars and Stripes Forever	10/27/60
Curses! If Only Jack Dalton Were Here	11/10/60
A Mustache, A Derby, a Cane and a Cop	11/11/60
Silents Please	11/11/60
(Alternate takes of tracks on "Rides, Rapes and Rescues.")	

LRP-3169	**Spike Jones as Leonard Burnside Discusses...**	9/20/61
LST-7169	(*Written by Bill Dana and Don Hinkley; narration by*	
	Jones. Recorded but not released; acetate extant.)	
	The Cymbal/The Kabuki Dance/The Zither	
	and Other Folk Music Instruments/The	
	Songwriter/ The Flamenco Dance/Drums	

Persuasive Concussion (*stereo basics*)

**	Carmen (*Arranged by Carl Brandt*)	2/6/61
#	Shh! Harry's Odd (Scherezade)	2/6/61
	That Old Black Magic	5/6/62
*	Holiday for Strings	5/6/62
	A Goose to the Ballet Russe	5/6/62
***	Powerhouse	5/6/62
***	Frantic Freeway (Beep-Beep Pachanga,	
	Sigalert Bossa Nova)	5/6/62
	Cocktails for Two	3/10/63
¥	Chloe (*Vocal by Red Ingle*)	3/10/63
	Powerhouse (*single, edited from LP version*)	1962
	Leonard Burnside Discusses the Ballet (*basic for LP*)	1962
	Leonard Burnside Discusses the Violin (*basic for LP*)	1962
**	Nyet! (*Written by Eddie Brandt and Carl Brandt;*	
	vocal by Shepard Menken. Stereo basic;	3/29/63
	complete mono with effects.)	
	Hootenanny Party (*Written by Eddie Brandt; stereo*)	1/25/64
	Hot Rod Bash (*Vocal by Doodles Weaver*)	c. 3/64
	Ghoul Days	3/11/64
	(*Written by Eddie Brandt; stereo, audition tracks for LP.*)	
	Ghoul Days/My Darling Frankenstein	

Planned But Not Recorded

	If You Knew Sousa	
	(*An album of John Phillips Sousa marches.*)	
	Ernest Hemingway Project	1961
	(*"An album featuring the biography of Hemingway."*)	
	Play Along With Spike	1961
	(*Intended for "Hangnails Hennessey and Wingy Brubeck."*)	
	Spike Jones Plays Rodgers and Hart	c. 1962
	$18.12 Overture	c. 1964
	Wonderful World of Suzie Poontong	c. 1964
	Jackie Gleason	c. 1964
	Pantomime Theme	c. 1964

#	*The dates of these sessions are in question.*
*	*Issued on the 1975 United Artists' LP "The Very*
	Best of Spike Jones" (LA439E).
**	*Issued on the 1994 Good Music CD "The Man*
	Who Murdered Music" (DMC1-1210).
***	*Issued on the 1994 Catalyst/BMG Classics' CD, "Spiked"*
	(09026-61982-2).
¥	*Issued on Capitol cassette "The Best of Spike Jones," and Capitol*
	CD of various artists "It's Been a Long, Long Time." (Both out of print).

Radiography

Pre-City Slickers (Jones as Sideman)

KFOX, Long Beach, Calif.
> Circa 1927-29. Long Beach Poly High Advanced Band.
> Circa 1927-29. Spike Jones and his Five Tacks.

KGER, Long Beach, Calif.
> Circa 1927-29. Long Beach Poly High Advanced Band.
> Circa 1927-29. Jones and his Five Tacks, alias "The Patent Leather Kids."
> 1930. Band: The California Revelers, led by Paul Harrison.

KNX, Los Angeles.
> 1936. Staff drummer. Orchestra: Jack Joy.

The Al Jolson Show (The Lifebuoy Program)
> CBS. Circa 1936-39. Orchestra: Victor Young; Lud Gluskin(?).

Rubinoff and his Violin
> CBS. Circa 1936-37. Orchestra: Dave Rubinoff.

The Burns and Allen Show
> CBS. Circa 1936-37. Orchestra: Henry King.

Kraft Music Hall (The Bing Crosby Show)
> NBC. Circa 1937-1942. Orchestra: John Scott Trotter.
> Mar. 27, 1941; Apr. 3, 1941: Novelty band backing Bob Burns.

The Eddie Cantor Show
> CBS. Circa 1938-39. Orchestra: Jacques Renard; Edgar Fairchild.

Tommy Riggs and Betty Lou
> NBC. Circa 1938-40. Orchestra: Freddie Rich.

CBS, Los Angeles.
> Circa 1938-39. Staff drummer. Orchestra: Lud Gluskin.

NBC, Los Angeles.
> Circa 1938-39. Staff drummer. Orchestra: Gordon Jenkins.

Screen Guild Theater
> CBS. Circa 1938-41. Orchestra: Oscar Bradley; Victor Young(?).

Fibber McGee and Molly
> NBC. Circa 1940-43. Orchestra: Billy Mills.

Guest Appearances (as Sideman)

The Academy Awards Show. KNX. Mar. 4, 1937.
Chrysler Shower of Stars. CBS. Late '30s. Orchestra: Lud Gluskin.
The Bob Hope Show. NBC. Circa 1938-39. Orchestra: Skinnay Ennis. •
Gilmore Circus. NBC. Circa 1938-39. Orchestra: Gordon Jenkins. •
Little Ol' Hollywood. NBC. Circa 1939. Orchestra: Gordon Jenkins. •
Birth of the Blues. Nov. 1, 1941. Bing Crosby. Orchestra: John Scott Trotter.
Lucky Strike Hit Parade. Mar. 28, 1942. Orchestra: Trotter.
Victory Parade. NBC. Aug. 8, 1942. Orchestra: Trotter.

• unconfirmed.

RADIO SERIES

The Arkansas Traveler (The Bob Burns Show)
> CBS. Show premiered Sept. 16, 1941. Jones and Slickers guested
> Oct. 14, 1942; appeared as house band Oct. 21, 1942 — Dec. 30, 1942,
> Wednesdays, 9 p.m.

Furlough Fun (The Gilmore Oil Show)
> NBC West Coast. Slickers guested Oct. 1, 1942; appeared as house band
> Nov. 2, 1942 — Feb. 8, 1943, Mondays; Feb. 19, 1943 — Jun. 23, 1944,
> Fridays, 9 p.m. Produced by Bradford Brown. With Beryl Wallace and
> George Riley.

The Bob Burns Show (The Lifebuoy Show)
> NBC. Jan. 7, 1943 — Jun. 23, 1944, Thursdays, 6:30 p.m.
> With Luther Roundtree.

The Chase and Sanborn Program
> NBC. Jun. 3, 1945 — Aug. 26, 1945, Sundays, 8 p.m. With Frances Langford.

Spike's at the Troc
> Mutual-Don Lee (KHJ, Los Angeles). Periodic broadcasts during
> engagement at the Trocadero. Mar. 22, 1946 — May 9, 1946. With Spike
> Jones and his Other Orchestra, Helen Grayco.

The Spotlight Revue (The Coke Show)
> CBS. Oct. 3, 1947 - Dec. 24, 1948, Fridays, 8:30 p.m. Produced by Hal
> Fimberg. Written by Fimberg, Eddie Brandt, Henry Taylor. With Dorothy
> Shay and Doodles Weaver. (Excerpts from the show were broadcast "live" on
> the public service program, *Here's to Veterans.*)

The Spike Jones Show
> CBS. Jan. 2, 1949 - June 25, 1949, Sundays. Produced by Joe Bigelow.
> Written by Jay Sommers, Eddie Brandt, Eddie Maxwell. With Doodles Weaver.

Guest Appearances

Point Sublime
>   NBC West Coast. Jul. 7, 1941 (the Slickers' radio debut); Jun. 17, 1942.

Kraft Music Hall
>   NBC. Numerous appearances, including: c. Apr. 1942; Jul. 2, 1942;
>   Oct. 12, 1944; Nov. 30, 1944; Jan. 11, 1945; Dec. 13, 1945; May 9, 1946.

USO Show.	NBC. May 30, 1942.
The Elgin Watch Show.	CBS. Nov. 26, 1942; Nov. 23, 1944.
Old Gold Show.	NBC. Dec. 14, 1942.
March of Dimes.	NBC. Jan. 23, 1943.
Treasury Song Parade.	Jun. 28, 1943. (Four 3-minute shows; unlimited b'cast).
The Adventures of Ellery Queen.	NBC. Sept. 4, Sept. 9, 1943. ***
Battle of New York.	NBC, New York. Sept, 11, 1943.
People Are Funny.	NBC. May 19, 1944. ***
The Chamber Music Society of Lower Regent Street.	BBC, London. Sept. 3, 1944.
Music America Loves Best.	NBC. Jun. 24, 1945; Aug. 12, 1945 (#378).
Bill Stern's Sports Newsreel.	NBC. Feb. 8, 1946; Feb. 7, 1947; May 13, 1949. ***
Request Performance.	CBS. Feb. 10, 1946.
Chesterfield Supper Club.	NBC. Apr. 18, 1946; May 2, 1946.
Tribute to the Shriners.	ABC. Apr. 27, 1946.
Philco Radio Time.	ABC. Oct. 23, 1946.
Sealtest Village Store.	NBC. Nov. 7, 1946.
Hawaii Calls.	Mutual. Circa Jul. 1948. ***
Truth or Consequences.	CBS. Dec. 11, 1948.
Salute to the Queen of the Rose Tournament.	CBS. Dec. 18, 1948.
The Louella Parsons Show.	ABC. Jul. 3, 1949; June 20, 1950; CBS. Jul. 4, 1954.
United States Coast Guard.	NBC. Aug. 3, 1949.
Sunday at the Chase.	CBS (KMOX), St. Louis. Nov. 6, 1949.
Don McNeil's Breakfast Club.	ABC, Chicago. Feb. 28, 1950. ***
The Hedda Hopper Show.	NBC. Dec. 17, 1950.
Ladies Day.	WHAS, Louisville. Mar. 12, 1951. ***
Saturday at the Chase.	CBS (KMOX), St. Louis. Mar. 24 , 1951; Mar. 31, 1951.
Juke Box Jury.	ABC. Sept. 1954. ***
Amos 'n' Andy Music Hall.	CBS. Jun. 16, 1955. ***
The AMPOL Show.	Australia. Circa Mar. 1955.
Art Linkletter's House Party.	Dec. 14, 1956. ***
Monitor.	NBC. 1960. (Two shows recorded; broadcast unconfirmed.) ***

>   *** *Guest appearances by Jones without the band.*

AUDITION SHOWS (UNSOLD PILOTS)

The Spike Jones Show *
>   NBC. Nov. 7, 14, 30, 1945.
>   Produced by Art Dailey. Written by Charlie Isaacs. With Red Ingle, Carl
>   Grayson, Ann Rutherford and Mabel Todd.

Spike Jones' Symphony Hall
>   Recorded Jul. 13, 1951.
>   Directed and written by Jay Sommers. With Dick Morgan, Freddy Morgan
>   and Earl Bennett.

Pilot
>   May 6, 1954. Made at Radio Recorders; no details available.

Use Your Head
>   NBC. Mar. 4, 1955. With George Rock, Billy Barty and others.

* *Two tracks ("Chloe" and "Hotcha Cornia") were released on M.F. Distribution's 1977
LP set, "The Complete Collection."*

ARMED FORCES RADIO SERVICE

Command Performance
>   Directed by Vick Knight. Numerous appearances, including: Sept. 29, 1942
>   (#33); Oct. 7, 1942 (#34); Oct. 27, 1942 (#39); Dec. 24, 1942; Mar. 27,
>   1943 (#59); Dec. 25, 1943 (#98?); Jan. 15, 1944 (#101); Apr. 1, 1944
>   (#113); Dec. 23, 1944 (#156); Jul. 5, 1945 (#182); Army Day (Apr. 6?),
>   1946; Aug. 25, 1948 (#346); Oct. 13, 1948 (#352). *Note: the band apparently
>   did not appear on the Oct. 14, 1944 program (#142) as generally accepted.*

Mail Call
>   CBS. Jun. 17, 1944 (#95).

Downbeat
>   Numerous programs were devoted to Jones' recordings (Standards, V-Discs,
>   etc.), including: Apr. 14, 1944 (#82); Apr. 19, 1944; Oct. 12, 1944 (#105);
>   Jan. 13, 1945 (#123); Feb. 1946 (#217). Spike was present to introduce the songs.
>   In addition to *Downbeat*, Jones' records were broadcast regularly on numerous
>   other AFRS shows—including *Basic Music Library, Purple Heart Album, G.I.
>   Jive, Melody Round-Up, Remember* and *Turn Back the Clock.*

>   Condensed editions of the band's two *Chesterfield Supper Club* appearances
>   were aired as *Supper Club.* Condensed versions of *The Chase and Sanborn
>   Program* and *Spotlight Revue* were also aired over AFRS stations (retitled
>   *Spike Jones* and *Corn's A-Poppin'*, respectively).

Vick Knight produced transcriptions with Spike Jones, Glenn Miller, Dinah Shore and Edward G. Robinson in England—for broadcast to the Allied Forces in France—during the entertainers' 1944 trip abroad. Jones' 20 transcriptions disappeared without a trace; one disc, "That Old Black Magic," surfaced in 2003.

Jones and the Slickers further served their country by recording various public service programs, including *Here's To Veterans*. The band's *Treasury Song Parade* transcriptions were aired "live" on two special New Year's Eve shows. They also recorded the following:

The Land's Best Bands
> U.S. Navy. Circa Nov. 27, 1950. (Four 15-minute shows: #3A, 5A, 8A, 11A; a 16" transcription mailed to radio stations to solicit enlistment in the Navy.)

COMMERCIALS & PROMOS

Butternut Bread. 1942. (17 jingles, written by producer John Guedel.)
The Musical Depreciation Revue. 1945, 1946, 1950, 1951, 1952. (Promos.)
KAYX, Waterloo, Iowa. 1948. (Station IDs excerpting "Chloe.")
WNEW, New York City. Circa 1949. (Time signals for DJs Rayburn and Finch.)
March of Dimes. 1951. (Fund appeal.)
Easter Seal. 1951. (Fund appeal.)
WWIN, Baltimore. 1952. (Station breaks for DJ Jackson Lowe.)
American Cancer Society. 1952. (Fund appeals with music from RCA record.)
Sister Elizabeth Kenny Foundation. 1952, 1953. (Fund appeals, as above.)
Robert Hall. 1954. (Spot for chain of clothing stores.)
Bob Spreen. 1956. (Spot for Calif. Oldsmobile and Cadillac dealer.)
Musical Insanities. 1956. (Promo for Jones' stage revue.)
WNEW, New York City. Circa 1957. (Station IDs: instrumental, sound effects.)
Magic Circle. Richard Ullman Inc. Circa 1957.
Renault Motors. 1959. (Two spots featuring Freddy Morgan.)

MISCELLANY
The following appearances are unconfirmed:

Blondie. CBS. May 18, 1942. Without band. (Camel commercial.)
Standard Brands Christmas Special. Dec. 21, 1943. (Guest appearance.)
Tommy Riggs & Betty Lou. NBC. Circa 1943. (Guest appearance).
Let Yourself Go. NBC. Circa 1944. (Guest appearance.)
Kraft Music Hall. NBC. Dec. 7, 1944. (Guest appearance.)
CBS Friday Night Lineup. Circa Sept. 1947. (Promo.)
Royal Canadian AF. July 1952. (15-minute programs for Recruiting Division.)
South African Broadcasting Corp. 1954. (Listener greetings for DJ Bill Prince.)

The hundreds of radio interviews Jones gave during the course of his career have been excluded.

Filmography

Pre-City Slickers

Vogues of 1938
> United Artists. Filmed Apr. 1937. Released Aug. 7, 1937. Directed by Irving Cummings. With Warner Baxter, Joan Bennett. Jones can be heard on the soundtrack, playing drums in the "El Morocco" sequence of this musical.

Sweet Sue (Six Hits and a Miss)
Jungle Drums (Carmen D'Antonio)
Parade of the Wooden Soldiers (The Music Maids with Stearns & Diane)
Song of the Islands (The Music Maids)
Row Row Row (Joy Hodges with the Rio Bros. Trio)
Darn That Dream (Martha Mears and Bill Roberts)
Havana Is Calling Me (Bernice Parks)
Hold That Tiger [Tiger Rag] (Victor Young and Orchestra)
> Globe Productions. Soundtracks recorded Jun. 23, 1940, at RCA Studios by Victor Young and his Orchestra, with Jones on drums (tracks only). Filmed Jul. 1-6, 1940, at International Studios, Los Angeles. Released Jan. 5, 1941. Executive produced by James Roosevelt. Directed by Reginald LeBorg (using various pseudonyms). The first Soundies session.

Hawaiian War Chant (Princess Momakai and the Hawaiian Ensemble)
Tuxedo Junction (Edna Mae Harris and the Lenox Lindy Hoppers)
> Globe Productions. Soundies recorded Jun. 23, 1940, as above. Filmed Dec. 8-9, 1942, in New York. Released Jan. 18, 1943. Produced by William F. Crouch. Directed respectively by John C. Graham and Crouch.

Road to Morocco
> Paramount Pictures. Filmed Mar. 1942. Released Oct. 5, 1942. Directed by David Butler. With Bing Crosby and Bob Hope. Jones backed the stars on the soundtrack, along with other *Kraft Music Hall* cohorts (including Slickers King Jackson and Perry Botkin).

SHORT SUBJECTS

Clink, Clink, Another Drink (vocal by Del Porter and Mel Blanc)
Pass the Biscuits, Mirandy (vocal by Del Porter)
> Soundies Distributing Corporation of America. Soundtracks recorded Feb. 20, 1942, at McGregor Studios. Filmed Feb. 20-24, 1942, at Hal Roach Studios. Released respectively Mar. 23 and May 4, 1942. Executive produced by Sam Coslow. Associate produced by Herbert Moulton. Directed by Reginald LeBorg. Written by Foster Carling. Musical direction credited to Phil Boutelje.

The Chool Song (The King's Men with Collins and Collette)
If He Can Fight Like He Can Love (Dorothy Cordray and Jim Mercer)
The Lamp of Memory (Yvonne DeCarlo and Russell Mercer)
Havin' a Time in Havana (Marvel Maxwell)
> Soundies Distributing Corporation of America. Recorded Feb. 20, 1942. Filmed Feb. 20-24, 1942 at Hal Roach Studios. Released Mar.-Jun. 1942. Executive produced by Sam Coslow. Associate produced by Herbert Moulton. Directed by Reginald LeBorg. Jones and the Slickers performed on the soundtracks of these Soundies in which the group was not seen.

The Blacksmith Song (vocal by Del Porter and King Jackson)
The Sheik of Araby (vocal by Del Porter and Carl Grayson)
> Soundies Distributing Corporation of America. Recorded on Jul. 6, 1942, at Radio Recorders. Filmed Jul. 13, 1942, at Hal Roach Studios. Released respectively Aug, 24 and Sept. 14, 1942. Produced and directed by Herbert Moulton. Written by Foster Carling. Musical direction credited to Phil Boutelje.

Idaho (Connie Haines)
Take Me (Kitty Kallen and Larry Carr)
My Great Great Grandfather (Connie Haines)
The Yankee Doodler (William Frawley)
Blackbird Fantasy (Dorothy Dandridge with Billy Mitchell)
The Sailor with the Navy Blue Eyes (Kitty Kallen and Billy Bletcher)
I Got a Little List (Billy Mitchell)
I'll Write Right Home to You (Kitty Kallen and Larry Carr)
A Lady with Fans (Faith Bacon)
> Soundies Distributing Corporation of America. Recorded Jul. 6, 1942. Filmed Jul. 9-13, 1942, apparently at Hal Roach Studios. Released Aug.-Oct. 1942. Produced and directed by Herbert Moulton. Jones and the Slickers on soundtrack only (Del Porter, Carl Grayson and Luther Roundtree appeared in *Idaho,* however.)

Hedda Hopper's Hollywood
> Paramount Pictures. Filmed at Pickfair, Beverly Hills, and released 1942. No. 6. Produced by Herbert Moulton. Spike served as the emcee in this short.

Der Fuehrer's Face
> 20th Century-Fox. Filmed Nov. 4, 1942 at NBC. Released 1942. Movietone News short.

Screen Snapshots
> Columbia Pictures. Filmed 1944, at U.S. Naval Hospital, Corona, Calif. Series 24, No. 3. Produced by Ralph Staub. Number: "Hotcha Cornia."

Army-Navy Screen Magazine
>Signal Corps. Filmed 1945. No. 70. Numbers: "Cocktails for Two," "Alexander's Ragtime Band," "Hotcha Cornia."

Screen Snapshots: Spike Jones in Hollywood
>Columbia Pictures. Released Dec. 15, 1952. One reel. Produced by Ralph Staub. Spike and family are shown watching clips from *Ken Murray's Hollywood* (the band was not involved).

FEATURES

Give Us Wings
>Universal Pictures. Filmed Sept. 1940. Released Dec. 4, 1940. Directed by Charles Lamont. Produced by Ken Goldsmith. Written by Arthur T. Horman and Robert Lee Johnson. With the Dead End Kids and the Little Tough Guys. The as-yet-unnamed City Slickers appeared in a brief sequence at a fish fry.

Thank Your Lucky Stars
>Warner Bros. Pictures. Filmed Nov. 5-16, 1942. Released Aug. 18, 1943. Directed by David Butler. Produced by Mark Hellinger. Written by Melvin Frank and Norman Panama. With Eddie Cantor, Dennis Morgan, Joan Leslie and Dinah Shore. Numbers: "Hotcha Cornia," "I'm Ridin' for a Fall" (vocal by Morgan and Leslie).

Meet the People
>Metro-Goldwyn-Mayer. Filmed May 17-Jun. 24, 1943. Released Apr. 21, 1944. Directed by Charles Riesner. Produced by E.Y. Harburg. Written by S.M. Herzig and Fred Saidy. With Lucille Ball, Dick Powell, Virginia O'Brien and Bert Lahr. Numbers: "Der Fuehrer's Face," "Schickelgruber" (vocal by Beau Lee).

Bring on the Girls
>Paramount Pictures. Filmed Mar. 6-Apr. 3, 1944. Released Feb. 23, 1945. Technicolor. Directed by Sidney Lanfield. Produced by Fred Kohlmar. Written by Karl Tunberg and Darrell Ware. With Veronica Lake, Sonny Tufts, Eddie Bracken and Marjorie Reynolds. The band's only color film. Number: "Chloe" (vocal by Red Ingle).

Breakfast in Hollywood
>United Artists. Filmed circa Oct. 1945. Released Jan. 14, 1946. Directed by Harold Schuster. Produced by Robert S. Golden. Written by Earl Baldwin. With Tom Breneman, Beulah Bondi, Raymond Walburn and Bonita Granville. Numbers: "Hedda Hopper's Hats" (vocal by Del Porter), "The Glow-Worm" (vocal by Red Ingle and Judie Manners).

Ladies' Man

> Paramount Pictures. Filmed Nov. 5-Dec. 20, 1945. Released Jan. 7, 1947.
> Directed by William D. Russell. Produced by Daniel Dare. Written by
> Edmund Beloin, Jack Rose and Lewis Meltzer. With Eddie Bracken, Cass
> Daley and Virginia Welles. Numbers: "I Gotta Gal I Love in North and
> South Dakota" (vocal by Jones and George Rock), "Hotcha Cornia,"
> "Holiday for Strings," "Cocktails for Two" (vocal by Carl Grayson).

Variety Girl

> Paramount Pictures. Filmed Nov. 5-18, 1946. Released July 15, 1947.
> Directed by George Marshall. Produced by Daniel Dare. Written by Edmund
> Hartman, Frank Tashlin, Robert Welch and Monte Brice. With Mary
> Hatcher, Olga San Juan, Bing Crosby and Bob Hope. Number: "I Hear Your
> Heart Calling Mine" (vocal by Hatcher).

Fireman, Save My Child

> Universal-International. Filmed Nov.-Dec. 1953. Released Apr. 27, 1954.
> Directed by Leslie Goodwins. Produced by Howard Christie. Written by Lee
> Loeb and John Grant. With Buddy Hackett, Hugh O'Brian, Adele Jergens
> and Tom Brown. Numbers: "Pass the Biscuits, Mirandy," "Dance of the
> Hours," "In a Persian Market," "A Hot Time in the Old Town Tonight,"
> "The Poet and Peasant Overture."

*Note: "Filmed" dates are dates of Jones' involvement (not the picture as a whole), as
confirmed by studio production files.*

UNREALIZED PLANS & PROJECTS

Siam
Boogie Woogie Cowboy
Come, Josephine, in My Flying Machine

> Soundies Distributing Corporation of America. 1942. Planned as additional
> Soundies but not filmed.

Untitled Project

> Walt Disney Productions. 1944. According to news reports, the band was slated
> to appear in "a short feature" at this time, probably *Make Mine Music* (released
> Aug. 15, 1946).

Unititled Project

> Columbia Pictures. 1944. A feature film was announced at this time.

Cocktails for Two

> Paramount Pictures. 1945. A deal with George Pal was prematurely
> announced, for a Puppetoon of the band's biggest hit; Jones apparently
> dropped out of the project due to financial reasons.

Duffy's Tavern
>Paramount Pictures. Released Aug. 20, 1945. Spike and the Slickers were announced for this all-star film version of the radio show when they returned from their USO tour.

City Slickers Project
>1946. Writer: Charles Isaacs. Jones tried to sell studios on a film featuring the band at this time.

Varieties of 1947
>RKO. 1946. Jones reportedly had a commitment with the studio for three features at this time, including this announced title, with Michael Kraike producing. None ever materialized.

Really, Mr. Greeley
>1950. Producer: Harry Sherman. Planned as a starring vehicle for Spike. Subsequently announced (1951) as a Tony Owen production to be released through RKO.

The Phantom of the Opera
>Universal-International. 1951. Jones approached Abbott and Costello and the studio about a remake. Subsequently announced (1954) with Liberace as possible co-star.

How the Circus Learned to Smile
>UPA. 1952. Writer: Frank Tashlin. Spike and Joe Siracusa approached the animation studio with the idea of turning the Slickers' children's album into an animated film.

W.C. Fields Project
>1960. Executive producer: Jones. Film biography of the comedian. Subsequently pitched as a TV special.

Billy Rose's Jumbo
>Metro-Goldwyn-Mayer. Released Dec. 1962. Produced by Joe Pasternak. Spike and the Slickers were considered for a "clown band act" sequence that was deleted from the script.

Rides, Rapes and Rescues
>1961. Executive producer: Jones. Writers: Les Ecklund, Buster Keaton. Arranger: Carl Brandt. Satirical documentary. Also pitched to publishers as a picture book.

MISCELLANY

Alexander's Ragtime Band
> 20th Century-Fox. Released May 28, 1938. Directed by Henry King. Jones' questionable appearance in the on-screen orchestra has been the subject of debate.

Dumbo
> Walt Disney Productions. Released Oct. 31, 1941. Jones-like instrumentation can be heard on the soundtrack, in the "Pink Elephants on Parade" number. (Spike occasionally worked freelance at Disney, according to animator Ward Kimball; union records were unavailable to verify his participation.)

Balinesa (Carmen D'Antonio)
The Dance of Shame (Faith Bacon)
The Aqua Waltz (Olive Hatch's Aquamaids)
> Soundies Distributing Corporation of America. Recorded and filmed in 1942. Released in 1942-43. Direction credited variously to Josef Berne or Herbert Moulton. Conflicting information in production files indicates possible participation by Jones and the Slickers on the soundtracks of these additional Soundies, near certain on the latter two.

Pass the Biscuits, Mirandy
The Greatest Man in Siam
> Walter Lantz Productions. Released respectively Aug. 23, 1943 and Mar. 27, 1944. Swing Symphonies series. Based on the Del Porter-Carl Hoefle songs recorded by Jones. Made without the bandleader's participation.

Boogie Woogie Man
> Walter Lantz Productions. Released Sept. 27, 1943. The bandleader was parodied as "Spook Jones" in this Swing Symphonies cartoon.

The Hick Chick
> Metro-Goldwyn-Mayer. Released Jun. 15, 1946. Directed by Tex Avery. The band was spoofed in this animated cartoon as "Spike Bones and his Chicky Slickers," during the time Avery was contributing gags to Jones' Paramount films.

Videography

TELEVISION SHOWS

Spike Jones and His Musical Depreciation Revue
Filmed July 1950. Two unsold 16mm pilots: *Wild Bill Hiccup*; *Foreign Legion*. Produced by Jerry Fairbanks. Directed by Eddie Cline. Written by Eddie Maxwell, Eddie Brandt, Sol Meyer, Cline. With the City Slickers, Billy Reed and Helen Grayco.

The Colgate Comedy Hour
NBC, Chicago. Feb. 11, 1951 (Jones' network TV debut). Produced by Ed Sobol. Directed by Kingman Moore. Written by Jay Sommers.
New York. Sept. 16, 1951. Produced by Ernie Glucksman. Written by Sommers. Hollywood. Feb. 6, 1955 (Co-hosted by Jones). Produced by Glucksman.

All-Star Revue
NBC. Jan. 12, 1952; May 31, 1952. Produced and directed by Ernie Glucksman.

The Spike Jones Show
NBC. Jan. 2, 1954 - May 8, 1954, Saturdays, 8-8:30 p.m. Produced by Ed Sobol. Directed by Bud Yorkin. Written by Freddie Morgan, Sol Meyer, Eddie Maxwell, Eddie Brandt, Victor McLeod, Tom Adair, Rick Vallaerts, Tex Avery. With the City Slickers and Helen Grayco.

The Spike Jones Show
CBS. Apr. 2, 1957 - Aug. 27, 1957, Tuesdays, 10:30-11 p.m. Produced by Dik Darley and Tom Waldman. Directed by Darley. Written by Waldman, Danny Arnold, Eddie Brandt. With The Band That Plays for Fun, Helen Grayco.

Club Oasis
NBC. June 7, 1958-Sept. 6, 1958, Saturdays, 9-9:30 p.m. (Jones' tenure as host.) Produced by Dik Darley and Tom Waldman. Directed by Darley. With Helen Grayco, Doodles Weaver, Joyce Jameson, Len Carrie, Ken Capps.

The Spike Jones Show (Swingin' Spiketaculars)
CBS. Aug. 1, 1960 - Sept. 19, 1960, Mondays, 9:30-10 p.m. Produced by Bill Dana. Directed by Bob Sheerer. Written by Dana, Don Hinkley. With Helen Grayco, Dana, Joyce Jameson, Lennie Weinrib.

The Spike Jones Show
CBS. Jul. 17, 1961 - Sept. 25, 1961, Mondays, 9-9:30 p.m. Produced by Perry Cross. Directed by Mack Bing. Written by Sheldon Keller, Don Hinkley, Mel Tolkin. With Helen Grayco.

GUEST APPEARANCES

Garroway at Large. NBC. Feb. 11, 1951. ***
This Is Your Life. NBC. Dec. 10, 1952; May 25, 1955; circa 1956; circa 1962. ***
The Peter Potter Show (Juke Box Jury). ABC. Dec. 20, 1953; Nov. 1956.
Martin & Lewis Muscular Dystrophy Telethon. ABC. Nov. 24, 1953; possibly others. ***
What's My Line? CBS. Jul. 4, 1954. ***
Masquerade Party. CBS. Jul. 19, 1954. ***
The Betty White Show. NBC. Aug. 12, 1954. ***
Place the Face. NBC. Sept. 18, 1954. ***
Talk show. (Hosted by Paul Coates; Los Angeles). Mid '50s. ***
The Sheila Graham Show. NBC. May 9, 1955. ***
Colgate Variety Hour. NBC. Oct. 30, 1955.
Queen For a Day. NBC. Jun. 12, 1956. ***
It Could Be You. NBC. Jun. 15, 1956; Dec. 21, 1956; Jul. 4, 1958; Nov. 4, 1960. ***
The Jack Benny Show. CBS. Oct. 7, 1956.
The Ford Show. NBC. Nov. 15, 1956.
The Perry Como Show. NBC. Dec. 8, 1956. (The band's only color broadcast.)
Truth or Consequences. NBC. Mar. 28, 1958; Jan. 16, Feb. 13, Mar. 27, 1962. ***
Club Oasis. NBC. Mar. 29, 1958.
The Frank Sinatra Show. ABC. Apr. 4, 1958.
Dinah Shore Chevy Show. NBC. Nov. 29, 1959.
Person-to-Person. CBS. Dec. 8, 1960. (A visit with the Jones family.) ***
The Ed Sullivan Show. CBS. Feb. 26, 1961. ***
I've Got a Secret. CBS. 1961. ***
Your First Impression. NBC. Aug. 13, 1962; Mar. 23, 1964. ***
Panorama Pacific (Los Angeles). Circa 1963.
The Edie Adams Show. ABC. Jan. 16, 1964.
Burke's Law. ABC. Jan. 17, 1964. (As a bookie). ***

*** *Guest appearances by Jones without the band.*

UNREALIZED PLANS & PROJECTS

Spike Jones and His Musical Depreciation Revue
> Circa 1949-50. Jones originally planned 39 half-hour programs, but filmed only two.

NBC Deal
> 1952. Jones reportedly signed a contract to appear on five 60-minute shows, but did only two.

Buster Keaton Project
> Circa 1953. Possibly for KTLA or KTTV, Los Angeles. Pilot. Director: Eddie Cline. With Keaton and the City Slickers. (Partially filmed; apparently never completed.)

Seven O'Clock Spiketacular
>CBS. 1955. Daytime variety series. With Helen Grayco, Minerva Pious and the City Slickers. (Three scripts and a lengthy proposal are extant.)

Ford Startime
>NBC. 1960. An alternate version of the W.C. Fields project (see Filmography) was pitched as a one-hour special for this variety series. With Jack Oakie as Fields.

From Tin-Foil to Stereo
>1960. Special. A musical documentary, eventually combined with *The Fabulous Phonograph* (see below).

Situation Comedy
>1961. Prime time series. With Spike and Helen as a show business couple. Producer: Danny Thomas.

The Fabulous Phonograph
>Early '60s. Mini-series, based on the book by Roland Gelatt. Writer: Eddie Brandt. Producers: Bud Yorkin and Norman Lear.

The Nutcracker Suite
>CBS. Early '60s. Special, using the 1945 RCA album as soundtrack material.

Spooktacular
>Early '60s. Special, based on the "Spike Jones in Stereo" album. Writer: Eddie Brandt.

Omnibust
>Early '60s. Special, based on the Liberty album. Writer: Eddie Brandt.

60 Years of Music America Hates Best
>Early '60s. Special, based on the Liberty album. With Red Ingle and others.

Gentlemen, Be Seated
>Early '60s. Special. A minstrel show. Writer: Eddie Brandt.

Scary Tales
>Early '60s. Special. A collection of horror-fairy tales. Writer: Eddie Brandt. Also intended as a picture book.

Spike Jones' Music Lovers
>Early '60s. Animated cartoon series.

Spike's Swinging Spiketacular of 1963
>1963. Special. Variety show.

MISCELLANY

NBC Comedy Hour.
> Jan. 15, 1956. (Slickers Billy Barty, Mousie Garner and Peter James appeared without Jones, alias The Gentlemaniacs. Erroneously listed in video catalogs as a 1962 Jones appearance.)

The Tonight Show.
> Dec. 1956. (Hosted by Ernie Kovacs. Jones was slated as a guest but forced to cancel.)

Hamm's Beer commercial.
> Jan. 4, 1961. (Spike supervised Slicker-style music for this animated spot.)

Hollywood Palace.
> NBC. Winter 1965. (Jones was announced as a guest but did not appear).

The following appearances are unconfirmed:

Local TV Show.
> Minneapolis-St. Paul. Circa 1950. (A performance of "Chinese Mule Train" with Freddy Morgan.)

Texaco Star Theater.
> NBC. Circa 1951-53. (Milton Berle recalled that Jones guest starred "two or three times.")

Philco Panorama.
> Circa 1956. (Commercial with Jones on camera; soundtrack excerpt from "Dinner Music" LP.)

The Ann Sothern Show.
> CBS. Fall 1960. (Jones was announced as a guest). ***

Dan Raven.
> NBC. Fall 1960. (Announced as guest). ***

What's My Line?
> CBS. Feb. 26, 1961. (Slated as a guest). ***

Canadian TV show.
> Toronto. Feb. 28, 1961. (Slated as a guest). ***

*** *Without band.*

Appendix D: The Essentials
A Collector's Guide

LPs and Cassettes

Dinner Music for People Who Aren't Very Hungry
(Verve MGV 4005, 1956)
> Spike's best LP, with "Black and Blue Danube Waltz" the standout track. CD reissues by Goldberg & O'Reilly and Rhino are out of print.

Thank You, Music Lovers!
(RCA LPM-224, 1960)
> Frequently reissued as "The Best of Spike Jones," this was the only compilation Jones lived to see. The original LP with the Jack Davis cover is still valued by collectors.

Spike Jones and his City Slickers Can't Stop Murdering, Vol. 3
(RCA PJM2-8021, Germany, 1974)
> This LP represented the first-ever release of "Alto, Baritone and Bass," "Rickeyshaw" and "Rum Tee Diddle Dee Yump," plus the rare "Fiddle Faddle" and the complete "Nutcracker Suite"—one highly collectable album.

Spike Jones Depreciation Revue
(Silver Swan, LP1002, 1975)
> This bootleg LP featured 16 tracks deriving from *The Land's Best Bands*, U.S. Navy radio transcriptions.

The King of Corn
(Cornographic 1001, 1975)
> A 17-track LP drawn from Spike's 1943-44 radio broadcasts, including *Furlough Fun* and *The Bob Burns Show*. Bootlegged on LP and cassette by Sandy Hook as "Spike Jones On the Air."

The Complete Collection
(MF Distribution, MF 205/4, 1977)
> Spike Jones Jr. compiled this four-disc album from his dad's 1943-1949 radio programs and 1956-57 TV shows. Also issued as a three-record set; reissued on LP and cassette as "The Craziest Show on Earth."

The Uncollected Spike Jones and His Other Orchestra
(Hindsight HSR-185, 1982)
> Spike's seldom heard (and hard-to-find) 1946 big band Standard Transcriptions comprised this 12-track LP and cassette reissue.

Spike Jones Presents World War II
(Goldberg & O'Reilly GO 10019, 1988)
> Ted Hering compiled these war-era tunes from various sources. No LP release; issued only on cassette.

CDs

Musical Depreciation Revue: The Spike Jones Anthology
(Rhino R271574, 1994)
> This 40-track double-CD is hard to beat for a comprehensive sampling from the maestro's legacy, including most of his best work and many lesser-known selections. Booklet with erudite liner notes by co-producer Dr. Demento; also issued on cassette.

Spiked! The Music of Spike Jones
(Catalyst/BMG Classics 09026-61982-2, 1994)
> Despite bizarre cover art by Art Spiegelman and odd liner notes by Thomas Pynchon, this 18-track CD is a must-have for the unedited "Nutcracker Suite" and the first release of Liberty recordings "Powerhouse" and "Frantic Freeway."

Spike Jones: The Man Who Murdered Music
(Good Music DMC1-1210, 1994)
> This 22-track CD includes first-time issues of "I Wuv a Wabbit," "My Cornet," "Nyet!" and the Liberty reject of "Carmen," plus other rarities; also issued on cassette. Caveat emptor: Produced by the author of this book.

Spike Jones and his City Slickers: The Bluebirds
(Harlequin HQ CD 100, 1998)
> In addition to the original 16 Victor Bluebird releases, this collection includes the rejected "Beautiful Eggs," several alternate takes and a few Standard Transcriptions. Plus a nicely illustrated booklet.

(Not) Your Standard Spike Jones Collection
(Collector's Choice CCM-329-2, 2002)
> This 3-CD 79-track compilation gathers all of Jones' 1941-1945 Standard Transcriptions. The Cindy Walker sides and the 1946 Other Orchestra recordings are absent.

Fonk
(Harlequin HQ CD 178, 2002)
> Rarities on this 23-track CD include RCA rejects "What Is a Disc Jockey?" and "Rum Tee Diddle Dee Yump," alternate takes, a disc jockey interview with Spike and airchecks from the band's 1941 radio debut.

Appendix E: Keeping Up With Jones
A Resource List

Many of the Spike Jones reissues and compilations released over the years are long out of print. This selective list was current at the time of publication; common "best of" albums and compilations of various artists have been generally excluded. Inclusion does not imply endorsement.

The larger companies (BMG, Paramount) do not fulfill orders. Try local music/video stores or order online; Amazon.com and other web shops offer nearly everything in print, plus some out-of-print items.

A-1 Video & Film Services
> (716) 731-2389; *www.a-1video.com.* On VHS: *Novelty Bands And Comedy Songs* includes three Jones Soundies, along with shorts by several of his competitors.

BMG Music
> On CD: *The Best of Spike Jones; Spike Jones is Murdering the Classics; Spiked! The Music of Spike Jones.*

Eddie Brandt's Saturday Matinee
> 5006 Vineland Ave., North Hollywood, CA 91606; (818) 506-4242. Jones videos available for on-site and mail order rental; photographs for sale.

Collector's Choice Music
> P.O. Box 838, Itasca, IL 60143-0838; (800) 923-1122; *www.collectorschoicemusic.com.* On CD: *(Not) Your Standard Spike Jones Collection; Spike Jones in Stereo; Omnibust/ 60 Years of Music America Hates Best.* Many other domestic and foreign Jones CDs available.

Congress Entertainment Ltd.
> P.O. Box 845, Tannersville, PA 18372; (800) 847-8273. On VHS: *World War II: The Music Video, Vol. 1* (includes "Cocktails for Two" from *Army-Navy Screen Magazine*); *Vol. 2* (includes "Hotcha Cornia" from same source).

eBay
> *www.ebay.com.* Online auction of Jones records and memorabilia, including out-of-print items.

Good Music Co.
> P.O. Box 637, Holmes, PA 19043-0637; (800) 538-4200; *www.yestermusic.com.* On CD: *Spike Jones: The Man Who Murdered Music.*

Greenwood Publishing Group
>   Customer Service, P.O. Box 6926, Portsmouth, NH 03802. (800)225-5800;
>   *www.greenwood.com.* In hardcover: *Thank You Music Lovers: A Bio-discography of
>   Spike Jones and His City Slickers, 1941 to 1965.*

Interstate Music Ltd./ Harlequin Records
>   P.O. Box 74, Crawley, West Sussex, RH11 0LX, England;
>   *www.interstatemusic.co.uk/Harlequin_Index.htm.* On CD: *Riot Squad; Louder
>   and Funnier; Corn's-a-Poppin'; The Bluebirds; The Ones You Always Wanted; Fonk.*

Navarre Corp.
>   On DVD: *The Spike Jones Story.*

Paramount Home Entertainment
>   On VHS: *The Best of Spike Jones, Vols. 1, 2, 3, 4* (compiled from Jones' TV shows).

Past Times Publishing Co.
>   *P.O. Box 661, Anaheim, CA 92815; (800) 677-1927; www.oldtimeshowbiz.com.*
>   Jones autographs, contracts, arrangements and sheet music for sale.

Rhino Records
>   (800) 432-0020; *www.rhino.com.* On CD: *Musical Depreciation Revue: The
>   Spike Jones Anthology.* On VHS: *Dr. Demento 20th Anniversary Collection*
>   (includes "Cocktails for Two" from *Ladies' Man*).

SPERDVAC (Society to Preserve & Encourage Radio Drama, Variety & Comedy)
>   P.O. Box 7177, Van Nuys, CA 91409; (877) 251-5771. Episodes of Jones'
>   *Spotlight Revue* and *Chase and Sanborn* shows are available via library loan to
>   members of this old-time radio organization.

spikejones.com
>   *www.spikejones.com.* The Jones' estate's official website was under construction
>   at press time.

SpikeJones Group
>   *http://groups.yahoo.com/group/spikejones/.* To subscribe: *SpikeJones-
>   subscribe@yahoogroups.com.* A discussion group/email digest for fans.

Spike Jones International Fan Club
>   304 E. Granada Ct., Ontario, CA 91764. SJIFC is inactive but club co-founder
>   Scott Corbett maintains archives and sells original Jones 78s, 45s, LPs, col-
>   lectibles and back issues of the discontinued club newsletter. In paperback: *An
>   Illustrated Guide to the Recordings of Spike Jones.*

Universal Home Video
>   On VHS: *Variety Girl.*

Warner Home Video
>   On VHS: *Thank Your Lucky Stars.*

Notes and Sources

PREFACE

iii   *If the real me:* SJ to Prideaux, Aug. 2, 1961, Jones papers, collection of the author.

DER FUROR

9   *This, brother:* Levin, *Down Beat,* Oct. 15, 1942.

10   *it was simply chosen:* Upon Jones' death, the Hollywood trade paper, *Variety,* asserted in an unsigned and unlikely report he had spent $400 of his own "on speculation" to cut the record. "He offered to sell it to Victor for slightly more than cost. Victor nixed that but said it would give the wax a San Diego [California] tryout and give Jones 5% of the retail sales." (*Variety,* May 3, 1965.)

11   *Wallace brought the tune:* Carl Hoefle, Jr. concurred that Wallace gave the tune to his father; Jones' statement (to Bob Crane, KNX, Los Angeles, Nov. 4, 1963) is bolstered somewhat by Winecoff's claim he was the middleman—as recalled by longtime Jones staff writer Eddie Maxwell. Winecoff was later General Manager of Jones' Oakhurst Music Publishing Co.

11   *someone in music publicity:* Frank Thomas to JY, Aug. 1, 1992.

11   *turn the number down:* Gabe Ward to JY, Oct. 6, 1991.

11   *the raspberry thing was obscene:* The raspberries, indicated in the published version of the song, were apparently Wallace's inspiration.

11   *legal advisers objected:* Frederick C. Othman, "He Plays Louder Than Anybody," *Saturday Evening Post,* Apr. 10, 1943. Many of the myths about Jones derive from this article, used as primary source material by journalists for decades.

11   *Donald Duck in Axis Land:* "the first title we find assigned to [the cartoon]... in June 1942." David R. Smith, Walt Disney Archives, letter to JY, Nov. 28, 1983.

12   *I don't think there:* Del Porter to Ted Hering, Jun. 3, 1971.

13   *It didn't seem like:* SJ cited by Othman, *Post,* Apr. 10, 1943.

13   *The Old Sow Song:* This number, which Vallee recorded for Bluebird, featured a raspberry even more raucous than "Serenade to a Maid." Jones covered the tune years later on "Dinner Music for People Who Aren't Very Hungry."

13   *from the top floor:* Walter Heebner to JY, May 13, 1993.

15   *We just couldn't get enough:* Novelist Herman Wouk built a scene around the tune in his 1978 bestseller, *War and Remembrance*—in which the record is played continuously at a desolate outpost.

15   *war bonds in the first week:* Bruno-New York Inc., letter to Victor record dealers, Sept. 25, 1942. Block had to call the RCA factory for a rush order pressing to fulfill all the demand, according to *Victor Record Review,* Nov. 1942.

15   *disc jockeydom to America:* Buddy Basch to JY, Mar. 24, 1992. Al Jarvis, who hosted a West Coast version of *Make-Believe Ballroom* on KFWB, Los Angeles, has been cited as Block's *predecessor*, beginning three years earlier in 1932. (Arnold Passman, *The Deejays,* Macmillan, 1971.)

15   *Within four weeks:* Jones claimed these events happened within five days of the record's release, another exaggeration reiterated for years (e.g., *Post,* Apr. 10, 1943; *True Story,* June 1949). The record was released September 18, 1942, according to *RCA Victor Phono-Graphic* newsletter. *Command Performance* was broadcast live on September 29. The NBC audition for his own show (*Furlough Fun*) took place October 1. The movie deal was first reported in a Warner Bros. in-house memo dated October 2, asking the legal department to draw up a contract. The *Bob Burns* guest shot took place October 14.

15   *Donald Duck in Nutziland:* The production title—which appeared on published sheet music prior to the final title change—was misspelled on Bluebird labels ("From the Walt Disney picture, *Nuttsey Land*").

15   *In October Disney did:* Victor Records, letter to distributors, Oct. 15, 1942.

16   *Best Cartoon:* The film, which was reportedly shown on ABC's *The Mickey Mouse Club* in the 1950s, surfaced on bootleg videos and websites before Disney finally made it available on DVD in 2004.

16   *It did the job:* Kinney, *Walt Disney and Other Assorted Characters* (Harmony Books, 1988).

16   *There is some discrepancy:* Total sales vary according to the source; *Time* (Dec. 17, 1945) and *Record Review* (Apr. 1949) both reported 1.5 million copies sold. BMG Music was unable to provide sales figures due to accidental destruction of RCA records.

DRUMMER BOY

17   *These are things he never:* Linda Jones to JY, Oct. 20, 1992.

17   *In an as-told-to:* "Spike Jones Tells His Own Story," *True Story,* Jul. 1949.

18   *Calexico, a sleepy little town:* Founded in 1900, the town was set up by surveyors diverting water from the Colorado River to the California desert.

18   *At school I was troublesome:* Michael Fitzgerald, "Spike Jones Says 'Momma, Yes.' " *Argus,* Wayville, Australia, May 26, 1955.

18   *Another day Mama:* Ibid.

18   *The only play I got:* SJ, *True Story.*

19   *Anybody in showbiz:* Rock to JY, Apr. 18, 1983.

19   *Having no piano:* SJ, *True Story.*

20   *I suppose if I... His father objected:* Ibid.

20   *the loudest four-piece:* Othman, *Post.*

20   *Spike wanted to be in Long Beach:* Bill Harris to JY, Oct. 7, 1991.

20   *By December 1926:* Although Harris recalled Jones attending a summer session at Poly High, school records indicate he attended Calipatria High through December.

20   *Poly was a terrific:* Hersh Ratliff to JY, June 19, 1983.

23   *Spike never asked for advice:* Dwight Defty to JY, July 2, 1983.

23   *a name allegedly suggested to Jones:* Carl Vidano to JY, Dec. 4, 1984. Vidano recalled Jones' group was originally named the California Revelers, apparently confusing it with the Paul Harrison band by that name, which he and Jones later joined.

23   *We played our music hard:* SJ cited by Fitzgerald, *Argus.*

24 *We all played in different groups:* Paul Harrison to JY, Aug. 5, 1993.

26 *I became so self-conscious:* SJ, *True Story.*

26 *The maitre d' comes over:* Vidano to Don McGlynn, 1988.

27 *Spike and I did:* Hall to JY, Feb. 23, 1992.

27 *In selecting Jones:* Unsourced clipping, circa 1928; Skip Craig collection.

Man About Town

30 *You can take such a let-down:* SJ, *True Story.*

30 *He would do anything:* Rex Finney to JY, Nov. 14, 1991.

30 *I was 18 and:* SJ, *True Story.* A possible distortion of the facts, since the Five Tacks of his high school days are not mentioned in this article.

31 *They probably got room... We went to see Spike:* Dorothy Buehler and Nell Michel to JY, Nov. 9, 1992.

31 *Aspiring drummer joined:* Sam Coslow, *Cocktails for Two* (Arlington House, 1977).

32 *Hoagland had the only real:* Kenton cited by Carol Easton, *Straight Ahead: The Story of Stan Kenton* (Morrow, 1973).

32 *not in Balboa:* However, Spike served as alternate drummer in "Brick" English's dance hall in Balboa, according to William Harris.

32 *Spike fell madly in love:* Willie Martinez to JY, Nov. 23, 1983.

33 *Ocean Park was a scene:* Harry Geller to JY, Sept. 20, 1983.

33 *Spike was a terribly funny:* Harriet Geller to JY, Dec. 11, 1983.

34 *They felt superior:* George Hackett to JY, Nov. 15, 1983.

35 *Willie Martinez, however:* Martinez, who did not remember Lyons at the Biltmore, vaguely recalled, "Patty was at the Paramount when we were there"—but insisted, "the Paramount has to be 1936 or '37." Geller, who seemed clearer and more lucid in his recall, was positive they worked at the Paramount in 1934-35.

35 *Spike met his wife:* Othman, *Post.*

37 *He backed Crosby on over 110:* Scott C. Corbett, *An Illustrated Guide to the Recordings of Spike Jones* (Corbett, 1989).

37 *Spike was about the top:* Harry Sosnik to JY, Oct. 22, 1992.

38 *A bandleader in name only:* Zep Meissner to JY, Aug. 22, 1983.

38 *network radio debut:* While Evelyn Bigsby stated (*Radio Life,* Dec. 1942) that Jones made his debut on the Jolson show on Jan. 6, 1938, there are indications to the contrary. The Henry King orchestra (with Spike on drums) appeared on *The Burns and Allen Show* from Sept. 1936 to Mar. 1937, according to John Dunning's scrupulous *On the Air: The Encyclopedia of Old-Time Radio* (Oxford University Press, 1998). Also, George Van Eps recalled meeting Jones in 1936 at NBC, "where he was working on a radio show."

39 *He hadn't actually crystalized:* Van Eps to JY, Feb. 3, 1992.

39 *One of the key reasons:* Spike Jones Jr. to Don McGlynn, 1988.

40 *a vocal quartet... audition record:* The 8" acetate appears to be the only recording of Spike actually singing. The fourth voice is unidentified. (Steve LaVere to JY, Oct. 30, 2003.)

40 *The union had a rule:* SJ cited by Othman, *Post.*

40 *There was a quota:* Wally Marks to JY, Nov. 26, 1983. Those who exceeded the quota were fined by the union, according to LaVere.

AND THEN ALONG CAME JONES

41   *Anybody who attacks:* William Glackin, unidentified Sacramento newspaper, Sept. 3, 1948.

41   *the lucrative field of corn:* "Corn might be defined as playing a style or lick that is out of date, not necessarily that it is wrong musically, but that the particular lick in question belongs with the bustle or the pegleg trousers," observed accordonist Jerry Shelton of Shep Fields' orchestra. (Shelton, "Being 'Corny' Is as Bad as Having Halitosis," *Down Beat*, Chicago, Feb. 1936).

41   *Spike Jones before his time:* David Cairns, "Orchestrated wit," *The Sunday Times,* London, Apr. 12, 1992.

41   *Johnson... reportedly originated the clown band:* George Bickel and Harry Watson have also been credited as the progenitors (*Billboard*, Nov. 29, 1952). But while the 1901 Adam Forepaugh & Sells Bros. route book lists Bickel as director of "The Original and Only Soo-See Ragtime Military Band," he and trombonist Watson are pictured as Johnson's sidemen in the 1897 Ringling Bros. route book. (Collection of Circus World Museum.)

42   *Vaudeville headliner Ted Lewis:* Anthony Slide, *The Encyclopedia of Vaudeville* (Greenwood Press, 1994).

42   *as accomplished as Waring's:* Reser did not achieve Waring's success, but was more prolific in making records. Both bands may be heard on CD compilations produced by The Old Masters.

42   *Like Ed Meeker before him:* an observation made by musicologist Mike Kieffer.

43   *cute, childlike vocals:* The voice heard on "He Ain't Done Right by Nell" (Victor, 1926) and other Aaronson records is remarkably similar to the one later employed by George Rock on Spike's recordings.

43   *fired pistols: The Whoopee Party,* a 1932 Mickey Mouse cartoon, is the earliest known use of gunshots in rhythm.

44   *We discovered a sure-fire laugh:* Britton cited by Robert Coleman, New York Daily News, June 19, 1937.

44   *maniacally smashing their instruments:* By the time Spike began using this attention-getter it was old hat. The Hoosier Hot Shots did it in their 1939 film debut, *In Old Monterey.*

44   *Meroff and Powell formed:* Meroff recorded with a straight jazz band in the '20s. Powell was a member of Meroff's comedy band before starting his own.

45   *When the Crash of '29:* Ward to JY.

45   *I Like Bananas... From the Indies:* Both numbers were reissued on the 1992 Columbia CD, "Hoosier Hot Shots: Rural Rhythm 1935-1942," along with 18 other tracks.

46   *Klaxon:* a trademarked device utilized for an electrically-operated horn or warning signal.

46   *potential of scrub-boards:* Country music legend Roy Acuff recorded such tunes as "Sixteen Chickens and a Tambourine" in the '40s and '50s with his Jug Band, which utilized a washboard with horns and gadgets. (Elizabeth Schlappi, *Roy Acuff,* Pelican, 1993.)

46   *a whole generation of corn bands:* Jhan Robbins, "Korn on the Kampus," *Varsity,* Apr. 1949.

46   *outlasted all their imitators:* Bob Skyles and his Skyrockets employed washboard, slide whistles and slap bass, in a merciless parody of the group on Bluebird ("We're Not the Hoosier Hot Shots"). The Skyrockets were one of many country and western units that enjoyed cutting up regularly, using whistles, saws, cowbells and piano-accordions to serve the campfire corn.

46   *The Schnickelfritzers... the Korn Kobblers:* The bands can be heard on a series of British CD compilations released by Sagamore Records (*www.sagamorerecords.com*).

46   *Freddie Fisher:* Not to be confused with composer Fred Fisher, who co-wrote "Come, Josephine, in My Flying Machine."

46   *One night some drunk:* Charlie Koenig to JY, Nov. 26, 1991.

47   *They planned to call themselves The Original:* Ibid; *Variety,* Aug. 2, 1939.

48   *It all started in the music hall:* Tony Hawes to JY, Oct. 10, 1993.

48   *Perhaps the preeminent act… the Nitwits:* Denis Gifford, *The Golden Age of Radio* (Batsford, 1985); *The Stage,* Aug. 11, 1962. The Nitwits were seen in America on *The Ed Sullivan Show* and *Hollywood Palace.* Surviving members of the band were touring as Nuts 'n' Bolts as late as 1999.

49   *They were two characters:* Arthur Ens to JY, Apr. 9, 1992.

49   *It was a real nut band:* Hall to JY.

50   *The duo had made such an impact:* Thomas A. DeLong, *Pops: Paul Whiteman, King of Jazz* (New Century, 1983).

50   *their sophomoric antics distressed:* Simon, *The Big Bands.*

50   *Kay didn't go for novelty:* Ish Kabibble to JY, Nov. 21, 1992.

51   *We did better than some:* Al Trace to JY, Nov. 4, 1991.

52   *copy down their routines:* Koenig to JY.

52   *Publicly, Jones rarely acknowledged:* In one interview he dryly noted there were bands that "copied us before we started." (SJ to Bob Crane, KNX, Los Angeles, Nov. 4, 1963.)

52   *That's the way he was:* Paul Trietsch, Jr. to JY, Oct. 6, 1991.

52   *Hoosier Hot Shots… made a substantial contribution:* "Spike Jones Covers the Hoosier Hot Shots," one of a series of compilation CDs available from the Hoosier Hot Shots Museum (*www.hhs.com*), offers an interesting comparison of the two bands.

52   *Slickers were a superior group:* "All those sound effects were made by schooled technicians. We didn't have any of that. The Korn Kobblers were not studio musicians," said the group's pianist, Marty Gold. "Spike didn't have any farmers; they were all studio guys. That was the basic difference." (Gold to JY, Nov. 18, 1991.)

52   *I think the reason none of them:* Rock to Don McGlynn, 1988.

BIRTH OF A BAND

53   *Spike wasn't getting anywhere:* Lud Gluskin to JY, Dec. 26, 1983.

53   *a mordant sense of humor:* Carl Brandt to JY, Jun. 22, 1983.

54   *at Bernstein's Grotto:* Harry Geller to JY. Sam Coslow asserted in his autobiography, *Cocktails for Two,* that Jones was using props as early as 1931. But Geller stated: "That's nonsense. He didn't start using that stuff until he put together the band at Bernstein's in 1934."

55   *Spike was a very moody guy:* Leighton Noble to JY, Aug. 7, 1983.

56   *All we ever did:* SJ, unidentified clipping, undated; Doc Birdbath collection.

56   *The girl singer:* Ray Erlenborn to JY, Jul. 12, 1992.

56   *Everything was going along… If people would roar:* SJ cited by Walter Ames, "A Clinker in Error Gave Spike Hunch; Now It's His Style," *Los Angeles Times,* Apr. 4, 1954.

57   *Veteran radio writer:* Carroll Carroll, *None of Your Business* (Cowles Book Co., 1970).

58   *Stravinsky had on some:* SJ to Bob Crane, KNX, Los Angeles, Nov. 4, 1963. Recalled Linda Jones: "My mother even told me that story, so I know it wasn't untrue."

58   *A lot of the guys in the sound effects:* Ward Kimball to JY, Oct. 18, 1991.

58   *The Gadget Band:* the film was never released, but some of the ideas were "cannibalized" and used elsewhere.

59   *In a less likely scenario:* Thurl Ravenscroft to JY, Sept. 25, 1992.

59   *the quartet... which Jones had backed on Decca records:* "Sweet Potato Tooters," a 1995 British compilation CD (Music & Memories), collected two dozen of the group's 1930s and '40s recordings, including many with Spike on drums.

59   *I had a long dry spell:* Porter to Ted Hering, Jun. 3, 1971.

59   *We put the two together:* Danny Van Allen to JY, May 28, 1984.

59   *They played dance halls:* Ray Johnson to JY, Dec. 8, 1983.

61   *appeared on three discs:* Scott Corbett, *An Illustrated Guide to the Recordings of Spike Jones.*

61   *John Cascales:* courtesy of Steve LaVere and American Federation of Musicians, Local 47.

62   *We had some good men:* George Boujie to JY, Oct. 8, 1992.

63   *Grayson was a contract:* Eddie Brandt to JY, Mar. 15, 1983.

63   *Grayson had a little following:* Grayson was identified as "featured band director of Universal Pictures and one of the outstanding orchestra leaders on the West Coast" in *The Jonathan* (Jan. 1941). According to union reports, Ray Lundale and Gene Miller (sax), Bert Harry (trumpet) and Jim Lynch (bass) were among those who played the long engagement at the club, along with the more durable King Jackson (trombone), Stan Wrightsman (piano) and Don Anderson (trumpet).

63   *Spike was a slick guy:* Porter to Ted Hering.

MAKING TRACKS

66   *Cindy Walker... claimed she was:* Ted Hering to JY, Jan. 8, 1984.

66   *the Local Yokels:* Joe Wolverton to JY, Nov. 13, 1991.

66   *lowbrow label:* Dr. Demento to JY, Apr. 27, 1984.

66   *It was a lot of fun:* Bruce Hudson to JY, Dec. 27, 1983.

66   *the de facto leader:* The contractor's report for August 8, 1941, identifies Jones as the leader, at a salary of $60—versus $30 for each of the sidemen. City Slicker Zep Meissner alleged, however, that Jones claimed leadership on union contracts without Porter's knowledge or approval. (Meissner to JY, Aug. 22, 1983.)

68   *first steady trumpet player:* Frank Wylie, Bert Harry, Bruce Hudson and others played trumpet on an irregular basis for the Slickers in 1940-41. Ralph Dadisman was an occasional substitute for Anderson, notably in *Thank Your Lucky Stars.*

69   *Employed by the government:* Don Ingle to JY, Jul. 23, 1983.

70   *He had an idea and he worked:* Dick Webster, May 12, 1983.

71   *ground to a halt:* The industry continued to make records sans musical accompaniment and reissue old recordings.

72   *Bostonians sat so tight-lipped:* Evelyn Bigsby, "Corn Takes Root," *Radio Life,* Jan. 9, 1944.

72   *Carl would get up:* Luther Roundtree to JY, Mar. 10, 1983.

74   *I wouldn't sign:* Don Anderson to JY, May 18, 1983.

74   *they made special records for the Morale:* Richard Sears, *V-Discs: A History and Discography* (Greenwood Press, 1980).

76   *Being unescorted, she had to:* Andrew C. Pinchot, "Spike Jones' Ad-Lib of All Ad-Libs," 1992, unpublished.

76   *A buzz bomb had hit:* Porter to Ted Hering.

76   *Dad roomed with Dick:* Don Ingle, email to JY, Sept. 22, 2003.

77   *We were sniped at:* SJ to Art Dorson, KHJ, Los Angeles, Oct. 14, 1944.

77   *I ran into a German:* Ibid.

77   *I remember my dad talking:* Beau Lee, Jr. to JY, Nov. 4, 1992.

77   *The band was given:* Lawrence Phillips, Executive Vice President of USO-Camp Shows, Inc., to Beauregard Lee, letter, July 12, 1944; collection of Beau Lee, Jr.

77   *They were asked to submit their scripts:* Ibid.

78   *The tune was a bit more salacious:* This verse appeared in Carling's original typescript but was excluded when the Slickers sang it on *Command Performance,* Jan. 15, 1944. On AFRS, the coda—"Jingle, jingle, steak on a shingle"—substituted "steak" for a four-letter word that *was* used on the tour, according to Beau Lee, Jr.

78   *On arriving in New York:* SJ, *Small World,* AFRS, Jan. 24, 1964.

78   *whose brilliant handiwork forever Spiked:* According to Eddie Brandt, Zep Meissner, Don Ingle and others, Washburne was the anonymous arranger of "Cocktails."

79   *Something happened between Spike and Del:* Eddie Brandt to Don McGlynn, 1988.

79   *When Spike started making:* Johnson to JY, Dec. 8, 1983.

80   *He and his wife, Pat:* News items, *Los Angeles Examiner,* Jan. 25, 1945; Aug. 21, 1945.

80   *that same month, the band:* Although Jones officially met his second wife in 1947, Helen's name appears on a printed program for the band's Aug. 28-Sept. 3, 1945 engagement at the Commercial Hotel in Elko, Nevada.

80   *Spike came in with his manager:* Helen Grayco to George Putnam, KIEV, Los Angeles, Dec. 17, 1984.

80   *She quickly found herself... there was a wall:* Grayco, "Just the Two of Us," *Radio Mirror,* Jan. 1949 (bylined "Helen Greco Jones").

81   *with Miriam LaVelle:* George Rock to JY, Eddie Brandt to JY.

81   *We all have our weaknesses:* Earl Bennett to Phil St. Martin, KLAF, Salt Lake City, Nov. 29, 1984.

VAUDEVILLE DAYS

84   *We always carried acts:* Brandt to JY, Oct. 17, 1993.

84   *Glow Worm:* Ingle and Manners preserved the number for posterity in the film, *Breakfast in Hollywood.* Manners—who impersonated Kate Smith on radio's novelty quiz show, *Which is Which?,* just prior to joining the band—recorded "Serenade to a Jerk" during her stint with Jones.

84   *The stage shows became:* Ingle to JY. On one occasion, an authentic American Indian supplied the punchline to the arrow gag, running onstage in full regalia.

85   *He kind of spoiled the flavor:* Porter to Ted Hering.

85   *Freddie Fisher never forgave Spike:* "I met Fisher one time in Hollywood," recalled Joe Siracusa. "I said, 'I know George Rock sends his regards.' And he said a four-letter word to George. I guess George didn't leave under the best conditions, or Fisher resented the fact that George left him to go with Spike. I certainly got that impression." (Siracusa to JY.)

86   *People don't understand this vaudeville:* Rock to Don McGlynn, 1988.

86   *You've got to be on your toes:* Beatrice Lee to JY, Nov. 4, 1992.

87   *Talk about hangovers:* Tommy Pederson to JY, Nov. 14, 1991.

88   *Spike told us when we went on:* Ratliff to JY.

88   *Decked out in garish:* The first Slicker outfits were rented from Western Costume in Hollywood, derbies and all. Custom-tailored costumes were later made by Max Koltz, Ernie Tarzia and others.

88   *the wildest wardrobe of all:* According to Ted Hering, an outfit identical to Jones' suit was depicted in Irving Berlin's 1942 Broadway musical, *This Is the Army.* The suit was pictured on a backdrop for the number, "What the Well-Dressed Man in Harlem Will Wear," set in the '20s. (Hering, "The Clothes Make the Man," *The Spike Jones Musical Depreciation Newsletter* No. 9, Fall 1989.)

89   *Spike would hire a musician:* Bill King to JY, Dec. 28, 1991.

90   *Kaye was a natural:* Brandt to JY. Ballard had no comment on the story.

91   *He was first ordained:* Dr. Horatio Q. Birdbath to JY, Sept. 20, 1981. Doc claimed his audition, which took place at Spike's house, lasted 17 hours.

91   *Spike made a profession:* Kabbible to JY.

91   *I went backstage when he was:* Frankie Little to JY, Mar. 26. 1983.

ON THE ROAD

95   *Harry James was the same:* Robert Robinson to JY, Aug. 13, 1983.

95   *Late in 1946:* A summer tour of South America did not take place as scheduled. "Maybe Peron will join me on second revolver," Spike quipped in announcing the plan (*Hollywood Note,* May 1946).

95   *I remember the first time:* Rock to JY.

96   *Ralph Wonders of General Artists:* Beau Lee remained Spike's personal manager when Jones joined General Amusement Company circa 1945; the firm changed its name to General Artists in 1946.

96   *Spike didn't want to be bothered:* Dick Webster to JY, May 12, 1983.

96   *Generally the top talents:* Eddie Metcalfe to JY, Jul. 23, 1983.

98   *start his own novelty band:* The Bear Family CD compilation "Red Ingle: Tim-Tayshun" features nearly all of Red's 1947-1953 recordings, including several rejects.

98   *George Rock was the fulcrum:* Joe Siracusa to JY, Mar. 15, 1983.

98   *Spike had asked me to join him:* Doodles Weaver to JY, Aug. 9, 1982. Jones first saw Weaver perform at the Pirate's Den, a Los Angeles nightclub.

98   *I didn't like vaudeville:* The revue reverted to vaudeville format for some 1947 engagements, doing abbreviated shows between film screenings. As Weaver noted, "Apr. 10: The opening in Buffalo (Shea's) went well, altho we all of us had almost no rest… Apr. 11: Hardly sound asleep when bango, over to Shea's for 5 more. Set record yesterday (box office)… Apr. 12: Too many today – 6 shows – everyone is being cut out but me – an honor to my act and my health." (Weaver diaries, 1947, courtesy of Win Weaver.)

99   *Doodles was a killer:* Mickey Katz to JY, Nov. 21, 1977.

101   *On those one-night stands:* Eddie Maxwell to JY, Oct. 6, 1991.

101   *She was a good poker player:* "Helen *lived* to play poker," said dancer Ruth Foster. "She was a gambler at heart; Spike wouldn't put one penny in anything." (Foster to JY, Aug. 13, 1983.)

101   *No matter where we stopped:* Eileen Gallagher to JY, Feb. 7, 1993.

103   *I once said to him:* Mickey Katz, *Papa Play For Me* (Simon and Schuster, 1977); Katz to JY, May 14, 1984.

103 *Before Katz left the group:* Mickey's parodies have been reissued on CD as "Greatest Shticks;" they have been performed in recent years by his son, Joel Grey, entertainer Avi Hoffman and the Boston-based Klezmer Conservatory Band. Katz's klezmer instrumentals have been reissued as "Simcha Time" and revived by Don Byron, KCB's one-time clarinetist, on CD and in concert.

103 *Freddy Morgan:* According to his widow, Morgan preferred "Freddie"—a spelling which often appeared on programs and sheet music. However, the comedian *signed* his name "Freddy" on contracts, per over a dozen found in Jones' files. The latter spelling predominated on record labels, from his Victor singles to his Liberty albums.

103 *I did some imitations:* Freddy Morgan, liner notes, "Mr. Banjo," Verve.

104 *I don't think he copied:* Carolyn Livingston to JY, Dec. 11, 1983. Jerry Lewis once acknowledged Morgan as an influence on *his* "idiot" persona, according to Livingston.

104 *accompanied by a squeal:* The sound was originally made by a maple key (leaf), a spring pastime among Missouri youngsters. But "when I went professional, I had to use a reed," said Earl Bennett. "I tried many things and wound up with a bit of leather that I would sand and shape very fine, and that had to be done before every show." (Bennett to JY, Nov. 18, 1991.)

104 *Sir Frederick Gas:* The original spelling of the gag credit on the record, "Our Hour." Bennett used both "Frederick" and "Fredric," but preferred the latter.

105 *personnel had pretty much stabilized:* Among the short-lived Slickers at this point were sax men Emilio Malione, who turned up on a few RCA sessions, and James "Jeff" Griffith, who sang briefly in Jones' stage revues before embarking on a prolific career as a movie character actor.

106 *Lottie Brunn:* "She was probably the best girl juggler in the world—the only other juggler Spike ever hired," said Bill King. "But I did everything comedy; she was no competition to me. Lottie worked in the first half of the show, and I did eight or nine minutes in the second half. She could never understand how I could follow her. She used to watch me work and say, 'You get away with murder.'"

106 *Saliva Sisters:* So-called because "they used to be with Phil Spitalny." The sister act was actually a trio of Slickers in blonde wigs.

107 *I grabbed it:* Souez cited by Fredric Milstein, "Mozart to Spike Jones—A Prima Donna Reminisces," *The Los Angeles Times,* Aug. 22, 1971.

108 *and Fee-tle-baum:* "I used to have a different ending for the race, when I was doing it in 1939, '40, at the clubs," recalled Doodles Weaver. "I'd use a funny word and everybody would laugh: '...And there goes the winner—Glibwicket... There goes the winner—Gackengoofer... There goes the winner—Pootwaddle.' But then I said 'Feetlebaum' one time, and everybody laughed about twice as much." (Weaver to JY). Weaver also said "*Beetle*baum" on at least one occasion – the 1947 Victor recording – thus a majority of people remember it this way. The comedian borrowed the name from the character of Mrs. Feitlebaum in humorist Milt Gross' 1925 book, *Nize Baby.*

109 *When Earl first came:* Siracusa, SPERDVAC Convention, Nov. 9, 1991.

109 *pigs slid down chutes:* Underscoring the line, "Down and down I go..." in "That Old Black Magic."

109 *I would sing:* Bernie Jones to JY, Jul. 19, 1983.

111 *Two decades earlier:* Olsen and Johnson teamed in 1914; by the early '20s they had developed most of the routines that became the basis of *Hellzapoppin,* which opened on Broadway in 1938. (Leonard Maltin, *Movie Comedy Teams,* Signet 1970).

111 *An excerpt from the script:* Mid-1950s, Jones papers.

112 *He was very hard on me:* Helen Grayco, *The Spike Jones Story* (Storyville Films, 1988).

113 *The theatre was over a fish market:* Grayco, *Radio Mirror,* Jan. 1949. Doodles Weaver observed: "At long last we hit a new all-time low in Wheeling, where the hotel was shabby, the eatery presented last year's chicken and ham, and then the real rock bottom crash came when we saw the Market Auditorium: a long thin barnish atrocity... the men's dressing room was a stone warehouse full of toilet suction pumps, the stage was as big as an orange crate and the audience consisted of 300 half-starved cadavers." (Weaver diaries, Mar. 30, 1947).

113 *The standard gag:* A joke with no basis in fact, apart from the odd quarrel. "Helen would never do anything deliberately to make my dad unhappy," noted Linda Jones.

114 *The tricks we'd play:* Jack Golly to JY, Apr. 12, 1992.

115 *We called the Spike Jones train:* Birdbath to JY, Apr. 19, 1983.

115 *One of the young guys in the band:* Eve Whitney to JY, Jan. 14, 1992.

117 *They kind of mothered us:* Gloria Gardner to JY, Nov. 10, 1992.

117 *After one of the shows:* Doodles Weaver, SPERDVAC banquet, 1976.

118 *The other big drinker:* Gardner to JY; Skip Craig to JY, May 12, 1983. Jones and Wonders eventually had a falling out, leading to Wonders' dismissal.

119 *expert marksman:* Rock honed his skills at the FBI's combat shooting school; at one point he served as firearms instructor for the Clark County (Las Vegas) Sheriff's Department.

120 *If Spike needed:* Billy Barty to JY, Aug. 2, 1983.

120 *He invested more time:* According to news reports, Spike sponsored a City Slickers basketball team, a football team and a little league team, none of which Joe Siracusa or Linda Jones recalled.

120 *own supermarket:* The Spike Jones Shop 'n' Save Market, which opened in La Crescenta, California, in 1952, was managed by his brothers-in-law, John and Ralph Greco. ("People have asked, 'Why not in Hollywood instead?' I have only one answer," quipped Jones. "People in Hollywood are too nervous to eat.")

122 *I looked at Locks:* Martin was often billed as Lock or Lockard in films, as Junior in the *Revue.* He was Locks to his friends.

123 *He broke all house records:* Gordon Schroeder to JY, Sept. 13, 1993. Sam Hanks drove the Spike Jones Special—powered by a Stutz Blackhawk engine—in the first post-war Indy 500. The car was later put on display in a museum at the Speedway. Jones also indulged his little-known hobby by sponsoring two of Schroeder's midget racers at regional tracks.

124 *In another week:* Tom Bernard, "Six Nights in a Madhouse," *American,* Jul. 1949.

124 *Dick Tracy:* The pretense of the strip—a gun borrowed from Spike is used to kill a man—was not that far-fetched: the bandleader's guns were actually stolen at least twice. The 1949 strip was reprinted in "The Case of the Madman's Mask," *Dick Tracy Comics* No. 114, Aug. 1957. Spike Dyke reappeared in the newspaper strip (in a new story) earlier that year.

124 *Al Capp:* The cartoonist apparently submitted a piece of material to Spike, who wrote him, "We again missed this year making a recording of your Sadie Hawkins song for Sadie Hawkins day. Would you kindly send it to my house, and we'll record it so far in advance this time that I know we can't miss." (Jones to Capp, letter, Nov. 10, 1951; Buddy Basch files.)

125 *There were a couple of hundred:* "Discord at Slapsy's; Spike Jones Quits," *L.A. Examiner,* Nov. 15, 1948.

126 *Blowing Bubble Gum:* Rock personalized the Del Porter-Carl Hoefle tune (later retitled "The Bubble Gum Song") for the occasion; when he began soliciting the sticky treat in his little boy persona from anyone who would listen, he tearfully pleaded, "Mr. President... bubble gum?" (Rock to JY.)

128 *The unsuspecting visitor:* A special surprise awaited the visitor to one of Jones' earlier residences, if he was well acquainted with the host. "The guest bathroom was at the far end of the living room," remembered Harry Geller. "There was a false hand sticking out from under the couch. Spike would occasionally step on this thing, if he knew the person, and the door would fly open." (Geller to JY.)

128 *by 1950 he was earning:* A Statement of Earnings prepared for the Joneses indicates their combined incomes for 1950 (salaries, royalties, dividends) totaled $245,932.69; they spent $62,543.98 on business expenses and paid $106,442.96 in Federal Income Tax for that year. (Statement of Earnings, Apr. 11, 1951, Jones papers.) However, the document does not account for the considerable monies earned by Jones' corporation, Arena Stars. Spike's *Revue* reportedly grossed between $1 million and $3 million a year, of which Arena Stars received 60-70%.

HOT WAX

131 *Spike talked… Harry Meyerson:* Walter Heebner to JY.

132 *odd batch of tunes:* "Red Wing" was recorded by Freddie Fisher for Decca, with similar instrumentation.

132 *The bandsmen whose presence:* Carl Grayson is not listed on the RCA data sheet but supplied backup vocals, according to Jack Mirtle (*Thank You, Music Lovers*).

132 *Only Spike Jones ever had anything:* Demento to JY.

132 *Bright Two-Step:* RCA was still using this designation for Spike's records when they released "Oh! By Jingo" and "The Sheik of Araby" two years later. By then, however, they were augmenting the description: "For knocked-out, slap-happy appeal, his… styling of these classics is in a musical category all its own." (Stephen H. Sholes, Victor Records, promotional letter to distributors, Mar. 31, 1943.)

133 *once they began recording:* However, according to Ted Hering, some Standards "show evidence of being *dubbed* compilations of good takes. If they got it direct to disc, all the better—but they *would* dub when they had to." (Hering to JY.)

133 *The earliest Standards featured vocalist:* The Slickers also backed Cindy Walker on a September 1941 Decca session.

136 *The pugnacious, roughhewn ex-trumpet:* Robert D. Leiter, *The Musicians and Petrillo* (Bookman Associates, 1953).

136 *Petrillo averred that:* Ibid.

137 *King of Corn:* Freddie Fisher was known as Colonel Corn years before *Down Beat* crowned Jones king.

137 *Priorities have me licked:* SJ to Neil Rau, *Los Angeles Examiner,* Jun. 11, 1944.

137 *Cocktails for Two:* Introduced by Danish entertainer Carl Brisson in the film, *Murder at the Vanities.*

137 *The first 30 seconds:* Brandt to JY.

137 *Due in part to a huge backlog:* Leiter, *The Musicians and Petrillo.*

139 *I hated it:* Sam Coslow, *Cocktails for Two.*

139 *I debated with my business manager:* SJ cited by Harold Heffernan, "Spike Jones: Bizarre Bandsman," *In Short,* May 1946.

139 *They used to have these idea conferences:* Ingle to JY, Apr. 8, 1992.

141 *I was told my dad really did:* Linda Jones to JY, July 21, 1993.

141 *The recording sessions were pretty cut:* Rock to JY.

142 *Jones Polka*: "After Mickey Katz, everything else sounds like amateur night," Earl Bennett remarked, after listening to a Jones compilation CD including the number.

142 *I am fed, gorged, stuffed*: SJ, cited in "Don't Call Me the Corn King," *Hollywood Note*, May 1946.

142 *No funny stuff*: Katz, *Papa, Play for Me*.

143 *People started complaining that a line*: The line in question has also been identified as, "Over and under and then up *her ass*," and "Over and under and then up *her rear*."

143 *I could never hear it*: Jim Hawthorne to JY, Jan. 19, 1993.

145 *The Man on the Flying Trapeze*: Weaver acknowledged spoonerism-spouting comedian Roy Atwell as an influence, but Joe Twerp's tongue-tangled rendition of "Trapeze"—as performed on a 1935 radio comedy-variety show—is the obvious source of this parody. Weaver performed it in his nightclub act as early as 1944, and did it on Rudy Vallee's radio show that year. Twerp (whose real name was Joseph Boyes) toured with Horace Heidt in the '50s, by which time he was collaborating with Weaver on song parodies.

145 *After the resolution of the 1942-44 ban*: Leiter, *The Musicians and Petrillo*.

145 *This time the all-powerful*: Ibid; Sigmund Spaeth, *The History of Popular Music in America* (Random House, 1948).

146 *My Old Flame*: Written for Mae West to sing—backed by Duke Ellington—in the film, *Belle of the Nineties*.

146 *Originally Spike just wanted me*: Paul Frees to JY, Apr. 21, 1983.

148 *There was great animosity between*: King to JY.

148 *all he got was the recording fee*: "It got him [Rock] fame. It got him a bigger salary," said Eddie Brandt. "George always got special things from Spike, 'cause he was the whole band." Recalled Rock: "They gave me a bonus for 'Two Front Teeth' and royalties after that. They thought I was going to leave the band, I guess, and Ralph Wonders came to me and said, 'If anybody makes an offer, give us a chance to better it.' Damn fool, I should've gone and told him about all the big offers I was getting." (Rock to JY.)

150 *Yiddish-accented pardner*: At Jones' request, Bennett mimicked radio actor Artie Auerbach's popular characterization of Mr. Kitzel, as heard on *The Jack Benny Program*.

150 *Monroe hit the ceiling*: Bennett to Phil St. Martin, KLAF, Salt Lake City, Nov. 29, 1984.

150 *The limited pressing of the objectionable*: RCA reportedly pressed 500 copies; when Monroe threatened to sue, they pulled it off the shelf. At least one Beverly Hills record store priced their remaining inventory at $5.00 a copy.

151 *The gentleman in charge*: Siracusa to JY.

153 *Basically, I think Spike did*: Bud Yorkin to JY, Mar. 22, 1984.

153 *I'd have done the same*: One-time band boy Skip Craig recalled, "Joe Colvin didn't feel that way. At the Navy show rehearsal [*The Land's Best Bands*, transcription disc, Nov. 1950], I found him off to the side *furiously* practicing 'Charlestono-Mio'... and mumbling to himself, 'I'll show that so-and-so how to play this stuff.' I don't think it was the session fee he missed, but pride. *He* was the Slicker trombonist." (*The Spike Jones Musical Depreciation Newsletter*, No. 13, Winter 1990.)

154 *Gil Bert and Sully Van*: The second voice was credited to Eddie Metcalfe in the first edition of this book; Metcalfe later attributed the voice to Eddie Maxwell, but neither Maxwell nor Walt Heebner, who produced the "Charleston" sessions, recognized the voice.

155 *Spike had a book the size*: Buddy Basch to JY, Mar. 24, 1992.

155 *One of the things we used to do*: Maxwell to JY.

156   *bull in a china shop:* Waring led the animal through a Fifth Avenue shop in Manhattan in 1939, after losing a bet on a football game.

156   *I dressed Nichols:* Jones wrote Basch, "I love your stunt with Barbara Nichols. I hope she blows a lot of kisses, and if she does the same for the disc jockeys, it's all right with me." (SJ to Basch, letter, circa Nov. 1952.)

156   *Six months ago it would have:* Ibid.

156   *I don't believe any record company:* L.W. Kanaga to SJ, letter, Nov. 24, 1950; Jones papers.

157   *dialect humor was beginning to fade:* Morgan continued doing his trademark Asian caricatures for the bandleader for years, as in his rendition of "Yes Sir, That's My Baby" on Jones' 1957 TV show.

157   *The original plan for the recording:* Hering, *The Spike Jones Musical Depreciation Newsletter,* No. 7, Spring 1989.

157   *Spike was very annoyed:* Bernie Jones to JY.

157   *blasted Katz for a parody:* Katz also got plenty of flak from managers of radio stations; he and Jones were apparently unaware of the criticism each other received. "There were many people who were frightened. If you said a Jewish word they'd start crawling... for fear that somebody was around the corner," observed Katz. "I had to do it first, then it was easy. By the time Allan Sherman came along, I'd softened things up a bit; it was much tougher for me." (Katz to JY.)

158   *We cut the record in Chicago:* Jethro Burns to Dr. Demento, 1977.

158   *Jack Webb's police drama:* Spike's co-star on the "Dragnet" parody was veteran radio character actor Jerry Hausner, whose baby cry (his specialty) was heard on Jones' "Baby Buggie Boogie."

158   *issued only as a gift premium:* "Fiddle Faddle" finally appeared on a German LP compilation in 1974.

159   *I was very surprised when Spike:* Cliffie Stone to JY, Sept. 29, 1992. The slap bass technique was pioneered in the early '20s by Steve Brown of the New Orleans Rhythm Kings.

159   *tongue in cheek:* Jones could never resist a joke. During the Country Cousins period he published a pair of country and western songs recorded by Arena Stars client Monte Hale; "The Key to My Door" and "Last Will and Testament" were credited to Eddie Maxwell and Russell Cattle (alias Jones, as revealed by the contract).

160   *It was strictly in self defense:* SJ, "Jones Spikes Rumors About His Not Playing Dance Music," *Down Beat,* circa May 1952.

160   *How in anyone's wildest:* SJ, "Spike Pens Rebuttal: Amazed at WHDH Ban on 'Wedding'—Cites Record," *Billboard,* Jan. 24, 1953.

161   *off-color... family-type show:* Cleveland critic Omar Ranney, who described Jones' vaudeville show as "definitely not for youngsters," might have influenced him in this regard: "...Jones has gained quite a juvenile following in the past several years, even making some popular children's records. Why he would court a following like that and then give them the sort of fare he dishes out in this show in a special arrangement of the sexy song, 'I Wanna Get Married,' I wouldn't know. He could get along very well without it—and does for at least three fourths of the bill." (Unidentified clipping, June 14, 1946; Doc Birdbath collection.) However, the revamped *Revue* had been touring for nearly a year when *The Los Angeles Examiner* noted in an Oct. 7, 1947 review: "There's little attempt to be subtle or refined, and a few of the lines are on the blue side."

163   *Disc jockey Bill Stewart:* SJ to Bernie Miller, RCA, letter, Oct. 23, 1954; Jones papers.

163   *at least four gold:* Joseph Murrell's *Book of Golden Discs* lists four gold records—"Der Fuehrer's Face," "Cocktails for Two," "Two Front Teeth" and "Glow Worm." Two more ("Chloe" and "The William Tell Overture") have been cited elsewhere; a 1959 UPI report noted "six gold

discs." The Record Industry Assn. of America did not begin certifying gold records until 1958; BMG was unable to provide information.

164   *fought a lengthy battle with A&R:* Dick Webster to Roy Gillespie, letter, Jun. 15, 1956; Jones papers.

164   *Christmas Story:* Gillespie's simple tale of "the first Christmas tree" so impressed Jones that he tried to sell it for years, to no avail.

164   *I wish I'd have been:* SJ to Eddie Cuda, WOPA, Oak Park, Ill., Oct. 24, 1959.

VANTAGE POINT: GEORGE ROCK

165   *The whole family was musically:* This "monologue" derives entirely from: George Rock to JY, Mar. 18, 1983.

165   *I was with Freddie Fisher:* Several Fisher tracks with Rock on vocals (taken from radio transcriptions) were included on Vintage Records' 1989 compilation, "Cornplastered."

166   *They couldn't call and have someone:* "George was damn near indestructible," said Eddie Metcalfe. "But this one time in Las Vegas he became ill, in the late '40s. Spike had Zeke Zarchy come up from L.A. and play for us, for about a week at the Flamingo Hotel." (Metcalfe to JY, Sept. 1, 1993.) On another occasion in Hollywood, "George had a minor operation on his nose," recalled Joe Siracusa, "but it affected the edge of his lip—of all things for a trumpet player. So Cappy Lewis played the show while George conducted and cued Cappy what to do." (Siracusa to JY, Jun. 29, 1993.)

168   *Our radio producer:* Bigelow produced *The Spike Jones Show,* CBS, January-June 1949.

168   *When we were working the Curran:* Bill King, who remembered the incident taking place at the Great Northern Theatre in Chicago, blamed it on a new pair of shoes with slippery soles. He recalled: "When I used to come out and juggle the axes, I'd make all kinds of flourishes, run back and forth, and go in a circle juggling them. I got down to the footlights and it was slick; I couldn't stop. I was going to jump in the orchestra pit, but there was a piano there, and I stepped down on it. They had that piano sitting up on wooden blocks—the blocks went out and it just fell right into the pit. You never heard such a damn noise in your life. Spike came out of the dressing room and said, 'What the hell did he do now?!' That was a great moment; I never did anything like that again." (King to JY.)

ON THE AIR

171   *Radio was such a different medium:* Bennett to JY.

173   *they were forced to substitute:* "King of Corn," *Bandwagon,* Mar. 1946. The tune was banned when it first came out; "The Nutcracker Suite" met a similar fate on the BBC. (Denis Gifford, *The Golden Age of Radio.*)

174   *What would you like me... to play next:* Excerpted from *The Chase and Sanborn Program,* June 10, 1945.

174   *You didn't have the time:* Frances Langford to JY, Nov. 14, 1991.

174   *Spike wanted a college premise:* Charlie Isaacs to JY, Feb. 22, 1993.

176   *The audition show was broadcast:* Renditions of "Chloe" and "Hotcha Cornia" from the 1945 pilot were included on the "Complete Collection" compilation album.

176   *When the union insisted his broadcasts:* Charlotte Tinsley to JY.

176   *MCA got Spike The Coke Show:* Brandt to JY.

178   *They'd work the dates like a wheel:* Golly to JY.

178 *The writers would be part of the advance:* Metcalfe to JY.

178 *Our clarinet player is making a fortune:* Excerpted from *Spotlight Review,* February 6, 1948.

179 *beyond description… Luckily we all got along:* Maxwell to JY.

179 *I remember one time he ad-libbed:* Rock to JY.

181 *Jones had a bit—it was going to be:* Bennett to JY.

181 *played at breakneck speed:* "It is hard to believe that what they played was written," asserted Jack Mirtle, "and harder to believe that what was written could be played!" (Mirtle, *Thank You, Music Lovers.*) Jack Golly observed: "It was all written. It had to be. Gardner and I used to sit and rehearse those parts all week, 'cause you couldn't read 'em; all those little reed parts are played verbatim." (Golly to JY.)

182 *We had the big orchestra:* Siracusa to JY. King Jackson, Rubin "Zeke" Zarchy and others were also employed to augment the Slickers.

182 *One of the more memorable shows:* The Lorre show (December 10, 1948) was issued on CD and cassette by Rhino Records (*Spike Jones and his City Slickers: The Radio Years, Vol. 1*).

183 *he was practicing Peter Lorre:* Brandt, SPERDVAC convention, Nov. 9, 1991.

183 *There was a routine with Kirk Douglas:* Siracusa, ibid.

184 *Dick Morgan was a heavy eater:* Siracusa to JY, Jun. 29, 1993.

185 *the sponsor asked the band:* Mirtle, *Thank You Music Lovers.*

185 *Philco Radio Time:* The band also did a reprise of "Hawaiian War Chant" with Mickey Katz (replacing Carl Grayson) on this 1946 broadcast; the selection was subsequently included in the "Complete Collection" album.

185 *For your consequence tonight:* Excerpted from *Truth or Consequences,* December 11, 1948.

186 *breakfast foods on the market:* excerpted from *Symphony Hall* script, 1951 (repeated from *The Spike Jones Show,* May 21, 1949).

VANTAGE POINT: JOE SIRACUSA

187 *I've been a City Slicker:* This monologue was assembled from: Siracusa to JY, Mar. 15, 1983; Jun. 29, 1993; Siracusa to Bob Ellis, KLAF, Salt Lake City, Nov. 29, 1984; SPERDVAC Convention, Nov. 9, 1991.

188 *He took it out for 30 days:* The tryout of the *Revue* began after the filming of *Variety Girl,* and ran from November 21 (Aberdeen, S.D.) to December 18, 1946 (Oklahoma City).

189 *the two-headed drummer:* In a treatise on how he made his records, Jones joked: "The musicians report for work at 9 o'clock in the morning. First, I check to see if they are all present. This is easy to do. I count heads and then divide by two." (*Billboard,* Nov. 12, 1949.)

189 *something he'd seen on The Jack Benny Show:* Theodore Norman, who played violin in Jones' Other Orchestra, claimed to have originated the idea. (Jack Mirtle, *Thank You, Music Lovers.*)

190 *Minka:* Recorded by the Korn Kobblers (featuring Nels Laakso), Harry James and others as "Trumpet Blues." Recorded by Wynton Marsalis as "Grand Russian Fantasia," which may be found on the CD "Carnaval."

MOVIE MADNESS

193 *I can't imagine him putting down:* Rock to JY.

193 *A bunch of the guys from Poly:* Ratliff to JY.

193 *A questionnaire:* Jones file, Academy of Motion Picture Arts & Sciences (AMPAS), Center for Motion Picture Study.

194 *the very first Soundies session:* Mark Cantor to JY, email, Sept. 28, 2003. Future Slicker Perry Botkin was the guitarist.

194 *Give Us Wings:* Jones, King Jackson and Stan Wrightsman are visible; Del Porter and Perry Botkin are present only on the soundtrack.

194 *As production head:* Coslow, *Cocktails for Two.*

195 *Spike was working down:* Duke Goldstone to JY, Nov. 22, 1992. Central Avenue, a black neighborhood, was the nucleus of Los Angeles' jazz scene in the '40s.

195 *schnickelfritz band:* Freddie Fisher's childhood nickname, Schnickelfritz—usually defined as "silly fellow"—had become generic by the early '40s, synonymous with musical corn.

195 *The fledgling bandleader agreed:* Ibid.

196 *Spike and his men received $5,000:* Warner Bros. Collection, University of Southern California (USC), Cinema-TV Library.

196 *production records do not indicate:* Ibid.

196 *written into a number of sequences:* MGM Collection, USC. Eleanor Keaton, who was working as a dancer on an adjoining soundstage, asserted, "Spike almost brought me to an untimely end. I had gone to lunch; I was going back to rehearsal and I was rounding a corner – and there was a big grizzly bear drinking a Coke. I almost ran right into it." (Keaton to JY, Sept. 6, 1992.) Although there were many scenes and songs planned for Jones, there is no grizzly bear indicated in the extant drafts of the script.

196 *We had to dance this silly dance:* Anderson to JY.

196 *In connection with the line:* Memo from Joseph Breen, MGM Collection.

197 *a reported seven-year contract:* According to the *Boston Post.*

197 *already in mid-production:* Paramount Collection, AMPAS. "That Old Black Magic" was also considered for filming.

197 *Lake was late virtually every day:* Ibid.

198 *battled a midget fireman:* an unbilled bit by Jerry Maren, one of the Lollipop Kids in *The Wizard of Oz.*

198 *They were slated for... also announced for:* Unsourced newspaper clipping, undated; Beau Lee, Jr. collection.

198 *unions were wreaking havoc:* Labor file, AMPAS; Ratliff to JY.

198 *Ladies' Man:* According to production files, the film was originally called *Manhattan at Midnight.* It was renamed *Big Town Blues* before receiving its final title. (Paramount Collection.)

199 *Jones and his men were paid $5,000:* Ibid.

199 *Those were the days of everybody stealing:* Brandt to JY.

199 *Spike was assigned...Another entry:* Paramount Collection.

199 *Ralph talked to me:* Isaacs to JY.

199 *receiving $10,000 a week:* Paramount Collection.

200 *Perhaps Paramount was kidding:* Peck, *PM,* undated review, AMPAS.

200 *the reporter sent west... now a period piece:* Louella Parsons, *Los Angeles Examiner,* Oct. 24, 1949; May 26, 1951. The disc jockey promo of "Wild Bill Hiccup" was labeled, "From the film..."

201 *The Phantom of the Opera:* Spike later announced he wanted to make the film with Liberace, probably as a joke.

201 *I had an idea for them to do a cartoon:* Siracusa to JY. The drummer left the band to work for UPA the same year. The studio's Oscar-winning cartoon, *Gerald McBoing Boing,* undoubtedly inspired Jones to record a tune by the same name in 1953; the number was never issued.

201 *a role that did not exist:* There is no mention of Jones' character or the band in the October 1952 draft by Lee Loeb. (Universal Collection, USC.)

201 *When Lou Costello collapsed:* Universal Collection; Bob Furmanek and Ron Palumbo, *Abbott and Costello in Hollywood* (Perigee, 1991). It is a widespread myth that A&C dropped *Fireman* in favor of *Abbott and Costello Meet Dr. Jekyll and Mr. Hyde.* Since the latter completed filming in February 1953 and was released in August—and *Fireman* began production as scheduled that November—this is scarcely possible.

201 *They got into a big fight:* Bennett to JY, Jun. 29, 1993.

202 *$75,000 apiece... $6,000 a week:* Universal Collection.

202 *Who is the comedian:* Bennett to Scott Corbett, *The Spike Jones Musical Depreciation Newsletter,* Spring 1988, No. 3. A truncated version of this scene remains in the film.

202 *Director Les Goodwins:* Bennett recalled that another director stepped in uncredited, possibly George Marshall.

203 *No matter what you and I:* SJ to Doll, letter, May 6, 1954; Jones papers.

204 *Although Universal ruined:* SJ to Friedman, letter, Feb. 8, 1955; Jones papers.

204 *life of W.C. Fields:* SJ, memos to himself, Feb. 8-11, 1960; Jones papers.

204 *I think you will agree that a new dimension:* SJ to Lloyd, letter, Oct. 3, 1961; Jones papers.

205 *Producer Joe Pasternak was considering:* John Genung to SJ, letter, Aug. 18, 1961; Jones papers.

VANTAGE POINT: EARL BENNETT

207 *I studied to be an artist:* This "monologue" derives primarily from: Bennett to JY, Nov. 18, 1991; Dec. 5, 1991; Jun. 29, 1993. Also: Bennett to Phil St. Martin, KLAF, Nov. 29, 1984; Bennett to Don McGlynn, 1988; Bennett, SPERDVAC Convention, Nov. 9, 1991.

211 *I just loved Frankie:* "This minute dwarf is a priceless gem," observed Doodles Weaver. "He waddles about the towns we visit as if he were a wandering king… What a picture he is at the poker table, with his little shoe full of money. One night after an argument in the game, he left the table in anger, stalked through the darkened Pullman sleeper complaining in stentorian tones: 'What this country needs is more midgets.' " (Weaver diaries, undated entry, Nov. 1946-Sept. 1947 book.)

212 *Flamingo Hotel:* Jones was one of the first entertainers to appear at the hotel, after making his Las Vegas debut at the Last Frontier.

212 *Spike had seen this bath mat:* Freddie Fisher employed the same prop in his act. *Time* magazine reported Fisher's "idea of jazz was to stand barefoot on a mat of falsies and tell dirty jokes." Fisher clarified: "That wasn't my idea of jazz—just a comfortable way to make a living. It was a hell of an act…broke 'em up every time." (*Time,* Apr. 17, 1964; *The Aspen Times,* Apr. 21, 1964.)

DOWN THE TUBE

215 *There was a big battle:* Bennett to JY.

215 *The Foreign Legion:* This sketch, which Billy Barty attributed to Milton Berle, was also trotted out in Spike's stage revue. In one town, "Spike got sick and couldn't do the show," recalled Barty. "I had to do the 'Foreign Legion' bit. From the time I was a boy, I used to watch all the acts; I could do every act that was on the bill. When it came to this, I said, 'I know it.' And I did it; I wore Spike's jacket."

216   *16mm Multicam:* The three-camera system developed by Fairbanks in 1947 at the behest of NBC gave birth to the more sophisticated system used to film "I Love Lucy." (Jon Krampner, "Myths and Mysteries Surround Pioneering of 3-Camera TV," *Los Angeles Times,* Jul. 29, 1991.)

216   *We always try to give:* "Foreign Legion" script, Jul. 25, 1950, Jones papers.

216   *I've just got to make:* SJ, "Wild Bill Hiccup," July 19, 1950.

216   *I think the shows were well done:* Siracusa to JY.

217   *Back here at Studebaker… A Jesus by the name:* Weaver diaries, Feb. 9-11, 1951.

218   *For his part, Weaver demonstrated:* The comedian was conspicuously absent from the 1950 pilots.

218   *That was no atomic:* Larry Wolters, *The Chicago Tribune,* Feb. 12, 1951.

218   *A new low:* Art Cullison, *The Akron Beacon Journal,* Feb. 13, 1951.

219   *He was so fast they missed everything:* Brandt to JY.

219   *let out a scream:* Memo, Apr. 16, 1951, Jones papers. The ad rep was Kay Callahan; the writer of the memo is identified only as "Wynn."

220   *The rest of the show:* SJ to Joe Finnigan, UPI, letter, Oct. 24, 1961; Jones papers.

220   *They had to try to take that set down:* King to JY.

221   *When Spike laughed, it would turn:* Bernie Jones to JY.

222   *Ray Heath:* "George Rock called him 'the best trombonist in the band,' over all the years," noted Skip Craig.

224   *Everybody would throw ideas:* Maxwell to JY.

224   *He knew I did impersonations:* Barty to JY.

225   *It was like an opening night:* Helen Grayco, *The Spike Jones Story.*

225   *Enjoyment of Spike Jones:* Freeman, *San Diego Union,* April 21, 1954.

225   *I don't think we should confine:* proposal, June 19, 1955; Jones papers.

225   *Ernie Kovacs:* Danny Welkes, MCA, to Dick Webster, letter, Dec. 13, 1956; Jones papers.

227   *It was, for Mr. Jones:* JPS, *The New York Times,* Apr. 3, 1957.

227   *Spike was always thinking what it was:* Gil Bernal, Oct. 15, 1983.

228   *We did something like four run-throughs:* Pederson to JY.

228   *Spike didn't pay anything extra:* Jad Paul, Sept. 22, 1992.

229   *Doodles… back in harness:* Weaver reprised his hit records on Jones' 1957 TV show but was not a regular.

229   *Maybe it's age:* Janet Kern, *Chicago American,* June 25, 1958.

230   *It was a thinking person's comedy:* Phil Gray to JY, Jan. 30, 1993.

231   *He could be very emotional:* Linda Jones to JY, July 21, 1993.

231   *When a Los Angeles lawyer wrote:* Correspondence, Sept. 13-22, 1960; Jones papers.

232   *I was an infantry soldier:* Bill Dana to JY, Sept. 21, 1992.

232   *A summer series gives me a chance:* SJ, "A Summer TV Series Can Save Your Life," *Los Angeles Mirror,* July 31, 1961.

233   *By the time you go on:* SJ to Bob Crane, KNX, Los Angeles, Nov. 4, 1963.

233   *Among the projects he tried but failed:* Eddie Brandt to JY.

234   *I do not feel that it is:* Jones to Doll, letter, Apr. 11, 1962; Jones papers.

234   *Today, Spike would have been a smash:* Yorkin to JY.

235   *I think the approach... I have in mind:* SJ, proposal, June 19, 1955.

ON THE ROAD AGAIN

237   *I'd buy a cheap seat:* Skip Craig to JY, May 12, 1983.

238   *When Spike advertised:* "Spike at the Flamingo," *Record Review,* Dec. 1950.

238   *Them Slickers weren't:* Thompson, *Fort Wayne Journal-Gazette,* Feb. 26, 1951.

239   *When we were ready:* Metcalfe to JY.

239   *The guys on stage right:* Gray to JY.

239   *It was a very funny routine:* Bennett to JY.

239   *He lifted it unhesitantly:* Joe Siracusa to JY; Ted Hering to JY.

240   *all-night poker sessions:* "It's a pleasant group, and playing cards is certainly as amusing and edu-
cational as 'suffering' thru long afternoons in graveyard towns like Ardmore [Oklahoma] etc.
The game has evolved itself into a decent little timepasser with 5-cent opener and 20-cent
limit," noted Doodles Weaver. (Weaver diaries, Jan. 19, 1949.)

241   *The constant parties:* Weaver diaries, 1974 addendum to 1951 book.

241   *lasted only 13 weeks:* Weaver's critically-lambasted Saturday night program was broadcast June 9-
Sept. 1, 1951. Writer Goodman Ace's review of the show: "Oh, brother."

242   *Spike really splurged:* Peter James to JY, Aug. 23, 1983.

242   *I didn't have to worry:* Gallagher to JY.

243   *He saw two barrels:* Jones to JY.

244   *He was like a big brother:* "Dick was probably one of the mainstays of the band as far as keeping
it on a level keel," said Hersh Ratliff. "When things got a little too wild, he had a sense of
calming it down a bit—a steadying influence."

244   *The heart attack was brought on:* Antabuse "alters the metabolism of alcohol in the body," causing
serious and sometimes severe reactions when alcohol is present. (*Columbia Encyclopedia,* 2001.)

245   *Spike and I hit it off:* Barty to JY.

246   *That salaries stayed:* The payroll for the Santa Clara Fair in San Jose, Calif., for Sept. 1955
indicates Freddy Morgan made $450 a week, Billy Barty and Peter James $400 each, George
Rock $375 and Bill King $350. By contrast, the payroll for the Riviera Hotel in Las Vegas for
Aug. 1957 reveals that Morgan and Barty were paid $600 each, Gil Bernal and Helen Grayco
$400 each, and Rock still $375.

246   *Spike was the best promoter:* Eddie Brandt to JY.

247   *The 46th Street Theatre:* Ralph Wonders to Larry Barnett, MCA, letter, Apr. 29, 1954; Jones
papers.

247   *Though neither Jones:* Ibid.

247   *Spike was willing to accept:* SJ to John Tranchitella, AFM, March 2, 1962, letter, Jones papers.

248   *The irrepressible bandleader:* UPI, Nov. 30, 1948.

248   *But Jones was ever anxious:* In 1958, he sought legal advice when the zany Las Vegas lounge act,
The Goofers, managed to get a booking in England. "Spike wants to sue the Queen or MCA or
somebody. In other words, he wants to go to England," manager Dick Webster told their attorney. Jones further railed against the unions in 1962—to no avail—when the veteran British
comedy band, the Nitwits, was booked into the Stardust Hotel in Las Vegas. (Webster to Loyd
Wright, letter, May 14, 1958; SJ to John Tranchitella, letter, March 2, 1962; Jones papers.)

248 *An offer for Spike:* Larry Barnett to Taft Schreiber, MCA inter-office communication, April 22, 1954; Jones papers. A 1959 offer for 15 days in Sweden, Finland and Denmark, at a guarantee of $12,500 tax free, also failed to materialize.

248 *In Adelaide, the show:* Rock to JY.

250 *Jones was guaranteed $163,000: Variety,* April 12, 1955. Nearly half the gross ($158, 380) was brought in by the 15 shows in Sydney.

250 *He always had sensational:* Yorkin to JY.

250 *I was straightman to Freddy:* Gray to JY.

251 *They were a little bit on the zooty:* Bernal to JY.

252 *Spike called me The Bosom:* Wilkinson to JY.

254 *the oxygen tank:* a 1959 UPI article reported Spike was using a tank and mask "to recuperate from a pneumonia attack."

254 *When he was diagnosed:* Linda Jones to JY.

255 *during the sensationalized trial:* Astonishingly, confusion persists to this day among the less worldly members of the general populace, e.g., "Spike Jones—isn't he the guy who killed his wife?"

255 *I tried to get him to retire:* Webster to JY.

IN THE GROOVE

257 *Among others turning out occasional:* A World War II era white-label pressing credited to the Coon Creek Boys contained a remarkable sound-alike version of "The Great Big Saw...." In 1959, the Will Bradley Jazz Septet (with Billy Butterfield on trumpet) cut a single titled "Who Cut the Gorgonzola" that smelled almost enough like the genuine article to be mistaken for Jones in his prime.

257 *comic sound effects:* "Ward had what we called the goodie box – sandpaper blocks, slapsticks, cowbells, all sorts of junk. If things got dull, he would reach in there and pull out something," recalled Frank Thomas. (Thomas to JY.)

257 *we were pretty serious:* Kimball was enough of a Spike Jones fan, however, that when he had a daughter in 1945 he named her Chloe. (Kimball to JY.)

257 *I loved Spike:* Stan Freberg to JY, Jan. 9, 1993. Freberg did use a gunshot, however, on "Abe Snake for President."

258 *Freberg was his idol:* Jones to JY.

258 *Capitol has always come up winners:* Stone to JY.

259 *The Christmas album:* A personal favorite of Spike's, along with the "The Nutcracker Suite."

259 *then you beat it to death:* Rock to JY. Jones returned to the well three years later, recording "I Want the War to Win the South for Christmas" for the Kapp label. "I should probably have my saliva tested for recording a Xmas single," he told the media, "however... I just couldn't resist trying for another 'Two Front Teeth.' "

260 *Every time I got ready to release:* SJ to George Church III, *Small World,* AFRS, Jan. 24, 1964.

260 *When medical research:* SJ, "Facts on Wax," *L.A. Examiner,* May 4, 1958.

260 *British humorist:* John Amis, liner notes, "Hoffnung Music Festival Concert" (Angel Records, 1956). In the same vein, The Guckenheimer Sour Kraut Band employed all manner of junkyard instrumentation, in debasing "Second Hungarian Rhapsody" and other classics on a 1958 RCA album, "Music for Non-Thinkers."

262 *Only after its release:* "Facts on Wax," *L.A. Examiner,* 1957.

262   *Spike had a nude gal:* Eddie Brandt to JY.

262   *a recording session for Billy Barty:* "I paid for it; it was my session. Spike supervised it," said Barty. "I took 'em to RCA, Capitol, they didn't want to do 'em..." (Barty to JY.)

262   *a prime influence on Haley:* Producer Milt Gabler modeled Haley's style on Jordan, whose records he also produced. However, musicologist Miles Kreuger asserted there was "an unbroken lineage from Freddie Fisher to Spike to Bill Haley," noting, "Haley did all kinds of things on stage obviously inspired by Jones." (Kreuger to JY.)

263   *What can a washboard and banjo:* SJ cited by Hal Humphrey, "Spike Jones Wants to Know How to Rib Today's Ditties," *Los Angeles Mirror,* Sept. 12, 1960.

263   *Every one takes themselves:* SJ to Norman Pringle, July 1959.

263   *never would get permission:* " 'Mack the Knife'... is owned by a composer and publisher who won't allow me to perform anything but a straight version," the bandleader lamented. (Ibid.)

263   *Spike Jones in Stereo:* Issued in mono as "Spike Jones in Hi-Fi."

263   *Teenage Brain Surgeon:* "That's come back to haunt me several times, just out of a clear blue sky. Pretty wild," noted Thurl Ravenscroft. "Spike was a screwball, but he was easy to get along with; he didn't drive us crazy like Stan Freberg." (Ravenscroft to JY.)

264   *Spike had a million voice tracks:* Carl Brandt to JY, June 22, 1983.

264   *The session, which cost him:* Alvin Bennett, Liberty Records, to SJ, letter, May 27, 1959; Jones papers.

264   *Ross Bagdasarian's Chipmunks:* Ironically, it was Bagdasarian (using the name David Seville) who saved Liberty Records from bankruptcy in 1958 with "Witch Doctor." Six months later, his "Chipmunk Song" became the fastest-selling record in history. (Bruce Nash and Allan Zullo, *The Wacky Top 40,* Bob Adams, Inc., 1993.)

264   *Allan Sherman:* When the parodist's first LP sold 65,000 copies in its first week of release in 1962, he quickly wrote material for two more. Ironically, he scored his biggest hit when he took a page from Spike's songbook – Ponchielli's "Dance of the Hours" – and reinvented it as "Hello Muddah, Hello Fadduh."

264   *Given his involvement on the board:* Jones also chaired NARAS' Awards and Nominating Committee for the Academy's first Grammy Awards in 1959.

265   *he was to remain with Liberty for the balance:* The aforementioned "Xmas" single and Bill Dana's "More Jose Jimenez" LP were the two exceptions, both for the Kapp label.

266   *Rides, Rapes and Rescues:* Disc jockeys gave the album considerable airplay, but announced it by the sub-title, "Music to Watch Silent Movies By"—lest they offend listeners. (*Hollywood Reporter,* Apr. 21, 1961.)

266   *claiming he himself played drums:* Jones to Soupy Sales, letter, March 21, 1961; Jones papers. John Cyr had replaced Spike on drums on *Eddie Cantor, Fibber McGee and Molly* and *Kraft Music Hall* two decades earlier when the City Slickers became a full time operation.

266   *Bobby Van Eps accompanied:* Marvin Ash played piano on one selection, "The Great Train Robbery." Trumpeter Mannie Klein and violinist Benny Gill, both key members of Mickey Katz's band, are also heard on the album.

266   *It's the real thing:* Van Eps to JY.

267   *Persuasive Concussion:* Five of the nine tracks from the unfinished album have been issued. See Discography: Liberty Rejects and Unrealized Projects.

267   *Raymond Scott:* The idiosyncratic artist has been called "the Spike Jones of Jazz." His surreal 1930s compositions—recycled in countless Warner Bros. cartoon soundtracks—have been reissued on CD by Stash and Columbia.

267   *Spike called him to do this record:* Ingle to JY.

267   *Everybody was ready to write Spike off:* Don Blocker to JY, June 4, 1984.

268   *Tommy Tedesco:* Best known for his guitar solo on the theme song for TV's *Bonanza,* Tedesco was "in all probability the most recorded guitarist in history," according to *Guitar Player* magazine.

268   *Brandt served as the bandleader:* Carl Brandt to JY.

268   *Dave Pell:* Head of A&R for Liberty, Pell once played tenor sax for Les Brown.

268   *Jones himself performed that function:* Brandt to JY.

269   *some pretty corny licks:* "Doo Wacka Doo" and "More Wacky Doodlin's," a pair of RCA albums from the early '60s featuring the Doowackadoodlers – arranged and conducted by Korn Kobblers alum Marty Gold, with former bandmate Nels Laasko on trumpet – blended dixieland with a much bigger helping of corn.

270   *They know they're in it:* SJ to Ballance, Apr. 5, 1964, KFWB, Los Angeles. Two decades earlier, Jones had ascribed the same motive to himself: "...it pays good dough. That's all I'm in this racket for and when it stops paying dividends I'll do something else." (SJ cited by Ken Alden, *Radio Mirror,* Nov. 1943.)

270   *I see absolutely no future:* SJ to Pringle, July 1959.

270   *We had three songs:* Eddie Brandt to Don McGlynn, 1988.

DOWN BEAT

271   *Maybe he figured if he stopped:* Linda Jones to JY, Jul. 21, 1993.

271   *He told me he knew he had emphysema:* Geller to JY.

272   *One of the saddest memories I have:* Dana to JY.

272   *a modified, scaled down:* As late as 1960, Jones turned down an offer to appear at the fabled Aragon Ballroom—which couldn't afford his troupe of 20—because "It would definitely not be a good policy for me to appear in Chicago, or any place for that matter, with fewer performers than the public is used to seeing..." (SJ to Andrew Karzas, letter, Aug. 26, 1960; Jones papers.)

272   *Spike was still the leader:* James to JY.

273   *Even on stage he had:* Siracusa to JY.

274   *He would work two shows:* Spike Jr. to Don McGlynn, 1988.

274   *My wife and I:* Rock to JY.

274   *People were walking out:* Mousie Garner to JY, Sept. 13, 1983.

274   *I went to see Spike at the Showboat:* Bob Vincent to JY, Jan. 28, 1993.

275   *We were all so glad when my dad:* Jones to JY, Oct. 20, 1992.

276   *Danny Thomas:* "He was someone who was considered far more than just a friend," said Linda Jones. "When my dad was very seriously ill in the hospital – on an evening when he was in critical condition – in walked Danny. He said, 'I called and the nurse said only family could be here. I'm family, so I came.' He sat in the corner for an hour, no cameras, no audience, he just sat there to be with us and then left. And that's how he was." (Jones to Don McGlynn, 1988.)

276   *Spike had lost so much:* Ruth Foster to JY, Aug. 13, 1983.

276   *He was weak, but quite lucid:* Yorkin to JY.

276   *The next morning... found by his nurse:* Harry Trimborn, *Los Angeles Times,* May 2, 1965; Jim Bennett, *Los Angeles Herald-Examiner,* May 4, 1965.

276   *Dr. Schwartz determined:* Certificate of Death, Los Angeles County.

277   *one Los Angeles newspaper:* Bennett, *Herald-Examiner.*

277   *Spike Jones wanted people... last year of his life:* John Devlin, cited in *Herald-Examiner,* May 4, 1965; *New York Times,* May 5, 1965; *Los Angeles Times,* May 5, 1965.

277   *outlived his mother:* Ada Armstrong Jones died Dec. 22, 1961, following a long illness. Spike's father, Lindley Murray Jones, died June 13, 1948, age 81.

278   *The last project to reach fruition:* An earlier restaurant-nightclub concept—which he had planned to call Spike's Speak, and hoped to open on the site of Mike Romanoff's famed Beverly Hills establishment—was never realized, despite elaborate sketches he commissioned. Yet another idea Jones had was to buy a ship. "This was a great idea—to do our show, to have a place to go— all out at sea," recalled Peter James.

278   *Jones' estate was estimated:* "First Wife of Spike Jones Shares Estate," *Los Angeles Times,* July 17, 1968.

280   *I was doing a hipper thing:* Miles Beller, "Spike Jones Jr. Carries the Torch for Loony Tunes," *Los Angeles Herald-Examiner,* Apr. 11, 1985. The band was billed variously as the Barstow Filharmonic and Rock Casualties.

280   *Because we have the records:* Gina Jones to JY, Oct. 17, 2003.

LIFE AFTER DEATH

281   *As Joseph Laredo observed:* "(Not) Your Standard Spike Jones Collection," Collector's Choice Music.

281   *Peter Schickele:* Schickele, "The Hills Are Alive, But What a Way to Live!," *The New York Times,* Apr. 10, 1994.

281   *Chick Corea:* Corea to JY, Feb. 26, 1995.

282   *Spike was a major inspiration:* Dr. Demento to JY, Aug. 9, 1982. The good doctor may be found at *www.drdemento.com.*

282   *Spike always made it a policy:* Siracusa to JY.

282   *It's surprising how many:* Miles Beller, "Spike Jones Jr. Carries the Torch for Loony Tunes," *Los Angeles Herald-Examiner,* Apr. 11, 1985.

283   *I always marvel at what:* Spike Jr. to George Stewart, WHYY, Wilmington, Del., 1983.

283   *compact discs since Jones' death:* Over 40 CDs have been released as of 2004. See Keeping Up with Jones for resources, The Essentials for recommendations.

283   *RCA's The Best of:* The album has been issued on LP, cassette and CD; it has been released in the U.S., Canada, England, France, Germany, Italy, Belgium, Holland, Australia, New Zealand and Japan.

284   *Rum Tee Diddle Dee Yump:* "That's the most embarrassing thing," admitted Earl Bennett. "Spike wanted to get me on the flip side of a hit record so I could get a little extra money. That's the best I could come up with; I'm not a writer."

284   *instrumental version of Carmen:* At the suggestion of archivist Ted Hering, engineer Mike Kieffer added missing sound effects. "There were three gunshots in the written arrangement of 'Carmen' which were not in the recording. Rather than round up a starter pistol with just the right timbre, I sampled two authentic Jones gunshots... I digitally combined them to get the best character- istics of both, and then fired the resulting composite gunshot into 'Carmen' by playing it through the mixing board," explained Kieffer. (*Past Times,* No. 17-18, Fall 1994.)

284   *Nutcracker Suite:* The album was available in whole only on the original 78s and 45s, until it was reissued on Vintage Records' 1992 CD, "For the Love of Spike."

285 *How innocent it all sounds:* "Spike Up the Band," Richard Corliss, *Time*, Jun. 13, 1994.

285 *first two Verve albums:* first reissued by Goldberg & O'Reilly on LP and cassette, subsequently on LP and CD by Rhino Records.

285 *The Spike Jones Story:* Don McGlynn's documentary, which included interviews with family members and former City Slickers, was released on DVD by Navarre Corp. in 2004.

285 *All Hail COINegie Tech:* Written by Mickey Katz and Howard Gibeling; vocal by Del Porter and The Boys in the Back Room. Reissued on an Evatone soundsheet at the Spike Jones International Fan Club's 1989 convention.

286 *It took four of us:* Levin, *rec.music.dementia,* May 16, 1995.

286 *We are very much doing Spike's stuff:* Bob Kerr, email to JY, Sept. 17, 2003.

286 *New York Jazz:* John J. Fialka, "Spike Jones Enjoys a Comeback of Sorts a Generation Later," *The Wall Street Journal,* Feb. 17, 1987; Mary Shaughnessy, "Oh My Aching Ear!," *People,* May 4, 1987.

286 *Ever since I was:* "He's Bringing Back the Late, Great, Demented Spike Jones," *Winston-Salem Journal,* Mar. 15, 1987.

287 *An Evening with Spike:* C. Robert Holloway to JY, July 14, 1992; Richard Dodds, "A Stage Spiketacular," *Times-Picayune,* New Orleans, June 26, 1992.

288 *Nobody is Spike Jones:* Basch to JY.

288 *He occupies a unique place:* Bernal to JY.

288 *Had he lived I think:* Geller to JY.

288 *I think his day was over:* Brandt to JY.

289 *It's unusual to have your father's name:* Jones to JY.

290 *do the right thing:* Mel Miller to Mayor David Dinkins, cited in *The New York Post,* Sept. 24, 1990.

290 *I will play as many as:* Skip Marrow to JY, Sept. 24, 2003.

291 *Working with Spike:* Metcalfe to JY.

OODLES OF DOODLES

293 *Doodles Weaver lived:* The comedian was profiled on cable TV's "Mysteries & Scandals" in 2000.

293 *commit suicide at noon:* "Doodles Weaver—Author," UPI report, *San Francisco Chronicle,* May 23, 1963; Earl Bennett to JY.

293 *Doodles' Nightclub:* Don Page, "Feetlebaum (Not Beetlebaum) Comeback," *Los Angeles Herald-Examiner,* Jun. 16, 1974.

293 *There was no end to the stories:* UPI report, *San Francisco Chronicle,* May 23, 1963; Steve Gruber, "Rumors Cloud Zany List of Doodles' Daring Deeds," *Stanford Daily,* Nov. 18, 1966; Ellie Williams, "Alumni Glorify Doodles Weaver Antics," *Stanford Daily,* Apr. 3, 1979; Boyd Haight, "The Stanford Legend of Doodles Weaver Had a Life of Its Own," *San Jose Mercury News,* Jan. 26, 1983.

294 *He spent a good part:* Haight, *San Jose Mercury News.*

294 *According to legend Doodles:* Ibid; Williams, *Stanford Daily.*

294 *stole five cupid figurines:* Weaver was widely believed to be the culprit in this incident, though his participation was never proven. "Only Doodles would have gone to the trouble to commit a felony for a practical joke," observed one-time Stanford secretary Frederic Glover. (Williams, *Stanford Daily.*)

294 *During the 35 years:* Weaver to Kay Daley, Stanford Alumni Assn., letter, circa Jan. 1973; cited by Haight, *San Jose Mercury News.*

294 *That was part of his glory:* Bennett to JY.

294 *Contrary to popular belief:* Weaver, *Stanford Mosaic;* cited by Haight, *San Jose Mercury News.*

295 *We used to go to Catalina:* Win Weaver to JY, Aug. 19, 1993.

295 *Doodles denied he painted... He admitted:* Gruber, *Stanford Daily;* Page, *Los Angeles Herald-Examiner.*

296 *signed picture of Jesus:* Radio-TV comedy writer Jack Douglas (*The Red Skelton Show*) had a portrait of Christ on *his* wall inscribed, "Thanks for punching up the Sermon on the Mount, J.C." (Hal Kanter to JY, Nov. 13, 1999.)

297 *the great thing was, they remembered me:* Weaver was not pleased when "wild and crazy guy" Steve Martin reprised his arrow-through-the-head gag and did what amounted to a take-off on him in the '70s. "I used to get more laughs in ten minutes than he gets in an hour," he asserted. (Weaver to JY, Aug. 9, 1982.)

297 *The most famous Stanford story:* The statue was of Stanford's first president, David Starr Jordan—or Herbert Hoover, according to different versions of the story. Weaver apparently got the idea for this prank from the opening scene of Chaplin's *City Lights.*

297 *He'd do the damnedest:* Jones to JY, Aug. 11, 1993.

299 *One day Doodles said:* Golly to JY.

299 *Weaver did care passionately about... sports:* At football games, Doodles often eschewed the stands for the scrimmage line. "Wherever he went, to games, he'd grab the megaphone; he'd be yelling and screaming and carrying on. I thought this was all normal," said Win Weaver. "I thought everybody's dad went to the game and got right on the field with all the players. He was a part of the team; everybody knew him." (Weaver to JY.)

300 *The butter-brained adolescents:* Weaver diaries, May 25, 1950.

302 *his older brother Pat:* Doodles and Pat were estranged at the time of the former's death; Pat accorded Doodles a one-sentence mention in his 1994 autobiography, *The Best Seat in the House.* Actress Sigourney Weaver is Pat's daughter, Doodles' niece.

303 *About the time Pat became:* Weaver diaries, Dec. 8-23, 1953.

303 *senior athletic contests:* Weaver's proudest moment in the Senior Olympics was perhaps a hundred-yard javelin toss in 1972. He reportedly won eight medals in a senior swim meet four months after his triple bypass operation in 1980.

304 *The sad joke is:* Weaver to JY.

WHO'S WHO IN THE SPIKE JONES DISORGANIZATION

305 The individuals themselves were the primary source of information for this appendix. Other sources include next of kin, AFM Local 47, death certificates and other public records, *Musical Depreciation Revue* program notes, Brian Rust's *Jazz Records 1897-1942* and *The Complete Dance Band Discography, Film Daily Yearbook, ASCAP Biographical Dictionary, The Los Angeles Times* and *Variety.*

DISCOGRAPHY

335 Ted Hering and Skip Craig were assisted in their efforts by John Wood and Spike Jones Jr. Jack Mirtle dated the Standard Radio transcriptions; Scott Corbett provided release dates for some of the singles. Larry Kiner contributed additional information.

335   "Pre-City Slickers" listings were compiled by the author from AFM Local 47 reports, supplied by Steve LaVere; *An Illustrated Guide to the Recordings of Spike Jones* by Corbett (drummer sessions by LaVere and Mirtle); *Jazz Records 1897-1942 and The Complete Entertainment Discography* by Brian Rust. Individual tracks and issue numbers may be found in the above references. "Rejects and Unrealized Plans" compiled by the author with the assistance of Hering.

RADIOGRAPHY

352   "Pre-City Slickers" and "Miscellany" compiled by the author. Additional guest appearances reported by Jack Mirtle and Wally Marks.

FILMOGRAPHY

357   Mark Cantor provided information on the Soundies, including the Victor Young and Spike Jones soundtrack-only sessions, from production records. Feature filming dates were obtained from studio production files at University of Southern California and Academy of Motion Picture Arts and Sciences; release dates from *Film Daily Yearbook*.

360   "Unrealized Plans" were compiled by the author, from Jones papers and news reports. Additional information supplied by of Steve LaVere.

VIDEOGRAPHY

364   "Unrealized Plans" were compiled by the author, with the assistance of Ted Hering and Eddie Brandt. Additional guest appearances reported by Jack Mirtle.

Selected Bibliography

Ames, Walter. "A Clinker in Error Gave Spike Hunch; Now It's His Style." *The Los Angeles Times*, Apr. 4, 1954.

Bernard, Tom. "Six Nights in a Madhouse." *American Magazine*, Jul. 1949.

Corbett, Scott C. *An Illustrated Guide to the Recordings of Spike Jones*. Monrovia, Ca.: Corbett, 1989.

Corbett, Scott C., ed. *The Spike Jones Musical Depreciation Newsletter*. 1987-1993.

Coslow, Sam. *Cocktails for Two*. New York: Arlington House, 1977.

Crane, Bob. Interview with Spike Jones. KNX, Los Angeles, Nov. 4, 1963.

Demento, Dr. Liner notes, *Dr. Demento Presents The Greatest Novelty Records of All Time*. Santa Monica, CA: Rhino Records, 1985.

Dorson, Art. Interview with Spike Jones. KHJ, Los Angeles, Oct. 14, 1944.

Dunning, John. *On the Air: The Encyclopedia of Old-Time Radio*. New York: Oxford University Press, 1998.

Fitzgerald, Michael. "Spike Jones Says 'Momma, Yes.'" *Argus*, Wayville, Australia, May 26, 1955.

Grayco, Helen. "Just the Two of Us." *Radio Mirror*, Jan. 1949.

Haight, Boyd. "The Stanford Legend of Doodles Weaver Had a Life of Its Own." *San Jose Mercury News*, Jan. 26, 1983.

Hardy, Phil, and Dave Laing. *The Faber Companion to 20th Century Popular Music*. London: Faber and Faber, 1990.

Hering, Ted. Interview with Del Porter. Unpublished. Jun. 3, 1971.

Hering, Ted. Spike Jones Discography. Unpublished. 1975.

Hal Humphrey, "Spike Jones Wants to Know How to Rib Today's Ditties." *Los Angeles Mirror*, Sept. 12, 1960.

Jones, Spike, as told to Joseph Kaye. "Spike Jones Tells His Own Story." *True Story*, Jul. 1949.

Katz, Mickey, as told to Hannibal Coons. *Papa Play For Me*. New York: Simon and Schuster,

1977 (reprinted by Wesleyan University Press, 2002).

Kinkle, Roger D. *The Complete Encyclopedia of Popular Music and Jazz 1900-1950*. New Rochelle, N.Y.: Arlington House, 1974.

Leiter, Robert D. *The Musicians and Petrillo*. New York: Bookman Associates, 1953.

Marshall, Jim. "A Night at the Uproar." *Collier's,* Jan. 10, 1948.

Mirtle, Jack, comp. *Thank You Music Lovers: A Bio-Discography of Spike Jones and His City Slickers, 1941 to 1965*. Westport, Ct.: Greenwood Press, 1986.

Othman, Frederick C. "He Plays Louder Than Anybody." *Saturday Evening Post,* Apr. 10, 1943.

Robbins, Jhan. "Korn on the Kampus." *Varsity,* Apr. 1949.

Rust, Brian. *The American Dance Band Discography 1917-1942*. New Rochelle, N.Y.: Arlington House, 1975.

Rust, Brian. *Jazz Records 1897-1942*. Chigwell, Essex, U.K.: Storyville Publications, 1982.

Schickele, Peter. "The Hills Are Alive, But What a Way to Live!" *The New York Times,* Apr. 10, 1994.

St. Martin, Phil. Interview with Earl Bennett. KLAF, Salt Lake City, Nov. 29, 1984.

Walker, Leo. *The Big Band Almanac*. New York: Da Capo, 1989.

Weaver, Doodles. Diaries. Unpublished. 1946-1951.

Young, Jordan R. "Jones: The Man Who Spiked Der Fuehrer in Der Face." *The Los Angeles Times,* Sept. 5, 1982.

Young, Jordan R. *Let Me Entertain You: Conversations With Show People*. Beverly Hills, Ca.: Moonstone Press, 1988.

Index

SONG AND RECORD INDEX

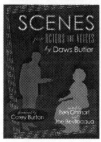

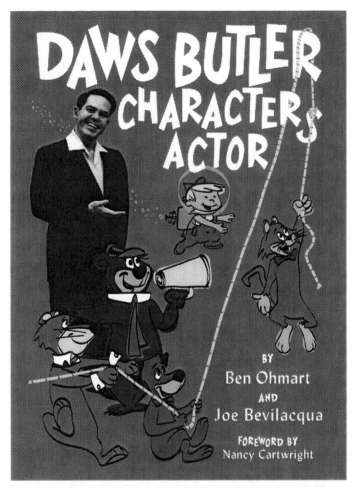

Daws Butler - Characters Actor

The official biography of the voice of Yogi Bear, Huckleberry
Hound and all things Hanna-Barbera. This first book on master voice actor Daws Butler has been assembled through personal scrapbooks, letters and intimate interviews with family
and co-workers. Foreword by Daws' most famous student,
Nancy Cartwright (the voice of Bart Simpson).

ISBN: 1-59393-015-1 $24.95.

CPSIA information can be obtained at www.ICGtesting.com
Printed in the USA
LVOW07s1231310116

473062LV00002B/455/P